John, the Son of Zebedee

Studies on Personalities of the New Testament

D. Moody Smith, General Editor

John, the Son of Zebedee
The Life of a Legend

R. Alan Culpepper

University of South Carolina Press

Copyright © 1994 University of South Carolina

Published in Columbia, South Carolina, by the
University of South Carolina Press

Manufactured in the United States of America

Library of Congress Cataloging-in-Publication Data

Culpepper, R. Alan.
    John, the son of Zebedee : the life of a legend / R. Alan
Culpepper.
        p. cm.
    Includes bibliographical references and index.
    ISBN 0–87249–962-6 (hardback : alk. paper)
    1. John, the Apostle, Saint. I. Title.
BS2455.C856   1994
225.9′2—dc20
    [B]   93–27796

To Hugo H. Culpepper in his eightieth year.
His life has been a fulfillment of 1 John 3:23—
Faith in Jesus Christ and service to others.

Contents

Preface

Writing has always been for me an adventure, a journey of discovery taking me to territories I had not previously explored. The experience of writing a book on the legends about the apostle John has been especially challenging and adventurous. When Moody Smith first approached me about writing a volume on the apostle, I wondered whether there was enough material to warrant a whole book on the subject. I reassured myself that it would be only a short manuscript. My original intent was to state what we know about the apostle, and then to collect some of the early legends about him. The assignment seemed manageable enough.

As I got into the project, however, four things happened. First, the reliability of the references to John in the Gospels and in Acts became increasingly suspect. I concluded that the making of the legend about John did not start after the writing of the Gospels. On the contrary, the characterization of the apostle John in the Gospels and in Acts was already shaped by the impulse to create stories about the apostles. Second, the terminus of the project began slowly to recede. At first I thought the book could end at the close of the second century. Then, it seemed necessary to extend the study through Eusebius and include consideration of the various Acts of John. The issue of what to do with material gleaned from others who had written on John finally led me to extend the project from Papias to the present. Third, while the project was growing, the time I had to give to it was being consumed by teaching and administrative responsibilities and commitments to other projects that I had made before I realized the full scope of this one. Fourth, I finally had to realize that it would not be possible to cover all of the stories and references to the life of the apostle. Like the redactor of the Gospel of John, I came to realize that everything that could be said about the subject could not be written in one book.

In keeping with the design for this series, I have sought to make the text readable and relatively free of material in foreign languages and the discussion of technical, textual matters, while at the same time supplying references in the notes that can lead the reader to the relevant sources. The tension between the impulse to write a more technical volume and the desire to produce a readable survey of the legends about John has forced compromises in every chapter. In principle, I have sought to collect English translations of the relevant texts, at times translating texts that were not available in English, and to provide enough introduction to allow the reader to follow the development of the legends about John. All biblical quotations are taken from the New Revised Standard Version unless a notation indicates otherwise. Those who wish to go further will find indispensable the fine work of Eric Junod and Jean-Daniel Kaestli, *Acta Iohannis,* Corpus Christianorum, 2 vols. (Turnhout: Brepols, 1983).

No journey of any consequence is possible without the help of a great many people. Moody Smith encouraged me to take up this project. The visionaries of the series itself, he and Ken Scott, Director of the University of South Carolina Press, repeatedly allowed me to extend my deadline for the manuscript, thereby enabling it to grow to its present scope and to become more than any of us had originally envisioned. Graduate students have provided invaluable assistance. The Southern Baptist Theological Seminary, using funds made available by the Lilly Endowment for faculty development, provided a stipend for a research assistant for one semester. During this time, David Gowler tirelessly pursued bibliographical references I had collected, and gathered material for future phases of the project. Opportunities to serve as Distinguished Lecturer at the New Orleans Baptist Theological Seminary and to give the Edward L. Beavin Memorial Lectures at Kentucky Wesleyan College in 1989 afforded me occasions to test and refine some of the material from the early chapters. I am also grateful to Marshall D. Johnson, editorial director of Fortress Press, for permission to adapt and reprint my essay "Guessing Points and Knowing Stars: History and Higher Criticism in Robert Browning's 'A Death in the Desert,'" which was originally written for *The Future of Christology: Essays in Honor of Leander E. Keck,* edited by Wayne Meeks and Abraham Malherbe (Minneapolis: Fortress Press, 1993).

During the summer of 1990, Donn Michael Ferris and the Duke Divinity School Library provided me with a study carrel and access to the library's exceptional collection of material. Chapter 5 was written during these enjoyable weeks of uninterrupted research. Finally, the generosity of Baylor University in providing me with a graduate assistant and a reduced teaching load during the fall of 1991 allowed me to bring the project to completion. Without the resources of the James P. Boyce Centennial Library at Southern Seminary and the Moody Memorial Library at Baylor, and the help of their able staffs, it would never have been possible to gather the materials needed for this project. Kevin Compton, my current graduate assistant, has demonstrated extraordinary research skills and scholarship in tracking down dozens of obscure references that were needed to fill out the latter chapters of the book. Edward Bolen also provided valuable help in tracking down obscure sources. The work of preparing the indexes was supported by funds from the Baylor

Research Committee. Along with Kevin Compton, my colleague Mikeal Parsons, and my mentor, Moody Smith, have been the first readers of the manuscript, and each has offered numerous valuable suggestions.

Throughout the writing of this manuscript, as in every other pursuit, my family has given me the kind of support and encouragement that cannot be appropriately or adequately acknowledged here. In particular, my father, Dr. Hugo H. Culpepper, has taken a keen interest in my work on "John, the Beloved." Both the gospel and the letters attributed to John have had a profound influence on his life, so it is to him that the book is dedicated, with affection.

Abbreviations

CBQ	*Catholic Biblical Quarterly*
CChr	Corpus Christianorum
CQR	*Church Quarterly Review*
CRTP	Cahiers de la Revue de théologie et de philosophie
CSEL	Corpus scriptorum ecclesiasticorum latinorum
ETL	*Ephemerides theologicae lovanienses*
EvQ	*Evangelical Quarterly*
ExpTim	*Expository Times*
FB	Forschung zur Bibel
FC	Fathers of the Church
GCS	Griechischen christlichen Schriftsteller
HDR	Harvard Dissertations in Religion
HibJ	*The Hibbert Journal*
HTCNT	Herder's Theological Commentary on the New Testament
HTKNT	Herders theologischer Kommentar zum Neuen Testament
HTR	*Harvard Theological Review*
IBS	*Irish Biblical Studies*
ICC	International Critical Commentary
IDB	*Interpreter's Dictionary of the Bible*
IDBSup	*Interpreter's Dictionary of the Bible*, Supplementary Volume
JBL	*Journal of Biblical Literature*
JEH	*Journal of Ecclesiastical History*
JETS	*Journal of the Evangelical Theology Society*
JhOAI	*Jahreshefte des österreichischen archäologischen Instituts in Wien*
JPT	*Jahrbücher für protestantische Theologie*
JR	*Journal of Religion*
JSNT	*Journal for the Study of the New Testament*
JSNTSup	Journal for the Study of the New Testament Supplement Series
JTC	*Journal for Theology and the Church*
JTS	*Journal of Theological Studies*
KPG	Knox Preaching Guides
LCL	Loeb Classical Library

LJS	Lives of Jesus Series
LXX	Septuagint
MNTC	Moffatt New Testament Commentary
NAB	New American Bible
NCB	New Century Bible
NEB	New English Bible
NHS	Nag Hammadi Studies
NIGTC	New International Greek Testament Commentary
NKZ	*Neue kirchliche Zeitschrift*
NovT	*Novum Testamentum*
NovTSup	Supplements to Novum Testamentum
NPNF	*Nicene and Post-Nicene Fathers*, ed. Philip Schaff and Henry Wace
NRSV	New Revised Standard Version
NTS	*New Testament Studies*
PG	J. Migne, *Patrologia graeca*
PL	J. Migne, *Patrologia latina*
RB	*Revue biblique*
RBén	*Revue Bénédictine*
RevQ	*Revue de Qumran*
RevScRel	*Revue des sciences religieuses*
RSV	Revised Standard Version
SAQ	Sammlung ausgewählter kirchen- und dogmengeschichtlicher Quellenschriften
SBA	Stuttgarter biblische Aufsatzbände
SBB	Stuttgarter biblische Beiträge
SBEC	Studies in the Bible and Early Christianity
SBLDS	SBL Dissertation Series
SBLMS	SBL Monograph Series
SBT	Studies in Biblical Theology
SNTSMS	Society for New Testament Studies Monograph Series
SPAW	*Sitzungsberichte der preussischen Akademie der Wissenschaften*
SRR	Studien zur Rechts- und Religionsgeschichte
ST	*Studia theologica*

ST	Studi e Testi
SWC	Sammlung wissenschaftlicher Commentare
TDNT	*Theological Dictionary of the New Testament*, ed. Gerhard Kittel and Gerhard Friedrich, trans. Geoffrey W. Bromiley
TextsS	*Texts and Studies*
TTS	Trierer Theologische Studien
TU	*Texte und Untersuchungen*
TW	Theologie und Wirklichkeit
TZ	*Theologische Zeitschrift*
USQR	*Union Seminary Quarterly Review*
Vict Poet	*Victorian Poetry*
WBC	Word Biblical Commentary
WUNT	Wissenschaftliche Untersuchungen zum Neuen Testament
ZKG	*Zeitschrift für Kirchengeschichte*
ZNW	*Zeitschrift für die neutestamentliche Wissenschaft*
ZST	*Zeitschrift für systematische Theologie*
ZTK	*Zeitschrift für Theologie und Kirche*

John, the Son of Zebedee

Introduction

The subtitle of this book, "The Life of a Legend," was of course deliberately chosen for its double entendre: both the life of the apostle John and the growth of the legends about him will concern us in the following pages. *Webster's Ninth New Collegiate Dictionary* defines *legend* as "a story coming down from the past, *esp:* one popularly regarded as historical although not verifiable." The term can be traced to the fourteenth century and derives from the Middle French *legende* and the Medieval Latin *legenda,* and it is related to the Latin gerundive *legere,* to gather, select, read, and to the Greek *legein,* to gather or say. Much of the life of the apostle John is popularly regarded as historical, including his days as a fisherman, the events reported in the Gospels, his exile to Patmos, and his writing of the five New Testament books attributed to him. How much of the life of John is "verifiable" from the New Testament and the earliest witnesses to his life and work? The evidence is compiled and reviewed in the present study in detail.

Our interest, however, is not confined to that portion of the material which may pass the modern canons of historical criticism. We shall also be interested in how the legends about John have grown and developed across the centuries. Legend-making is not necessarily delayed until after one's death. Indeed, it begins in one's own memories and in those of associates and successors. As an initial—and very general—outline of the generative process of legends, I would suggest the following.[1]

1. *Selection.* Memories are selected. Some events, sayings, and teachings are forgotten; others are retained. Each individual shapes his or her memories of a significant figure. Those memories, particularly if they become part of a shared memory or a community memory, ultimately begin to take on a life of their own.

2. *Embellishment.* As the memories are recalled, repeated, and integrated into a corpus of memory that defines the hero figure, those memories are embroidered and enlarged. Often this process occurs through the act of interpretation. Earlier traditions are interpreted through commentary. Gaps in the tradition are filled in, and obscure references are explained. Interpretation and embellishment are aspects of an ongoing process, however, since later interpreters of the tradition then interpret and embellish the earlier interpreta-

1

tions and embellishments. The work of each generation is subject to review, interpretation, and enhancement by the next. Corporate memories enhance the significance of the hero, and the significance of the hero in turn fosters further embellishment of the traditions.[2]

3. *Fabrication.* As the legend continues to grow, anecdotes and quotations begin to be fabricated. At first, these accretions to the legend may be variants of established stories or sayings in the tradition. They may also be fabrications that illustrate some aspect of the hero's character, wit, or work. Finally, the legend-making breaks free of the constraints of memory, and fabrication of material like that which has surrounded other heroes lionizes the legendary individual.

4. *Canonization.* As the legend grows, the community that enshrines the hero may begin to exert some direction in the shaping and preservation of the legend. When the legend becomes institutionalized, whether in liturgy or writings, the community authorizes certain elements of the legend while discarding others as apocryphal. The authoritative legend thereby achieves a degree of permanence, though embellishment and fabrication continue.

This book is concerned with both the life of the apostle John and the life of the legend that formed around him. Assuming that the historical data regarding John has come through some such process, what do we actually know about the apostle, and how did the legend develop? These questions will lead us on an intriguing odyssey in the chapters that follow. Our aim is to collect as many of the legends about John as possible. Most of the material in this book is available elsewhere, but never has so much of the tradition about John been collected and made available in English. Where space permitted, an English translation of the stories, references, and pertinent texts has been reproduced, and the sources containing the original-language texts have been noted. More lengthy accounts of the apostle's life are summarized. The volume may serve, therefore, as a sourcebook for the traditions about John. An effort has also been made, however, to keep the text relatively free of references so that the collection of the traditions about John can be read without constantly alluding to the more technical discussions. On the other hand, readers interested in delving more deeply into the tradition will find that the notes serve as a guide to primary texts, translations, and most of the important discussions in the scholarly literature. Some of the texts are analyzed in detail, while others receive little or no analysis. This unevenness is dictated both by the relative significance of the texts and by the limitations of the author.

Inevitably, some judgments about the development of the tradition had to be made. The primary purpose of the book, however, was to collect and assess the development of the legends about John rather than to propose a novel solution to the issues related to the development of the traditions. As the book amply illustrates, the history of scholarship is littered with the remains of countless efforts to unravel the issues posed by the Johannine traditions. Efforts will (and should) continue to be made to resolve the problems associated with the authorship and canonization of the five New Testament writings attributed to the apostle John. It is my hope that this collection of the relevant texts will enable the story to be told more fully. At the same time, an enhanced appreciation for the powerful currents at work in the development of the legends about John should also serve to caution those who would venture to resolve questions about the apostle with too much confidence.

The last paragraph of the last article published by B. W. Bacon, after he had pursued the traditions about John for all of his career, betrays a remarkable confidence:

> Nevertheless historic truth is mighty and will prevail. Gradually, as criticism moves backward beyond the time of the Ephesian canon-makers, the actual son of Zebedee, the fisherman of Galilee, co-"pillar" with James the Just of the mother church in Jerusalem and James' fellow-martyr, will come to his own. Even the late, confused, and distorted traditions of the post-apostolic age will be compelled to yield their meagre contribution to the dawning reality. The John whom Paul knew and mentions *once* will emerge at last from the crowd of Pseudo-Johns of ecclesiastical legend and higher-critical mythology.[3]

After reviewing the history of the legends about the apostle, the reader may not share Bacon's confidence, but where there is loss, there is also gain. Understanding the development of the legends about John richly enhances our appreciation for the role the apostle has played in Christian tradition, liturgy, and folklore. If we cannot work back to the origin of the Johannine tradition with confidence, at least we can appreciate the richness of its later developments.

A brief overview of the course we will follow will no doubt help the reader to fit the following chapters into a meaningful whole. Chapter 1 surveys the setting of the apostle's early life: his physical surroundings, the meaning of his name, and the traditions concerning his family background. Later sources supply clues as to the equipment, conditions, and techniques that probably characterized the Galilean fishing industry in the first century. In this context, the synoptic traditions of the call of James and John to be "fishers of men" can be seen in a fresh light.

One of the misperceptions about the life and character of John common to many of the earlier works on the apostle is that the legend-making did not begin until late in the second century. As a consequence of this assumption, what is said about John in the Gospels was often taken as historical fact while the later traditions were questioned. In chapter 2 a close reading of the gospel traditions about John reveals that the legend-making process was already at work by the time the Gospels were written. Several observations emerge from a review of the reports about John in the Gospels. First, one notes that the positions given to John in the lists of the Twelve reflect varying assessments of his role as an apostle. John is remembered as one of the group of three (Peter, James, and John), one from the two sets of brothers who were called to leave their nets (Peter and Andrew, James and John), and as Peter's companion (Peter and John). Then one notes that the group with which John is identified correlates closely with the way he is characterized. The group of the three disciples is present at private manifestations of Jesus' power (the raising of Jairus's daughter, the transfiguration, the instruction on the Mount of Olives, where Andrew is also mentioned, and the arrest in Gethsemane). The characterization of John as one of the "sons of thunder" is propelled by events in which John is accompanied by his brother James (restraining the unauthorized exorcist, calling down fire on a Samaritan village, and requesting the left- and right-hand seats in the kingdom). The interpretation of John as a hothead draws heavily on material in the Gospel of Luke, but the name *Boanerges* occurs only in Mark. In Acts, John appears exclusively as Peter's companion, while in Galatians, he is one of the three "pillars" of the early church: James, Cephas, and John.

Chapter 3 examines the role of the Beloved Disciple in the Gospel of John, analyzing the passages in which he appears and then surveying the range of suggestions as to the identity of this idealized but unnamed disciple. The indications that the Beloved Disciple was an actual person, as well as the idealization of his role in the Gospel, must be taken into account. The result is a heightened appreciation for the work of an otherwise unknown Judean disciple, probably not one of the Twelve, who served as the apostolic authority for the Johannine community and mediated to it the tradition of the words and works of Jesus.

The next chapter continues the pursuit of the question of the apostle's relationship to the writings attributed to him. Here the internal evidence and the attestation of the Epistles and the Apocalypse are examined. How are the elder of the Epistles and the seer of the Apocalypse to be related to one another and to the Beloved Disciple of the Gospel? Traditionally, the three have all been identified as the apostle John, but that identification is by no means certain.

Chapter 5, therefore, turns to the reception of the Gospel and the emergence of the view that the Gospel and the other Johannine writings were penned by the apostle. For three-fourths of the second century, there are only echoes, hints, and allusions. Hence, the chapter is entitled "Obscurity: The Apostle in the Second Century." The chapter traces the testimony concerning the apostle and the reception of the Gospel from the earliest papyrus text of a portion of John through Irenaeus, Polycrates, and the oldest Gospel prologues. By the end of the second century, the place of John as the author of at least the Gospel was secure, and the emergence of legends about the later life of the apostle was already under way.

Chapter 6 contains a rather miscellaneous collection of traditions about the apostle spanning the third to the fourteenth century, the period of the early Church through the Middle Ages. Isolated stories are preserved as early as the writings of Tertullian and the heads of the Christian school at Alexandria: Clement of Alexandria, Origen, and Dionysius. The last raised questions about the authorship of Revelation and reported that there were two Johns in Ephesus and two tombs of the apostle. Interrupting the survey of stories about the apostle, the chapter at this point introduces the material related to the tombs of John in Ephesus. The references to John in the writings of Western and Greek church fathers and the later, medieval sources are summarized in roughly chronological order. Some of the traditions are clearly marginal, fanciful, or idiosyncratic, while other sources report traditions that were widely accepted as historical.

The next chapter traces the development of the various apocryphal acts of the apostle John. The earliest account of acts of John dates back to the second century. This chapter contains summaries of the *Acts of John* from Leucius, a document called the *Acts of John at Rome,* and the *Acts of John by Prochorus.* A summary of the Syrian *History of John* and synopses of the *Apocalypse of John the Theologian* and John's role in various accounts of the assumption of Mary are also included. A review of the content of the *Book of John the Evangelist,* a translation of the *Homily of Pseudo-Chrysostom,* and a summary of the Irish *Life of John the Evangelist* round out the discussion.

The eighth chapter examines the impact of the legends about John on early and medieval art, the poetry of Adam of St. Victor, and the works of nineteenth-century German, English, and American poets. By the nineteenth century, the modern historical consciousness would not allow the creation of further legends about John except in literature, primarily poetry. This chapter surveys the fascinating representations of John in the works of Herder, Hölderlin, Klopstock, Longfellow, and Browning.

The period from about 1870 to 1930 marks a time of phenomenal interest in the life of the apostle. Numerous lives of the apostle were written in German and English during this time, as a glance at the first section of the bibliography will confirm. Generally, these lives are fairly conservative and cautious in their scholarship, assembling information that can be gleaned from the biblical material and sometimes analyzing the second-century writers also. In these works we see a modern expression of the same historical interest that fueled the life of the legend through earlier centuries, constrained now by the analysis of sources and the canons of late nineteenth-century and early twentieth-century historiography. These works too, however, constitute a chapter in the development of the legends about John since they certify portions of the legend as critically acceptable to scholarship and the modern mind.

The tenth chapter picks up the most recent developments in the *Nachleben* or "afterlife" of the apostle: the resurgence of interest in John the Elder in such different scholars as B. W. Bacon, Robert Eisler, and Martin Hengel; the critical reconstructions that result from the quest for the Johannine school in the 1960s and 1970s, and the reaffirmation of the traditions about the apostle in the works of Leon Morris, John A. T. Robinson, Stephen Smalley, and D. A. Carson.

In a sense, the book remains unfinished both because there are gaps in the material and because the legends about John continue to grow and develop. Ultimately, of course, this book itself represents one further episode in the life of the legend of John, the son of Zebedee. By tracing the development of the legend, however, we can see in fresh ways the interplay between history, tradition, and interpretation that contributed to that development. We may also see how elusive historical data are, how freely the tradition floats, and how powerful the impulse to develop legends remains. What follows, therefore, is more the biography of a legend than a life of the apostle.

NOTES

1. See H. Delehaye, *The Legends of the Saints: An Introduction to Hagiography,* trans. V. M. Crawford (New York: Longman, Green, and Co., 1907), esp. chap. 2, "The Development of the Legend," 12–59.
2. For a brilliant analysis of this process in reference to the various accounts of the death of John, see Jean-Daniel Kaestli, "Le rôle des textes bibliques dans la genèse et le développement des légendes apocryphes: Le cas du sort final de l'apôtre Jean," *Augustinianum* 23, nos. 1–2 (1983): 319–36.
3. B. W. Bacon, "John and the Pseudo-Johns," *ZNW* 31 (1932): 150.

CHAPTER 1

Fisherman
The Setting of the Apostle's Early Life

Mist rising over a lake early in the morning is an appropriate image with which to begin the odyssey of John, the son of Zebedee, for he first appears in the gospel accounts as a Galilean fisherman working on his nets. Although the call of the two sets of brothers—Simon and Andrew, and James and John—is reported in only a few verses in each of the synoptic Gospels, the idyllic picture of the fishermen with the boats and nets is indelibly imprinted in Christian imaginations.

This chapter will sketch what we may learn about the picture etched by these accounts. What do we know about the family of Zebedee or the life of a Galilean fisherman? What is meant by the call to become "fishers of men"? These are the questions that will concern us first.

JOHN, THE SON OF ZEBEDEE: WHAT'S IN A NAME?

John is commonly identified as the "son of Zebedee" and the brother of James. From the names alone, we may begin to form an impression of the apostle's cultural and religious background.

John, or *Johanan,* was a common Hebrew name meaning "God has been gracious" (1 Chron. 26:3; Ezra 10:6). The currency of the name among Jewish families is attested by the observation that there are four other persons named John in the New Testament: (1) John the Baptist (Mark 1:4; Luke 1:13, 60; 3:2–20); (2) John the father of Simon Peter (John 1:43; 21:15–17);[1] (3) John Mark (Acts 12:12, 25; 13:5, 13; 15:37); and (4) John the relative of Annas, an otherwise unknown member of the high-priestly family, who is mentioned in Acts 4:6.

James (*Iakobos*) is a Hellenized form of *Iakob* or Jacob, again a common Jewish name. Zebedee (*Zebedaios*) means "gift of Yahweh." The Aramaic or

7

Hebrew name is closely related to Zebadiah, which means "Yahweh has given."[2] A column of the synagogue in Capernaum (fourth century A.D.) provides evidence of the continued popularity of the name in Galilee. It bears an Aramaic inscription naming a certain "Zebida bar Jochanan" as the maker of the column.[3] According to later legend, Zebedee was from the tribe of Levi and his wife was from Judah.[4]

In most accounts James is mentioned first, and at times John is identified as his brother: "he saw James son of Zebedee and his brother John" (Mark 1:19; cf. 3:17), or "James and John the sons of Zebedee" (Mark 10:35). Because James is mentioned first, the suggestion has been made that he was the older of the two brothers. On four occasions in Luke-Acts, however, John is named before James (Luke 8:51; 9:28; Acts 1:13; 12:2), and in the last James is identified as the brother of John. This sequence may indicate that Luke knew that John was the more famous of the two brothers.[5] On the other hand, the identification of James as the brother of John in Acts 12:2 serves to distinguish him from James the brother of Jesus, who plays a more prominent role in Acts (12:17; 15:13; 21:18).

The mother of James and John is named among the women at the cross in Matthew 27:55–56: "Many women were also there, looking on from a distance; they had followed Jesus from Galilee and had provided for him. Among them were Mary Magdalene, and Mary the mother of James and Joseph, *and the mother of the sons of Zebedee*" (italics mine). Some interpreters, both ancient and modern, have confidently identified the mother of the sons of Zebedee as Salome on the basis of the parallel account in Mark 15:40:[6] "There were also women looking on from a distance, among them were Mary Magdalene, and Mary the mother of James the younger and of Joses, *and Salome*. These used to follow him and provided for him when he was in Galilee; and there were many other women who had come up with him to Jerusalem" (italics mine). Salome is mentioned elsewhere only in Mark 16:1. The variations in the lists of the women at the cross, at the burial, and at the empty tomb should caution us, however, about putting much weight on identifications based on the parallel accounts.

John 19:25 lists either three or four women at the cross: "Meanwhile, standing near the cross of Jesus were his mother, and his mother's sister, Mary the wife of Clopas, and Mary Magdalene." The question posed by this verse is whether the sister of Jesus' mother was Mary the wife of Clopas. If so, the sister's name was Mary. But, since the synoptics and Acts identify Jesus' mother as Mary, it is unlikely that her sister was also named Mary. Most interpreters have therefore concluded that John lists four women at the cross. Neither Jesus' mother nor her sister is identified by name. Which (if any) of the four women was the mother of James and John? Mary Magdalene appears in all the lists. Mary the mother of James the younger and Joseph (or Joses) would be the mother of Jesus (cf. Mark 6:3; 15:40; Matt. 13:55; 27:56). Salome (the mother of James and John, the sons of Zebedee) could not also be the wife of Clopas, so attempting to harmonize these lists leads to the inference that the mother of James and John was named Salome and that she was the sister of Mary, the mother of Jesus. That would make James and John the maternal first cousins of Jesus and also the relatives of John the Baptist (see Luke 1:36). Such relationships might help to explain why these early disciples of Jesus were followers of John the Baptist, if such were the case, and why Jesus gave the keeping of his mother to the Beloved Disciple. Each of these items involves further inferences and assumptions (as we will see) so that finally the whole structure of inferences becomes too shaky to inspire confidence.

The uncertainty of the names of the women at the cross and the tomb of Jesus seems to have led Luke to choose caution by not attempting to give all of their names:

> But all his acquaintances, including the women who had followed him from Galilee, stood at a distance, watching these things. . . . The women who had come with him from Galilee followed, and they saw the tomb, and how his body was laid. . . . Now it was Mary Magdalene, Joanna, Mary the mother of James, and the other women with them who told this to the apostles. . . . Moreover, some women of our group. . . . (Luke 23:49, 55; 24:10, 22)

We must conclude, therefore, that while John the son of Zebedee's mother may have been named Salome, it is precarious to build other inferences on the basis of these lists.[7] Surely, if John had been Jesus' first cousin, this relationship would have been recognized more prominently in the early Christian traditions about the apostle.

GALILEAN FISHERMAN

Mark and Matthew identify the brothers by saying simply, "for they were fishermen" (Mark 1:16; Matt. 4:18). This note has often conjured up an idyllic picture of simple, hard-working men, but that picture has recently been challenged. A vigorous fishing industry had developed around the Sea of Galilee. While a knowledge of this industry does not answer all our questions, it can help us to understand something of the life of a first-century Galilean fisherman.

Fishing in the Sea of Galilee

The Sea of Galilee (or Gennesaret: Luke 5:1) is an inland lake fed by the Jordan River on its way south to the Dead Sea. Its surface lies about 680 feet below sea level. The pear-shaped lake is thirteen miles long and eight miles across at its greatest width. The waters along its north shore are relatively shallow, while its greatest depths (around 150 feet) are found along the river channel. Josephus provides the following description of the area:

> The lake of Gennesar takes its name from the adjacent territory. It is forty furlongs broad and a hundred and forty long. Notwithstanding its extent, its water is sweet to the taste and excellent to drink: clearer than marsh water with its thick sediment, it is perfectly pure, the lake everywhere ending in pebbly or sandy beaches. Moreover, when drawn it has an agreeable temperature, more pleasant than that of river or spring water, yet invariably cooler than the great expanse of the lake would lead one to expect. . . . The lake contains species of fish different, both in taste and appearance, from those found elsewhere.[8]

The frequent references to fish in the New Testament indicate that fish was an important part of the diet of first-century Galileans and Judeans. They ate fish, fresh and processed, more than any other meat: "Bread and fish, with the addition of olive-oil and wine, formed in ancient times the most substantial parts of the diet of the people, rich and poor. Fish, fresh and salted, pickled and dried, was consumed in large quantities, the poor classes being almost entirely dependent for their *opson* [sustenance] on the cheaper qualities and especially on salted and dried fish."[9] A hungry boy might ask his father for fish (Matt. 7:10; Luke 11:11), or carry a lunch of bread and fish (Mark 6:38). Accounts of the appearances of the risen Lord relate that he ate broiled fish in Jerusalem (Luke 24:42) and fresh fish with the disciples in Galilee (John 21:9, 14). Galilee was the food basket of Palestine. Galilean farmers produced grain in the fertile soil of the plain of Gennesaret, and Galilean fishermen harvested fish from the lake. The population was so dependent upon the supply of fish that when the fishermen interrupted the supply by observing religious feast days, there were complaints.[10]

The importance of the fishing industry is evidenced by some of the names around the Sea of Galilee. Bethsaida means "House of the Fisher" or "Fishville." Magdala, the home of Mary Magdalene, was located on the western shore, north of Tiberias. It is identified by the Talmud as *migdalnunaiya*,[11] which means "Fish Tower." It is probably to be identified with the site known as Dalmanutha (Mark 8:10) or Tarichea, which means "processed fish" or *tarichos.* Strabo, the ancient geographer, reports that "at the place called Taricheae the lake supplies excellent fish for pickling."[12] One may suppose that fish were brought here to be dried, pickled, or salted for export. Although the report may be exaggerated, Josephus claims that he commandeered 230 fishing boats at Tarichea—"all the boats he could find on the lake."[13] Each boat carried four sailors, and with these boats he pretended to prepare an attack on Tiberias from the water.

The eighteen species of fish in the Sea of Galilee fall into three main groups.[14] The *Cichlidae,* called *Musht* by the Arabs, include the Tilapia or "St. Peter's fish," a mouth-breeding fish of Ethiopic origin that looks something like an American panfish (crappie or bluegill). Also found are the *Cyprinidae,* the carp family, which range from the large Barbels to the small fresh water "sardines" (*Acanthrobrama terrae-sanctae*). This latter variety were probably the "small fish" in the boy's lunch (John 6:9). Finally, there are the *Siluridae,* or catfish (*Clarias lazera*), called *Barbut* in Arabic, which were also common in the Nile River and in lakes around Alexandria.

Various explanations for the close relationship between the fish of the Jordan valley and East Central Africa have been offered. Josephus recalls the legend that the spring near Capernaum was considered to be a branch of the Nile because it produced the catfish (or *coracin*) found in the lake of Alexandria.[15] Seán Freyne surmises that the presence of this African species may be evidence that "the waters of the lake were re-stocked as part of a government fisheries' policy."[16] Alternatively, it has been suggested that the two river systems were once connected, perhaps in the early Tertiary period.[17]

Jewish law stated that "whatever has fins and scales" is clean (Lev. 11:9–12; Deut. 14:9–10). Catfish were thereby excluded as unclean. In Jesus' parable, "the kingdom of heaven is like a net that was thrown into the sea and caught fish of every kind; when it was full, they drew it ashore, sat down, and put the good into baskets but threw out the bad" (Matt. 13:47–48). The rabbis debated whether it was permissible to sell unclean species, but some of the more tolerant teachers did permit the practice: "If hunters of wild animals, birds and fishes chanced upon species that are unclean, they may sell them. R. Judah says: Also if a man came upon such by accident he may buy or sell them provided that this is not his trade. But the Sages forbid it."[18] Processed fish could be presumed clean, but fish brine was always unclean.[19] Similarly, there were laws pertaining to fish caught on the Sabbath:

> If traps for wild animals, birds or fish were set on the eve of a Festival-day, what are caught may not be taken out on the Festival-day unless it is known that they were caught during the eve of the Festival-day. A gentile once brought fish to Rabban

Gamaliel [Paul's teacher, according to Acts 22:3]. He said, "They are permitted but I have no wish to accept them from him."[20]

Deuteronomy 33:23 specifies that the tribe of Naphtali shall "possess the lake and the south" (RSV). According to traditional interpretation this meant that only the tribe of Naphtali could fish the Sea of Tiberias,[21] but it is doubtful that this law was enforced in the first century. The Talmud interprets the verse in Deuteronomy as follows:

> "That it be permitted to fish with an angle in the Sea of Tiberias provided that no sail is spread, as this would detain boats." It is, however, permitted to fish by means of nets and traps. . . . Our Rabbis taught: The Sea of Tiberias was included in the portion of Naphtali. In addition, he received a rope's length of dry land on the southern side to keep nets on, in fulfillment of the verse, *Possess thou the sea and the South.*[22]

According to the *Tosefta,* what must be a universal law among fishermen was obeyed on the Sea of Galilee also: "A man may not lay out his fishing net or set up his boat in the area of another person."[23]

According to Matthew 17:27, Jesus instructed Peter to "go to the sea and cast a hook; take the first fish that comes up; and when you open its mouth, you will find a coin." Sometimes a hook was pulled quickly through the water in an effort to impale a fish. Fishing by hook and line, apparently with bait, is also mentioned in the Pseudo-Clementine *Recognitions:*

> When I was at Capernaum, occupied in the taking of fishes, and sat upon a rock, holding in my hand a hook attached to a line, and fitted for deceiving the fishes, I was so absorbed that I did not feel a fish adhering to it while my mind eagerly ran through my beloved Jerusalem . . . when I did not perceive, through the occupation of my mind, that I had caught a very large fish which was attached to the hook, and that although it was dragging the hook-line from my hand, my brother Andrew, who was sitting by me, seeing me in a reverie and almost ready to fall, thrusting his elbow into my side as if he would awaken me from sleep, said: "Do you not see, Peter, what a large fish you have caught? Are you out of your senses, that you are thus in a stupor of astonishment? Tell me, what is the matter with you?"[24]

More commonly, nets were used. According to tradition, the fishermen made their own nets from flax.[25] There is almost certainly a close correlation between the kinds of nets used by Arab fishermen until recent decades and the various words for nets found in the Gospels.[26] The casting net (in Greek, *amphiblēstron* [Mark 1:16]; in Arabic, *shabaka*) is a circular net up to twenty feet across with weights along the circumference. The fisherman wades out, watches for signs of fish, casts the net in a circle and, drawing it in by means of a center cord, entraps the fish. The trammel net, or *diktyon* (though this is a generic word for nets in Greek; in Arabic, the word is *mubattan*) is a compound net—three nets of equal length suspended from a rope. The outer two have a wide mesh, but the mesh of the center net is fine. The top of the net is held up by floats, while the bottom is anchored with weights. Fish can swim through the outer nets but become entangled in the center net and cannot retreat. The largest of the nets is the *sagēnē* (in Greek [Matt. 13:47]; in Arabic, *jurf*). It may be 400 yards long. The net is set out by boat in a large semi-circle with the two ends near the shore. As with the *diktyon,* the top is held up with floats, and the bottom is anchored with weights. Men on the shore then draw the net in by means of ropes attached to its upper and lower corners. Care is taken to keep the net in uninterrupted motion while it is being retrieved.[27] These fishing operations were often carried on near shore. In John 21:7, Peter is stripped, ready to jump into the lake to free the net when it catches on the bottom.[28]

A relatively large boat is required to pull the *sagēnē,* and thanks to the vigilance of amateur archaeologists in the region, an example of this class of boat was discovered in January 1986.[29] The shell of the boat, which is 26.5 feet long, 7.5 feet wide, and 4.5 feet high, was buried in the mud near the edge of the Sea of Galilee between Kibbutz Ginnosar and Migdal. Initially there was speculation that the boat may have been one of those used in the Battle of Migdal (A.D. 67), for Josephus reports that the Jews "were sent to the bottom with their skiffs" and "the beaches were strewn with wrecks."[30] Detailed observation, however, revealed that the boat had been stripped of reusable parts before it was pushed out into the lake. The mast block, stempost, and sternpost had been removed.

The boat could be either rowed or sailed. Just as the boat depicted in a first-century mosaic from Migdal, the boat was designed for a crew of four rowers and a helmsman, who would have stood on a large stern platform. Both the size of the vessel and contemporary accounts indicate that it could have carried about fifteen people. The shell itself was made by a master craftsman using cedar planking and oak frames. These were held together by mortise and tenon joints, a construction technique found in other ancient Mediterranean vessels. By the converging evidence of the building techniques that were used, the pottery found around the boat, and the carbon 14 test, the wood used for the boat has been dated to 40. B.C. plus or minus 80 years, hence from 120 B.C. to A.D. 40. It is uncertain, however, how long the boat was in use before it was scuttled. By all accounts, it appears to have been a typical fishing vessel used during the period of Jesus and the disciples.[31]

The Economic Status of Fishermen

The New Testament says nothing about the life of the family of Zebedee prior to Jesus' call to the brothers to follow him. Judged from the sole fact that they were fishermen, the economic and social status of the family has been described in varying terms. According to A. T. Robertson, for example, "It was a simple home beyond doubt, without many luxuries and without means for higher education."[32] On the other hand, G. W. Buchanan places the family among the upper class in Galilee.[33]

Understanding the economic system as it affected the fishing industry may help us to gain a clearer understanding of the family's situation. Since the Herods adhered to the model of the Ptolemaic administrations in Egypt, fishing rights were probably controlled by the state. Those with sufficient means would purchase fishing rights from Herod Philip, the son of Herod the Great, who ruled Gaulanitis from 4 B.C. to A.D. 34. His wife was also named Salome (the daughter of Herodias), and in contrast to his father, he was known as a mild and peaceful ruler.[34]

As we have seen, fishing was one of the region's major industries. Recent developments in processing, marketing, and exporting the fish had stimulated a greater demand for the fisherman's catch. Philip would have sold fishing rights to those who were willing to pay his price in order to develop their own commercial interests. Those who purchased the fishing rights from Philip, and who also served as tax collectors, would in turn lease fishing permits to fishermen for a share of what was caught. Wilhelm Wuellner suggests that as a tax collector, Matthew-Levi had fishermen working for him.[35] The fisherman—and here we probably find Zebedee's place in the system—would hire servants to help him with the hard work of maintaining the nets, catching the fish, sorting them, and transporting them to the market.

Specialties developed as some men became more expert with various nets or with boat handling than others. Origen, for example, identified James and John as sailors: "When he [Celsus] calls them indiscriminately sailors, he probably means James and John, because they left their ship and their father Zebedee, and followed Jesus; for Peter and his brother Andrew, who employed a net to gain their necessary subsistence, must be classed not as sailors, but as the Scripture describes them, as fishermen."[36] In Egypt at least, the tax collector could be entitled to thirty or forty percent of the catch.[37] Seán Freyne assumes that similar arrangements prevailed in Palestine also: "At all events, given this overall state of affairs related to the fish industry, it is unlikely that small Galilean fishermen would profit from the new markets and better techniques of preservation, even if these were carried out on such a scale that one of the older settlements along the lake front, Magdala, received a Greek name from the new industry."[38]

Mark 1:20 says that James and John "left their father Zebedee in the boat with the hired men,"[39] and Luke 5:7, 10 supplies the added detail that they were partners with Simon Peter. While this information places the family a step above the hired servants, caution dictates that we refrain from building too many inferences on such a slender base. Eric F. F. Bishop, for example, has teased these particular data into a detailed picture of the disciples' activities:

> Incidentally, Zebedee seems to have been able to employ day labor which might imply a substantial business, and perhaps some other commercial partnership in a Mediterranean port. If so, their business would have taken St. James and St. John to Jerusalem and Caesarea more often than the other pair of brothers. This does not necessarily imply that the latter could not afford day-labor, but it would give the sons of Zebedee a greater chance to get in touch with important people. Did their "syndicate" for instance supply the high-priestly family with fresh and cured fish? They might have been in charge at times of caravans, taking salted fish from Taricheae, loaded on mules or donkeys. More than probably Our Lord and the Apostles took this "fish" trip, when occasion offered, which would certainly be at feast times.[40]

At most, we can say that the fishermen operated a small fishing business that involved boats and hired workers. The evidence is insufficient to show that they were among the families of the upper class, but neither did they share the desperate lot of hired servants and day laborers.

Bethsaida and Capernaum

The Gospels tell us that Peter maintained a house in Capernaum (Mark 1:29) and that Peter and Andrew and Philip were from Bethsaida (John 1:44). On this basis, Bethsaida has been named as John's home also. William Dallmann, for example, writing in 1932, could claim with no apparent hesitation, "John was born at Beth Saida."[41]

Bethsaida was a fishing village located on the east side of the Jordan, two kilometers from where it flows into the Sea of Galilee. Josephus tells us that Philip had recently rebuilt Bethsaida and renamed it Julias: "He [Philip] also raised the village of Bethsaida on Lake Gennesaritis to the status of city by adding residents and strengthening the fortifications. He named it after Julia, the emperor's daughter."[42] It has generally been supposed that the Julia in question was the daughter of Augustus, who was banished 2 B.C. That being the case, Philip must have conferred the name Julias on the town between 4 and 2 B.C.[43] On the basis of the coin evidence, it has recently been argued, however, that this Julia was Livia-Julia, the wife of Augustus and the mother of Tiberius.[44] Josephus, therefore, was in error.

The building and the influx of new settlers probably did not change the character of the village greatly, however. Seán Freyne evaluates the impact of Philip's work at Bethsaida as follows:

> On the other hand Bethsaida Julias situated on the lake did allow for much more frequent contacts, especially with the Galilean villages and settlements along the lakefront such as Caphernaum and Corozain, but its threat to an essentially Jewish way of life seems to have been much less. Despite Philip's renaming it after Augustus's daughter Julia, in all probability it never enjoyed full city status. The extra population that Philip attracted there (*Ant.* 18:28), probably some lesser officials for the most part, was not likely to have appreciably changed its character from that of fishing village to hellenistic city.[45]

Theories that there was a second, western Bethsaida based on John 12:21, which locates Bethsaida in Galilee rather than Gaulanitis, have been abandoned. The name "Galilee," used loosely, could encompass the nearby town of Bethsaida.[46] Debate as to the exact location of Bethsaida continued until recently with three sites in contention: et-Tell, a prominent hill two and a half kilometers north of the lake; khirbet el-Araj, at the edge of the lake about a thousand meters east of the current river bed; and khirbet el-Mesadiyeh, a ruin one kilometer southeast of el-Araj that is too small to have been a city.[47] Excavations in 1987 revealed only one level of occupation (fourth to fifth century A.D.) at el-Araj, leaving et-Tell as the only reasonable site for Bethsaida. In all likelihood, alluvial deposits have filled in the marshlands south of et-Tell over the centuries, pushing the lake further from the site. Excavations at et-Tell in 1988, 1989, and 1990 showed that, though the site has been severely disturbed and plundered, it was inhabited from the time of the Early Bronze Age. In the stratum from the second century B.C. to the first century A.D., there is a large paved courtyard surrounded by rooms. Fishing paraphernalia recovered from the area suggest that it was connected with fishing activity, either as a public plaza or as the courtyard of an affluent family.[48]

As early as A.D. 530, a pilgrim by the name of Theodosius wrote (exaggerating the distance) that it was six miles from Capernaum to Bethsaida, "where the apostles Peter, Andrew, Philip and the sons of Zebedee were born."[49] About A.D. 725, Willibald saw a church in Bethsaida which was reportedly located on the site of the house of Zebedee.[50] The growth of legend and the confusion of sites is evident in the itinerary of Daniel (A.D. 1106): "The village of Zebedee the father of John was near the lake, so too, the house of John the Divine. It was here that Christ drove out a legion of devils from a man, ordering them to enter a herd of swine which were drowned in the lake. A little distance from here is the village of Capernaum."[51]

Clemens Kopp concludes that Daniel identified the Tabgha hospice at the cape of Tell el-'Oreimeh as "the village of Zebedee."[52] From this time forward, pilgrims mistakenly identified el-Minyeh, a site on the western shore, south of Capernaum, as Bethsaida. Bethsaida was situated near the shallow waters of the northern end of the lake, "the richest fishing-ground" on the lake.[53] The two best fishing spots on the lake, it is claimed, were the mouth of the Jordan near Bethsaida and the site of the seven springs, just south of Capernaum.[54] Bethsaida and Capernaum were also located on the major roads that led north to Caesarea Philippi, south to Tiberias, and west to Cana, Nazareth, and Sepphoris. The population of the area was mixed, Syrian and Jewish, and the Gospels indicate that Jesus met Pharisees in the villages around the Sea of Galilee. As the provenance of John's early life, Bethsaida, along with Capernaum, probably offered him a measure of prosperity and stimulation, but the excavations of Peter's house at Capernaum suggest that it was the home of a poor family.[55]

"FISHERS OF MEN": THE CALL TO DISCIPLESHIP

The four Gospels contain as many as three different accounts of John's call to discipleship. In Mark and Matthew, Jesus calls the two sets of brothers while they are "mending their nets." According to Luke, the call to discipleship followed the miraculous catch of fish. Luke's interest is focused on Peter, however, and the calling of the sons of Zebedee is mentioned almost as an afterthought. If one identifies the unnamed disciple in John 1:35ff. as the Beloved Disciple, as is often done, and if the Beloved Disciple is John, the son of Zebedee, then the Fourth Gospel provides a third account of the call to discipleship, as well as evidence that John had earlier been a follower of John the Baptist. The question of the identity of the Beloved Disciple and his relationship to the unnamed figure in John 1:35ff. will be treated in chapter 3. Here we will examine the synoptic accounts of John's call to discipleship.

The Call in Mark and Matthew

The calling of disciples is the first public act of Jesus' ministry in the Gospel of Mark. Its position in the Gospel is undoubtedly important. Mark 1:14–15 is a summary statement which places the beginning of Jesus' ministry after the arrest of John the Baptist. Mark also provides a summary of Jesus' teaching: "The time is fulfilled, and the kingdom of God is at hand." Just as the call of the disciples follows this summary statement, so the appointment of the Twelve follows a summary statement in Mark 3:7–12.

Matthew follows the same sequence, placing the call of the disciples after Jesus' temptation. The report that Jesus withdrew to Galilee is supported by a quotation from Isaiah 9:1–2. In neither Gospel is there any report of previous contact between Jesus and the sons of Zebedee. Earlier it was common to harmonize these accounts with Luke and John, so that there was some psychological preparation for the forceful call to discipleship in Mark and Matthew. Such harmonizing, however, is artificial and fails to recognize the significance of the way in which each gospel reports this part of the ministry of Jesus.

Attempts to locate the precise spot where the calling occurred, such as that of J. Garrow Duncan, who chose the bay at Tabgah, must also be rejected as fanciful:

> This larger bay is probably the place where Peter was fishing when he was called by Jesus. It is well known that the fishes come up to it in shoals on account of the water from the springs, and there is no other place on the shore of the Lake where the *amphiblēstron* or "throw-net" could be used to greater advantage, since here the fishes are known to come close in large shoals.[56]

In response, Wuellner argued that (1) casting nets were used by fishermen in boats as well as by those wading in the water, (2) the term *amphiblēstron* could be used for "just about any kind of net," and (3) the use of casting nets was restricted during the summer, when the water was low.[57] It is difficult to arbitrate such debates, but clearly the Gospel records do not locate the site except to say that it was "by the lake" (Mark 1:16).[58]

The meaning of the phrase that is commonly translated "mending their nets" has also been debated. G. R. Wynne collected occurrences of the verb in Seneca, Appian, and Cicero, as well as translations of the term into Latin in the Vulgate and in a medieval scholia. On the basis of these data, he rejects

Luther's translation, which says that the disciples were "patching" broken nets: "It is submitted, then, that we may fairly question the common opinion and adopt the more probable sense of *componentes, farcientes* or *complicantes,* and imagine the hands in the boat carefully placing in neat folds the net they carried, always in view of the next haul."[59] The Greek verb *katartizein* seems to carry the general sense of making ready or preparing—hence, of cleaning, mending, and folding the nets. Again, attempts to define the meaning too precisely should be abandoned.

In Mark and Matthew, the evangelist does not state Jesus' call to James and John in direct discourse. The text merely says, "he called them" (Mark 1:20; Matt. 4:21). The reader naturally assumes that the call to the sons of Zebedee was the same as the call to Simon and Andrew in the previous verses. That call contains two parts, which together convey the meaning of this strange invitation: "follow me" and "I will make you fish for people."

The imperative "follow me" has corollaries in both the Graeco-Roman philosophical tradition and the Jewish prophetic tradition. The closest parallel to our passage in the Graeco-Roman philosophical tradition is Socrates' invitation to Euthydemus.[60] Socrates goes to the saddler's shop and challenges Euthydemus to become his disciple-companion. Both passages present a three-step process: command, promise, and response. Similarly, Socrates calls Strepsiades, saying: "but come [*deuri*] and follow me [*akoloutheseis emoi*]."[61] Diogenes Laertius reports Xenophon's call to be Socrates' disciple in words similar to those of the Gospels: "'Then follow me,' said Socrates, 'and learn.' From that time onward he was a disciple of Socrates."[62]

The classic, and often-cited, parallel to the call of the disciples, however, is Elijah's call to Elisha:

> So he set out from there, and found Elisha son of Shaphat, who was plowing. There were twelve yoke of oxen ahead of him, and he was with the twelfth. Elijah passed by him and threw his mantle over him. He left the oxen, ran after Elijah, and said, "Let me kiss my father and my mother, and then I will follow you [LXX: *kai akoloutheso opiso sou*]." Then Elijah said to him, "Go back again; for what have I done to you?" He returned from following him, took the yoke of oxen, and slaughtered them; using the equipment from the oxen, he boiled their flesh, and gave it to the people, and they ate. Then he set out and followed Elijah [LXX: *kai eporeuthe opiso Eliou*], and became his servant. (1 Kings 19:19–21)[63]

The language of this account is similar to the language of calling in the Gospels, but as Vernon Robbins points out, many features of the Gospel story are absent: Elijah does not issue a command or expect Elisha to follow him, and there is no promise that Elijah will make Elisha into something different.[64] Robbins, therefore, mounts a persuasive argument that the calling of the disciples in Mark reflects a merger of the Graeco-Roman and Jewish traditions.[65]

A further question concerns the relationship between the vocation of the fishermen and the meaning of discipleship. The metaphor "fishers of men" is striking both because it arises out of the situation and because it is a clever play on words. The fishermen are caught by Jesus and given a new vocation. J. Manek found the meaning of the metaphor in "old cosmological myths" in which the waters represent chaos; therefore, "to fish out a man means to rescue him from the kingdom of darkness."[66] Such overtones, however, are not explicit in the Gospel accounts and lead to unfounded allegorization.[67] Charles W. F. Smith demonstrated that in the Old Testament and the Dead Sea Scrolls, fishing is used metaphorically for gathering people for judgment:[68]

> The Lord God has sworn by his holiness: The time is surely coming upon you, when they shall take you away with hooks, even the last of you with fishhooks. (Amos 4:2)

> You have made people like the fish of the sea. . . . The enemy brings all of them up with a hook, he drags them out with his net, he gathers them in his seine; so he rejoices and exults. (Hab. 1:14–15)

> I am now sending for many fishermen, says the Lord, and they shall catch them. . . . " (Jer. 16:16)

> And Thou hast set me in a place of exile among many fishers that stretch a net upon the face of the waters, and [among] hunters [sent] against the sons of perversity. (1QH 5.7–8)[69]

On the basis of these texts, Smith argued that "the figure of the fishers is one of judgment and the fishermen are its agents." The call to the disciples, therefore, is "a commission to gather the people for the judgment."[70] Rudolf Bultmann's suggestion that the whole scene is woven out of the metaphor "fishers of men" must be rejected as improbable.[71] The provenance of Jesus' ministry (esp. Capernaum and Bethsaida) and the repeated references to fishing in the Gospel traditions make it highly unlikely that the identification of these disciples as fishermen originated from the metaphor rather than from historical fact.

On the other hand, whereas Smith declares that "as 'fishers' their call was to an eschatological task which would virtually preclude learning and teaching in the ordinary sense,"[72] the parallels adduced by Wuellner and Robbins show that the call was understood in light of both the prophetic and the Graeco-Roman school traditions: "While fishing for men in biblical tradition usually refers to an act of judgment by God, fishing in Greek literature is a well-established metaphor for teaching and learning in relation to philosopher-teachers."[73] In the Gospels, the call to become fishers of men becomes a call to gather men and women for the kingdom. It retains eschatological overtones from the biblical traditions, authorizes the disciples as representatives of their teacher and agents of the kingdom, and looks on to the church's evangelistic mission.

The Call in Luke

In Luke, the call of the fishermen (5:1–11) is set in the context of the miraculous catch of fish. Its climax is Jesus' call to Simon Peter: "Do not be afraid; from now on you will be catching people" (5:10b). The call of James and John, on the other hand, is subordinated to the call of Simon Peter. They are mentioned only in verse 10 and presumably included in verse 11: "When they had brought their boats to shore, they left everything and followed him." The Lukan account explains why the fishermen were willing to leave everything to follow Jesus, so it provides a psychologically more plausible account than Mark and Matthew.

Luke 5:1–11, however, seems to depend on a traditional story found also in John 21:1–14, where a strikingly similar catch of fish is reported in a post-resurrection context. Raymond E. Brown has listed ten points shared by the two accounts: (1) the disciples have fished all night with no results, (2) Jesus challenges them to let down the nets, (3) the disciples then enclose an enormous catch in their nets, (4) the effect this catch has on the nets is observed, (5) Peter's reaction is described, (6) Jesus is called Lord, (7) other fishermen take part in the catch but say nothing, (8) the theme of following Jesus is introduced, (9) the catch of fish "symbolizes a successful Christian missionary endeavor," and (10) the same words for "getting on board," "net," etc., appear at various points in the two stories.[74]

Four theses have been advanced to account for these similarities: (1) both are historically correct—there were two miraculous catches of fish, one at the calling of Peter and one at his restoration to discipleship following his denials in the courtyard;[75] (2) there was one catch of fish—at the call of the disciples, as Luke has it;[76] (3) the catch of fish was originally a post-resurrection appearance tradition, as John has it;[77] and (4) no historical event lies behind this tradition.[78] The issues are not easily resolved,[79] and a good case can be made for each of the alternatives.

It is noteworthy that Peter is called "Simon Peter," for this is the only occurrence of the double name in Luke. Moreover, James and John are named in the traditional sequence rather than in the reverse as in Luke 8:51 and 9:28 and in Acts 1:13. These details confirm Luke's dependence on tradition— tradition that has apparently gone through an extended process of development. Without attempting a detailed analysis, we may indicate that the similarities are sufficient to point to a common tradition lying behind both Luke 5 and John 21. Two considerations tilt the balance in favor of the hypothesis that Luke has taken a post-Easter appearance tradition and placed it back in the ministry of Jesus. First, following Luke's geographical scheme (ministry in Galilee, journey to Jerusalem, passion and resurrection, and mission beginning from Jerusalem), the appearances in Luke 24 take place in and around Jerusalem. There is no place for a Galilean appearance. Second, Peter's response, "Depart from me, for I am a sinful man," has particular force if the scene follows his denials in the courtyard. It is not clear, however, that the miracle story was originally an appearance tradition. No other appearance takes the form of a miracle story. Whatever the original function of the miracle story, it was used as a post-Easter-appearance account before it became part of the Fourth Gospel. Luke retrojected the appearance into the ministry of Jesus as a call narrative.

The connection of the call to the catch of fish is therefore secondary and probably dependent on Mark 1:16–20.[80] Whatever is made of the intricacies of these arguments, it is nevertheless clear that Luke 5:1–11 cannot be used with any confidence as a source of information regarding John the son of Zebedee's call to discipleship. Indeed, if John were the Beloved Disciple who was responsible for the tradition of the Fourth Gospel, and if the catch of fish were the occasion of his calling to discipleship, one would certainly expect the account to be presented in this way in the Gospel of John. In all likelihood, however, neither of these "ifs" should be taken as historical fact.

CONCLUSION

What may be seen through the mists that surround the Sea of Galilee is that John was a fisherman, and the son of a fisherman, who probably spent his early life in Bethsaida, Capernaum, or another village at the north end of the lake. As a fisherman, John's lot was that of neither the rich nor the destitute. Recent excavations have confirmed the site of Bethsaida and retrieved a fishing boat from the Sea of Galilee. A great deal is also known about the nets and techniques used by ancient fishermen, so a surprisingly full picture of the early days of John's life can be constructed, though we have no reports of specific events prior to his call to discipleship. The call to be a "fisher of men," as it stands in the Gospels, is a call to follow Jesus as teacher and to devote himself to proclaiming the advent of the kingdom. The role of John as a disciple of Jesus is recorded in the synoptic Gospels, and it is to that period of his life that we turn next.

NOTES

1. John 1:42 and 21:15–17 read "Simon, the son of John [*Iōannou*]." Matthew 16:17 reads "Simon, son of Jonah [*Bariōna*]. The similarity between the two names probably led to the development of two different traditions regarding the name of Simon Peter's father.
2. Josephus, *Ant.* 5.33, identifies Achar (Josh. 7:1), as "son of Zebedee, of the tribe of Judah." *Josephus,* trans. H. St. J. Thackeray et al, LCL (Cambridge, Mass.: Harvard University Press, 1934), 5:17.
3. Gustaf Dalman, *Sacred Sites and Ways: Studies in the Topography of the Gospels,* trans. P. P. Levertoff (London: S.P.C.K., 1935), 143.
4. See the Ethiopic text "The Genealogies of the Twelve Apostles"; English translation, Ernest A. Wallis Budge, *The Contendings of the Apostles* (Amsterdam: Apa-Philo Press, 1976), 2:40. Jean-Daniel Kaestli has called my attention to other traditions regarding Zebedee's tribe of origin in the prologue of the *Acts of John by Prochorus* in Vatican Gr. 654, fol. 88ᵛ–89. In this account, Zebedee was a priest from Jerusalem who had moved to Capernaum. His wife, the mother of James and John, was Maria, the cousin of Mary the mother of Jesus. See Eric Junod and Jean-Daniel Kaestli, *Acta Iohannis,* CChr (Turnhout: Brepols, 1983), 1:10, 35.
5. If Luke has reversed the sequence of the two names because he knew John to be the more famous, did he also know of Gospel traditions associated with John? See the interesting parallels distinctive to Luke and John cited in F. Lamar Cribbs, "St. Luke and the Johannine Tradition," *JBL* 90 (1971): 422–50; and "The Agreements that Exist between John and Acts," in *Perspectives on Luke-Acts,* ed. Charles H. Talbert, Special Studies Series 5 (Danville, Va.: Association of Baptist Professors of Religion, 1978), 40–61.
6. Salome is identified as the mother of the sons of Zebedee and the daughter of Joseph in the *Chronikon* of Hippolytus of Thebes, in *Hippolytus von Theben,* ed. Franz Diekamp, 4th ed., TU (Münster: D. Aschendorff, 1898), 20, ll. 3–5 (a passage interpolated from the *Encomium* of Sophrinus of Jerusalem [A.D. 560–638]). Cf. Migne, *PG* 117:1033. See below, p. 174.
7. See Ronald Brownrigg, *The Twelve Apostles* (New York: Macmillan, 1974), 89: "James and John had a close familial link both with Jesus and even with John the Baptist. The mothers of James and John, and of Jesus, were the two sisters Salome and Mary, daughters of Joachim and Anna." The tradition that Joachim and Anna were the parents of Mary the mother of Jesus is based on the Protoevangelium of James, an apocryphal work that is dated about A.D. 150. Salome is mentioned as a witness of the virgin birth, but she is not identified as Mary's sister in the Protoevangelium of James.
8. Josephus, *Jewish War* 3.508 (LCL 2:719).
9. Michael I. Rostovtzeff, *The Social and Economic History of the Hellenistic World* (Oxford: Clarendon Press, 1941), 2:1177.

10. Salo Wittmayer Baron, *A Social and Religious History of the Jews* (New York: Columbia University Press, 1952), 1:254–55.

11. b. Pes. 46a.

12. Strabo, *Geography* 16.2.45; *The Geography of Strabo,* trans. Horace Leonard Jones, LCL (Cambridge, Mass.: Harvard University Press, 1954), 7:297.

13. Josephus, *Jewish War* 2.635 (LCL 2:567); cf. *Life* 163–68 (LCL 1:63–65).

14. See Mendel Nun, *The Sea of Galilee and Its Fishermen in the New Testament* (Kibbutz Ein Gev: Kinnereth Sailing Co., 1989), 6–11; P. Franz Dunkel, "Die Fischerei am See Gennesareth und das Neue Testament," *Biblica* 5 (1924): 383–86; Ernest W. Gurney Masterman, *Studies in Galilee* (Chicago: University of Chicago Press, 1909), 43–48; F. S. Bodenheimer, "Fish," in *IDB* (Nashville: Abingdon Press, 1962), 2:272–73.

15. Josephus, *Jewish War* 3.520 (LCL 2:723).

16. Seán Freyne, *Galilee from Alexander the Great to Hadrian, 323 B.C.E. to 135 C.E.: A Study of Second Temple Judaism* (Wilmington, Del.: Michael Glazier, 1980), 174.

17. Roland K. Harrison, "Fish," in *International Standard Bible Encyclopedia* (Grand Rapids: Wm. B. Eerdmans, 1982), 2:309.

18. *m. Shebiith* 7.4. Herbert Danby, trans., *The Mishnah* (London: Oxford University Press, 1933), 47.

19. *m. Makshirin* 6.3 (Danby, 765).

20. *m. Betzah* 3.2 (Danby, 185); cf. *m. Shabbath* 1.6 (Danby, 101).

21. *t. Baba Qamma* 8.18, in Jacob Neusner, *The Tosefta: Neziqin* (New York: KTAV, 1981), 49.

22. *b. Baba Qamma* 81a, in *Talmud: Bava Kamma,* trans. E. W. Kirzner, ed. I. Epstein (London: Soncino Press, 1935), 461.

23. *t. Baba Qamma* 8.17, in Neusner, *The Tosefta,* 49. See further Daniel Sperber, "Some Observations of Fish and Fisheries in Roman Palestine," *Zeitschrift der Deutschen Morgenländischen Gesellschaft* 118 (1968): 265–69.

24. *Recognitions of Clement* 2.62–63; in *The Ante-Nicene Fathers,* ed. Alexander Roberts and James Donaldson (Grand Rapids: Wm. B. Eerdmans, 1986), 8:114.

25. Louis Ginzberg, *The Legends of the Jews* (Philadelphia: Jewish Publication Society of America, 1968), 4:221. For descriptions of fishing in antiquity and the various nets employed on the Sea of Galilee, see further William Radcliffe, *Fishing from the Earliest Times* (Chicago: Ares Publishers, 1974); Nun, *The Sea of Galilee and Its Fishermen in the New Testament,* 16–48.

26. Dunkel, "Die Fischerei," 375–81. Dunkel also reports that the period from the middle of December to the middle of April is the best season for fishing. Among the most productive areas of the lake, he lists (see 381–82) Capernaum (Tell Hum) and Tabgha.

27. Masterman, *Studies in Galilee,* 39–42; Eric F. F. Bishop, "Jesus and the Lake," *CBQ* 13 (1951): 401; Wilhelm H. Wuellner, *The Meaning of "Fishers of Men"* (Philadelphia: Westminster Press, 1967), 39, 232–33.

28. Masterman, *Studies in Galilee,* 43; Bishop, "Jesus and the Lake," 401–2; cf. Marion L. Soards, *"ton ependytēn diezōsato, ēn gar gymnos,"* *JBL* 102 (1983): 283–84.

29. For information regarding the "Galilee boat," see the report of the director of the excavation, Shelley Wachsmann: "The Galilee Boat—2,000-Year-Old Hull Recovered Intact," *BAR* 14, no. 5 (1988): 1833.

30. Josephus, *Jewish War* 3.525, 530 (LCL 2:725).

31. For further information on the boats of this period and region, see Daniel Sperber, *Nautica Talmudica* (Leiden: E. J. Brill, 1986).

32. A. T. Robertson, *Epochs in the Life of the Apostle John* (New York: Fleming H. Revell, 1935), 16.

33. G. W. Buchanan, "Jesus and the Upper Class," *NovT* 7 (1964): 206.

34. Emil Schürer, *The History of the Jewish People in the Age of Jesus Christ*, rev. and ed. G. Vermes, F. Millar, and M. Black (Edinburgh: T. and T. Clark, 1973), 1:339.

35. Wuellner, *The Meaning of "Fishers of Men,"* 43. John R. Donahue argues that the *telōnēs* of the Gospels were toll collectors; see "Tax Collectors and Sinners: An Attempt at an Identification," *CBQ* 33 (1971): 39–61. The normal toll was two to five percent of the value of goods, except on the eastern frontier, where rates were higher. Capernaum was one of the toll collection points in Roman times (Otto Michel, "*telōnēs*," *Theological Dictionary of the New Testament*, ed. Gerhard Kittel and Gerhard Friedrich, trans. Geoffrey W. Bromiley (Grand Rapids: Wm. B. Eerdmanns, 1972), 8:88–105, esp. 98–99 and n. 118). "Collectors at the fishery tollhouse" (*tois epi tō telōnion tēs ichthyikēs*) are mentioned in an Ephesian inscription dated during the reign of Antoninus Pius (138–161 A.D.). See E. L. Hicks, *Priene, Iasos, and Ephesos*, vol. 3 of *The Collection of Ancient Greek Inscriptions in the British Museum*, ed. C. T. Newton (Oxford: Clarendon Press, 1890), 167; and Wilhelmus Dittenberger, *Orientis Graeci Inscriptiones Selectae* (Lipsiae: S. Hirzel, 1905), 134–35 (496, 8–11).

36. Origen, *Contra Celsum* 1.62 (*ANF* 4:423).

37. The primary source here is P. Teb. 701 (235 B.C.). *The Tebtunis Papyri*, ed. Arthur S. Hunt and J. Gilbart Smyly (London: Oxford University Press, 1933), 3:46–63; see esp., comments on ll. 86–90 and 202–8. See also Rostovtzeff, *Social and Economic History of the Hellenistic World* 1:296–97, 2:1177–79, 3:1387 n. 101.

38. Freyne, *Galilee*, 174.

39. Hippolytus of Thebes calls Zebedee "proprietor of the boat" (*idionauklypos*) and first among the eminent men (*tōn episēmōn*) of Galilee; see Migne, *PG* 117:1032, 1039, 1052.

40. Bishop, "Jesus and the Lake," 402.

41. William Dallmann, *John: Disciple, Evangelist, Apostle* (St. Louis: Concordia Publishing House, 1932), 3. See the aberrant tradition that John was from Zebede in Epiphanius the Monk, *The Life of the Virgin* (Migne, *PG* 120:204, 208–9).

42. Josephus, *Ant.* 18.28 (LCL 9:25); cf. *Jewish War* 2.168, 3.57 (LCL 2:387–89, 593).

43. Schürer, *History of the Jewish People* 2:172.

44. Heinz-Wolfgang Kuhn and Rami Arav, "The Bethsaida Excavations: Historical and Archaeological Approaches," in *The Future of Early Christianity: Essays in Honor of Helmut Koester*, ed. Birger A. Pearson (Minneapolis: Fortress Press, 1991), esp. 87–90.

45. Freyne, *Galilee*, 137.

46. C. H. Dodd, *Historical Tradition in the Fourth Gospel* (Cambridge: Cambridge University Press, 1963), 310 n. 1.
47. See Clemens Kopp, "Christian Sites Around the Sea of Galilee: II. Bethsaida and El-Minyeh," *Dominican Studies* 3 (1950): 10–40; Kopp, *The Holy Places of the Gospels,* trans. Ronald Walls (Freiburg: Herder and Herder, 1963), 180–86; Jack Finegan, *The Archaeology of the New Testament: The Life of Jesus and the Beginning of the Early Church* (Princeton: Princeton University Press, 1969), 60; Schürer, *History of the Jewish People,* 2:171–72.
48. Kuhn and Arav, "The Bethsaida Excavations," 91–107; Rami Arav and John J. Rosseau, "Elusive Bethsaida Recovered," *The Fourth R* 4 (January 1991): 1–4.
49. Geyer, *Itinera Hierosolymitana saeculi,* IIII–VIII [*sic*] (Vindebonae, 1898), 138; cited in Kopp, "Christian Sites," 17.
50. Tobler, *Descr. T. S.,* 26; cited in Dalman, *Sacred Sites and Ways,* 164.
51. Khitrowo, *Itinéraires Russes en Orient* (Geneva, 1889), 64; cited in Kopp, "Christian Sites," 27.
52. Kopp, "Christian Sites," 29.
53. Masterman, *Studies in Galilee,* 38.
54. Dalman, *Sacred Sites and Ways,* 139.
55. For accounts of the excavations at Capernaum, see Virgil Corbo and Stanislaus Loffredda, *New Memoirs of Saint Peter by the Sea of Galilee,* trans. G. Bushell (Jerusalem: Franciscan Printing Press, n.d.); Virgilio Corbo, *The House of St. Peter at Capharnaum,* trans. S. Saller, Publications of the Studium Biblicum Franciscanum 5 (Jerusalem: Franciscan Printing Press, 1972); and Finegan, *Archaeology,* 51–56.
56. J. Garrow Duncan, "The Sea of Tiberias and Its Environs," *Palestine Exploration Fund Quarterly* (1926): 20.
57. Wuellner, *The Meaning of "Fishers of Men,"* 39.
58. Epiphanius the Monk, in *The Life of the Virgin* (Migne, *PG* 120:208A), reports that Jesus went to Zebede, ate with Zebedee, and took James and John as his disciples. Their mother asked that they might have the left and right hand seats in the kingdom (cf. Matt. 20:20–28).
59. G. R. Wynne, "Mending Their Nets," *The Expositor* 7th ser., 8 (1909): 285.
60. Vernon K. Robbins, "Mark 1.14–20: An Interpretation at the Intersection of Jewish and Graeco-Roman Traditions," *NTS* 28 (1982): 220–36, analyzes the parallels between Mark 1:14–20 and Socrates' invitation to Euthydemus in Xenophon, *Memorabilia* 4.1.5–4.2.39.
61. Aristophanes, *The Clouds* 497–517; cited in Robbins, "Mark 1:14–20," 227.
62. Diogenes Laertius, *Lives* 2.48; cited in Robbins, "Mark 1:14–20," 227.
63. Cf. Josephus, *Ant.* 8.354 (LCL 5:763).
64. Josephus, *Ant.* 8.228–29 (LCL 5:695).
65. Martin Hengel, however, rejects A. Schulz's view "that the call to follow is to be understood as the establishment of a teacher-pupil relationship between Jesus and his disciples on the analogy of the activities of a rabbinical school"; see *The Charismatic Leader and His Followers,* trans. J. Greig (New York: Crossroad, 1981), 13–14.

66. Jindrich Manek, "Fishers of Men," *NovT* 2 (1957): 139.

67. Joseph A. Fitzmyer, *The Gospel According to Luke,* AB 28 (Garden City: Doubleday, 1981), 568–69.

68. See Charles W. F. Smith, "Fishers of Men," *HTR* 52 (1959): 187–203, esp. 189–90.

69. A. Dupont-Sommer, *The Essene Writings from Qumran,* trans. Geza Vermes (Cleveland: World Publishing Co., 1961), 214.

70. Charles W. F. Smith, "Fishers of Men," 190–91.

71. Rudolf Bultmann, *The History of the Synoptic Tradition,* rev., ed., and trans. J. Marsh (New York: Harper and Row, 1963), 28. Hengel responds: "It is . . . perverse to think that the whole anecdote in Mk. 1.16, 17 has been 'spun out of' this saying" (*The Charismatic Leader,* 77).

72. Charles W. F. Smith, "Fishers of Men," 193.

73. Robbins, "Mark 1:14–20," 230; see Wuellner, *The Meaning of "Fishers of Men,"* 70–72.

74. Raymond E. Brown, *The Gospel According to John,* AB 29a (Garden City: Doubleday, 1970), 1090.

75. See I. Howard Marshall, *The Gospel of Luke,* NIGTC (Grand Rapids: Wm. B. Eerdmans, 1978): "While few scholars would allow that Luke has recorded a tradition separate from that incorporated in Jn. 21, there is no real evidence that forbids this possibility. There are other examples in the Gospels of pairs of similar but distinct incidents (cf. 7:36–50) where the parallel features have led to some modification of each narrative in the light of the other, and this may well have been the case here" (200).

76. Eduard Schweizer, *The Good News According to Luke,* trans. David E. Green (Atlanta: John Knox Press, 1984), 103; cf. Reginald H. Fuller, *The Formation of the Resurrection Narratives,* 2d ed. (Philadelphia: Fortress Press, 1980), 147–52, 160–61.

77. Brown, *John,* 1091; cf. John A. Bailey, *The Traditions Common to the Gospels of Luke and John,* NovTSup 7 (Leiden: E. J. Brill, 1963), 12–17.

78. Rudolf Pesch, *Der reiche Fischfang* (Düsseldorf: Patmos-Verlag, 1969), 111, 126–30. Both accounts rest on an earlier, legendary miracle story: "die ganze Erzählung ist reichlich legendär (und novellistisch) angelegt" (128).

79. Pheme Perkins comments, "It is not possible to decide whether the miraculous catch of fish should be seen as a resurrection tradition that Luke has retrojected into his gospel or whether it is a miracle tradition from the life of Jesus that the Johannine community has linked to the tradition of a Galilean appearance of the Lord"; see *Resurrection: New Testament Witness and Contemporary Reflection* (Garden City: Doubleday, 1984), 181.

80. Pesch, *Der reiche Fischfang,* 72–76. Cf. Marshall, *Luke:* "On the whole, it seems more probable that Luke has incorporated the miracle story in a framework based on Mk., and in so doing he may have replaced the original ending of the miracle story with Marcan material" (201).

CHAPTER 2

Son of Thunder
The Apostle in the Synoptic Gospels and Acts

The last several decades have brought significant changes in the way in which interpreters view the Gospels. Whereas books on the apostle John once sought to harmonize the Gospels in order to present a coherent account of his early life, recent scholarship has demonstrated that each Gospel presents a distinctive view of the ministry of Jesus. The Gospels also reflect differing perspectives on the role of the disciples.[1] In this chapter, each reference to the apostle in the synoptic Gospels will be examined. Although the synoptics are treated together here, the distinctive themes of each Gospel will be recognized as they impinge on the scenes in which John appears. The role of the Beloved Disciple in the Gospel of John is the subject of the next chapter.

One of the peculiarities of the Gospel accounts is that John is featured alone with Jesus in only one scene, when John had ordered a man to stop casting out demons in Jesus' name (Mark 9:38; Luke 9:49). Even here, John speaks as one of a group of the disciples: "Teacher, we saw someone casting out demons in your name, and we tried to stop him because he was not following us." In every other reference, John appears as one of the Twelve, one of the inner three or four, with his brother or with Peter. Moreover, there is a clear relationship between the type of scene in which John appears and the identity of his companions. As a result, the groups in which the apostle appears offer a convenient way of organizing the synoptic Gospels' references to John.

JOHN AND THE TWELVE

John appears in each of the lists of the twelve disciples (Mark 3:17; Matt. 10:2; Luke 6:14; and Acts 1:13). Each of these lists places the two sets of fishermen brothers first, so John always appears among the first four names:

28

Mark	Matthew	Luke	Acts
Simon	Simon	Simon	Peter
James	Andrew	Andrew	John
John	James	James	James
Andrew	John	John	Andrew

Interesting implications arise from the variations in the sequence of names in these four lists. Simon Peter is always named first. Mark then lists James and John, thus placing the "inner three" disciples first in the list. Only these three are given a special name, and only in Mark does the name *Boanerges* appear in the list of the Twelve. Mark has evidently arranged the names in this order and supplied the Semitic nicknames.[2] Andrew, who was called at the same time and who appears with the other three at the eschatological discourse on the Mount of Olives (Mark 13:3), is named in fourth place. Mark's list, therefore, sets up the first three as a significant group which will appear in important scenes later in the Gospel.

Throughout this chapter, the priority of Mark and Q (a hypothetical collection of Jesus' sayings used by Matthew and Luke) is assumed as the working hypothesis for handling Matthew and Luke's interpretation of the synoptic traditions. Matthew and Luke, who wrote after Mark and independently of one another, agree in moving Andrew to second place, preserving his position as Simon's brother. James and John then follow in the normal sequence, with James first. These two lists, therefore, reflect the tradition of the call of the two sets of brothers as we find it in Mark 1:16–20 and Matthew 4:18–22. The call of the two sets of brothers was apparently more important to Matthew and Luke than was the special role of the "inner three" disciples.

The list in the first chapter of Acts uses the name "Peter" rather than "Simon" and moves John to second place in the list. The lesser-known brothers follow. Peter and John appear together on several occasions in the succeeding chapters. In fact, John is mentioned in Acts only as Peter's silent, apostolic companion. The only exception is in Acts 12:2, where James is identified as John's brother. The list in Acts, therefore, features Peter and John as the apostolic leaders of the early church, the role they play in the first part of the book.

Three traditions are reflected in these lists: the call of the two sets of brothers, the role of the inner three, and the importance of Peter and John in the early church. The first of these is examined in chapter 1; the other two are discussed below. Before we turn to the role of the inner three, however, the contrasting roles given to the disciples in the synoptic Gospels should be noted.

In the Gospel of Mark, the disciples are portrayed as moving from a lack of understanding to complete failure to understand. They do not comprehend the parable of the sower (see Mark 4:10–13). Their greatest success comes when they follow Jesus' instructions after they are sent out by twos (6:7–13), but then they do not grasp the meaning of the feeding of the five thousand or the feeding of the four thousand. Jesus challenges them: "Do you still not perceive or understand? Are your hearts hardened? Do you have eyes, and fail to see? Do you have ears, and fail to hear? And do you not remember?" (8:17–18; compare the plight of the outsiders in Mark 4:10–12). Mark indicates that indeed their hearts were hardened (6:52).

Even following Peter's confession at Caesarea Philippi, the disciples do not understand what Jesus is doing. Three times, Jesus tells the disciples that he is going up to Jerusalem, where he will be killed and rise on the third day. Each time, the disciples (Peter in Mark 8:32–33, all the disciples in 9:33–34, and then James and John in 10:35–37) show not only that they do not understand but that they were pursuing the self-centered objectives of glory and reward (10:28–29). Only those to whom sight is given can follow Jesus (10:52). In Jerusalem, Jesus instructs the disciples to watch so that they will be ready for the trauma of the destruction of Jerusalem and the coming of the Son of Man, but in the Garden of Gethsemane, they cannot watch with Jesus for even one hour (14:34–42). When Jesus is arrested, they flee into the night, abandoning him and their call to be his followers (14:50). The failure of the disciples could hardly be more complete; only the promise of a meeting with the risen Lord holds out hope for their future usefulness (16:7; see also 13:9–13).[3]

Although Matthew and Luke contain some of these same scenes, the failure of the disciples is softened in these books. Each Gospel offers its own portrait of the disciples. In Matthew, the disciples are characterized as those who are taught by Jesus. Shortly after calling the first disciples, Jesus delivers the Sermon on the Mount to the disciples and the crowd following him. One who hears Jesus' teaching and lives by it is like the wise man who built his house upon the rock (7:24). Whereas others may not hear and respond to Jesus' teachings (13:11–15), Jesus assures the disciples: "But blessed are your eyes, for they see, and your ears, for they hear. Truly, I tell you, many prophets and righteous people longed to see what you see, but did not see it, and to hear what you hear, but did not hear it" (13:16–17). Jesus explains the parables privately to the disciples and then likens their role to that of a scribe: " 'Have you understood all this?' They answered, 'Yes.' And he said to them, 'Therefore every scribe who has been trained for the kingdom of heaven is like the master of a household who brings out of his treasure what is new and what is old' " (13:51–52).

Matthew further softens Mark's judgment on the failure of the disciples by changing the conclusion of the story of Jesus' walking on the water. Whereas Mark wrote, "And they were utterly astounded, for they did not understand about the loaves, but their hearts were hardened" (6:51–52), Matthew reports that Peter walked on the water with Jesus, "and those in the boat worshiped him, saying, 'Truly you are the Son of God'" (14:33). Neither here nor anywhere else in the Gospel of Mark do the disciples confess that Jesus is the Son of God. Jesus confers the keys to the kingdom to Simon Peter in Matthew 16:17–20 (cf. Mark 8:29–30). Matthew also includes an account of the disciples' meeting with the risen Lord in Galilee. Those who have been taught are commissioned to become teachers and to make disciples "of all nations . . . teaching them to obey everything that I have commanded you" (28:19–20). For Matthew, therefore, the disciples are those who are called to receive and to follow Jesus' teachings and in turn to make disciples of others.

The Gospel of Luke presents Jesus as a model to be imitated: he prays (5:16; 6:12; 9:18, 28), has compassion on the outcasts (5:27–32; 7:36–50), and dies an ideal martyr's death (23:32–47). The principle at work is that "A disciple is not above the teacher, but every one who is fully qualified will be like the teacher" (6:40). The disciples, as his followers, also set an example for the Gospel's Christian readers. Luke therefore, like Matthew, softens Mark's sharp words on the obtuseness of the disciples. For example, Luke has no parallel to Mark 4:13—"Do you not understand this parable? Then how will you understand all the parables?" Neither does Luke have anything comparable to Mark 6:51–52 (quoted above) or 8:17–21, which concludes with the sharp question: "Do you not yet understand?" Luke also omits any reference to the flight of the disciples when Jesus was arrested. Instead, he says "Peter was following at a distance" (22:54). Similarly, Luke's redaction of Mark 8:34 conveys something of his concept of discipleship as well as the change from Mark's setting of persecution and eschatological fervor to a more settled situation: "If any want to become my followers, let them deny themselves and take up their cross *daily* and follow me" (9:23). Not surprisingly, we find that in the Book of Acts, the disciples are pictured as continuing the ministry of Jesus by means of their preaching and healing miracles (Acts 2:43; 3:1–10; 5:12–16).[4]

JOHN AND THE INNER THREE

The Gospels record three scenes in which Jesus left the other nine disciples and took with him only Peter, James, and John: the raising of Jairus's daughter, the transfiguration, and the Garden of Gethsemane. The role of this group of disciples seems to have been more important for Mark than for either Matthew, who does not single them out at the raising of Jairus's daughter, or Luke, who does not separate them from the others at Gethsemane. Neither Matthew nor Luke introduces this group into any other scene.

One may conjecture, therefore, that the inner three had special significance for Mark, perhaps in conjunction with the Gospel of Mark's secrecy motif. On several occasions, Jesus teaches the disciples privately (Mark 4:10, 34; 8:27; 9:33; 10:32). In a justly famous dictum, the German New Testament scholar Martin Dibelius described Mark as a Gospel of secret epiphanies.[5] To the disciples was given "the secret of the kingdom of God, but for those outside, everything comes in parables" (4:11). The special group of three disciples served as witnesses to the most secret events of Jesus' ministry: the only raising of a dead person in Mark, the transfiguration, and Jesus' agony in the garden.

In addition to their being identified by name in these scenes, the first four disciples whom Jesus called are named in two other places in Mark—the healing of Peter's mother-in-law (1:29) and Jesus' eschatological discourse on the Mount of Olives (13:3)—but not in either Matthew or Luke. The first of these scenes in Mark is different from the others in that it lacks the character of a secret epiphany. The explanation for the presence of the four disciples may be as simple as the observation that this first healing follows shortly after the call of the two sets of brothers and precedes the calling of any of the other disciples. The names of James and John appear as an appendage in Mark 1:29, just as their calling to discipleship is a doublet of the calling of Simon and Andrew (Mark 1:16–20).

Jesus went from the synagogue to Peter's house, where Peter's mother-in-law "was in bed with a fever." Jesus touched her hand, and the fever left her. The next morning, Peter "and his companions" (1:36) went out in search of Jesus, who had gone out alone to pray. The brief exchange that follows is the first hint that the disciples do not, and perhaps cannot, understand who Jesus is or what he is doing.

Andrew unexpectedly reappears with the inner three at the discourse on the Mount of Olives. Even here, Andrew is added to the group of three rather than being named immediately after his brother is mentioned. The function of the group of four disciples in Mark 13 is the same as that of the inner three in the other three Markan scenes. They are witnesses to secret disclosures— here, Jesus' prophecy of the destruction of the temple, the coming of false prophets, and the coming of the Son of Man.

Jairus's Daughter

The healing of the woman with a flow of blood is sandwiched inside the account of the raising of Jairus's daughter in Mark 5:37 and Luke 8:51. Scholarship is still divided on the question of whether this sandwiching is Markan or had already occurred in the pre-Markan tradition.[6]

According to Mark, Jesus allowed only the three disciples to accompany him to Jairus's house (5:37). When they arrived at the house, he allowed only the girl's parents "and those who were with him" to enter the room where the child was (5:40). Matthew reports the story but does not mention either the three disciples or the child's parents. In Matthew's handling, therefore, the story loses its character as a secret manifestation of Jesus' power. Luke changes both the sequence of names and the point at which the three disciples are separated from the others. Once Jesus arrived at the house, "he did not allow anyone to enter with him, except Peter, John, and James, and the child's father and mother" (Luke 8:51). The sequence here agrees with the sequence of the names in the list of the Twelve in Acts 1:13.

Various assessments have been made of the relationship of the three disciples to this and the other events at which they appear. Rudolf Bultmann recognized the tendency of the tradition to give names to unidentified participants, but declared: "I think it probable that those sections of the tradition which use the names of individual disciples come from an earlier time when the idea of the Twelve as Jesus' constant companions had not yet been formed or carried through. I further think that in the following passages the naming of the disciples is original: [Mark] 5:37, 9:38, 10:35 and probably 13:3 as well."[7]

Others have challenged this view, maintaining that Mark introduced the group of three into this scene,[8] but no explanation is given for why the privileged witnesses should be this group of three disciples. If there is not some historical basis for the recollection that these three disciples were Jesus' closest associates, how did the "inner three" enter the tradition? If the call narratives were the basis for the tradition, we would expect the group to include Andrew (as in Mark 13:3).

The Transfiguration

Peter, James, and John are again singled out in all three synoptic Gospels as the witnesses of the transfiguration: Mark 9:2, Matthew 17:1, Luke 9:28. Few passages have been more intractable to critical evaluation,[9] the range of interpretations spanning the analytical spectrum. The historicity of the event has been defended.[10] Symbolic interpretations have related the transfiguration to the Feast of Tabernacles, the Parousia, and the Exodus and wilderness period.[11] Although it has found contemporary defenders, the thesis that the transfiguration is a post-resurrection appearance retrojected into the ministry of Jesus has been convincingly rejected by a series of British and American scholars.[12] Although we may never be able to determine the nature of the event that gave rise to this tradition, attempting to explain its origin as a post-resurrection appearance merely adds further complications.[13]

In a seminal article, Bruce Chilton distinguishes traditional and redactional material in the Markan account of the transfiguration.[14] Chilton identifies the list of the three names as Markan redaction, but nevertheless concludes that the transfiguration added authority to these three "pillars of the church" (Gal. 2:9): "the Pauline evidence is consistent with the view that Peter, James and John were responsible for the traditional shape of the Transfiguration narrative."[15] Paul responded to this tradition by defining his apostolic authority with reference to the Mosaic revelation (2 Cor. 3:7–4:6). Chilton therefore suggests that the three disciples are cast in the roles of Aaron, Nadab, and Abihu (see Exod. 6:23; Lev. 10:1; Exod. 24:1, 9). Building on Chilton's analysis, John Anthony McGuckin theorizes that the tradition of the transfiguration began as a homily delivered by Peter, who cast himself in the role of Aaron. James and John were given the subsidiary roles of Nadab and Abihu.[16]

Fascinating as the thesis of Chilton and McGuckin is, the group of three disciples included James the son of Zebedee, whereas the James of the "pillars of the church" is uniformly understood to be James the brother of Jesus. Confusion between these two groups can be traced back to the second century. The best texts of Galatians 2:9 name the apostles as "James, Cephas, and John," but the traditional list of the inner three has left its mark on the textual tradition. Most notably, Codex Claromontanus, Tertullian, and Ambrosiaster list the three as "Peter, James, and John."[17] In view of such confusion, one must recognize the possibility that the role of the three disciples in Mark has been shaped by the memory that three apostles were leaders of the church in Jerusalem after Jesus' death.

The Petrine tradition, which relates the transfiguration to the Parousia, does not mention James and John.[18] Nevertheless, the repeated references to "we" in 2 Peter 1:16–19, especially following the first-person singular references in the previous verses, may be a vestige of the tradition that the transfiguration was witnessed by the group of three. The Apocalypse of Peter (Ethiopic 15–16), which has been dated to A.D. 135, is dependent upon the synoptic accounts, but it does not mention the sons of Zebedee.[19] Instead, "the disciples" accompany Jesus to the mountain, and Peter's role is extended by legendary details.

In a detailed analysis of the reference to the three disciples at the transfiguration, Maria Horstmann argues that the list of the Twelve in Mark 3:14–16—which names Peter, James, and John first—rests on pre-Markan tradition. The role of the inner three, moreover, is akin to the organization at Qumran, which featured a council of twelve and three priests (1QS 8:1). As Horstmann notes, it is not clear from the Manual of Disciple whether the three were part of the twelve or in addition to them. Finding the group of three in the tradition, Horstmann argues, Mark then used it to underscore the secrecy motif.[20]

An alternative position maintains that the naming of the three disciples at the transfiguration is an element of Markan redaction.[21] The scene originally included either Peter only or "the disciples." Indeed, it has been argued that Mark is responsible for all of the references to the group of three disciples.[22]

Nothing in the transfiguration scene requires that the group of disciples who withdrew with Jesus "apart by themselves" (9:2) was limited to the three. The Markan handling of the narrative, however, uses the separation of Jesus and the three from the other disciples as an occasion for private instruction (9:9–13). It also allows Mark to underscore the failure of the disciples to help the boy with an unclean spirit (9:14–29). There is good reason, therefore, to conclude that Mark has inserted the names of the three disciples into a unit of traditional material. Nevertheless, one cannot escape the question that if the three were not connected with one or more of the events with which their names are linked, how did they enter the Gospel traditions?[23] The alternatives seem to be the following: (1) Mark created this group of three and inserted them into the transfiguration scene as well as into the other Gospel scenes where he names these three; (2) the group of three had been featured in a memorable scene, probably the transfiguration, and Mark included them in the other Gospel scenes in order to enhance his portrayal of the secret revelations of Jesus' divinity; (3) the group was named in the pre-Markan tradition at each point where Mark refers to the "inner three."

Although the origin of this group remains debatable, it is clear that Mark shows a special interest in them and may therefore have added the names of Peter, James, and John to scenes which did not originally cite individual names at all. It is also possible that the memory of the leadership of James, Cephas, and John helped to foster a role for Peter, James, and John in the Gospel materials. If the latter were the case, however, one might have expected to find this group featured more prominently in either Matthew or Luke, both of which portray the disciples in a more favorable light than Mark does.

The Mount of Olives

The Gospel of Mark names "Peter, James, John, and Andrew" as Jesus' interlocutors on the Mount of Olives (Mark 13:3). Neither Matthew nor Luke identifies any of the disciples by name at this point. Matthew specifies that the question was raised by "the disciples" (Matt. 24:3), but Luke, who identifies the questioners only as "some" of the people, allows Jesus' response to be addressed to all, not just the disciples (21:5). Apart from the call of the disciples in Mark 1:16–20 and its parallels, this is the only other passage in the Gospels where these four disciples are singled out as a group. Their questions reveal a keen interest in the signs that will accompany the destruction of the temple. Jesus distinguishes the destruction of the temple from the time of the coming of the Son of Man, but the discourse does not tell us whether the disciples had related these two events to one another.

The four disciples appear as a group in Mark 1:16–20, where the two sets of brothers are called to follow Jesus, and in Mark 3:16–17, where they are named first. As in the list of the Twelve in Mark 3:16–17, Andrew is added to the list of the three disciples in Mark 13:3.[24] Again we face the question of the reliability of the list of names attached to this tradition. Did the pre-Markan eschatological discourse name these disciples, or are they part of Mark's redactional framing of the discourse? What, if anything, can be made of the absence of the names in the other two Gospels? Did the tradition move from naming the individuals at an early period to elevating the role of the Twelve as Jesus' companions? Or did Matthew and Luke have sources other than Mark which did not contain the names of the four disciples?

The passage is consistent with Mark's technique of having the disciples or a group of disciples question Jesus privately. Again, this observation can cut in two directions, and possibly both are correct. Mark may have introduced the select group of four in order to heighten the private nature of this teaching. On the other hand, Matthew and Luke—who do not attach such significance to the distinction between insiders and outsiders and do not present Jesus' ministry as a series of secret epiphanies—allow Jesus' teachings to be addressed to a wider group by removing the restrictive identification of the four disciples.

The key question, then, is whether Mark attached the names to the discourse or whether they were already identified with it in the pre-Markan material. Vincent Taylor, who introduced form criticism to British and American scholarship, recognized that the vocabulary of verses 3 and 4 suggests Markan composition, but protests that "it is not a mere literary setting for 5–37; it is more probable that he is using oral or written tradition."[25]

Assuming that the names were part of the early tradition, one may suspect that the original group was composed of only Peter, James, and John. The name of Andrew was added subsequently, not by Mark, who uses the group of three elsewhere, but by someone who assumed that the group would have been the original fishermen brothers. The placement of Andrew's name at the end of the list rather than after Peter's remains as evidence of the earlier tradition that the disciples who raised the question that triggered this discourse were the inner three—Peter, James, and John.

Gethsemane

Mark reports that when Jesus went to Gethsemane, he told the larger group of disciples to sit and pray while he took "Peter and James and John" and went further (14:33). He left them with the instructions "remain here and watch" while he prayed by himself. Matthew follows Mark closely, changing the designation of the disciples to "Peter and the two sons of Zebedee" (26:37). This change gives less prominence to the individual roles of James and John. Presumably, their names were at least as well known in the tradition as that of their father, Zebedee.

Matthew diminishes the role of John noticeably. Whereas John is named ten times in the Gospel of Mark, his name appears only three times in Matthew (the call of the fishermen, 4:21; the list of the Twelve, 10:2; and the transfiguration, 17:1). John, the son of Zebedee, therefore, seems to have been less important for Matthew than for any of the other Gospel writers. Not irrelevant is the further observation that Matthew elevates the position of Peter more than any of the other Gospels do. Peter's name appears twenty-three times in Matthew. Matthew also contains scenes adding luster to Peter's reputation which are not found in the other Gospels: Peter's walking on the water (14:28–31), his receiving the keys of the kingdom (16:16–19), his catching the fish with a coin in its mouth (17:24–27), and his asking about forgiveness (18:21).

As he does in other scenes, Luke simplifies the story line and omits the mention of the special group of disciples at Gethsemane. The disciples follow Jesus to Gethsemane as a group, and his words are addressed to all the disciples (22:39–40). Here again, one faces the question of whether Luke had a second source of passion material, separate from Mark, and if so, whether in this instance he preserves a more original version, while the separation of the three disciples is again due to Markan redaction.[26]

The pattern is remarkably consistent. Mark makes greater use of the group of three than any of the other Gospels. Matthew retains the group only at the transfiguration (which may be evidence that the group was firmly attached to this story), while elevating the role of Peter elsewhere. Luke omits references to the group at the Mount of Olives and Gethsemane, so that all the disciples function for the later church as models for those who seek to follow Jesus.

In Mark, the inner three serve as Jesus' closest companions, who witness the most secret, intimate events of Jesus' ministry. They see his power to raise the dead, the glory of his transfiguration, the prophecy of the destruction of the temple and the coming of the Son of Man, and the agony of his prayer in the garden.[27] In the end, they—along with all the rest—abandon him. In contrast to Matthew and Luke, however, Mark does not seem to exalt these disciples as the apostolic authorities of the later church. Instead, they enhance two of Mark's major themes: the secrecy surrounding Jesus' messiahship and the failure of the disciples.

The identification of the inner three as the group closest to Jesus can be traced to Mark with some confidence. The group appears in the other Gospels only in scenes derived from Mark. Only in Mark does the separation of these three with Jesus fit the larger structure of the Gospel. The reasons for Mark's interest in these three disciples are unknown, and the question of why James and John were chosen as members of this group remains unanswered. Mark probably found this group in the early tradition, but we are unable to locate which scene or scenes featured this group in the pre-Markan traditions. Some have conjectured that the memory of the group of three leaders of the church in Jerusalem led Mark to insert the three disciples into pivotal scenes in his Gospel. The similarity of the list in Galatians 2:9 (James, Cephas, and John) is such that the possibility of confusion or the suggestion of a group of three leading disciples cannot be excluded, even though the James in question is different in the two groups.[28] On the whole, however, it is dubious that the "pillars of the church" were the origin of the "inner three" in the synoptic tradition.

THE SONS OF THUNDER

The passages which mention James and John without Peter are quite different in character from those we have just examined. They do not depict intimate experiences with Jesus or secret manifestations. On the contrary, they portray John as intolerant and hot-tempered, one of the "sons of thunder" as this name is popularly understood.

Boanerges

Only Mark 3:17 records that Jesus called James and John "Boanerges, that is, Sons of Thunder." In several other passages, Mark also retains an Aramaic term or phrase which is omitted by the other two synoptics:

> *talitha cumi* (Mark 5:41; omitted in Matt. 9:25 and Luke 8:54)
> *Corban* (Mark 7:11; omitted in Matt. 15:5; no parallel in Luke)
> *ephphatha* (Mark 7:34; no parallel in Matthew or Luke)
> *Abba* (Mark 14:36; omitted in Matt. 26:39 and Luke 22:42)
> *Golgotha* (Mark 15:22; Matt. 27:33; John 19:17; omitted in
>   Luke 23:33)
> *Eloi Eloi, lama sabachthani* (Mark 15:34; Matt. 27:46
>   [Hebrew]; omitted in Luke)

The Aramaic name may therefore have been omitted by Matthew and Luke because its meaning was uncertain. Luke, especially, avoided Mark's Aramaic terms.

Two issues must be distinguished: (1) the etymology and meaning of the Aramaic *Boanerges,* and (2) the meaning of the interpretation "sons of thunder." Scholars have withheld neither energy nor imagination in attempts to explain the etymology of *Boanerges.* The word is clearly a transliteration of a Semitic expression which should be divided *Boane- rges.* The first part derives from the Hebrew (and Aramaic) word *b^{e}ne,* "sons of," but the transition from *b^{e}ne* to *boane-* has been explained in several ways. James A. Montgomery suggests that *boane-* stems from a Galilean dialect form which used a "double-peaked vowel," such as is found in South Arabic.[29] Responding to C. C. Torrey's assertion that *boane-* is a combination of two acceptable transliterations of *b^{e}ne* (*bone-* and *bane-*),[30] and to Arndt and Gingrich's conclusion that "the difficulty pertaining to the vowels of Boa is not yet solved,"[31] Randall Buth suggests that a Greek-speaking scribe introduced the reading *boane-* as a play on the Greek word *boan,* which means to shout or cry (cf. Mark 1:3, 15:34). The same scribe altered the second word to the root *erg- es,* which means "workers." The resulting construction would have meant "shout-workers" or "loud-voiced."

Five possibilities for the Semitic origin of *-rges* have been advanced:

(1) רגשׁ (*regesh:* "commotion");
(2) רגז (*r ges:* "anger, agitation, excitement, hot-tempered");[32]
(3) רעשׁ (*r'sh:* "earthquake, noise");
(4) רעם (*r'm:* "thunder");[33]
(5) a conjectured, unattested meaning for one of these words.

An *ayin* (ע) in ancient Hebrew names was occasionally transliterated by a *gamma* (ג). John T. Rook favors the third option listed above, translating the Semitic original as "Sons of (the) quaking (heavens)."[34] The same argument is applicable to the fourth option,[35] since it also requires that an *ayin* was transliterated as a *gamma.* A similar but independent interpretation maintains that the explanation "sons of thunder" is correct; the original Semitic was the word for thunder, *r'm* (רעם), but transliterated as *regem.*[36] A consensus seems to be building, therefore, that *Boanerges* is derived from either *b^{e}ne regem* or *b^{e}ne r'sh* and that the explanation "sons of thunder" is therefore an accurate translation of the Semitic expression that lies behind the corrupt transliteration.

Interpretations of the Hebrew or Aramaic words that lie behind *Boanerges* do not explain why Jesus called the two by this name. Unfortunately, Mark gives no clues. Explanations have ranged from the suggestion that James and John spoke with loud voices to the conjecture that as followers of John the Baptist, they had witnessed the voice from heaven, spoken in thunder. Generally, however, interpreters have concluded that the name was given to the brothers because of "the impetuosity of their natural character."[37] Earlier books on John advanced colorful descriptions of John's character and personality based on this term. For example, James Stalker (1895) referred to John's "infirmity of temper,"[38] and D. A. Hayes (1917) wrote: "Jesus gave him this name because he had that in him which could flash fire at times. A man cannot flash fire unless he has some flint in him. It runs up and down his backbone and it shows in his face."[39]

The meaning of "sons of thunder" has been sought in both Graeco-Roman and Jewish religious traditions. Mining the Graeco-Roman legends for supporting data, Ronald Brownrigg contended that *Boanerges* was "a title exactly equivalent to 'the heavenly twins,' Castor and Pollux, the sons of Zeus the Sky-God, who sit on each side of him as the 'children of the sky' controlling thunder and lightning. The name may have been a playful allusion on the part of Jesus to their duality in appearance or conduct; the sons of Zebedee were not actually known to be twins but the possibility must not be discounted."[40] Schlatter contended that there were traits in John which are evidence of his close contact with Zealotism.[41] Otto Betz cited occurrences of the verb in the hymn scroll from Qumran. As a translation of *Boanerges,* he proposed "Sturmgesellen" (storm companions) and linked this designation of the role of the sons of Zebedee to the Simeon-Levi tradition. Like James and John, Simeon and Levi are given second and third place in the list of the twelve tribes of Israel, and Levi follows Simeon even though he is the more famous (Gen. 49:5–7). Like Levi (Deut. 33:9), James and John must forsake father and mother. They were noted most, however, for their zeal, which is evident in the censure of the unauthorized exorcist and their offer to call down fire on the Samaritan village. The name *Boanerges,* Betz concludes, belongs to early tradition, deriving even from Jesus himself. The early church would have had no interest in giving its "pillars" such an ambiguous name.[42]

Alternatively, Jesus may have called the brothers "sons of thunder" not as a disparaging nickname but as a promise of what they could become.[43] Peter is the only other example of a disciple to whom Jesus gave a new name. In his case, the name is ironic. Peter was anything but rock-like in his faithfulness to Jesus, but he would become the leader of the disciples and a leading figure in the early church in Jerusalem. The suggestion that the name, as in the case of Peter, is a promise or a forecast of the greatness of the sons of Zebedee has a great deal of merit. By the giving of the name *Boanerges,* Jesus announced that James and John would become "sons of thunder," mighty witnesses, voices as from heaven.[44]

Only the inner three, Peter, James, and John, are given new names. In Jewish tradition, names were often given either as a promise or as an act of laying upon the recipient a specific task.[45] Accordingly, the "sons of thunder" were probably recognized by Jesus for their potential as thundering witnesses, not because they were hot-tempered.

The Unauthorized Exorcist

Mark and Luke contain the only scene in the synoptic Gospels in which John is named alone as the speaker for the disciples. The unit is a pronouncement story that is linked to its context by the phrase "in your name" (Mark 9:37; Luke 9:48). John reports, "we saw someone casting out demons in your name, and we tried to stop him, because he was not following us." Jesus' response corrects the disciples' effort to retain sole authority for the use of Jesus' name: *"Do not stop him;* for no one who does a deed of power in my name will be able soon afterward to speak evil of me. *Whoever is not against us (you) is for us (you)"* (Mark 9:39; Luke 9:50). Luke shortened the logion in Mark, retaining only the words italicized above. Matthew omitted the entire pericope, perhaps because its demand for tolerance cut against the authority that he invested in Peter and the Twelve.

Three questions must be addressed. (1) Does this pericope stem from the ministry of Jesus or the early church? (2) Is the name John original or a secondary addition to the pericope? (3) If the name is a secondary addition, why was it added to this story?

The debate over whether this pericope recounts an event in the ministry of Jesus or was created by the early church to speak to a significant issue of ecclesiastical authority has produced strong advocates of both perspectives. Those who contend that the pericope was formed by the early church maintain that it is a response to the activity of ecstatic prophets outside the church who called upon Jesus.[46] Would exorcism in the name of Jesus have been practiced during his lifetime? The parallel story of the unauthorized prophets in Numbers 11:27–29 is often cited. More importantly, the formula "in Jesus' name," which is so prominent in Mark 9:38, 39, and 41, was a formula of authority used by the early Christians (cf. Acts 2:38; 3:6, 16; 4:10, 18, 30; 5:28, 40–41). The issues of authority and control seem to point to an ecclesiastical setting. If that is the case, does the problem reflect Mark's concern, or can it be traced to a pre-Markan church setting?[47]

On the other hand, a setting in the ministry of Jesus has been defended on the grounds that the activity of unauthorized exorcists in the early church does not prove that the story was created by the church. The background of the story may lie in the appointment of the Twelve to mission.[48] The use of Jesus' name by those who had heard of his successes would not be surprising. Again, one may question whether the church would have created a story expressing such a liberal perspective.[49] The following factors have been adduced in support of the "substantial historicity" of the tradition: the Palestinian matrix of the text, the unusual term *kakologein* ("to speak against"), the criticism of the disciples over an opinion divergent from Jesus', and the liberal, non-ecclesiastical view expressed by Jesus.[50] Of these, the last is the most significant.

A judgment on this matter involves prior decisions about a number of other factors—the nature of Jesus' ministry, the role of the Twelve, and the development of the synoptic tradition in general. Although it is difficult to deny the impression that this pronouncement story, at least in its present form, reflects an ecclesiastical setting, the liberality of Jesus' response argues forcefully for a historical core for this pericope.

The association with the aphorism in Mark 9:40 is probably secondary. The point of the story is stated in Mark 9:39—"Do not stop him; for no one who does a deed of power in my name will be able soon afterward to speak evil of me."[51] This logion supplies a sufficient response to the situation described in verse 38. The aphorism in Mark 9:40—"Whoever is not against us is for us" (cf. Luke 9:50)—is a more tolerant form of the logion in Matthew 12:30— "Whoever is not with me is against me" (cf. Luke 11:23). Which of these forms is more original? As has been pointed out, the church is unlikely to have advocated the openness of Mark 9:40. On the other hand, Matthew 12:30 makes a radical demand for the necessity of discipleship which also has parallels in the teaching of Jesus. A choice between the two forms of the saying is therefore difficult, but in either case, it is more likely that Mark 9:40 was a secondary addition to the pronouncement story than that the story was generated by the aphorism. If the aphorism gave rise to the story, Mark 9:39 would represent a further expansion, and Luke's form would be the more original. Mark 9:38–39, however, is probably a traditional unit that subsequently attracted verse 40 because of the similarity of theme. Mark 9:39 may have been the kernel around which the pronouncement story was fashioned. Verse 38 serves only to provide a setting for the following sayings, but it may have been transmitted with the saying in verse 39 as an original unit.

Was John involved in this incident, or was his name added to the story at a later time? Following each passion prediction in Mark, one of the inner three disciples responds and is rebuked: Peter (8:32–33), John (9:38), and James with John (10:35–37).[52] Bultmann—though he noted the tendency of the tradition to supply names for nameless groups or individuals—decided that the name of John was not a secondary addition in this pericope.[53] Others have claimed that the abrupt beginning of the story indicates "a good knowledge of what happened, since otherwise we cannot see how John's name came to be attached to the story."[54]

If the story of the unauthorized exorcist originally involved the disciples as a group and the naming of John is a secondary addition,[55] was the name of John chosen for any reason other than that he was a well known figure? One may conjecture that this story attracted the name of John because it fit well with the story of the brothers' wanting to call down fire on the Samaritan village. If that be the case, the story of the unauthorized exorcist is evidence of the way in which John was viewed. Early Christians saw in this story an example of John's character as one of the "sons of thunder."

The story of the unauthorized exorcist cannot be used with confidence as an example of John's intolerant or fiery temperament, as is so often thought. The data can be explained by assuming that Jesus did not give John the name "son of thunder" as a disparaging nickname. On the contrary, a name conveying a promise was interpreted by the later church—and perhaps as early as Mark—as a description of John's fiery character. His name was therefore attached to this story because it illustrates that popular interpretation.

Calling Down Fire on the Samaritan Village

Only Luke, who omits the name *Boanerges* (see Luke 6:14), includes this story concerning the calling down of fire. It is set at the beginning of Jesus' journey to Jerusalem, and introduced by the Lukan formulation in Luke 9:51. Jesus sent messengers ahead to make arrangements for the group of travelers. The Samaritans would not receive Jesus, however, because he was on his way to Jerusalem. In response, James and John said, "Lord, do you want us to command fire to come down from heaven and consume them?" (9:54). Jesus rebuked them, and some manuscripts supply an appropriate rebuke: "You do not know what spirit you are of, for the Son of Man has not come to destroy the lives of human beings but to save them" (9:55–56).

The question James and John ask echoes the words of Elijah in 2 Kings 1:10 and 12, "If I am a man of God, let fire come down from heaven and consume you and your fifty." Jesus therefore rejects the spirit of Elijah. Throughout this section of Luke, Jesus is shown to be one who does works like Elijah but is greater than the prophet (see 9:8, 19, 30, and 33). This pericope further distinguishes Jesus' role as Savior from the role of Elijah. Parallels can also be observed between this pericope and the destruction of Sodom and Gomorrah in Genesis 19:24ff.: "Then the Lord rained on Sodom and Gomorrah sulfur and fire from the Lord out of heaven."[56] The evidence for detecting echoes of the destruction of Sodom and Gomorrah is not as clear in Luke, however, as are the parallels with the words of Elijah. The influence of the latter is evident even in the gloss in verse 54, "even as Elijah did," which is contained in some manuscripts from various textual traditions.[57]

More importantly for our purposes, the introduction of the names James and John following the references to "the disciples" is sufficiently awkward that it has led many scholars to conclude that the names were a later addition to the story.[58] One clue to the insertion of the names here is the surprising frequency of the names of disciples in Luke 8 and 9: Peter (8:45; 9:20, 33), the group of three (8:51; 9:28), John (9:49), and James and John (9:54).

Luke did not construct the pericope to explain or illustrate how James and John came to be called *Boanerges*—he never mentions this name. The names of James and John were introduced into a unit of tradition that originally spoke only of "the disciples" (see Luke 9:54) either by someone other than Luke as a result of the popular understanding of *Boanerges* or by Luke himself, who had used their names elsewhere in chapters 8 and 9.[59] In either case, this pericope tells us nothing about James and John. It may serve, however, as evidence of the early currency of the belief that the "sons of thunder" received their name because of their intemperate spirit.

The Request for Glory

Following the third passion prediction in Mark 10:32–34, there is yet another incident in which the disciples show that they do not understand what Jesus has just told them (Matt. 20:20; Mark 10:35, 41). James and John (or, according to Matthew, their mother) seek special places of honor. Their first request is open-ended and undefined: "whatever we ask of you." When Jesus asks what it is they want, the response is "Grant us to sit, one at your right hand and one at your left, in your glory" (Mark 10:37). Jesus answers that they do not know what they are asking for: could they "drink the cup" he is about to drink? Those who share his glory will be those who have shared his suffering. The cup was often used as a symbol for suffering or for meeting one's fate. Again the disciples persist in asserting that they are able to drink the cup and be baptized with Jesus. Jesus assures them that they will drink the cup and be baptized with his baptism, but the seats of glory are not his to grant. When the other ten heard of the brothers' request, they were indignant, not because they were above such ambition but apparently because James and John sought the prizes they also coveted.

Although the sayings in Mark 10:42–45 may be a secondary addition to this unit, the unit itself seems to be traditional and to have contained the names of James and John. The traditional character of the names is disputed, however. S. Légasse concludes that this pericope derives from early catechetical material which taught the future glory of Christ and his disciples, and the testing of all of his disciples. James and John either are typical of all the disciples or are mentioned simply for narrative embellishment.[60] The additional identifying phrase, "the sons of Zebedee," may have been a traditional tag, but it is unnecessary in Mark (following references to Zebedee in 1:19–20; 3:17). John and his brother appear in Mark 9:2–8 and John in 9:38 without the tag, so the tag and the names were apparently part of the tradition prior to Mark.

Matthew's alteration of the story, in which the request is brought by the mother of James and John, is plausible in that their mother appears in the lists of the women who follow Jesus from Galilee to Jerusalem.[61] On the other hand, the disciples are still present (see Matt. 20:20, "with her sons"; and

20:22, "they said to him"). The Matthean account follows the form of the Markan: the disciples (or their mother) approach Jesus with an unspecified request. Jesus asks, "What do you want?" and the request for the seats of honor follows. Matthew therefore follows Mark closely with the exception of attributing the request to the disciples' mother. Did Matthew have an independent, more authentic tradition, or did he modify Mark, perhaps to relieve the disciples of the scandal of such a request? In the absence of further evidence, the latter alternative is to be preferred.

The disciples' request is sufficiently open to allow for various interpretations: the places of honor at the messianic banquet, the places of honor at the Parousia, or the places of honor when Jesus establishes the kingdom in Jerusalem. William Lane raises a provocative but unanswerable question: "Were James and John asking for confirmation that the places they occupied in the fellowship meals which the Twelve shared with Jesus would be their seats when his glory was openly unveiled? Cf. Jn. 13:23–25 (where John appears to be reclining on Jesus' right hand)."[62] Fascinating as the question is, it rests entirely on the evidence of John 13:23–25 and on the identification of the Beloved Disciple with John.

Jesus' metaphorical answer has also generated an elaborate history of interpretations. The basic questions are whether the cup and the baptism are to be understood as (1) general metaphors for sharing in Jesus' sufferings, (2) a *vaticinium ex eventu* of the martyrdom of James and John, or (3) an allusion to the importance of baptism and the Eucharist. Among recent interpreters, Best champions the sacramental interpretation, arguing that it allows James and John to serve as typical believers: "all believers participate sacramentally in the passion of Jesus; there cannot then be special seats in glory for special believers."[63] The first alternative, however, also permits one to view the disciples as representative of all believers. The suffering of the believer does not carry the same significance as Jesus' suffering. It is, rather, a participation in Jesus' passion. The words of Jesus regarding the cup and the baptism are therefore neither predictions of the martyrdom of James and John nor references to baptism and the Lord's Supper. They are, rather, paradoxical and metaphorical sayings that challenge the disciples to understand that both Jesus and they must inevitably experience suffering.[64]

Acts 12:2 records the martyrdom of James, but the tradition of the martyrdom of John does not appear until much later and is probably derived from Mark 10:39. The issue of the martyrdom of John will be treated in chapter 6.

JOHN AND PETER

John also appears paired with Peter in the Gospel traditions and Acts. This pairing is particularly interesting since the Beloved Disciple and Peter appear together in several passages in the Gospel of John.

Preparation of the Passover Meal

Luke 22:8 names Peter and John as the two disciples sent to prepare the Passover Meal for Jesus and the rest of the disciples. This pericope is an edited form of the Markan account of the same event (Mark 14:12–16), but Mark leaves the two disciples unnamed. The prominence of Peter and John early in Acts supports the conclusion that the appearance of their names in Luke 22:8 is a Lukan insertion into the tradition that Luke takes over from Mark. If the Lukan form were the more original, one wonders why Mark would have omitted the names.

The Gospel of John does not contain an account of the preparations for the last supper. On the other hand, in John one does find the Beloved Disciple and Peter together around the table (13:23–24), at the tomb (20:3–10), and at the appearance in Galilee (21:2–8). The reference to "the other disciple" (18:15), who was known to the high priest and who helped Peter get into the courtyard, should probably be added to this list. Only the "race to the tomb" in John 20:3–10 has parallels in the synoptic tradition, and there, only in Luke, which does not connect John with this event. The references are tantalizing:

> But Peter got up and ran to the tomb; stooping and looking in, he saw the linen cloths by themselves; then he went home, amazed at what had happened. (Luke 24:12; omitted in Codex Beza)

> Some of those who were with us went to the tomb and found it just as the women had said; but they did not see him. (Luke 24:24)

One could argue that the "some" mentioned in Luke 24:24 were Peter and the Beloved Disciple. As we will see in the next chapter, however, it is more likely that John has inserted references to the Beloved Disciple into contexts which originally contained no such references. If the tradition contained any recollection that Peter and John had run together to the tomb, one would expect that Luke would have included their names here, since he inserted their names in 22:8 and mentioned them together repeatedly in Acts. The absence of any reference to John may mean that the earliest form of the tradition named only Peter as the disciple who ran to the tomb. Alternatively, the Johannine account may rest on early tradition that Peter and one or more others ran to the tomb (Luke 24:24). Clearly, John has inserted the reference to the Beloved Disciple, but did the tradition once contain his name and it was dropped out later because he was a lesser known disciple? While this line of reasoning is plausible, the retention of the name of Cleopas in the same context (24:18) makes it dubious that the tradition contained any name other than Peter.

Work in Jerusalem and Samaria

Peter and John appear together in Acts in scenes describing the healing of the crippled man in the temple (3:1–10), the hearing before the council (4:1– 22), and their working among the Samaritans (8:14–25). John is also mentioned in passing as the brother of James, who was martyred (12:2).

As with some of the synoptic references discussed above, scholars have questioned the authenticity of the references to John as Peter's companion in Acts. In all of these passages in Acts, John remains silent. In regard to the healing in Acts 3, Ernst Haenchen contends that "originally John must have been absent," citing Morgenthaler's judgment that this pair of names is a peculiarity of Lukan style (doubling, or the "rule of two") and Harnack's assertion that Luke "smuggled John in as a stowaway."[65] Haenchen notes in particular the awkwardness with which John's name appears in Acts 3:4— "And Peter looked intently at him, as did John, and said, 'Look at us.' "[66]

In Acts 4:13, when Peter and John appear before the council of "rulers, elders, and scribes" gathered in Jerusalem, Luke records: "Now when they saw the boldness of Peter and John and realized that they were uneducated and ordinary men, they were amazed and recognized them as companions of Jesus." Here too, the addition of John's name seems to be an afterthought. In the Greek text, the term for "boldness" follows the name Peter, so that the name of John is quite secondary. The apostles are called "uneducated" (*agrammatoi*) and "ordinary" (*idiōtai*). The former adjective was applicable to anyone who could not write, and the latter either could be synonymous with the former or could distinguish the layman from the expert or priest. In this context, the terms convey the idea that the council recognized the apostles had not been trained in the law.[67] The description fits what we have seen of the status of fishermen in Galilee; it is hardly surprising that the council in Jerusalem would have had such disdain for fishermen. Nevertheless, Peter and John serve for Christian readers as models of fearless witnesses for the Gospel. Readers are likewise challenged to judge whether it is right to serve God or fear men (4:19).

The only other reference to these two leading apostles together is in Acts 8:14, where in response to the work of Philip in Samaria, the church in Jerusalem sends Peter and John to this region. Echoing the language of Harnack cited above, Gerd Lüdemann concludes that the references to Peter and John are redactional: Luke "smuggled" Peter and John into the story of Philip to demonstrate the endorsement of the Samaria mission by the Jerusalem apostles.[68] In view of the numerous parallels between Luke and Acts, it may be significant to observe that in both Luke 22:8 and Acts 8:14 the two disciples who are sent are Peter and John and that the verb *apesteile/an* is used in both references. Here again, only Peter speaks. John does not appear in any other passage in Acts. The last we hear of John in the tradition of the synoptics and Acts is that he returned to Jerusalem after "proclaiming the good news to many villages of the Samaritans" (Acts 8:25). This episode can be juxtaposed in intriguing ways with the pericope in Luke in which James and John offer to call down fire on a Samaritan village (Luke 9:54). When the passages in Luke and Acts are taken together, one observes that Luke's characterization implies something of a change in John's temperament in that his last reported act is the calling down of the Holy Spirit—not fire—on the Samaritans. The scene in Samaria in Acts 8 is also suggestive when considered in light of the special attention given to Samaritans in John 4. It may well be that the church's traditions reflect the memory of John's work in Samaria.

Whatever their basis in tradition, the references to John in the Book of Acts show that he was remembered as one of the leading apostles of the early church, ranking second only to Peter in his importance in the church in Jerusalem prior to the Jerusalem conference and the emergence of James as the leading voice of the Christian community in Jerusalem.

THE "PILLARS OF THE CHURCH"

The most illuminating glimpse of the role of the apostle John in the early church comes from Galatians, a letter unquestionably written by Paul, probably in the mid-fifties. In the first two chapters, Paul responds to the accusation that he is not an apostle but received his gospel from those who had been with Jesus. In the course of this defense, Paul recalls the only two occasions when he went to Jerusalem between the time of his conversion to Christian faith and his writing of Galatians. On his first visit to Jerusalem, Paul saw only Cephas (Peter) and James, the Lord's brother (Gal. 1:18–19). Fourteen years later, he returned to Jerusalem with Barnabas and Titus and laid before "the acknowledged leaders" (2:2) the gospel which he preached among the Gentiles. Paul's disdain for the authority of the Jerusalem apostles is scarcely concealed: "And from those who were supposed to be acknowledged leaders (what they actually were makes no difference to me . . .)" (2:6). Paul boasts, however, that these apostles laid no constraints on him: "and when James and Cephas and John, who were acknowledged pillars, recognized the grace that had been given to me, they gave to Barnabas and me the right hand of fellowship, agreeing that we should go to the Gentiles and they to the circumcised" (2:9).

Numerous features of this verse have attracted attention: the repeated use of "acknowledged" in this context, the meaning of "pillars," and the role of James, Cephas, and John. C. K. Barrett concluded that "pillars" originally had an eschatological sense. The apostles, and these three in particular, were regarded as pillars of the new temple in the New Age.[69] Eventually, the institutional sense replaced the eschatological. Paul recognizes the necessity of conferring with these three, even though in this context he finds it difficult to acknowledge their role as the supreme authorities within the church. Barrett suggests that it is these circumstances which explain the repeated use of "acknowledged" (*dokein*) in this paragraph.[70]

Günter Klein interprets the past tense in Galatians 2:6—"what they were"—as indicating a change in the positions of these three between the time of Paul's visit and the writing of Galatians. The "protocol" of the Apostolic Council is reflected in 2:7–8. Whereas during Paul's first visit to Jerusalem, Peter was in full control, the "up-and-coming" men at the Council were James and John. At the time of the writing of Galatians, the three formed a triumvirate led by James.[71] These three were called "pillars" by the Jerusalem church, apparently because the church was regarded as a heavenly building or a new temple.[72] R. D. Aus has proposed that these three were selected by the Aramaic-speaking Jerusalem church "on the basis of the model of the three Patriarchs, Abraham, Isaac and Jacob, thought of in rabbinic sources as the three pillars of Israel, indeed of the entire world," which made the title all the more offensive to Paul because it implied the continuing "merit" of the Patriarchs.[73] David Hay, however, finds such speculations unnecessary, arguing instead that Paul subjected the authority of these pillar apostles to the test of whether they recognized the genuineness of the gospel given to him by revelation. If they had not recognized his gospel, they would not have exercised authority as apostles, at least in his eyes.[74] The significance of the role of the three pillar apostles is also suggested by the correspondence of the sequence of the epistles attributed to them in the New Testament. The canonical order—James; 1 and 2 Peter; 1, 2, and 3 John—corresponds to the sequence of the names in Galatians 2:9—James, Cephas, and John.[75]

For our purposes, the significance of Galatians 2:9 is that it provides unimpeachable evidence of the role of John, the son of Zebedee, in the leadership of the early church in Jerusalem. While it does not confirm the accuracy of the stories about John in the Book of Acts, it does show that they at least derive from the memory of John's place among the leading apostles, Peter and James. Moreover, the Acts account links John more closely with Peter than with James, an observation that may be significant in view of James's association with the Pharisaic Christians in Jerusalem (see Acts 15 and Gal. 2:11–14).

At this point John fades out of the tradition preserved by the synoptics and Acts. He is not named among the apostles present at the conference in Jerusalem (Acts 15), a fact which some have explained by appeal to the late traditions that both James and John were martyred under Agrippa (Acts 12:2, Mark 10:38). On the other hand, the silence of Acts 15 regarding John may mean that he no longer ranked among the leaders of the church in Jerusalem or that he had already moved from Jerusalem to some other Christian center.

CONCLUSION

Within the synoptic Gospels, Acts, and Galatians, we find historical data pertaining to both the life of John, the son of Zebedee, and the ways in which he was remembered by the early church. As a member of the Twelve, he is always listed among the first three or four. Only once does John appear alone with Jesus in the Gospels. More characteristically, he is one of the group of four (the two sets of brothers) or one of the inner three (Peter, James, and John), or he is Peter's silent partner.

Mark gave greater prominence to the inner three, arranging his list of the Twelve in order to feature these three first and recording the names they were given by Jesus (Peter, *Boanerges*). Most scholars who have given attention to the matter are agreed that the names of these three have been inserted by Mark into the scenes in which they appear. Opinion regarding the connection of the names of these three with the transfiguration is significantly divided, however.

If Mark is primarily responsible for the elevation of the three in the synoptic tradition, the reasons for this development are less clear. The group of three clearly serves to advance the secrecy motif at the raising of Jairus's daughter (Mark 5:37) and at the transfiguration (9:2). Their role at Gethsemane (Mark 14:32–42), on the other hand, heightens the impact of the failure and flight of the disciples in Mark's account. Presumably, Mark did not arbitrarily select these three names to identify the inner group of disciples present with Jesus on these occasions. Either they were already distinguished from the larger group of the disciples in the early traditions or Mark chose these three because he confused them with the group of three leaders of the church in Jerusalem (James, Cephas, and John; Gal. 2:9). The latter is not impossible, but the sequence of the names and the use of *Peter* rather than *Cephas* in Mark point to the greater probability that the group of three was already established in the pre-Markan Gospel traditions.

The name *Boanerges* was probably given to the brothers as a sign of what they could become, "sons of thunder," rather than as a nickname disparaging their impetuosity or hot temper. They would be mighty voices, powerful witnesses. The scene which is most often used to illustrate the "hot temper" of James and John, the offer to call down fire on the Samaritan village, is in Luke, not Mark; and Luke makes no reference to the name *Boanerges*. The name was carried over in a corrupted form into Greek, and its meaning was not understood. The interpretation of *Boanerges* as an indication that the brothers were hot-tempered probably arose before the writing of Matthew and Luke, leading the evangelists to omit the ambiguous nickname. Such a development could also account for the association of the brothers with the scenes in which they appear together: the calling down of fire on the Samaritan village (Luke 9:54), the request for the seats of honor (Mark 10:35ff.), and possibly the episode of the unauthorized exorcist (Mark 9:38), if James was once named with John in this pericope. John appears as Peter's silent partner in Luke 22:8 and in Acts. Together these two serve as the leaders of the apostles in the Jerusalem church before the ascendancy of James, which is already evident in Galatians 2:9.

In sum, the synoptic tradition portrays John as one of the leaders of the disciples called by Jesus, but only a few statements are attributed to John himself (Mark 9:38; 10:35, 37, 39; Luke 9:54). He remains a shadowy figure, alternately portrayed as impetuous, ambitious, and intolerant, but nevertheless as one chosen to be among the disciples closest to Jesus during his ministry and to be a "pillar of the church" in the years that followed.

NOTES

1. See the fine collection of essays edited by Fernando F. Segovia, *Discipleship in the New Testament* (Philadelphia: Fortress Press, 1985), esp. the introductory essay by Segovia; and the earlier volume by Seán Freyne, *The Twelve: Disciples and Apostles, A Study in the Theology of the First Three Gospels* (London: Sheed and Ward, 1968).

2. Ernest Best, *Following Jesus: Discipleship in the Gospel of Mark*, JSNTSup 4 (Sheffield: JSOT Press, 1981), 180.

3. Mark's treatment of the disciples has generated a flood of books and articles in recent years, of which the following are a sample: Best, *Following Jesus;* Ernest Best, "Mark's Use of the Twelve," *ZNW* 69 (1978): 11–35; Ernest Best, "The Role of the Disciples in Mark," *NTS* 23 (1976–1977): 377–401; Robert C. Tannehill, "The Disciples in Mark: The Function of a Narrative Role," *JR* 57 (1977): 386–405.

4. On the role of the disciples in Luke, see Brian E. Beck, " 'Imitatio Christi' and the Lucan Passion Narrative," in *Suffering and Martyrdom in the New Testament,* ed. W. Horbury and B. McNeil (Cambridge: Cambridge University Press, 1981), 28–47; Wolfgang Dietrich, *Das Petrusbild der lukanischen Schriften,* BWANT 94 (Stuttgart: W. Kohlhammer, 1972); George E. Rice, "Luke's Thematic Use of the Call to Discipleship," *AUSS* 19 (1981): 127–32; Charles H. Talbert, "Discipleship in Luke-Acts," in *Discipleship in the New Testament,* 62–75.

5. Martin Dibelius, *From Tradition to Gospel,* trans. Bertram Lee Woolf (London: Ivor Nicholson and Watson, 1934), 297.

6. Paul J. Achtemeier holds that the sandwiching is Markan; see "Toward the Isolation of Pre-Markan Miracle Catenae," *JBL* 89 (1970), 276–79. See also Achtemeier, *Mark,* Proclamation Commentaries, 2d ed. (Philadelphia: Fortress Press, 1986), 22–26. Rudolf Bultmann judges that the sandwiching is pre-Markan; see *History of the Synoptic Tradition,* rev., ed., and trans. J. Marsh (New York: Harper and Row, 1963), 214.

7. Bultmann, *History of the Synoptic Tradition,* 345.

8. See, for example, Rudolf Pesch, *Das Markusevangelium*, HTKNT (Freiburg: Herder, 1976), 1:307; Burton L. Mack, *A Myth of Innocence: Mark and Christian Origins* (Philadelphia: Fortress Press, 1988), 231.

9. See Thomas F. Best, "The Transfiguration: A Select Bibliography," *JETS* 24 (1981): 157–61.

10. William L. Lane, *The Gospel According to Mark* (Grand Rapids: Wm. B. Eerdmans, 1974), 316–17; Allison A. Trites, "The Transfiguration of Jesus: The Gospel in Microcosm," *EvQ* 51 (1979): 68.

11. Ernst Lohmeyer, "Die Verklärung Jesu nach dem Markus-Evangelium," *ZNW* 21 (1922): 185–215; J. A. Ziesler, "The Transfiguration Story and the Markan Soteriology," *ExpTim* 81 (1970): 263–68.

12. Bultmann, *History of the Synoptic Tradition*, 259–61. The thesis has been defended by C. E. Carlston in "Transfiguration and Resurrection," *JBL* 80 (1961): 233–40; and by George W. E. Nickelsburg in "Enoch, Levi and Peter: Recipients of Revelation in Upper Galilee," *JBL* 100 (1981): 575–600. In the following, however, convincing arguments are advanced against this interpretation: G. H. Boobyer, *St. Mark and the Transfiguration Story* (Edinburgh: T. and T. Clark, 1942); Boobyer, "St. Mark and the Transfiguration," *JTS* 41 (1940): 119–40; C. H. Dodd, "The Appearances of the Risen Christ: An Essay in Form-Criticism of the Gospels," in *Studies in the Gospels: Essays in Memory of R. H. Lightfoot*, ed. D. E. Nineham (Oxford: Basil Blackwell, 1955), 25; Robert H. Stein, "Is the Transfiguration (Mark 9:2–8) a Misplaced Resurrection Account?" *JBL* 95 (1976): 79–86.

13. Morton Smith interprets the transfiguration as an initiation ceremony, which probably involved hypnosis. He also contends that the list of the three disciples is a later addition to the tradition; see "The Origin and History of the Transfiguration Story," *USQR* 36 (1980): 39–44. See further Joseph A. Fitzmyer, *The Gospel According to Luke*, AB 28 (Garden City: Doubleday, 1981): "Just what sort of incident in the ministry of Jesus—to which it is clearly related—it was is impossible to say" (796); and Pheme Perkins, *Resurrection: New Testament Witness and Contemporary Reflection* (Garden City: Doubleday, 1984): "we should not write the story off as imaginative fiction even though we can no longer recover its historical contours" (99). Nickelsburg, in "Enoch, Levi and Peter," cites the fascinating tradition of revelatory experiences in upper Galilee, but these do not argue for a post-resurrection appearance setting over against a mysterious event in the ministry of Jesus.

14. See Bruce D. Chilton, "The Transfiguration: Dominical Assurance and Apostolic Vision," *NTS* 27 (1980): 115–24. Chilton concludes: "it is beyond reasonable doubt that the Transfiguration is fundamentally a visionary representation of the Sinai motif of Exod. 24. In the sense that it is the reinterpretation of a literary motif, it is inappropriate to reduce the Transfiguration narrative in its present form to historical events or to psychological conditions" (122).

15. Chilton, "The Transfiguration," 124. Cf. John Anthony McGuckin, *The Transfiguration of Christ in Scripture and Tradition*, SBEC 9 (Lewiston, N.Y.: Edwin Mellen Press, 1986), 13.

16. McGuckin, *The Transfiguration*, 14.

17. See the textual apparatus of Nestle-Aland, *Novum Testamentum Graece*, 26th ed. (Stuttgart: Deutsche Bibelstiftung, 1979). Dieter Lührmann shows that whereas Jerome correctly identified James as the Lord's brother (Migne, *PL*, 26:362), Augustine confused the two Jameses: "Petrus autem et Iacobus et Ioannes honoratiores in Apostolis erant, quia ipsis tribus se in monte Dominus ostendit in significatione regni sui" (Migne, *PL*, 35:2113); see "Gal 2:9 und die katholischen Briefe: Bemerkungen zum Kanon und zur regula fidei," *ZNW* 72 (1981): 71.

18. Bultmann held that originally only Peter was mentioned in Mark 9:2 and that the other two names were added later; see *History of the Synoptic Tradition*, 260, 345–46.

19. Edgar Hennecke, *New Testament Apocrypha*, ed. Wilhelm Schneemelcher, trans. R. McL. Wilson (Philadelphia: Westminster Press, 1965), 2:664, 680–81.

20. Maria Horstmann, *Studien zur markinischen Christologie* (Münster: Aschendorff, 1969), 83–85. See also Stein, "Is the Transfiguration (Mark 9:2–8) a Misplaced Resurrection-Account?" 92–93, where it is agreed that the names come from pre-Markan tradition.

21. Bultmann, *History of the Synoptic Tradition*, 260, 345–46; Johannes M. Nützel, *Die Verklärungserzählung im Markusevangelium: Eine redaktionsgeschichtliche Untersuchung*, FB 6 (Würzburg: Echter Verlag, 1973), 91–92. Ernest Best allows that Mark may have "replaced an earlier reference to Peter or to the disciples generally with the names, Peter, James and John"; see *Following Jesus*, 55–56.

22. Ludger Schenke, *Studien zur Passionsgeschichte des Markus: Tradition und Redaktion in Markus 14, 1–42*, FB 4 (Würzburg: Echter Verlag, 1971), 480–85.

23. Günther Schmahl holds that the three were part of the pre-Markan tradition in 9:2, but that Mark inserted the three in Mark 5:37 and 14:33, see *Die Zwölf im Markusevangelium: Eine redaktionsgeschichtliche Untersuchung*, TTS 30 (Trier: Paulinus Verlag, 1974), 133–34.

24. See Schmahl, *Die Zwölf im Markusevangelium*, 140.

25. Vincent Taylor, *The Gospel According to St. Mark* (London: Macmillan, 1952), 502.

26. Schenke, *Studien zur Passionsgeschichte des Markus*, 480–85; Werner Kelber, "Mark 14:32–42: Gethsemane. Passion Christology and Discipleship Failure," *ZNW* 63 (1972): 169–70; Werner Mohn, "Gethsemane (Mk 14:32–42)," *ZNW* 64 (1973): 197; Best, *Following Jesus*, 147.

27. See Anthony Kenny, "The Transfiguration and the Agony in the Garden," *CBQ* 19 (1957): 444–52.

28. See also Schmahl, *Die Zwölf im Markusevangelium*, 138.

29. James A. Montgomery, "Brief Communications," *JBL* 100 (1981): 94–95.

30. Charles Cutler Torrey, *The Four Gospels*, 2d ed. (New York: Harper and Brothers, 1947), 298

31. Walter Bauer, *A Greek-English Lexicon of the New Testament and Other Early Christian Literature*, trans. and ed. William F. Arndt and F. Wilbur Gingrich, 2d ed., rev. Frederick W. Danker (Chicago: University of Chicago Press, 1979), 144.

32. This option was favored by Gustaf Dalman and Vincent Taylor; see Taylor, *Mark*, 232.

33. This solution can be traced to Jerome (on Dan. 1:7); cited in Taylor, *Mark*, 232.

34. John T. Rook, "'Boanerges, Sons of Thunder' (Mark 3:17)," *JBL* 100 (1981): 94–95.

35. Randall Buth, "Mark 3:17 *BONEREGEM* and Popular Etymology," *JSNT* 10 (1981): 29–33.

36. D. R. G. Beattie, "Boanerges: A Semiticist's Solution," *IBS* 5 (1983): 11–13.

37. A. T. Robertson, *Epochs in the Life of the Apostle John* (New York: Fleming H. Revell, 1935), 43, citing Henry Barclay Swete, *The Gospel According to St. Mark* (London: Macmillan, 1898), 57.

38. James Stalker, *The Two St. Johns of the New Testament* (New York: American Tract Society, 1895), 88.

39. D. A. Hayes, *John and His Writings* (New York: Methodist Book Concern, 1917), 47.

40. Ronald Brownrigg, *The Twelve Apostles* (New York: Macmillan, 1974), 94.

41. A. Schlatter, *Geschichte der erst. Chr.*, 65; cited in Albrecht Stumpff, "*zeloō*," *TDNT* 2:886.

42. See Otto Betz, "Donnersöhne, Menschenfischer und der davidische Messias," *RevQ* 3 (1961): 41–70.

43. Jürgen Roloff, *Apostolat—Verkündigung——Kirche* (Gütersloh: Gerd Mohn, 1965), 148.

44. Hans Bietenhard, "*onoma*," *TDNT* 5:281.

45. Bietenhard, "*onoma*," *TDNT* 5:254.

46. Bultmann, *History of the Synoptic Tradition*, 24–25, 54; Eduard Schweizer, *The Good News According to Mark*, trans. Donald H. Madvig (Atlanta: John Knox Press, 1970), 194.

47. Fitzmyer, *Luke*, 820.

48. I. Howard Marshall, *The Gospel of Luke*, NIGTC (Grand Rapids: Wm. B. Eerdmans, 1978), 398.

49. E. A. Russell, "A Plea for Tolerance (Mk. 9.38–40)," *IBS* 8 (1986): 154–60; these arguments are also advanced by Eino Wilhelms in "Der fremde Exorzist," *ST* 3 (1950–51): 162–71.

50. J. Schlosser, "L'exorciste étranger (*Mc*, 9, 38–39)," *RevScRel* 56 (1982): 237–38.

51. See Bultmann, *History of the Synoptic Tradition*, 24–25.

52. Lane, *Mark*, 342.

53. Bultmann, *History of the Synoptic Tradition*, 345. E. P. Sanders concludes that the study of details in the tradition, such as names, teaches caution; the priority of one Gospel to another cannot be demonstrated on the basis of such evidence; see *The Tendencies of the Synoptic Tradition*, SNTSMS 9 (Cambridge: Cambridge University Press, 1969), 188.

54. Taylor, *Mark*, 406; cf. Karl L. Schmidt, *Der Rahmen der Geschichte Jesu* (Berlin, 1919), 236.

55. Schlosser, "L'exorciste étranger," 232–33.

56. See Otto Betz, "Donnersöhne," 50.

57. J. M. Ross argues for retaining these variants (see "The Rejected Words in Luke 9:54–56," *ExpTim* 84 [1972–1973]: 85–88), but they are absent from p[45] and p[75] and have been rejected by most critical editions of the New Testament and most commentators. Cf. Fitzmyer, *Luke,* 830.

58. See Bultmann, *History of the Synoptic Tradition,* 346; Marshall, *Luke,* 406; E. A. Russell, "A Plea for Tolerance," 158. In contrast, Michi Miyoshi maintains that the names of the disciples were part of the tradition; see *Der Anfang des Reiseberichts Lk 9,51–10,24: Eine redaktionsgeschichtliche Untersuchung,* AnBib 60 (Rome: Biblical Institute, 1974), 12, 15.

59. See also Marshall, *Luke,* 406.

60. S. Légasse, "Approche de l'épisode préévangélique des Fils de Zébédée (Marc x.35–40 par.)," *NTS* 20 (1974): 174–77.

61. See above, chap. 1.

62. Lane, *Mark,* 379.

63. Best, *Following Jesus,* 124.

64. A. Feuillet, "La coupe et le baptême de la passion (Mc, x, 35–40; cf. Mt, xx, 20–23; Lc, xii, 50)," *RB* 74 (1967): 389–91; Lane, *Mark,* 379–81.

65. See Ernst Haenchen, *The Acts of the Apostles: A Commentary* (Philadelphia: Westminster Press, 1971), 199.

66. *The Acts of the Apostles,* 199. Gerd Lüdemann agrees: "The mention of John here [Acts 3:1] is redactional. John is a bystander throughout and the verbs in v. 4 (*eipen*) and v. 7 (*egeiren*) are in the singular. Luke needs *two* witnesses later before the Supreme Council. Moreover, he has a preference for mission in pairs"; see *Early Christianity According to the Traditions in Acts* (Minneapolis: Fortress Press, 1989), 50.

67. See F. F. Bruce, *The Acts of the Apostles* (Grand Rapids: Wm. B. Eerdmans, 1951), 122.

68. Lüdemann, *Early Christianity According to the Traditions in Acts,* 96.

69. C. K. Barrett, "Paul and the 'Pillar' Apostles," in *Studia Paulina in honorem Johannis de Zwaan* (Haarlem: Erven F. Bohn N.V., 1953), 12–13. See also John Schütz, *Paul and the Anatomy of Apostolic Authority,* SNTSMS 26 (Cambridge: Cambridge University Press, 1975), 142–46.

70. Barrett, "Paul and the 'Pillar' Apostles," 17. See also James D. Hester, "The Use and Influence of Rhetoric in Galatians 2:1–14," *TZ* 42 (1986): 400.

71. Günter Klein, "Galater 2,6–9 und die Geschichte der Jerusalemer Urgemeinde," *ZTK* 57 (1960): 287–90; Hans Dieter Betz, *Galatians,* Hermeneia (Philadelphia: Fortress Press, 1979), 94.

72. Ulrich Wilckens, "*styloi,*" *TDNT* 7:734–35.

73. R. D. Aus, "Three Pillars and Three Patriarchs: A Proposal Concerning Gal 2:9," *ZNW* 70 (1979): 255, 260–61.

74. David M. Hay, "Paul's Indifference to Authority," *JBL* 88 (1969): 36–44.

75. Lührmann, "Gal 2:9 und die katholischen Briefe," 71.

CHAPTER 3

Beloved Disciple
The Apostle in the Fourth Gospel

Surprisingly, John the son of Zebedee is mentioned only once in the Gospel attributed to him. At the beginning of John 21, the narrator explains that seven of the disciples were fishing at the Sea of Tiberias. Among these seven were the sons of Zebedee: "Simon Peter, Thomas called the Twin, Nathanael of Cana in Galilee, the sons of Zebedee, and two others of his disciples" (21:2). Three points regarding this reference to John are notable.

First, this initial and only reference to John occurs very late in the Gospel, in the last chapter. Moreover, John 21 is widely regarded as an epilogue to the Gospel. The Fourth Gospel seems to reach a natural conclusion at the end of chapter 20, only to reopen the narrative in John 21. All of the evidence for regarding John 21 as an epilogue, afterthought, or later addition to the Gospel is internal.[1] None of the early manuscripts of the Gospel ends with chapter 20. Nevertheless, the absence of any reference to John earlier in the Gospel is curious. It means that the sons of Zebedee appear in John only in a minor role, but that they were recognized by the Johannine community as two of Jesus' disciples.

The second point is that the sons of Zebedee are mentioned in Luke 5:10 as having been with Peter at the miraculous catch of fish. The association of the sons of Zebedee with Peter is only one of several features that link the stories of the miraculous catch of fish in Luke 5 and John 21.[2] The parallel in Luke 5 may indicate, however, that the author of the Fourth Gospel had no particular interest in the sons of Zebedee but merely listed them because they were named as Peter's companions in the early tradition. The association of the sons of Zebedee with Peter may also be a vestige of the account of the calling of the two sets of brothers (Mark 1:16–20).[3]

Third, one of these seven disciples (other than Peter) was the Beloved Disciple. John 21 reports the miraculous catch of fish as a post-resurrection appearance. The Beloved Disciple, who was in the boat with Peter, was the

56

first to recognize the risen Lord. This conjunction of references to the sons of Zebedee and the Beloved Disciple in the same passage has naturally led either to the easy assumption that the two were one and the same or to the question of whether the Beloved Disciple was John the son of Zebedee or one of the two unnamed disciples. This question will be explored in detail later in this chapter. Presumably, the first readers of the Gospel knew who the Beloved Disciple was, but we are left with only a tantalizing set of references. John 21, therefore, appears to promise us more information than it actually delivers.

Older books about John identified the apostle as the Beloved Disciple and hence relied heavily on the Fourth Gospel. As we have seen, however, the Gospel of John does not identify the Beloved Disciple as John the son of Zebedee. Caution dictates, therefore, that this identification can no longer merely be assumed. The approach taken below will be to examine each of the Fourth Gospel's references to the Beloved Disciple, then to survey the various attempts that have been made to identify this fascinating figure.

THE BELOVED DISCIPLE IN THE FOURTH GOSPEL

The Beloved Disciple emerges in the Fourth Gospel as the disciple closest to Jesus—the one who reclined on the breast of Jesus at the Last Supper, the one to whom Jesus gave his mother at his death, the first of the disciples to reach the empty tomb, the first to believe in the resurrection, and the first of the disciples to recognize the risen Lord at the miraculous catch of fish in Galilee. Except for the scene at the cross,[4] the Beloved Disciple always appears as Peter's companion. The later followers of the Beloved Disciple also credit him with bearing a true witness.

The first explicit reference to the Beloved Disciple appears in John 13:23, where he is introduced to the reader: "One of his disciples—the one whom Jesus loved—was reclining next to him." In Greek, the clause "whom Jesus loved" is *hon agapa* (a verbal form of the noun *agapē*). The same statement appears in other references to the Beloved Disciple (19:26; 21:7, 20). Nevertheless, some references to the Beloved Disciple use a different verb: "Simon Peter and the other disciple, the one whom Jesus loved" (20:2). The reference to the Beloved Disciple is a relative clause in both instances—"whom Jesus loved"—but in John 20:2, the clause is *hon ephilei*. The syntax of these references raises the question of whether there are other references to the Beloved Disciple besides those which use the full formula: some form of the word "disciple" together with "whom Jesus loved," using either the verb *agapa* or the verb *ephilei*. John 20:2 refers to the Beloved Disciple first as "the other disciple" (*ton allon mathētēn*) and then identifies this unnamed disciple as "the one whom Jesus loved."

One of the disputed passages is John 18:15–16, which reports Peter's entry into the courtyard on the evening of Jesus' trial:

> Simon Peter and another disciple [*allos mathētēs*] followed Jesus. Since that disciple was known to the high priest, he went with Jesus into the courtyard of the high priest, but Peter was standing outside at the gate. So the other disciple [*ho mathētēs ho allos*, which is merely a variation of *ho allos methētēs*], who was known to the high priest, went out, spoke to the woman who guarded the gate, and brought Peter in.

Is this "other disciple" the Beloved Disciple, or is he, as some have suggested, Judas Iscariot?[5] The case for Judas is not strong. Judas appears in the same scenes with Peter after the footwashing (13:21–30) and at the arrest of Jesus (18:1–11), and he had had some previous contact with the priests. Nonetheless, is it credible that Peter, who had just slashed off the ear of the high priest's servant at the arrest scene, would allow Judas to accompany him? The supposition that "the other disciple" was Judas requires, at a minimum, that Peter did not know of Judas's treachery, even though Peter had been in the garden with Jesus at the time of the arrest.

While John 18:15–16 does not explicitly identify "the other disciple" as the Beloved Disciple, such an identification seems to be supported by the way in which the Beloved Disciple is referred to as "the other disciple" in John 20:2 and the verses which follow: "So she ran, and went to Simon Peter and *the other disciple,* the one whom Jesus loved. . . . Then Peter and *the other disciple,* set out and went toward the tomb. The two were running together, but *the other disciple* outran Peter. . . . Then *the other disciple,* who reached the tomb first, also went in, and he saw and believed" (20:2–8; italics mine). The clause "whom Jesus loved" in John 20:2 appears to be an added appositional identification which confirms for the reader that "the other disciple" of John 18:15–16 was the Beloved Disciple of John 13:23 and 19:26.[6] While recognizing that the reference is still open to debate, we will treat John 18:15–16 as a scene involving the Beloved Disciple.

The clause in John 20:2, "whom Jesus loved" (*hon ephilei ho Iēsous),* has a close parallel in the reference to Lazarus in John 11:3, where Lazarus is spoken of as "he whom you love"—*hon ephileis* (cf. John 11:36). John 11:3 is the only other verse in the Gospel which uses a relative clause to refer to one whom Jesus loved. Lazarus is actually named as "he whom you love" before the disciple "whom Jesus loved" is introduced in John 13:23. A fascinating case can be made for identifying the Beloved Disciple as Lazarus, but before we evaluate the arguments in favor of this possibility, let us survey what the Gospel tells us about the Beloved Disciple.

One other uncertain reference remains to be considered first, however. In John 1:35–40, John the Baptist directs two of his disciples to Jesus, calling him "the lamb of God who takes away the sin of the world." One of these original disciples is later identified as Andrew, the brother of Peter (1:40). The other disciple is unnamed. On the strength of the accounts of the calling of the two sets of brothers in the other Gospels and the priority of their names in the lists of the Twelve, it has often been suggested that Andrew's unnamed companion was John the son of Zebedee.[7]

It is prudent to treat this identification with some skepticism, however. Nothing in the passage or later in the Gospel suggests that this unnamed disciple was John. Neither is there any suggestion that this was the disciple "whom Jesus loved." Philip and Andrew appear together in later scenes (6:5–9; 12:20–22; cf. 1:43–44), but Andrew never appears with either John or the Beloved Disciple. Such an identification of the unnamed follower of John the Baptist rests heavily on assumptions that harmonize the Gospel of John with the synoptics: that the sons of Zebedee were among Jesus' first disciples and that the Fourth Gospel's account of the calling of the first disciples runs parallel to the synoptic accounts. Actually, the only similarity is that Peter appears among the first disciples in all four Gospels. Andrew is not mentioned in Luke 5:1–11, and the sons of Zebedee are not mentioned in John 1. In the synoptic Gospels, the calling of the first disciples takes place at the Sea of Galilee. In John, the calling of the first disciples takes place at Bethany across the Jordan (1:28). In view of these differences, the Fourth Gospel should be left free to tell its own story without our attempting to impose any prior assumptions upon it.[8]

Even if there is some common ground between the traditions of the synoptics and the Fourth Gospel at this point, the synoptics can be used to support only the conclusion that the unnamed disciple was John, not that John was the Beloved Disciple. The latter requires a second inference, namely that John was not identified because he was the author and intentionally concealed his name. But there is early material that may be pertinent. Papias, who wrote five books early in the second century, refers to the disciples in the same sequence in which they appear in John: "Andrew, or Peter, or Philip." This sequence of names is striking both because it parallels John and because it displaces Peter as the disciple traditionally named first in lists of Jesus' disciples. James and John do not appear until later in Papias' list.[9] Some interpreters, treating the matter without regard to the synoptic call stories, have suggested that the unnamed disciple was Philip.[10] Andrew then found Simon, and Philip found Nathanael. The present study therefore will not treat John 1:35–40 as a part of the growing body of tradition about John, though the passage has been incorporated into that tradition by many interpreters of the Gospel.

Reclining on Jesus' Breast

The first explicit reference to the Beloved Disciple appears in John 13:23. Its context is that of Jesus' prediction of his betrayal. Jesus' statement—"Very truly, I tell you, one of you will betray me"—is one of the few sayings in John (13:21) that is a verbatim parallel of the synoptic version (Mark 14:18; Matt. 26:21). Only the doubling of "truly" (*amēn*) is different in John. Matthew, Mark, and John each make note of the reactions of the disciples, but John's account differs from the synoptics at this point, and the introduction of "one of the disciples—the one whom Jesus loved" follows.

The first reference to the Beloved Disciple appears, therefore, as a distinctively Johannine addition to tradition common to John and the synoptics. Moreover, he is introduced as one who may not otherwise be known, and there is no hint that this character has appeared previously in the Gospel narrative.

The Beloved Disciple was reclining "in the bosom" of Jesus, a position that signals a privileged relationship. Moreover, because the prologue of the Gospel reported that the son was "in the bosom" of the Father (1:18), the repetition of this description implies that Jesus' relationship to the Father was a model for the Beloved Disciple's relationship to Jesus. Just as the Son had come from the Father and revealed the Father, so the Beloved Disciple came from the bosom of Jesus and revealed him to later believers. The reader is then told that Peter was somewhere further removed from Jesus and that Peter motioned to the Beloved Disciple to ask Jesus whom he was talking about. The request implies that the Beloved Disciple has a privileged access to Jesus. Why did not Peter merely ask Jesus himself? The Beloved Disciple's privileged position is confirmed by the narrator's interpretive comment that the Beloved Disciple was lying "next to Jesus" (13:25).

At this point, the Johannine account returns to the common tradition that Judas shared a bowl with Jesus (Mark 14:20; Matt. 26:23; cf. Luke 22:21). John's account is even more dramatic, however. Jesus answered the Beloved Disciple: "It is the one to whom I give this piece of bread when I have dipped it" (13:26). Then he dipped the piece of bread in the sauce and gave it to Judas. The Beloved Disciple is not mentioned again in this scene, so the narrator leaves an ambiguity unresolved. Did the Beloved Disciple understand Jesus' gesture? Did he share with Jesus the knowledge that Judas was the betrayer? Perhaps the Gospel does not answer this question because there is no satisfying answer. If the Beloved Disciple did not understand, then his characterization as one who was close to Jesus and who was a reliable mediator of the tradition about Jesus would be undermined. On the other hand, if the Beloved Disciple did understand, then one faces the question of why he did not tell the others or do anything to stop Judas. Naturally, one could conjecture that the Beloved Disciple is presented as a disciple so close to Jesus that when Jesus shared with him the knowledge of his coming death and its significance, the Beloved Disciple guarded Jesus' divine knowledge. Yet the Gospel account hardly prepares readers to make such an inference so soon after the first introduction of the Beloved Disciple. The Beloved Disciple fades from the scene as soon as his privileged position has been defined in relationship to both Jesus and Peter.

Known to the High Priest

John 18:15–16 is particularly significant for the question of the identity of the Beloved Disciple because it is the only reference that tells us something about "the other Disciple" apart from his relationship to Jesus, Peter, Jesus' mother, or the later Christian community.

These verses report that the other disciple was known to the high priest, Caiaphas (11:49–53; 18:3), who was appointed from one of the leading families of Jerusalem. The question that naturally arises is whether it is plausible that a Galilean fisherman, John the son of Zebedee, could have known the high priest. Several interesting considerations emerge from the efforts to answer this question affirmatively. Some scholars have suggested that the Zebedees' fishing business involved exporting fish to Jerusalem and that John may have brought fish to the high priest's house. The antiquity of such an interpretation may well be reflected in a paraphrase of this passage in John from the mid-fifth century (Nonnus) which identifies the other disciple as a young fisherman.[11] In addition, a fourteenth- or fifteenth-century manuscript, *Historia passionis Domini,* reports that the Gospel of the Nazarenes contained this same explanation: "In the Gospel of the Nazareans the reason is given why John was known to the high priest. As he was the son of the poor fisherman Zebedee, he had often brought fish to the palace of the high priests Annas and Caiaphas."[12]

Alternatively, Hippolytus of Thebes relates that after Zebedee's death, John gave away his father's property in Galilee and acquired a place in Jerusalem, "from which, as it says concerning him, he was known to the high priest."[13] Similarly, *The Life of the Virgin* by Epiphanius the Monk (ca. A.D. 1015) reports that after the death of his father, John sold his vast property in Zebede, and, having come to Jerusalem, bought the holy Zion, the highest part of Jerusalem.[14] According to the prologue to the *Acts of John by Prochorus* (Vatican Gr. 654), Zebedee was a priest who had lived in Jerusalem, near the temple.[15] The high priests, who changed each year, came from various provinces. Caiaphas was from the province of Kio in Bithynia and, while serving as high priest, stayed at the estate of John the Theologian. This is Epiphanius the Monk's explanation of how John was "known to the high priest."[16] Others have cited the report of Polycrates of Ephesus (ca. A.D. 190) that John himself was a priest,[17] but that report may itself be a later interpretation based on these verses in John. Again, it has been suggested that if John was the nephew of Mary, Jesus' mother, he had priestly relatives (see Luke 1:5, 36), which might again explain how he could have been known by the high priest. This explanation too, however, is based on the conclusion that the "other disciple" was the Beloved Disciple and that this disciple was John the son of Zebedee.

On the other hand, the situation described in John 18:15ff. virtually requires that the other disciple was not a well-known figure. The story of Peter's denials requires that neither the other disciple nor Peter was known to be a disciple. Some have contended that the other disciple could not have been the Beloved Disciple because his close relationship to Jesus would have been known, but such a conclusion does not necessarily follow. Surely Peter was as well known publicly as any of the disciples. The issue in the other Gospels and Acts, however, is that Peter (and the others) were Galileans (Mark 14:70; Matt. 26:69; Luke 22:59; Acts 1:11; 2:7). The other disciple may have been above suspicion because he was not a Galilean but a Judean, one who was known in Jerusalem, even by the high priest.

While it is not impossible that John the son of Zebedee was known by the high priest, John 18:15–16 must be considered to be among the difficulties for the traditional interpretation that the Beloved Disciple was John the son of Zebedee. Let us return to the question of the role of these particular verses in the Gospel. The introduction of the other disciple provides an answer to a question that is left unaddressed by the synoptic accounts: how did the most vocal of the apostles get into the high priest's courtyard? It may have been felt that a Galilean fisherman obviously would not have an entrée to the high priest's house. The Fourth Gospel fills this gap in the story by introducing another disciple, presumably a Judean, who secured Peter's entrance into the courtyard. If these were the considerations that led to the Fourth Gospel's expansion of the story of Peter's denials, they serve as further considerations in favor of rejecting the identification of this disciple as also a Galilean fisherman.

Nevertheless, the Beloved Disciple regularly appears in scenes where he is given some priority or advantage over Peter. If we identify the other disciple as the Beloved Disciple, then this scene shows that the Beloved Disciple was not only the one closest to Jesus but was also able to come and go in the high priest's house. Moreover, it implies the faithfulness of the Beloved Disciple in contrast to Peter's failure. The Beloved Disciple was there too, in the high priest's courtyard, but he did not deny Jesus. Hence, the credibility of the Beloved Disciple is heightened further.

Whereas the synoptic Gospels report that the Twelve abandoned Jesus and fled (Mark 14:50), the Fourth Gospel reports that the Beloved Disciple was standing near the cross and witnessed Jesus' death. This contrast in the Gospel accounts may also serve as a point in favor identifying the Beloved Disciple as one who was not included among the Twelve, in other words, someone other than the apostle John.

Mother and Son

The scene at the cross (John 19:26–27) is one of the most poignant in the Fourth Gospel. From the cross, Jesus sees his mother and the Beloved Disciple standing nearby and, with a simple statement, gives the Beloved Disciple as a son to his mother and gives his mother to the Beloved Disciple. By this ceremonial act, a new relationship is formed; a new family is created. The significance of this scene becomes clearer when it is set in the context of the Gospel's designation of believers as "children of God."

The term "children of God" first appears in the prologue: "But to all who received him, who believed in his name, he gave power to become children of God" (1:12). A new birth, "from above," sets the children of God apart from the world (3:3, 5). Nicodemus misunderstands, thinking that in some way he must be born again physically. The birth from above, however, is birth by the Spirit that gives the believer eternal life. This life is marked by the believer's knowledge of God and obedience to God's commands. The life of the children of God is sustained by bread and water that the world cannot see. Just as Jesus had food "that you do not know about" (4:32), so those who receive him have living water (4:10, 14; 7:37–39) and bread of life (6:27, 33, 35, 51). Following Caiaphas' unwitting declaration that it is better that Jesus should die than that the whole nation should perish, the narrator explains that Caiaphas was actually prophesying "that Jesus was about to die for the nation, and not for the nation only, but to gather into one the dispersed children of God" (11:51–52). It is not surprising, therefore, that at Jesus' death, a new family unit is formed—a home, a community for "the dispersed children of God." The final step in this development occurs when the risen Lord instructs Mary Magdalene to tell his "brothers" that he is ascending "to my Father and your Father, to my God and your God" (20:17). Mary Magdalene understands. She goes not to his brothers, who do not believe in him (7:5), but to his disciples (20:18), the children of God, brothers and sisters in the new community of faith.

When seen in this perspective, the scene at the cross is intelligible without the use of artificial symbolic interpretations.[18] The mother of Jesus, who is never named in the Fourth Gospel, appears only in this scene and the wedding at Cana (2:1–11). In both scenes, Jesus addresses her as "woman." In the earlier scene, Jesus asks his mother, "What concern is that to you and to me? My hour has not yet come," and she does not appear again until the hour of

Jesus' death. The theme of the "hour" recurs at intervals in the following chapters (2:4; 7:30; 8:20; 12:23, 27; 13:1; 16:32; 17:1; 19:14). Following Jesus' declaration to his mother and the Beloved Disciple, the narrator ties the meaning of what has just happened to the theme of the hour by reporting that "from that hour the disciple took her into his own home" (19:27).

The primary significance of this comment is that it confers on the Beloved Disciple—and, by implication, on the Johannine community—the authority of succession. The New Testament reflects a struggle among various Christian communities for the right to claim that they were authorized by Jesus' family. This claim appears clearly in Luke and Acts. Luke portrays Mary in a positive light in the birth narrative, where Mary is designated as "the handmaid of the Lord" who says to the angel of the Lord, "Let it be with me according to your word" (Luke 1:38). Later, Luke presents a subtly more positive version of Mark's sharp question, "Who are my mother and my brothers?" (Mark 3:31–35). According to Luke, Jesus instead says, "My mother and my brothers are those who hear the word of God and do it" (8:21). In light of the annunciation (Luke 1:38), Jesus' physical mother and brothers are included among those who "hear the word of God and do it."

Jesus' mother and brothers also figure prominently among those who "were constantly devoting themselves to prayer" in preparation for Pentecost (Acts 1:14). According to Luke and Acts, therefore, the Jerusalem church claimed the authority of Jesus' family, and James, the brother of Jesus, later became the leader of the church in Jerusalem (Acts 15:13; 21:18). In contrast, Mark and Matthew seem to dismiss the authority of Jesus' family. Jesus forms a new family by saying, "Whoever does the will of God is my brother and sister and mother" (Mark 3:35; cf. Matt. 12:46–50). The earthly family of Jesus is thereby displaced, and Jesus begins to gather a new family. The earthly family of Jesus does not figure in the resurrection community. They are not mentioned in Mark 13 nor in the angel's command, "tell his disciples and Peter that he is going ahead of you to Galilee; there you will see him" (Mark 16:7). In Matthew, the role of the family is displaced by the primacy of Peter, to whom the keys to the kingdom are given (Matt. 16:18–19).

The Fourth Gospel dismisses the role of the brothers of Jesus by identifying them as unbelievers and then transferring the designation "brothers" to Jesus' disciples (7:5; 20:17–18). Unlike Mark and Matthew, however, the Fourth Gospel retains the importance of Jesus' mother. She is given to the Beloved Disciple, and together they become the nucleus of the new community. The comment that from that hour the Beloved Disciple took Jesus' mother to his own home has been cited as evidence that the Beloved Disciple was a Judean who had a home in Jerusalem. Such an interpretation accords well with the earlier report that the "other disciple" was known by the high priest (18:15), and it may be harmonized with Luke's claim that Jesus' mother was among the believers who gathered in Jerusalem following the resurrection (Acts 1:14). Nevertheless, the Greek term *ta idia* in John 19:27 is not the word for house (*oikos*) but a broader term that means one's "own," one's goods and possessions. The primary function of this verse may be to attribute to the Beloved Disciple and the Johannine community the authority of Jesus' mother. The reference to "that hour" does not necessarily mean that the Beloved Disciple's home was in the immediate vicinity. It may have been, but the "hour" links the Beloved Disciple's relationship to Jesus' mother to the "hour" of Jesus' death. This note is central to the contention that the Beloved Disciple was John Mark (see below), whose mother had a home in Jerusalem. This verse may have also given rise to the legend that the apostle John took Jesus' mother with him to Ephesus, where the remains of a house south of the city are identified by local tradition as the home of Jesus' mother. Caution should be exercised in drawing inferences about the Beloved Disciple's home from these verses, but if any inferences are to be drawn, they support the identification of the Beloved Disciple as a Judean rather than as a Galilean.

Witness to Jesus' Death

John 19:35 does not make explicit mention of the Beloved Disciple, but the close similarity between this passage and John 21:24, together with the prior note that the Beloved Disciple was standing near the cross (19:26–27), make it virtually indisputable that the passage is referring to the Beloved Disciple.

The pattern of noting the Beloved Disciple's presence at crucial moments in the passion of Jesus continues. Not only is the Beloved Disciple present at the Last Supper, in the courtyard, and at the cross; he also witnesses Jesus' death. In this regard, the Beloved Disciple usurps the role of the centurion who, in the synoptic accounts, sees how Jesus dies and responds with a climactic confession (Mark 15:39). In the Fourth Gospel, the Beloved Disciple has borne witness, and his witness is now conveyed by the written Gospel itself.

The Beloved Disciple is presented as an eyewitness; he had seen how Jesus died. As in the discovery of the empty tomb, seeing does not always lead to believing, but sight does mean faith for the Beloved Disciple. He saw, and he has borne witness, and his witness is true. Each of these affirmations is important in the Fourth Gospel.

The close parallels between John 19:35 and 21:24 are evident in the following table:

John 19:35	*John 21:24*
He who saw this	This is the disciple
has testified—	who is testifying to these
	things,

	and has written them,
so that you also	(Cf. 20:31)
may believe.	
His testimony is true,	and we know that his testimony
and he knows that he	is true.
tells the truth.	

Since it is evident that John 21:24 was written by the editor or redactor who refers to the Beloved Disciple, it is likely that John 19:35 was inserted by the redactor also. The secondary nature of the references to the Beloved Disciple, and indeed the designation itself, has led to the widely accepted conclusion that all the references to the Beloved Disciple were added to the Gospel by the redactor. The Disciple did not refer to himself as the "Beloved." Instead, it was the tribute paid to him by a community that had accepted his testimony as true and that looked to him as their link with the ministry of Jesus.

This verse signals the significance of the Beloved Disciple. He was the witness to later believers. Describing his presence at the key moments in the passion narrative was a way of affirming both his authority as a true witness and, by implication, the authority and credibility of the Gospel. The Gospel may be believed because it rests on the testimony of the disciple who was closest to Jesus, who was present at his death and saw the risen Lord, and who has borne a true witness.

Witness to the Empty Tomb

The next reference reports that the Beloved Disciple was the first to believe in the resurrection of Jesus (20:3–10). In order to grasp the full significance of this report, however, one needs to understand it in the context of the development of the traditions related to the resurrection of Jesus.[19]

The earliest strata in the New Testament contain reports of the resurrection of Jesus. Assuming that there is a historical core to the preaching of the apostles in Acts, we find evidence there that the earliest Christian proclamation was that "this Jesus God raised up" (Acts 2:32; cf. 2:23–24; 3:15; 4:10; 5:30). The kerygma was then formulated into a confession, such as we find in 1 Corinthians 15:3–8. Paul wrote 1 Corinthians around A.D. 54, but says that he had taught this confession to the Corinthians when he was with them (51–52). The words "deliver" and "receive" are technical terms for receiving and handing on oral tradition. This well-formed confession contains four balanced clauses followed by a list of appearances:

> *that Christ died* for our sins in accordance with the scriptures,
> *that he was buried,*

that he was raised on the third day in accordance with the
scriptures, and
that he appeared
to Cephas, then to the twelve.
Then he appeared to more than five hundred brothers and
sisters at one time, most of whom are still alive, though some
have fallen asleep.
Then he appeared to James, then to all the apostles.
Last of all, as to one untimely born, he appeared also to me.

(1 Cor. 15:3–8)

These extraordinary verses contain one of the earliest confessions in the New
Testament. They show that the early kerygma, or preaching of the church,
took the form of reports of Jesus' death and resurrection. Moreover, the
resurrection appearances were viewed as authorizing the work of those to
whom the Lord had appeared. For this reason, no women are mentioned in this
list of appearances.

Mark and Matthew suggest that the empty tomb tradition and the appearance traditions were originally separate and distinct. Women went to the tomb
in Jerusalem and were told that the Lord would appear to the disciples in
Galilee. The interpreting angel(s) who appear at the empty tomb repeat the
kerygma, with notable parallels to the confession in 1 Corinthians 15. According to Matthew, the disciples went to Galilee, where the Lord appeared to
them. Matthew also shows that the empty tomb tradition could be related to
the appearance traditions not only by having an appearance foretold by the
angel(s) but by reporting an appearance to the women at the tomb (Matt.
28:8–10) in which Jesus repeats what the angel has already said.

Luke adapts the material further. In Luke's scheme, Jesus ministered in
Galilee, then journeyed to Jerusalem, where he died and was raised; the
disciples were told to remain in Jerusalem and, after Pentecost, went forth
from Jerusalem to "the ends of the earth" (Acts 1:8). This geographical pattern
allows no room for appearances in Galilee, so all the appearances reported in
Luke and Acts take place in or around Jerusalem. The two men (angels) at the
tomb did not charge the women to send the disciples to Galilee but reminded
the women of what Jesus had said while he was in Galilee. In addition, the
appearance by the Sea of Galilee is reported earlier in the Gospel as Peter's
call to discipleship.[20]

Luke 24:12 is one of several verses at the end of Luke that are omitted by
Codex Bezae, a fifth-century manuscript that often contains interpolations or
expansions not found in other manuscript traditions.. Westcott and Hort assigned it to the Western tradition and spoke of these verses as "Western non-
interpolations." The discovery of papyrus text^ which contain these verses has

led to reappraisal of Westcott and Hort's omission of these verses from the text of the New Testament. This trend toward accepting Luke 24:12 is important for our purposes because it reports that Peter ran to the tomb, peered in, saw the burial cloths, and went away amazed. Whereas Matthew includes an appearance to the women at the tomb, Luke shows that there was the counter tendency to join the empty tomb and appearance traditions by bringing the disciples to the empty tomb.

The parallels between Luke 24:12 and John 20 are readily apparent: "Peter [John 20:3] got up and ran to the tomb [John 20:3]; stooping and looking in [John 20:5, where it is the Beloved Disciple who stoops and looks in], he saw the linen cloths by themselves [John 20:6]; then he went home [John 20:10], amazed at what had happened." With exception of the final clause, "amazed at what had happened," each element of Luke 24:12 appears in John 20:2–10. The differences in the Gospel of John reveal a distinctive Johannine interest. The Beloved Disciple is added to the tradition known to Luke; the Beloved Disciple arrived at the tomb before Peter, looked in, and saw the linen cloths; the position of the linen cloths is described in more detail; and when the Beloved Disciple stepped into the tomb, "he saw and believed."[21] The final clause of Luke 24:12 is omitted because it would create tension following the report of the Beloved Disciple's belief. The result of these alterations to the tradition is that the Beloved Disciple becomes the first of the disciples to arrive at the empty tomb and the only one to see and believe.

As we have seen, the development of the resurrection traditions shows that the empty tomb and appearance traditions were originally separate—one Judean, the other probably Galilean; one involving the women, the other the disciples. The list of appearances in 1 Corinthians 15 also shows that the reports of appearances were used to defend the authority of the apostles. Similarly, Paul defended his authority as an apostle by arguing that his experience too was an appearance of the risen Lord (see 1 Cor. 9:1).

The tradition of Peter's running to the tomb (Luke 24:12) serves both as a secondary link joining the empty tomb tradition to the appearance tradition and as a further demonstration of the authority of Peter. Not only was he the first to see the risen Lord (Luke 24:34; 1 Cor 15:5; Mark 16:7); he was the first apostle to get to the empty tomb. Luke still maintains that it was only the appearances, not the discovery of the empty tomb, that brought faith in the resurrection.

This background allows us to see clearly the significance of the adaptation of the tradition in John 20:2–10: the authority of Peter is subordinated to that of the Beloved Disciple, who not only beat Peter to the empty tomb but then "saw and believed." By implication, Peter saw but did not understand the significance of what he saw. The Beloved Disciple, therefore, becomes the only figure in the New Testament of whom it is said that he believed in the resurrection because of what he saw at the empty tomb.

In short, the tradition of Peter's running to the empty tomb is a secondary development in the empty tomb/appearance traditions, but it can be traced to tradition known to both Luke and the Fourth Evangelist.[22] The Fourth Evangelist then added the role of the Beloved Disciple with the effect that his authority was elevated over that of Peter.

Witness to the Risen Lord

The story of the great catch of fish (John 21:1–14) has been discussed earlier.[23] Here, it is sufficient to recall that the stories in Luke 5 and John 21 probably stem from a common tradition. The expansion of this tradition in John 21 is parallel to what we have just seen of the development of the empty tomb tradition in John 20:2–10. The Johannine account is based on tradition known also to Luke, which features the apostle Peter. In the Johannine version, the Beloved Disciple has been added to the tradition and takes precedence over Peter.

The Beloved Disciple actually plays only a small role in John 21:1–14, being mentioned only in verse 7: "That disciple whom Jesus loved said to Peter, 'It is the Lord!'" With this one verse, the Beloved Disciple is given the honor of being the first of the disciples to recognize the risen Lord. This observation grows in significance when one considers the possibility that this story originally circulated separately, not as the third appearance to the disciples as it is in its present location. Indeed, John 21:1–14 may be an account of the appearance promised in Mark 16:7 since John 21 reports an appearance to "the disciples and Peter" in Galilee. If this account originally reported the first (or only!) appearance, the effect of the Johannine redaction is striking: the Beloved Disciple, not Peter, was the first to recognize the risen Lord. It may well be that "the Lord has risen indeed, and he has appeared to Simon" (Luke 24:34), but according to John it was the Beloved Disciple who first recognized the risen Lord and told Peter who it was.

"What about This Man?"

The last word on the relationship between Peter and the Beloved Disciple is recorded in John 21:20–23, which has no parallel in the other Gospels. It appears, rather, as an appendix or epilogue to the account of the conversation between Peter and the risen Lord in which Peter is restored and given a pastoral role as a good shepherd. Not only will he shepherd the sheep; he will lay down his life for his Lord (John 21:18–19).

As the Gospel winds toward its conclusion, therefore, it allows the reader to look ahead to the role that Peter will play, and even to his death. But what about the Beloved Disciple? Surely the Gospel could not end with the elevation of Peter to the role of shepherd and martyr with no word about the role of the Beloved Disciple, not after the role of Peter had been systematically subordinated to that of the Beloved Disciple. Something like verses 20–23 and 24–25 had to be added.

The Beloved Disciple is reintroduced in verse 20 by reminding the reader of the scene in which the Beloved Disciple was first introduced—reclining next to Jesus. While it may seem odd to reintroduce a character who has appeared in so many significant scenes, we may recall that Nicodemus was reintroduced in 7:50 and 19:39, and that Caiaphas was reintroduced in 18:14. Moreover, by reintroducing the Beloved Disciple in this way, the Gospel reminds the reader that this disciple, the one whom Jesus loved, had the place of honor next to Jesus.

Jesus' response reasserts the conviction of the early church that Jesus would come again soon. The preaching of the Parousia or the coming of Jesus plays a relatively minor role in John, which emphasizes that the hopes for the future which had been associated with the coming of the Day of the Lord, or the resurrection and last Judgment, were already being realized in the incarnation and in the resurrection of Jesus. Just as the promise of the Parousia is reasserted in 1 John (3:2), so it also recurs here, in one of the latest strata of the Gospel tradition. Moreover, these verses indicate that the longevity of the Beloved Disciple had been tied to the hope of the Lord's coming. Apparently some believed that the Beloved Disciple would not die until the Lord returned. The increasing longevity of the Beloved Disciple, therefore, became an indication of the proximity of the Lord's coming. Then, evidently, the Beloved Disciple died, and some in the community were thrown into consternation because they believed that the Lord had said that the Beloved Disciple would not die until he came. As a result, the author explains that the risen Lord had not actually said that the Beloved Disciple would not die. These verses, therefore, explain the death of the Beloved Disciple and correct the report that Jesus had promised that this disciple would not die.

This chain of implications leads to several significant conclusions. First, it strongly suggests that the Beloved Disciple, whose role in John up to this point has always been a secondary addition to tradition known to the other evangelists, was not just a legendary accretion to earlier tradition but a real human being who had died by the time these verses were written. Such a conclusion is not quite accurate, however, since we know the Beloved Disciple only from the "legendary accretions to earlier tradition" in John. It is more accurate to say that the Beloved Disciple, as he appears in the crucial scenes late in the Gospel, is an idealized and legendary description of the role attributed to a significant member of the Johannine community. Indeed, John 19:35 and 21:24–25 show that the Beloved Disciple was the community's eyewitness and link to the ministry of Jesus.

In a subtle fashion, these verses also elevate the authority of the Beloved Disciple over that of Peter. The risen Lord had commanded Peter to follow him (21:19); then Peter turned and saw the Beloved Disciple already following (21:20). The point of the Lord's hypothetical question to Peter was to reiterate the command that Peter was to follow him (21:22). The Beloved Disciple, of course, was already following.

Authority for the Gospel

John 21:24–25 is an editor's concluding statement which echoes both John 19:35 and John 20:30–31 and draws the Gospel to a close. It continues the affirmation of the authority of the Beloved Disciple from the preceding verses. Peter might die a martyr's death, but the Beloved Disciple would bear a true witness (in Greek, *martyria*).

The next claim is even stronger. The author says that it is the Beloved Disciple who "has written these things." The question immediately arises as to whether "these things" means the entire Gospel or only chapter 21. Obviously the claim cannot be literally true for the conclusion of the Gospel because the sentence continues "and we know that his testimony is true" (19:35). Either "has written these things" means that the author was using the Beloved Disciple's writings as a source for the Gospel or that the Beloved Disciple wrote the bulk of the Gospel and the present writer was simply an editor who added the final touches, including these final verses. One other alternative merits consideration: the verb "has written" could have had a causative force, meaning "he has caused these things to be written." The three alternatives are not sharply different. In any interpretation of the ending of the Gospel, the author attributed a prior and formative role to the Beloved Disciple. What stands written in the Gospel owes its origin, definition, and authority to the Beloved Disciple.

The reference "we know" signals that there was a community which attested to the truth of the Beloved Disciple's witness and, by implication, to the truth of the Gospel. There is no need, nor any evidence, to maintain that this group had some official standing, as a group of apostles or presbyters. To the contrary, the pronoun is adequately explained as a reference to a community of believers who had gathered around the Beloved Disciple. They had heard his witness, and they knew it was true. The writer, who later speaks in first person (21:25), of course, counted himself as a member of this community. The community knew that their disciple's witness was true, and they spoke of him as "the Beloved Disciple." They also honored him and explained the origin of his authority by describing the role they imagined for him at key points in the Gospel story. The Beloved Disciple was next to Jesus at the Last Supper, in the courtyard with Peter, at the cross (where he was given charge of Jesus' mother and witnessed the death of Jesus), at the empty tomb (where he perceived what had happened), and at the appearance in Galilee (where he was the first to recognize the risen Lord). Such developments in the tradition may indeed suggest that a number of years had passed since the death of the Beloved Disciple, long enough for his reputation to grow into this privileged role in the Gospel story.

As a conclusion to this survey of the references to the Beloved Disciple in John, we may underscore the point that each of them seems to be a secondary addition to earlier tradition. Although it has been argued that the Beloved Disciple passages actually constituted an early core or source narrative composed by the Beloved Disciple,[24] it is far more likely that the opposite is the case. They are relatively late, Johannine additions to earlier tradition. The Beloved Disciple first appears in the traditional context of Jesus' reference to his betrayer at the Last Supper, then at the courtyard where Peter denies Jesus, at the cross with the women, and at the empty tomb. These are the pivotal, memorable moments of the passion narrative, which, in light of the absence of any reference to the role of the Beloved Disciple in the parallel synoptic passages, cast suspicion over the historical credibility of these passages. They serve to validate the authority of the Gospel, and they tell us a great deal about the Johannine community's regard for the witness who stood behind their traditions, but they tell us little about events at the death and resurrection of Jesus.

WHO WAS THE BELOVED DISCIPLE?

If the Beloved Disciple was not just a fictional character designed to give authority to the Gospel, if he was a disciple who was known to the evangelist or redactor of the Gospel but who died some time before it was completed, then who was he? The traditional answer, of course, has been that the Beloved Disciple was John, the son of Zebedee. In later chapters we will see how John came to be identified as the Beloved Disciple. Here we will survey the evidence and arguments that can be brought for and against the view that the Beloved Disciple was the apostle John. Then we will assess the strength of the arguments that have been advanced for other candidates—Lazarus, John Mark, Benjamin, Philip, the rich young ruler, Matthias, Paul—and for the view that the Beloved Disciple was simply a symbolic figure.

The Apostle John

The issues of the authorship of the Fourth Gospel and the testimony of Papias, Polycarp, and Irenaeus can hardly be separated from the issue of the identity of the Beloved Disciple, but these issues are dealt with in the next two chapters. Only the bearing of evidence from the Gospel itself on the identification of the Beloved Disciple as John, the son of Zebedee, will be considered here. As a general observation, it is significant that the trend in Gospel studies has been to turn away from the importance of the early church's testimony regarding the authorship of the Gospels while relying increasingly on evidence from the Gospels themselves. One indication of this trend is that leading commentators who once identified the Beloved Disciple with John have subsequently abandoned that position. Both Raymond E. Brown and Rudolf Schnackenburg, who once held that John was the Beloved Disciple, have more recently claimed that this figure was an eyewitness of the ministry of Jesus but not one of the Twelve.[25] It is further significant that both of these commentators considered the question in the context of discussion concerning the authorship of the Gospel and that even in their earlier positions, both claimed the evangelist was not the Beloved Disciple but someone who had been close to him.

What then can be said in support of the traditional identification of John as the Beloved Disciple from the Gospel itself?

1. Whereas in the Gospel of John, Peter and the Beloved Disciple appear together in several scenes, in Acts (1:13; 3:1, 3, 4, 11; 4:13, 19; 8:14) John is named as Peter's companion. The only place in Acts where John is not named as Peter's companion is 12:2, and Peter is mentioned in the next verse. The comparative evidence from Acts, therefore, supports the conclusion that Peter's unnamed companion in the Fourth Gospel was the apostle John.

2. As we have seen, Mark and Matthew preserve the tradition of the calling of the two sets of brothers. Even Luke 5 mentions the sons of Zebedee in connection with the call of Peter to discipleship. An analogy could be drawn to the Gospel of John if one is prepared to make certain assumptions. The first line of assumptions is that the unnamed companion of Andrew in John 1:35 and 40 was the Beloved Disciple. If that were the case, then by analogy with the synoptic traditions, one could argue that the Beloved Disciple was John the son of Zebedee. The other line of reasoning concerns the story of the great catch of fish in John 21. Since Luke 5 mentions the sons of Zebedee as Peter's associates, it is sometimes suggested that the Beloved Disciple in John 21 must be John the son of Zebedee. This line of reasoning is strained, however, since the sons of Zebedee are included in the list of disciples who went with Peter but there is no way to know whether the Beloved Disciple was John or

one of the two unnamed disciples. Neither the evangelist nor the redactor seem to feel any need to identify the Beloved Disciple by name.

3. The presence of the Beloved Disciple at the Last Supper has been interpreted as evidence that the Beloved Disciple must have been one of the Twelve, and if so, then probably he was John. Difficult as it may be to put Leonardo da Vinci's painting out of our minds, the Gospels are not unambiguous about the number or identity of those present at the Last Supper. John implies that Jesus shared the supper with "his own" (13:1). In the discourses that follow, we learn that Peter, the Beloved Disciple, Judas, Thomas, Philip, and Judas (not Iscariot) were present. The Twelve are not mentioned at this point in John, but assuming that this Judas (not Iscariot) was Judas the son of James (named among the Twelve in Luke 6:16 and Acts 1:13), then each of those named appears elsewhere in a list of the Twelve. Mark says that "when it was evening he came with the twelve" (14:17), and Matthew, that "he took his place with the twelve" (26:20). Luke seems to agree. Although Luke uses the term "apostles" in 22:14, one cannot say that here "apostles" includes others besides the Twelve as it does in 1 Corinthians 15:7 because Luke 6:13 identifies the Twelve as apostles. While the synoptics indicate that the Twelve were present, therefore, they neither mention others nor say specifically that only the Twelve were present. The Johannine tradition may coincide with the synoptics at this point, but there is nothing in John to suggest that only the Twelve were present. The Twelve are mentioned in John only in 6:67 and 70–71, and in 20:24, and John never lists the Twelve by name. The references to Jesus' close relationship with Mary, Martha, and Lazarus, who lived nearby, raises the possibility that John may have thought of these friends as being included among "his own."

Even if one concludes that only the Twelve were present, there is nothing in John to indicate that the Beloved Disciple was John. One might reason that because the Beloved Disciple is not identified by name, he could not have been Peter (which is clear), or Judas Iscariot (which is also clear), Thomas, Philip, or the other Judas. While this inference seems reasonable, the premise that the Beloved Disciple was not among those identified by name, if applied to John 21, would exclude the sons of Zebedee (21:2).

4. The giving of Jesus' mother to the Beloved Disciple has also been cited as a basis for identifying him with John. If the mother of the sons of Zebedee was Salome, who was also the sister of Jesus' mother,[26] then the sons of Zebedee would have been Jesus' first cousins. Such a family relationship might explain why Jesus formed a new relationship between his mother and Beloved Disciple. This line of reasoning depends on inferences drawn from the other Gospels and does not explain why Jesus' brothers would not have assumed the care of their mother. John says earlier that Jesus' brothers did not

believe in him (7:5), but the relationship between Jesus and the Beloved Disciple is sufficient to explain Jesus' act apart from any family relationship.

5. Again, by comparison with the synoptics and Acts, one can argue that John the son of Zebedee, who was one of the inner three, is such an important figure that the Fourth Gospel could not simply overlook him.[27] The absence of any explicit reference to John (until 21:2) must be deliberate: John's name was suppressed because he was the author. He referred to himself only as the "other disciple," and his followers later inserted the honorific tag "the Beloved Disciple."[28]

The arguments for identifying the Beloved Disciple with John are not strong. Indeed, they rely heavily not on internal evidence but on comparisons with the synoptics and Acts. On the other hand, significant considerations have been advanced in opposition to the traditional identification.

1. The Gospel of John does not mention any of the special scenes at which John is present in one or more of the synoptics: the raising of Jairus's daughter, the transfiguration, the discourse on the Mount of Olives, or Jesus' prayer at Gethsemane. John records the arrest of Jesus but does not say that Jesus was in agony, that he prayed in the garden, or that the garden was named Gethsemane. Yet the force of this consideration is diminished if one traces the origin of "the inner three" to Mark rather than to the ministry of Jesus.[29]

2. The Gospel of John does not record the calling of the two sets of brothers, as the synoptics do. And if the calling of the disciples involved a miraculous catch of fish (Luke 5), it is strange that the Gospel of John would not also record the great catch of fish as a call experience rather than as a resurrection appearance. The strength of this point is weakened if one agrees that the catch of fish was originally a resurrection appearance which Luke has placed back in the ministry of Jesus.[30] Nevertheless, the absence of the calling of the two sets of brothers from their nets is still a consideration that challenges either the historicity of that tradition or the identification of the Beloved Disciple as John.

3. Assuming that the "other disciple" in John 18:15–16 is the Beloved Disciple, as we have argued above,[31] it is difficult to explain how a Galilean fisherman would have been known by the high priest in Jerusalem. Explanations that the disciple was known only to the servant, or that John delivered fish to the house of the high priest, or that, after all, Palestine was a small country hardly overturn this difficulty.

4. Similarly, the detailed knowledge of Judean geography reflected in John may be a fact that indicates the Beloved Disciple was himself a Judean. Again, the force of this consideration depends on how much of the Gospel one attributes directly to the Beloved Disciple and how much of its familiarity with Judea might be explained by concluding either that after the resurrection

the Beloved Disciple remained in Judea for a period of time (see the references to Peter and John in Acts) or that the community standing behind the Gospel originated in Judea.

5. According to the synoptic Gospels, none of the disciples was present at the cross: "all of them deserted him and fled" (Mark 14:50). Yet, according to John, the Beloved Disciple stood with the women at the cross. The implication is that the Beloved Disciple was not one of the Twelve. Again, however, this argument relies on comparisons of the Fourth Gospel with the synoptics.

From such considerations, it is clear that the Gospel of John does not identify the Beloved Disciple as John the son of Zebedee and that there are aspects of the characterization of the Beloved Disciple which are difficult to square with the traditional identification. These difficulties, presented by the Gospel's internal evidence, have led both to an intensive review of the external evidence from the church fathers and to a search for other candidates. Among these, some of the most interesting arguments focus on Lazarus.

Lazarus

The identification of the Beloved Disciple as Lazarus draws heavily upon evidence within the Gospel itself, but these arguments are not without difficulties, and there is no corroborating external evidence.[32]

The story of the raising of Lazarus begins with the report to Jesus: "Lord, he whom you love is ill" (John 11:3; in Greek, *hon phileis*). No further identification seems to be necessary. Two verses later, the narrator explains: "Jesus loved [*ēgapa*] Martha and her sister and Lazarus" (11:5). Then, when Jesus wept and asked to be taken to Lazarus' tomb, the Judeans said, "See how he loved [*ephilei*] him" (11:36). These are the only places in the Fourth Gospel (other than the Beloved Disciple passages) where the reader is told that Jesus had a special love for another person. These statements also occur just shortly before the introduction of the Beloved Disciple in John 13:23. The presence of Lazarus at table with Jesus in chapter 12 also prepares the reader to understand that the one whom Jesus loved, who was reclining next to him, was Lazarus. The information that Lazarus was from Bethany, where he or his sisters had a house (11:20), accords well with the report that the Beloved Disciple was known to the high priest and that he took Jesus' mother to his home (19:27). Being a Judean, Lazarus would also have known the topography of the area, which is described in some detail in the Fourth Gospel.

The identification of the Beloved Disciple as Lazarus casts an interesting light on two other passages. It would explain why some believed that the Beloved Disciple would not die until the Lord came: he had already been raised from the dead. This hypothesis also adds significance to the reference to the burial wrappings in the empty tomb. John 11:44 says that Lazarus came out of the tomb still bound by the wrappings. If it was Lazarus who saw the burial wrappings in the empty tomb, that fact provides an interesting explanation of why the cloths led him to believe in the resurrection of Jesus.

Serious objections can be raised against this intriguing solution, however. The first has to do with the disparity between the explicit identification of Lazarus in chapters 11 and 12 and the anonymity of the Beloved Disciple. The hypothesis that the Beloved Disciple was Lazarus works best on the assumption that the intended readers of the Gospel were in the same position as we, that they did not know who the Beloved Disciple was and were forced to rely on clues within the Gospel. On the other hand, if they knew who the Beloved Disciple was, why would the author have introduced him with explicit references in chapters 11 and 12 and then hidden his identity in later passages? Another difficulty arises when one observes that the Beloved Disciple is introduced as a new character in John 13:23. There is no hint in this passage that the Beloved Disciple has appeared previously in the Gospel, as there is in other passages where a character is reintroduced. Is this part of a deliberate riddle, or does it in fact mean that the Beloved Disciple was not Lazarus? Finally, one faces the issue that no ancient church authority identifies the Beloved Disciple as Lazarus. Was the Beloved Disciple a minor character, whose authority could not have been set in opposition to the tradition that claimed Peter as its authority? If so, one might suppose that the Johannine community shielded his identity while magnifying his authority. But the fact remains that the identification of the Beloved Disciple as Lazarus is a modern solution that, though intriguing, remains questionable.

John Mark

If John the son of Zebedee does not fit easily into the profile of the Beloved Disciple, it has been suggested that another John does. As surprising as it may be on first consideration, the argument that the Beloved Disciple was John Mark has much to commend it. John Mark was not one of the twelve disciples, but he was from Jerusalem. Therefore, some of the objections confronting the traditional view that John the son of Zebedee was the Beloved Disciple would not apply to John Mark. The synoptic Gospels neither affirm nor deny that John Mark was a disciple or that he was at the cross. Those who identify John Mark as the unnamed young man who fled naked from the garden (Mark 14:51–52) would presumably need to conjecture that shortly thereafter, John Mark, reclothed, escorted Peter into the courtyard and later stood with the women at the cross.

Since John Mark was from Jerusalem, where his mother had a house (Acts 12:12), he would have been familiar with the geography and topography of Jerusalem and Judea. Virtually all of the events of Jesus' ministry reported in the Fourth Gospel occur in Judea. Whereas in the synoptic Gospels, all of Jesus' ministry takes place in and around Galilee (until his only journey to Jerusalem at the end of his life), in the Fourth Gospel, only the wedding at Cana (2:1–12), the healing of the official's son (4:46–54), and the feeding of the multitude (6:1–7:9) occur in Galilee. The Judean orientation of the Gospel raises questions about the traditional view while supporting the argument for either Lazarus or John Mark as the Beloved Disciple.

Since early Christians gathered in the home of John Mark's mother, it has been conjectured that her home was the site of the Last Supper and that John Mark may have served as the host on that occasion. Such a scenario would explain why the Fourth Gospel says nothing about preparations for the Last Supper and why John Mark, who was not one of the Twelve, would have occupied the place of honor near Jesus.

John Mark's cousin, Barnabas, was a Levite (Col. 4:10; Acts 4:36), so he may have had priestly connections and could have been known by the high priest. John Mark also had contacts with both Luke and Peter that could explain the common tradition found in Luke and John and the association of the Beloved Disciple with Peter in the Fourth Gospel.[33] Every time Mark's name appears in Paul's letters, Luke is named also (Col. 4:10, 14; Philemon 24; 2 Tim. 4:11). Two New Testament references link John Mark with Peter. When Peter was released from prison, he made his way directly to the home of John Mark's mother (Acts 12:12–17). The conclusion of 1 Peter also provides evidence of some connection between the two, for it refers to Mark as "my son" (1 Pet. 5:13). Assuming that these two oblique references do indicate some special relationship between Peter and John Mark, we can understand Papias' statement that John Mark was Peter's interpreter. The Gospel of Mark says less about Peter than any of the other Gospels. In the Fourth Gospel, however, the Beloved Disciple and Peter are together at the crucial moments in the passion narrative.

All of this takes on further significance when one reexamines references to John Mark in early Christian writings. Mark has traditionally been viewed as the author of the second Gospel, but second-century sources never identify John Mark with Mark the evangelist. Moreover, John Mark and John the son of Zebedee were occasionally confused with one another.[34] Could John Mark have been the Beloved Disciple and the Fourth Evangelist while John the Galilean fisherman was the author of the Gospel of Mark?[35]

Intriguing as these threads of evidence may be, they are all circumstantial. The arguments that John the Son of Zebedee could not have been the Beloved Disciple are stronger than the arguments that John Mark was. The arguments regarding the Judean orientation of the Gospel, the Beloved Disciple's home in the area, the role of the host at the Last Supper, and the acquaintance with the high priest are significant but work equally well in favor of Lazarus or some unknown believer from Judea.

The difficulties with each of the proposals discussed above have led scholars to propose still other candidates—Matthias, the rich young ruler, Paul—and to seek various other interpretations of the symbolic significance of the Beloved Disciple.

Matthias

The case for Matthias begins with his being chosen as the twelfth apostle after the death of Judas.[36] Who would be a better choice than one who was beloved by the Lord? The criteria for the selection were that the disciple should have been a witness to the ministry of Jesus from the baptism of John to the resurrection (Acts 1:21–22). If Andrew's unnamed companion in John 1 was the Beloved Disciple, then he certainly met the first criterion. Moreover, according to John, the Beloved Disciple was not just a witness but the foremost witness to the resurrection, the one who saw the contents of the empty tomb and believed.

The identification of Matthias as the Beloved Disciple casts an interesting light on the scene of the Last Supper. The Beloved Disciple, although he knew who the betrayer was, did nothing to stop Judas, and was later chosen to take his place among the Twelve. Obviously the Beloved Disciple has some symbolic significance. Accordingly, Judas can represent the failure of Judaism, while Matthias represents the church.

Again, one must grant that this argument has fascinating implications. Nevertheless, it also illustrates the fact that *something* could be said in favor of the identification of almost any New Testament character as the Beloved Disciple. In all cases, the evidence is neither conclusive nor persuasive.

The Rich Young Ruler

A minor figure from the synoptic Gospels—the rich young ruler—has also been proposed.[37] The merits of the case are that Jesus is said to have loved him (Mark 10:21), that he may have been a Judean, and that he presumably owned a home in the vicinity of Jerusalem and therefore could have been known to the high priest. It is unclear whether the rich young ruler was a Judean or not. Mark reports that Jesus met him as Jesus was "setting out on a journey" (10:17), and both Matthew and Luke agree in reporting that Jesus met the man before Jesus arrived in Jerusalem. Only Luke calls him a "ruler" (Luke 18:18).

All the rest is conjecture. We do not know for a fact that he was a Judean.

We do not know that he owned a home in Jerusalem or that he was the host at the Last Supper (Mark 14:13–15). Only the fact that he was rich suggests any connection with the high priest. Finally, since the Gospel of John does not report Jesus' encounter with the rich young ruler, we would have to surmise that the encounter is omitted in the Fourth Gospel because of the author's reticence. But the argument from reticence or humility is hardly convincing in a Gospel which refers to this figure as "the disciple whom Jesus loved." We must conclude therefore that the rich young ruler is a figure from the synoptic tradition that is unknown to the Johannine tradition. The evidence for his being the Beloved Disciple is so sparse that it is pointless to press such a conjecture.

Paul

The argument that the Beloved Disciple was Paul is intriguing and more nuanced than one might assume.[38] The first step is to recognize that the portrayal of the Beloved Disciple is not a report of actual events. How could the Beloved Disciple have known who the betrayer was and have done nothing to stop him? This ideal disciple appears only in scenes connected with the death and resurrection of Jesus. Paul interpreted the Lord's Supper as the means by which one appropriates Christ's spirit, but unworthy eating of the supper brings dire spiritual and physical consequences. For the unworthy, the supper is a "sacrament of judgment." This Pauline interpretation, it is argued, is presented in John by means of Judas's betrayal. The Beloved Disciple is "the *interpreter* of the 'Petrine' story of the announcement of the betrayal. And he interprets it on the basis of the Pauline doctrine of the sacrament of judgment."[39] The method of the Fourth Evangelist was to create ideal, composite, representative characters, but "a very real man has sat for the portrait" of the Beloved Disciple.[40] The Beloved Disciple enters the Gospel story only at the cross and the resurrection (the heart of Paul's preaching), stands in some antithetic relation to Peter, and enters the eternal life by appropriating the mind "that was in Christ Jesus" (Phil. 2:5). The Beloved Disciple is one who can say: "I have been crucified with Christ; and it is no longer I who live, but it is Christ who lives in me. And the life I now live in the flesh I live by faith in the Son of God, *who loved me* and gave himself for me" (Gal. 2:19–20). In this sense, Paul is the first and foremost model of the Beloved Disciple.

The argument continues: this was only the evangelist's view. The redactor, who added interpolations to the Gospel and composed chapter 21, mistakenly interpreted the Beloved Disciple passages as references to John the son of Zebedee. This traditional identification, it is argued, can therefore be traced all the way to the redactor of the Gospel. In contrast, the novel and fanciful suggestion that Paul was the Beloved Disciple has rightly been rejected by later scholars as "impossible"[41] and "grotesque":[42] the connections between the Fourth Gospel and Pauline Christianity or Pauline theology are simply not strong enough to support it.

Benjamin

Since the Beloved Disciple appears in ideal situations in the Gospel, and since each of the efforts to identify him with some figure known from the other Gospels or Acts confronts significant difficulties, it is not surprising that some interpreters have concluded that the Beloved Disciple is an ideal or symbolic figure rather than an actual historical person. Even here, interpretations of the symbolic significance of this figure vary.

An interesting case has also been made for recognizing that the Beloved Disciple evokes the figure of Benjamin.[43] The foundation for the argument is the well-established assumption that the Gospel was written for Jewish readers and that it builds on the expectation of a prophet like Moses. This expectation is grounded in Deuteronomy (18:15, 18), which is Moses' farewell address to Israel. Since the Beloved Disciple first appears in the context of Jesus' farewell address, it is reasonable to search for some precedent for his role in the Book of Deuteronomy.

The clue is found in Deuteronomy 33:12: "Of Benjamin he said, 'The beloved of the Lord rests in safety—the High God surrounds him all day long—the beloved rests between his shoulders.'" This verse offers three assurances to Benjamin: (1) he is beloved by the Lord; (2) he will dwell securely in the Lord; and (3) he will make his dwelling in the Lord. Benjamin had been the best-loved son of Jacob-Israel, and the reference to the "disciple whom Jesus loved" could evoke the memory of this assurance to Benjamin. This verse also provides the clue to the report that the Beloved Disciple would remain until the Lord came (John 21:22–23). It is an echo of Moses' promise to Benjamin: "The Lord shelters him all the day" (NAB). The third assurance, which can be read that God would "make his [God's] dwelling between his [Benjamin's] shoulders," has also been interpreted (NAB, NEB, NRSV) as meaning that Benjamin would abide securely between the Lord's shoulders. In this reading of Deuteronomy, the promise to Benjamin is mirrored in the privileged position of the Beloved Disciple, who reclined "in the bosom" of the Lord (13:23; 21:20). Since all three features of the blessing on Benjamin are evoked by the sparse references to the Beloved Disciple in a context in which Deuteronomy and the Mosaic traditions serve as the background for the Gospel story, these correspondences can hardly be accidental.

The value of this proposal is that it moves the discussion beyond the search for a name in the New Testament with which to identify the Beloved Disciple and recognizes that the symbolism of this ideal disciple is significant. More-over, the significance of that symbolism is related to the Mosaic/ Deuteronomic motifs in the Gospel. Whether the links between the figure of the Beloved Disciple and the promise to Benjamin are strong enough to bear the weight of the role of the Beloved Disciple in the Gospel is doubtful, but this proposal may provide one piece to the puzzle.

Gentile Christianity

Rudolf Bultmann made crucial distinctions among the various explicit and possible references to the Beloved Disciple. He dismissed from consideration John 1:35ff. and 18:15–16 as references to other disciples. John 19:35 and chapter 21 are the work of the redactor, who identified the Beloved Disciple with, in Bultmann's words, "a particular historical figure, clearly an authorita-tive one for the circle which edits the Gospel." The redactor regarded the Beloved Disciple as the author of the Gospel (21:24), yet the Beloved Disciple is not a historical figure but rather "an ideal figure." On the basis of the scene at the cross, Bultmann suggested that Jesus' mother "stands for Jewish Christendom. And the Beloved Disciple therefore represents Gentile Christen-dom . . . in so far as it is the authentic Christendom which has achieved its own true self-understanding." Only in a general sense, open to others also, does the Beloved Disciple represent the evangelist of the Gospel.[44]

An Itinerant, Prophetic Community

Another influential interpretation views the Beloved Disciple as representa-tive of the community that produced the Johannine writings.[45] The bases for this interpretation are the judgments (1) that John 1:35–40 and 18:15–16 are to be considered along with the explicit references to the Beloved Disciple; (2) that these references are not part of the pre-Johannine tradition; and (3) that the central concern of these passages is the relationship between the Beloved Disciple and Peter. If Peter is representative of the apostolic church, then the Beloved Disciple must have represented a rival ecclesiastical movement. One of the primary tensions in the first-century church developed over the conflict between the growing authority of church offices and the freer, Spirit-led communities. When the Johannine writings are interpreted against such a background, the Beloved Disciple appears as the representative of itinerant, prophetic community that found itself in conflict with the official leadership of the apostolic church. 3 John in particular reflects the conflict of the community with Diotrephes, who may have been a church official. The result is that while the term *Beloved Disciple* may refer to an individual, it also has a symbolic, representational function. The Beloved Disciple embodies the work of the Paraclete and represents the prophetic community that produced the Johannine writings.

This view has a great deal to commend it. It recognizes the symbolic or representational role of the Beloved Disciple in relation to Peter and seeks to interpret the representational significance of this figure in relation to the historical setting of the Gospel and the other Johannine writings. It also relates the issue of the identity of the Beloved Disciple to the distinctive place of the Paraclete in the Gospel of John and the conflict with ecclesiastical authority in 3 John. Even if one takes a somewhat different view of the role of Diotrephes,[46] and even if one is more inclined to see the Beloved Disciple as representing an actual figure who had played a foundational role in the life of the Johannine community, the view that the Beloved Disciple represents the Johannine community contributes an essential ingredient for understanding the role of the Beloved Disciple in the Fourth Gospel.

The Elder Who Wrote 2 and 3 John

The mix of historical allusions and symbolism in the figure of the Beloved Disciple requires that interpreters account for both. The characterization of the Beloved Disciple in John builds on reflection upon both the significance of a historical person, whose authority had confirmed the traditions about Jesus for the community, and the symbolism evoked by the Fourth Gospel's portrayal of the Beloved Disciple. The Beloved Disciple had borne witness to Jesus, a witness which the community accepted as true, and this disciple was regarded as an authority at least equal to Peter. His testimony, moreover, answered speculation that Jesus merely seemed to be human (see 1 John 4:2), or perhaps that the Spirit had left Jesus before his death. It was important for the community that the Beloved Disciple was a witness both to Jesus' death and to his resurrection.

This portrayal of the Beloved Disciple's role, his authority for the community, and his opposition to a docetic Christology match the profile of "the elder" who wrote 2 and 3 John. The suggestion that the Beloved Disciple is a literary representation of the elder has much to commend it, since it takes seriously the role of the Beloved Disciple in the history of the Johannine community.[47] The proposal does raise certain questions of chronology, however. It requires that 2 and 3 John were written before the final redaction of the Gospel and that the elder died before the redactor of the Gospel inserted the references to the Beloved Disciple.[48] This sequence of events is not impossible, but again it raises the question of the place of 1 John in the history of the Johannine writings. Was the elder who wrote 2 John also the author of 1 John, and do both 1 and 2 John refer to the same controversy in the community? If so, the writing of the Epistles must have preceded the completion of the

Gospel. Again, this is not impossible, just contrary to most current interpretations of the Johannine Epistles. On the other hand, identifying the Beloved Disciple as a later representation of the elder does explain why the Epistles never appeal to the authority of the Beloved Disciple.

CONCLUSION

The search for the Beloved Disciple has not been in vain. Although the effort has led New Testament interpreters to some false trails, dead ends, and surprising twists, the profile of a consensus is emerging. First, we can recognize that the figure of the Beloved Disciple is both individual and representational. Solutions that seek merely to identify an individual fail to take seriously the idealized nature of the scenes in which he appears and the way in which they are appended to earlier traditions. Solutions that interpret the Beloved Disciple solely as a symbolic figure do not satisfactorily explain the concern in John 21:20–23 over the death of the Beloved Disciple. As has often been remarked, symbolic figures do not die. What we have then is a historical figure who has been given an idealized role in the crucial scenes of the farewell discourse, trial, death, and resurrection of Jesus.

When we look for the profile of the individual, we find that he was probably a Judean who knew the geography of Judea and Jerusalem, who may have had a house in Jerusalem, and who could have been known to the high priest. These descriptors pose serious problems for the traditional view that the Beloved Disciple was John the son of Zebedee, but none of the other proposals that the Beloved Disciple was someone who appears elsewhere in the Gospels or Acts has gained widespread acceptance. It seems best, therefore, to conclude that the Beloved Disciple was an otherwise unknown disciple, an eyewitness, but one about whom nothing is known except through the Fourth Gospel's idealized portrayal of his role at the death and resurrection of Jesus.

We are on more solid ground in recognizing that the Beloved Disciple bore witness to events reported in the Gospel and that the Johannine community received his witness as true, even Spirit-inspired. Perhaps it is not stretching the point too much to say that in the work of the Beloved Disciple the Johannine community saw the Paraclete at work among them. At least it is clear that the community attributed the Gospel to the witness of the Beloved Disciple and believed that the Paraclete, the Spirit of Truth, validated the Gospel also.

The relationship between the Beloved Disciple and Peter suggests further that the former was the Johannine community's apostolic authority, the one from whom the community had received its teachings. He was their link with the earthly Jesus and their witness to the risen Lord. The community recognized the role of Peter, but nevertheless maintained that the Beloved Disciple had been given a unique role. He is portrayed in the Gospel as the one whom Jesus loved, who had reclined next to Jesus. He was the one who had first grasped the reality of the resurrection and who had recognized the risen Lord. He was their apostolic authority, and they knew that his testimony was true. In the Beloved Disciple the Johannine community witnessed the work of the Paraclete, who reminded them of all that Jesus had said and who bore witness to the world. The Beloved Disciple serves, therefore, as an important figure, legitimating and authorizing the distinctive teaching of the Johannine community in the face of the rising authority of Peter in other traditions.[49]

By identifying the Beloved Disciple as John the Son of Zebedee, tradition filled out the character of John in such a powerful way that he would thereafter be known as John the Beloved. As we have seen, the rest of the New Testament preserves little information about John. John the fisherman, one of the group of three, became John the disciple whom Jesus loved. The tensions between these diverse interpretations of John the son of Zebedee were overshadowed by the power of the figure that had emerged in the imagination and tradition of the church. But we have yet to trace the way in which this development occurred.

NOTES

1. Paul S. Minear contends that the chapter is an integral part of the Gospel, not a later appendix; see "The Original Functions of John 21," *JBL* 102 (1983): 85–98.
2. See above, p. 21.
3. See above, pp. 18–21.
4. John's portrayal of the relationship between these two apostles is the subject of the recent volume by Kevin Quast, *Peter and the Beloved Disciple: Figures for a Community in Crisis,* JSNTSup 32 (Sheffield: JSOT Press, 1989).
5. For proponents of this view since 1730, see the sources cited in F. Neirynck, "The 'Other Disciple' in Jn 18,15–16," *ETL* 51 (1975): 120 n. 41. Most recently, t⊦ identification of the other disciple as Judas has been endorsed by Thomas L. B in *The Gospel According to John: A Literary and Theological Commentary* York: Oxford University Press, 1993).
6. Neirynck, in "The 'Other Disciple' in Jn 18,15–16," 139–40, reaches thi⯑ conclusion.
7. Cf. Raymond E. Brown, *The Gospel According to John,* AB 29 (Garden (⟩ Doubleday, 1966),73.
8. C. K. Barrett has written: "It is natural that the church should wish to know something of the way in which its best-known leaders came to be disciples and the growth of diverse legends of their call is therefore not surprising; nor is it surprising that the Johannine narrative should reflect the situation of the church after Easter"; see *The Gospel According to St. John,* 2d ed. (Philadelphia: Westminster, 1978), 179.
9. Eusebius, *E.H.* 3.39.4. *Eusebius: The Ecclesiastical History,* trans. Kirsopp Lake (Cambridge, Mass.: Harvard University Press, 1926), 1:293.

10. See, for example, Rudolf Schnackenburg, *The Gospel According to St. John,* vol. 1, trans. Kevin Smyth, HTKNT (New York: Herder and Herder, 1968), 310.

11. Brown, *John,* 823, citing W. Drum, "The Disciple Known to the High Priest," *ExpTim* 25 (1913–1914): 381–82.

12. Edgar Hennecke, *New Testament Apocrypha,* ed. Wilhelm Schneemelcher, trans. R. McL. Wilson (Philadelphia: Westminster, 1963), 1:152.

13. Hippolytus of Thebes, "Syntagmate chronologico" (Migne, *PG* 117:1032B, 1052B).

14. Epiphanius the Monk, *The Life of the Virgin* 18 (Migne *PG* 120:208). See below, pp. 174–75.

15. Prologue to the *Acts of John by Prochorus* in Vatican Gr. 654, fol. 88v. See Eric Junod and Jean-Daniel Kaestli, *Acta Iohannis,* CChr (Turnhout: Brepols, 1983), 1:10, 35.

16. Epiphanius the Monk, *The Life of the Virgin* 20 (Migne, *PG* 120:210).

17. Eusebius, *E.H.* 5.24.3 (LCL 1:507).

18. Regarding the symbolic interpretations that have been suggested for the role of Jesus' mother, see my *Anatomy of the Fourth Gospel* (Philadelphia: Fortress Press, 1983), 133–34.

19. In addition to the standard commentaries, fine treatments of John 20:1–10 can be found in Robert Mahoney, *Two Disciples at the Tomb: The Background and Message of John 20.1–10,* Theologie und Wirklichkeit 6 (Bern: Herbert Lang, 1974); and Pheme Perkins, *Resurrection: New Testament Witness and Contemporary Reflection* (Garden City: Doubleday, 1984).

20. See above, p. 21.

21. See Sandra M. Schneiders, "The Face Veil: A Johannine Sign (John 20.1–10)," *BTB* 13 (July 1983): 94–97; and Brendan Byrne, "The Faith of the Beloved Disciple and the Community in John 20," *JSNT* 23 (1985): 83–97, who identify the position of the face cloth as a sign.

22. This conclusion accords with the position of Rudolf Schnackenburg, who has a full discussion of the issues in "Der Jünger, den Jesus liebte," in *Evangelisch-katholischer Kommentar zum Neuen Testament, Vorarbeiten* (Neukirchen-Vluyn: Neukirchener-Verlag, 1970), 2:102–5. John A. Bailey holds what seems now to be a minority view—that Luke 24:12 is an interpolation based on John's account; see *The Traditions Common to the Gospels of Luke and John,* NovTSup 7 (Leiden: E. J. Brill, 1963), 85.

23. See above, p. 21.

24. See N. E. Johnson, "The Beloved Disciple and the Fourth Gospel," *CQR* 167 (1966): 278–91.

25. For their early positions, see Brown, *John,* xcviii and c; and Rudolf Schnackenburg, *The Gospel According to St. John,* vol. 1, trans. Kevin Smyth (New York: Herder and Herder 1968), 97–104. For their later positions, see Brown, *The Community of the Beloved Disciple* (New York: Paulist Press, 1979); and Schnackenburg, *The Gospel According to St. John,* vol. 3, trans. David Smith and G. A. Kon (New York: Crossroad, 1982), 383–87, which summarizes the position articulated in "Der Jünger, den Jesus liebte," published in 1970.

26. See above, p. 8.

27. See Bruno de Solages, "Jean, fils de Zébédée et l'énigme du 'disciple que Jésus aimait,'" *BLE* 73 (1972): 41–50.

28. Brown, *John,* xciv.

29. On the historicity of the role of the "inner three" disciples, see above, p. 37.

30. See above, pp. 21–22.

31. See above, pp. 61–63.

32. For advocates of the theory that Lazarus was the Beloved Disciple, see B. Grey Griffith, "The Disciple whom Jesus Loved," *ExpTim* 32 (1920–1921): 379–81; Robert Eisler, *The Enigma of the Fourth Gospel* (London: Methuen, 1938); Floyd V. Filson, "Who Was the Beloved Disciple?" *JBL* 68 (1949): 83–88; J. N. Sanders, "Those Whom Jesus Loved (John XI, 5)," *NTS* 1 (1954–1955): 29–41; Sanders, "Who Was the Disciple Whom Jesus Loved?" in *Studies in the Fourth Gospel,* ed. F. L. Cross (London: A. R. Mowbray, 1957), 72–83, where it is argued that the Beloved Disciple was Lazarus, but that "the other disciple whom Jesus loved" (John 20:2) was John of Ephesus (John Mark), the son of the Mary who had a house in Jerusalem; K. A. Eckhardt, *Der Tod des Johannes als Schlüssel zum Verständnis des johanneischen Schriften,* Studien zur Rechts- und Religionsgeschichte 3 (Berlin: De Gruyter, 1961), where it is suggested that the name "Lazarus" became a pseudonym for John the son of Zebedee after he was raised from the dead. See also, most recently, Vernard Eller, *The Beloved Disciple: His Name, His Story, His Thought* (Grand Rapids: Wm. B. Eerdmans, 1987), esp. 53–73.

33. See Bailey, *The Traditions Common to Luke and John.*

34. See J. Edgar Bruns, "The Confusion between John and John Mark in Antiquity," *Scripture* 17 (1965): 23–26, who cites Chrysostom, Alexander the Monk, the *History of the Patriarchs of Alexandria,* and the *Witness of John the Baptist.* Most famous is Chrysostom's comment on Acts 12:12 in which he erroneously explains that Peter's constant companion (John the son of Zebedee) was John Mark. From this confusion grew the legend that John the son of Zebedee bought a house in Jerusalem where Christians gathered. (See also Bruns, "John Mark: A Riddle within the Johannine Enigma," *Scripture* 15 [1963]: 91.)

35. This reversal of tradition is advocated by Pierson Parker in "John and John Mark," *JBL* 79 (1960): 97–110; and in "John the Son of Zebedee and the Fourth Gospel," *JBL* 81 (1962): 35–43—the latter being the most cogent rejection of the tradition that John the Son of Zebedee was the author of the Fourth Gospel. Representing a variation of the view that the Beloved Disciple was John Mark, J. N. Sanders has argued that Lazarus was the Beloved Disciple, but that John Mark was the fourth evangelist; see "St. John on Patmos," *NTS* 9 (1962–1963): 75–85; and "Who Was the Disciple Whom Jesus Loved?" in *Studies in the Fourth Gospel,* ed. F. L. Cross (London: A. R. Mowbray, 1957), 72–83. Bruns contends that John the Presbyter was John Mark; see "The Confusion between John and John Mark in Antiquity," 25–26. Three notes regarding the thesis that the Beloved Disciple was John Mark appeared in *ExpTim* 77 (1966): Lewis Johnson, "Who Was the Beloved Disciple?"

157–58; J. R. Porter and Donald G. Rogers, "Who Was the Beloved Disciple?" 213–14; and Lewis Johnson, "The Beloved Disciple—A Reply," 380.

36. See Eric L. Titus, "The Identity of the Beloved Disciple," *JBL* 69 (1950): 323–28.

37. H. B. Swete, "The Disciple Whom Jesus Loved," *JTS* 17 (1916): 371–74. Frank Warburton Lewis suggested that the rich young ruler, Lazarus, and the Beloved Disciple were all one and the same person; see "The Disciple Whom Jesus Loved," *ExpTim* 33 (1921–1922): 42.

38. The argument was originally advanced by Benjamin Wisner Bacon in "The Disciple Whom Jesus Loved and His Relation to the Author," *Expositor,* 7th ser., 4 (1907): 324ff., an essay republished in his *The Fourth Gospel in Research and Debate* (London: T. Fisher Unwin, 1910), 301–31.

39. Bacon, *The Fourth Gospel,* 317.

40. Bacon, *The Fourth Gospel,* 325.

41. Rudolf Bultmann asserted: "if one has to posit an actual historical figure who represented this free Christendom for the Evangelist, Bacon's view that Paul is intended is the best as regards his subject matter. It is of course impossible . . . "; see *The Gospel of John: A Commentary,* trans. and ed. G. R. Beasley-Murray et al. (Philadelphia: Westminster Press, 1971), 484 n. 5.

42. Barnabas Lindars, *The Gospel of John,* NCB (London: Oliphants, 1972), 33.

43. Paul S. Minear, "The Beloved Disciple in the Gospel of John: Some Clues and Conjectures," *NovT* 19 (1977): 105–23.

44. Bultmann, *John,* 483–85.

45. See Alv Kragerud, *Der Lieblingsjünger im Johannesevangelium* (Oslo: Universitätsverlag, 1959).

46. See my *1, 2, 3 John,* Knox Preaching Guides (Atlanta: John Knox Press, 1985), 132–35.

47. See Hartwig Thyen, "Entwicklungen innerhalb der johanneischen Theologie und Kirche im Spiegel von Joh. 21 und der Lieblingsjüngertexts des Evangeliums," in *L'Évangile de Jean: Sources, rédaction, théologie,* BETL 44 (Gembloux: J. Duculot, 1977), 259–99, esp. 296.

48. These points are nuanced by Bernhard Bonsack in "Der Presbyteros des dritten Briefs und der geliebte Jünger des Evangeliums nach Johannes," *ZNW* 79 (1988): 45–62, so that the objections of chronology do not apply.

49. See the perceptive work by Joachim Kügler, *Der Jünger, den Jesus liebte: Literarische, theologische und historische Untersuchungen zu einer Schlüsselgestalt johanneischer Theologie und Geschichte. Mit einem Exkurs über die Brotrede in Joh 6,* SBB 16 (Stuttgart: Verlag katholisches Bibelwerk, 1988), esp. the conclusions he reaches on 474–88.

CHAPTER 4

Elder and Seer
John in the Epistles and the Apocalypse

If the evidence that John the apostle wrote the Fourth Gospel is ambiguous at best, can we with more confidence affirm that the apostle was the author of the Johannine Epistles or the Apocalypse (the Revelation of John)? Closely related to this question is the credibility of the assumption that the elder of the Epistles and/or the seer of the Apocalypse may be identified with the apostle. This chapter will review the issues and evidence related to the elder and the seer and the question of whether either of them was the apostle.

Neither the Johannine Epistles nor the Apocalypse explicitly claims to be written by the apostle John, but ecclesiastical tradition eventually attributed all four of these writings to him. First John makes no reference to its author; 2 and 3 John identify their author merely as "the elder"; and the author of the Apocalypse indicates that his name is John and that he was on the island of Patmos when he wrote the Apocalypse. The John of the Apocalypse does not claim to be an apostle, however, and none of the five Johannine writings makes any explicit reference to any other of these writings. Each, therefore, remains distinct. The Gospel does not identify the apostle or the Beloved Disciple as the elder of the Epistles or the seer of the Apocalypse, and the latter make no reference to the apostle or the Beloved Disciple. Yet, once the Epistles and Apocalypse were accepted along with the Fourth Gospel as the work of the apostle, references to the elder and the seer were mingled indiscriminately with references to the apostle. An important chapter in the history of the legends of John, therefore, concerns the process by which the elder and the seer were identified as the apostle. The relevant references within the Epistles and the Apocalypse, the early traditions about their authorship, and the issues related to the authorship of each of these writings are examined in this chapter. Later chapters collect the references to John in patristic and medieval sources.

THE ELDER OF THE EPISTLES

For the sake of clarity and precision, each of the three Epistles needs to be considered separately. We will look first at the references to the author and the author's forms of address to the readers in each of the Epistles.

Internal Evidence

Only in the two shorter Epistles does the sender identify himself as "the elder." The two shorter Epistles are written in the common letter form, but 1 John is not so clearly a letter. It lacks both the formal opening, with identification of the sender and the addressee and a greeting, and a formal closing, with greetings or the promise of a visit. First John, therefore, has the appearance of an exhortation or treatise rather than a communication to a community or individual separated some distance from the writer. Nevertheless, 1 John presumes a written rather than an oral medium of communication.

Although the author does not refer to himself by name or title, there are numerous first-person references in 1 John and enough clues to shed some light on the relationship between the author and those whom he addresses. First John opens with a volley of first-person plural references. The New Revised Standard Version, for example, contains the word "we" twenty-two times in the first chapter, with other references to "our" and "us." Some of these references include the readers with the writer (e.g., "If we say we have fellowship with him," in verse 6), while in other instances the use is exclusive (e.g., "This is the message we have heard from him and proclaim to you," in verse 5).

The first occurrence of the first-person singular appears in 1 John 2:1 along with an endearing address to the readers: "My little children, I am writing these things to you. . . . " Both singular and plural first-person references continue throughout the letter, but with one exception, the first-person singular is used only with the verb "to write" (2:1, 7, 8, 12–14[6 times], 21, 26; 5:13). The exception is in 5:16, "There is sin that is mortal; I do not say that you should pray about that." The first-person plural in the opening verses conveys the authority of established tradition, while the inclusive first-person plural references establish rapport with the addressees.

The author's favorite terms for the addressees are "my little children" (*teknia;* 2:1), or simply "little children" (*teknia;* 2:12, 28; 3:7, 18; 4:4; 5:21), "beloved" (2:7; 3:2, 21; 4:1, 7, 11), and "children" (*paidia;* 2:18; 3:7). First John 2:12–14 contains a series of assurances to the readers, characterizing them as little children, fathers, and young people. In addition, the author repeatedly calls his readers "children of God" (*tekna theou* or *ta tekna tou theou;* 3:1, 2, 10; 5:2). The rhetoric of 1 John, therefore, appeals to the relationship between author and addressees as one characterized by care and parental concern. The author makes no overt appeal to office or authority. Instead, he exhorts and encourages. Authority resides in the tradition (1:1, 3:11) and the commandments (5:2–3), especially the commandment of love (2:7; 3:23; 4:21).

While the first-person plural references at the beginning of 1 John could be interpreted as a claim to apostolic authority (e.g., "what we have seen with our eyes, what we have looked at and touched with our hands" in 1:1), the other exclusive and inclusive first-person plural references in the opening chapter, and the later appeals to tradition rather than apostolic authority, point away from such an interpretation. Instead, it appears that the writer is identifying himself and his community with the tradition received from the apostles. Similarly, the endearing references to the addressees as "little children" could imply that the writer is the aged apostle, but the use of "children of God" in the letter and also in the Gospel (1:12; 11:52) indicate that this was a well-established term for the Christian community or communities addressed by these writings. The terms of endearment are equally appropriate coming from an "elder" of the church.

Second John opens with an address from "The elder to the elect lady and her children" (v. 1). First-person singular references are common in the letter: "whom I love in the truth, and not only I but also all who know the truth" (v. 1); "I was overjoyed" (v. 4); "But now, dear lady, I ask you, not as though I were writing you a new commandment" (v. 5); and in the closing greetings and promise of a visit (v. 12). Moreover, the first-person plural references are all inclusive (vv. 4, 5, 6, 8). Just as in 1 John, the elder appeals here to tradition and the commandments (vv. 5–6, 9). The picture that emerges is of an elder who addresses a sister church (vv. 1, 13) to warn it of the false teachings it will encounter. Again, there is no claim of apostolic authority; the appeal for cooperation is made on the basis of goodwill, tradition, the authority of the commandments, and perhaps the warning that he will visit them in the near future. The relationship between the elder and the elect lady and her children is more distant than the relationship with the addressees in 1 John; he does not address them as his children or as "beloved."

Similarly, 3 John opens with the address "The elder to the beloved Gaius, whom I love in truth" (v. 1). In this letter, the term "beloved" is repeated in verses 2, 5, 11 as an address to Gaius. Other believers are called "my children" (v. 4), "brothers" (vv. 3, 5, 10) and "friends" (v. 15). Assessments of the relationship between the elder and his opponent, Diotrephes, have run the gamut from viewing the elder as the authorized representative of the church and Diotrephes as a rebellious local leader, to the opposite situation in which Diotrephes is the bishop and the elder is a charismatic rebel against ecclesiastical authority.[1]

The Reception of the Johannine Epistles

Each of the Epistles followed a different path toward its ultimate reception as an apostolic writing. Raymond E. Brown, who has written the definitive commentary on the Johannine Epistles, has collected the possible allusions to 1 John prior to Irenaeus. Parallels or possible echoes in 1 Clement, Ignatius, and the Didache he judges to be inadequate to establish knowledge of the Epistles. Suggested parallels in Barnabas, 2 Clement, the Shepherd of Hermas, Justin Martyr, the Epistle to Diognetus, and Polycarp's Epistle to the Philippians are judged by Brown to be more adequate.

The last of these is the most important. In the Epistle to the Philippians 7:1, Polycarp (ca. A.D. 140) says, "For everyone who does not confess Jesus Christ to have come [perf. infin.] in the flesh is Antichrist," which is a distinct echo of 1 John 4:2–3 and 2 John 7. The next line in Polycarp contains the phrase "belong to the devil," which again may echo 1 John 3:8. Brown's conclusion is that by the middle of the second century, "ideas, themes, and even slogans of the Johannine Epistles (or at least, of I John) were being cited in other Christian works."[2] Papias may have used 1 John even earlier, for Eusebius records that Papias "used quotations from the first epistle of John."[3] The earliest use of 1 John, therefore, appears to have come through the tradition from Papias to Polycarp and then to Irenaeus. From Irenaeus, we have the first explicit citations from both 1 and 2 John, though he may have known of only one Epistle, which he cites as the work of "John, the disciple of the Lord."[4]

By the beginning of the third century, 1 John is cited by Tertullian and Clement of Alexandria, the latter speaking of 1 John as "the greater epistle" and 2 John as being addressed to "Virgins."[5] The *Muratorian Canon,* once dated in the second century but now often assigned to an eastern provenance in the fourth century, quotes from the beginning of 1 John and includes two Johannine Epistles in the canonical list.[6] The first references to 3 John date to the third century and come to us secondhand through Eusebius, who records that Origen knew of not only one Epistle, but a second and a third, but reported that "not all say that these are genuine."[7] Similarly, Eusebius tells us that Dionysius, Origen's successor, knew of 2 and 3 John.[8] Eusebius himself lists 1 John among the "recognized books" and 2 and 3 John among the "disputed books."[9] Jerome acknowledged that the two shorter Epistles were said to be the work of John the Elder rather than the apostle, but he himself seems to have attributed all three to the apostle.[10]

Even in the late fourth century and early fifth century, universal acceptance of the two shorter Epistles cannot be confirmed. John Chrysostom (d. A.D. 407) and Theodore of Mopsuestia (d. A.D. 428) made no reference to 2 or 3 John. A list from the Roman Council under Pope Damasus (A.D. 382) accepts only one Epistle from John the apostle and two from John the Elder.[11] Nevertheless, their canonicity was assured in their acceptance by Athanasius (A.D. 367), the Synod of Hippo (A.D. 393), and the Council of Carthage (A.D. 397).[12] In Syria, the Peshitta included only 1 John, whereas 2 and 3 John were accepted only in the later Philoxenian version (A.D. 508).

That 2 and 3 John are cited with less frequency and in later sources and were accepted into the canon more slowly than 1 John has been explained both by reference to their brevity and by evidence that the author's calling himself "the Presbyter" created doubts about his identity. Both the internal evidence and the history of the reception of the Epistles, therefore, raise the question of whether they were written by the apostle John, by Papias's John the Elder, or by some other elder who may not even have been named John.

The Authorship of the Johannine Epistles

The question raised by the patristic writers, whether 2 and 3 John were written by the apostle or by another who identified himself as "the elder" has taken different forms in modern scholarship. The prevailing view, at least in English scholarship, was that 1 John was written by the author of the Fourth Gospel, so those who attributed the Gospel to the apostle John also maintained the apostolic authorship of 1 John. The grammatical and lexical evidence regarding the relationship between the Gospel and the Epistles was amassed in the late nineteenth century by H. J. Holtzmann, who identified fifty "peculiarities" in the style of 1 John, which he concluded was written by a different author.[13] A. E. Brooke and R. H. Charles subsequently reviewed Holtzmann's list of stylistic peculiarities and came to the opposite conclusion, favoring common authorship.[14] Brooke concluded in 1912 that "there are no adequate reasons for setting aside the traditional view which attributes the Epistle and the Gospel to the same authorship," but "the differences of thought and expression make it probable that some interval of time should be placed between the composition of the two writings."[15]

The next major advance—and indeed for many, a decisive reversal of perspective—came with an article published by C. H. Dodd in 1937 in which he refined the argument from the style of the writings by proposing comparisons of minor points: specifically, prepositions, conjunctions, and particles, compound verbs, idioms and rhetorical figures, and Aramaisms.[16] For example, the Gospel employs 23 prepositions, while only 14 appear in 1 John. The Gospel has a total of 36 adverbial particles, while 1 John uses only 9. The number of compound verbs is even more disproportional: 105 to 11. Not only the variety but also the frequency with which particles are used is much greater in the Gospel than in the Epistle: "for" (*gar*) occurs 68 times in the Gospel, 3 times in 1 John; "therefore" (*oun*) occurs 194 times in the Gospel, but only once in 1 John.[17] Moreover, although the Epistle is much briefer than the Gospel, it contains 39 terms or expressions, many of them technical or theological terms, which are not found in the Gospel.

The second step in Dodd's argument was to show that there is an equally striking difference in thought between the Gospel and 1 John in three areas: eschatology (in which the emphasis on realized eschatology is much stronger in the Gospel, while the Epistle asserts a more traditional emphasis on the future); the significance of the death of Christ (which is interpreted in terms of glorification and exaltation in the Gospel but as expiation in the Epistle); and the doctrine of the Holy Spirit (in which the Epistle does not follow the Gospel's distinctive interpretation of the Spirit as Paraclete, applying the term instead to the risen Lord). Dodd also judged that the Epistle stood closer to Gnosticism than the Gospel. Finally, Dodd noted in the Fourth Gospel "a richness, a subtlety, a penetrating quality about the style which is missing in the Epistle."[18] Still, the similarities between the Gospel and Epistle are undeniable. Dodd's conclusion, therefore, sought to account for the similarities while, on balance, favoring separate authorship: "I conceive the First Epistle of John, then, to have been written by an author who was quite possibly a disciple of the Fourth Evangelist, and certainly a diligent student of his work. He has soaked himself in the Gospel, assimilating its ideas and forming his style upon its model."[19]

In his commentary on the Epistles, Dodd reaffirmed this position and added the judgment that the two shorter Epistles were written by the author of 1 John. Hence, if the author were John the Elder, then the elder could not be considered as a candidate in the search for the author of the Gospel.[20]

A series of articles responded to Dodd, arguing that other considerations could explain the stylistic differences he had noted: the Gospel is the result of a long process of composition, whereas the Epistle responded to a special situation; the subject matter of the Gospel covers a wider range than the Epistle; the evangelist drew on oral and written sources; the Aramaisms in the Gospel may stem from its underlying tradition; the amanuensis of the Epistle may have been given greater freedom.[21] Reassessments of the stylistic data showed that the Gospel and Epistle are more closely related in matters of style than are Luke and Acts or the undisputed Pauline Epistles. New considerations, such as word order, were also adduced to weaken further the argument that difference of authorship can be demonstrated from differences in the styles of the writings.[22] It now appears that the argument over stylistic differences has proved inconclusive.

The differences in thought between the Gospel and 1 John have not received the same vigorous rebuttal. Nevertheless, similarities have been observed between the perspectives of sections of the footwashing and the farewell discourse in the Gospel and the emphases of 1 John which suggest that some of the later sections of the Gospel may have been the work of the author of the Epistles. Even this argument has been nuanced to the point of maintaining only that the redaction of the Gospel probably took place in the same historical situation as the writing of the Epistles, but was not necessarily the work of the same writer.[23] Raymond Brown introduced the additional consideration of the greater grammatical obscurity of the Epistles.[24] When taken together, the various factors (style, thought, life setting, and grammatical obscurity) still favor the view that the Gospel and 1 John were composed by different authors.[25]

For our purposes, it is sufficient to observe that there has not been an effort to attribute the Epistles to the apostle John apart from common authorship with the Gospel. Even those who have dated one or more of the Epistles earlier than or contemporaneous with the composition of the Gospel have not argued that the Epistles derive from the apostle.[26] Apostolic authorship of the two shorter Epistles depends first on the assumption that the three Epistles were written by the same author and, second, that they were written by the evangelist. Indeed, 2 and 3 John were slow in gaining entry into the canon, apparently because they were attributed to the elder rather than to the apostle. The case for apostolic authorship of the Epistles, therefore, hangs entirely on the prior argument that the Epistles and the Gospel were composed by the same person—a point that is now much in doubt.

THE SEER OF THE APOCALYPSE

The place of the Apocalypse among the Johannine writings has been viewed with considerable ambivalence since the third century, when Dionysius argued that it could not have been written by the author of the Fourth Gospel. Ironically, however, the Apocalypse is the only one of the five Johannine writings to identify its author with the name John. As in our treatment of the Epistles, we will summarize the internal evidence and the record of the reception of the Apocalypse before turning to the question of its authorship.

Internal Evidence

The name "John" appears four times in the Apocalypse, three times in the opening verses (1:1, 4, 9) and once in the conclusion to the book (22:8). In none of these references does the author claim that he is an apostle. The first verse refers to John in the third person as "his [God's] servant." The fourth verse is written in the form of an epistolary address—"John to the seven churches that are in Asia . . . "—but does not identify John further with a title such as "the apostle" or "the elder," as Paul often did in the address of his letters. The third reference supplies more information, setting the scene for the vision which follows. John identifies himself as "your brother who share[s] with you in Jesus the persecution and the kingdom and the patient endurance, [who] was on the island called Patmos because of the word of God and the testimony of Jesus" (1:9). Again, the reference "brother" says nothing about either an official position or apostolic status. If the Apocalypse were written by the apostle and fourth evangelist, one might have expected the term "the disciple whom Jesus loved." On the other hand, where the Apocalypse does refer to the apostles, they are referred to as figures of the past, founders of the church: "And the wall of the city has twelve foundations, and on them are the twelve names of the twelve apostles of the Lamb" (21:14; cf. 18:20). Similarly, if the Apocalypse was written around the time of the Epistles and by the same author, one would expect the author to refer to himself as "the elder." Neither of these terms occurs in the opening of the Apocalypse, however—a fact lending support to the conclusion that the author was an early Christian prophet named John, about whom nothing else is known. The last reference (22:8) adds nothing to our knowledge of the author.

Revelation 1:9 adds that John was "on the island called Patmos because of the word of God and the testimony of Jesus." The traditional view has been that John had gone to Patmos in exile, not as a free itinerant evangelist, and the grammar favors the view that John was on Patmos "because of" rather than "for the sake of" the gospel. Patmos is one of the Sporades islands, ten miles long and five miles wide, lying thirty-seven miles southwest of Miletus.[27] Tacitus reports instances of banishment by the Romans.[28] Tertullian, who was himself a lawyer, indicates that John was sent to Patmos "*in insulam relegator*,"[29] which was a lenient form of banishment that could be imposed by a provincial governor and did not involve loss of rights or property.[30]

The picture sketched by the Apocalypse, therefore, is that John, an early Christian prophet who is close to the churches in Asia Minor, has been banished to Patmos, probably by a local governor, and writes his vision to the churches to strengthen them in a time of threatening persecution.

The Reception of the Apocalypse

The story of the reception of the Apocalypse moves from early reception in the West to doubts in Alexandria about its authorship and lingering questions in the East about its place in the canon. The first uncertain echoes of the language of the Apocalypse occur in the *Visions* of the Shepherd of Hermas.[31] Eusebius never says that Papias knew of the Apocalypse, but it is possible that his own opposition to the book led him to suppress information from Papias on this point.[32] Indeed, a sixth-century commentary by Andreas of Caesarea reports that Papias maintained that the Apocalypse was dependable.[33] Regardless of the situation with Papias, Tertullian claims that Marcion rejected the Apocalypse.[34]

The first attribution of the Apocalypse to the apostle John appears in the *Dialogue with Trypho* of Justin Martyr, who had lived in Ephesus before moving to Rome: "And further, there was a certain man with us, whose name was John, one of the apostles of Christ, who prophesied, by a revelation that was made to him, that those who believed in our Christ would dwell a thousand years in Jerusalem; and that thereafter the general, and, in short, the eternal resurrection and judgment of all men would likewise take place."[35] Shortly after Justin Martyr, Melito of Sardis (160–190) wrote a commentary on the Apocalypse.[36] The position of Revelation was being debated vigorously. Gaius, a leader of the church in Rome, denied the apostolic authorship of both the Gospel and Revelation, attributing the latter to Cerinthus.[37] Irenaeus responded with a defense of the apostolic authority of Revelation, the Gospel, and the first two letters.[38] Thereafter, the authority and authorship of Revelation were never seriously questioned in the West.

Eusebius refers to the use of the Apocalypse by Theophilus, bishop of Antioch, and the anti-Montanist writer Apollonius (ca. A.D. 210).[39] The *Muratorian Canon,* which is usually traced to the same period (to Rome, late second century), also attributes the Apocalypse to the apostle John.[40] Tertullian, who worked in Carthage early in the third century, cites Revelation extensively, saying for example: "Now the Apostle John, in the Apocalypse. . . ."[41]

The tradition of the Alexandrian school is mixed. Clement cites the Apocalypse as scripture,[42] as does Origen.[43] The first real challenge to the apostolic authorship of the book, however, came from their successor Dionysius, who introduces his discussion of the authorship of the Apocalypse by reporting: "Some indeed of those before our time rejected and altogether impugned the book, examining it chapter by chapter and declaring it to be unintelligible and illogical, and its title false."[44] Dionysius then proceeds to argue that the authentic Johannine writings do not have an explicit attribution to John and reveal sharp differences in character, language, and style. Dionysius knew of two tombs of John in Ephesus, but he obviously did not know of Papias's allusion to John the Elder. It was left for Eusebius, who shared Dionysius's reservations about the authorship of the Apocalypse, to suggest that the second John—not the apostle—was the author of Revelation.[45] Consequently, Eusebius lists Revelation both among the "recognized" books and among the "spurious."

The debate over the canonicity of Revelation was settled in favor of receiving the book, but uncertainty about its authorship continued. Cyprian cited the Apocalypse repeatedly, while Cyril of Jerusalem (315–386) excluded it from his canon and forbade its use in public or in private.[46] R. H. Charles reports that the Apocalypse is also omitted from the lists of canonical writings from the Synod of Laodicea (ca. A.D. 360), the Apostolic Constitutions, and Gregory of Nazianzus (d. A.D. 389).[47] Neither was it cited by Chrysostom (d. A.D. 407), Theodore of Mopsuestia (350–428), or Theodoret (386–457). Jerome seems to have been doubtful about its canonicity,[48] but Athanasius received it along with the other four Johannine writings as the work of the apostle.

Thereafter, its place in the canon of the Western church remained secure—though over a millennium later, Martin Luther maintained that it was "neither apostolic nor prophetic."[49] In the East, Revelation was excluded from the Peshitta, and only later included in the Philoxenus edition of the Syriac version. Debate continued. Revelation was accepted by the Armenian church in the twelfth century, but even then, not by the Nestorian church.

This lengthy ecclesiastical debate about the place of the Apocalypse can be read variously. Supporters of the apostolic authorship of the book can appeal to Hermas, Papias, Justin Martyr, and Irenaeus, a strong line of increasingly more certain testimony. On the other hand, those who doubt that Revelation was written by the apostle can argue that it was misattributed early on because it carried the name John. As in other matters, the interpretation of Papias's place in this debate is quite uncertain, and an equally strong line of witnesses can be summoned for the rejection of apostolic authorship: Marcion, Gaius, Dionysius, and Eusebius.

The Authorship of the Apocalypse

Debate over the authorship of Revelation has continued in modern scholarship, where varieties of four positions can be identified: (1) the apostle John wrote both the Gospel and the Apocalypse (and the Epistles),[50] (2) the apostle wrote the Gospel but not the Apocalypse, (3) the apostle wrote the Apocalypse but not the Gospel, and (4) neither the Gospel nor the Apocalypse was written by the apostle. Since Eusebius, the Elder John has been suggested as a likely candidate for the authorship of either the Gospel, the Apocalypse, or both. Theories of a Johannine school have also served to relate the apostle to the elder, the seer, or other unnamed Johannine writers.[51] The factors adduced by Dionysius—attribution, language and style, and theology—have continued to attract scrutiny in this debate.

Although Dionysius judged that the Apocalypse "has no connexion, no affinity, in any way with them [the Gospel and 1 John]; it scarcely, so to speak, has even a syllable in common with them,"[52] even those who agree with his conclusion recognize that he overstated the case. The Gospel and Revelation are both marked by a pervasive dualism. They are also the only two books in the New Testament to call Jesus the Word of God (John 1:1; Rev. 19:13). Similarly, only in these two books in the New Testament do the images of the apocalyptic warrior lamb and the Passover lamb coalesce in a title for the Christ (John 1:29; Rev. 5:6). The common climate of the two writings is further demonstrated by the prevalence of the use of terms for witness, life, death, thirst, hunger, and conquering in a moral or spiritual sense.[53]

Those who have held out for common authorship of the two writings have usually suggested as explanations for the books' differences one of the following theories. (1) There was a significant lapse of time between the two writings—Revelation usually being assigned an early date and the Gospel a later one.[54] The prevailing arguments for dating both writings in the 90s make this view look like special pleading with little supporting evidence. (2) The differences may be explained by postulating the use of different amanuenses. This explanation does not account for the differences in thought as adequately as it does the divergence of language and style. (3) The differences in language and style are due to the difference in genre. The difference in genre may explain the difference in language, and even some aspects of the style and thought of Revelation, but on the whole such variations are so substantial that they cannot be explained on this basis. (4) The theology of the two books is complementary rather than contradictory. Most interpreters, however, now conclude that the differences between the Gospel and the Apocalypse indicate that they come from different authors, and that the similarities between them are the result of a shared context rather than a common author.[55]

Following Erasmus, Johann Salomo Semler (1725–1791), the Tübingen school, and R. H. Charles, contemporary scholars have generally favored Dionysius's conclusion that the Gospel and the Apocalypse could not have been written by the same author. The argument from vocabulary and style has been pivotal. Dionysius observed that the Gospel and 1 John "are not only written in faultless Greek but also show the greatest literary skill in their diction, their reasonings, and the constructions in which they are expressed. There is a complete absence of any barbarous word, or solecism, or any vulgarism whatever." When Dionysius examined the style of Revelation, however, he commented: "I observe his style and that his use of the Greek language is not accurate, but that he employs barbarous idioms, in some places committing downright solecisms."[56]

R. H. Charles even proposed that Revelation was written in a Greek with its own grammar,[57] though this assessment of the language has since been substantially modified.[58] Among the differences in vocabulary the most frequently noted include the following. Revelation and John use different words for "lamb" (Rev., *arnion;* John, *amnos*), and "Jerusalem" (Rev., *Ierousalēm;* John, *Ierosolyma*). They use the same word—*ethnos, ethnē*—differently

(Rev., "gentile nations"; John, "the Jewish nation"); and only John uses "world" and "Jews" in a hostile sense. Words common in one are lacking in the other: "truth," "true," and "joy" are recurrent in John but do not occur in Revelation; "faith," "faithful," "patience" (or "endurance"), and "wisdom" occur repeatedly in Revelation but are absent from John.[59] These differences led Charles to conclude that the mix of similarities and differences between the Gospel and Revelation is best explained by tracing the works to different authors who were closely related to one another as members of an early Christian school in Ephesus.[60]

Differences in thought reinforce the consensus that the writings come from different authors. Whereas John emphasizes the present realization of eschatological hopes, the orientation of the Apocalypse is futuristic. The Gospel retells the ministry of Jesus, whereas the ministry of Jesus holds virtually no significance for the Apocalypse. While both works use symbolism extensively, the imagery and symbolism of the Apocalypse is similar to that found in other apocalypses but different from the Gospel's. The Gospel's penchant for irony is missing from the Apocalypse—or, at a minimum, is employed quite differently there.

As a result of such considerations, most scholars conclude that Revelation must be assigned to a different author. On the other hand, there is no reason to deny that Revelation was written by someone named John. Consequently, some scholars have argued that this John was the apostle and that the character of the book accords well with the character of the apostle who was given the name *Boanerges.* On the other hand, John the seer never claims to be an apostle, does not give any evidence of having been with Jesus during his ministry (which he scarcely mentions), makes little or no use of the sayings of Jesus, and when he does refer to the apostles, it is to a group in the past with whom he has had no direct contact (Rev. 18:20; 21:14). It therefore appears that John the seer was not the apostle John but a prophetic teacher of Asia Minor.[61] This conclusion has led to vigorous debate over what sort of prophet John was, and whether he wrote as an individual or as the leader of a school, guild, circle, or association of prophets.

Elisabeth Schüssler Fiorenza has rigorously rejected the theory that the similarities and differences between John and Revelation can be explained by tracing the two to different authors within the Johannine school. In her opinion, the same sort of linguistic data that can be used to argue for affinities between the Gospel and the Apocalypse can be used to argue for an even closer affinity with the Pauline writings:

> Whereas Rev. and the Fourth Gospel have only eight words common to them alone, Rev. and Paul share thirty-three such words and Rev. and Luke have almost the same number in

common. The closer affinity of Rev. to Pauline vocabulary comes even more to the fore when we compare those words which both authors use at least twice. Whereas Rev. and the Fourth Gospel share forty-six such words, Rev. and Paul have 157 in common. The affinity of Rev. to Pauline language can be observed in its use of small particles such as prepositions and conjunctions.[62]

Schüssler Fiorenza's point is well taken, but some of the criticisms of Dodd's use of statistics in the comparison of the vocabulary and style of the Gospel and 1 John apply here also. In particular, one suspects that comparing Revelation to a larger corpus (the Pauline letters as opposed to the Gospel) would be likely to yield a higher correlation than comparing it to a smaller corpus. For example, arguing that there are more terms common only to Revelation and the Gospel than terms common only to Revelation and 3 John would prove nothing.[63] Schüssler Fiorenza's solution is that Revelation was written by the head of a prophetic-apocalyptic school in Asia Minor, who had access to both Pauline and Johannine school traditions. In particular, the reference in Revelation 22:16, she argues, is a reference to a "special group of *Gemeindepropheten*" whose function is to teach and guard the content of the book.[64] Schüssler Fiorenza also argues that "Jezebel," "Balaam," and the Nicolaitans are rival prophetic schools.

David Aune has similarly contended that although the seer never calls himself a prophet, he describes his book as prophecy (1:3; 22:7, 10, 18, 19) and says that he is "your fellow servant, and the fellow servant of your brothers the prophets" (22:9). Aune therefore agrees that the seer was a member of a prophetic guild or circle that opposed "Jezebel" and the Nicolaitans.[65] As models for such groups of prophets, Aune points to the prophetic community that produced Q, the prophets in the Corinthian church (1 Cor. 14:29–33), the inspired singers of the Odes of Solomon, and the prophetic school that may lie behind the Ascension of Isaiah.[66]

Adela Yarbro Collins responded to the arguments that John was the head of a prophetic-apocalyptic school or the member of a prophetic guild or circle by arguing that the use of Old Testament materials and apocalyptic materials in Revelation is not the product of school activity but of freer transmission and proclamation. Neither does Revelation 22:16 require the supposition that there was a special group of prophetic interpreters. While Collins agrees that the seer does seem to have been an itinerant early Christian prophet (of the sort attested by Matthew and the Didache) who had worked in each of the seven communities he addresses, "the frequently advocated thesis that he was a member or the head of a prophetic school or local circle of prophets is without foundation."[67] John apparently came from a Jewish background in Palestine and was bilingual. Nevertheless, he appears to have deliberately rejected what was considered good Greek style to write, as an act of resistance, in a Semitic style. His use of allusions to the scriptures in a form similar to the Hebraizing *kaige* version and the similarity of his work to the fourth book of the Sibylline Oracles support such a view of the seer's background and social location.[68]

CONCLUSION

The internal evidence, including self-designations and considerations of thought, language, and style, point to the conclusion that the evangelist, the elder, and the seer were three different persons. Many would also distinguish the Beloved Disciple from the evangelist. On the other hand, distinct similarities in style and thought, especially between the Gospel and the Epistles, point to a close relationship between these writings. The most likely explanation seems to be that they originated in the same community, from a school of early Christian writers who had access to the same traditions and who provided guidance for a loosely related group of churches within the same general geographic area.

The Apocalypse is clearly tied to the seven churches in Asia Minor. If the Gospel and the Epistles are traced to Ephesus, the Johannine writings all emerged from the same area at about the same time. Apart from the later legends about the life of the apostle and tradition that the apostle was the author of the Johannine writings, however, there is no evidence from the writings themselves and no evidence prior to the middle of the second century to connect the Gospel and the Epistles with Ephesus. Nevertheless, if the ecclesiastical tradition regarding the authorship of the Johannine writings is thrown in doubt, the basis for tracing the Gospel and the Epistles to Asia Minor must be reexamined.

Moreover, it appears that the majority of New Testament scholars are now convinced that none of the works traditionally attributed to the apostle John were actually written by him. If that is the case, then how did the tradition of apostolic authorship emerge in the second century? The next chapter will take up the story of how the five Johannine writings came to be traced to the same figure—the apostle John.

NOTES

1. On this issue, see Raymond E. Brown, *The Epistles of John,* AB 30 (Garden City: Doubleday, 1982), 732–39, where six alternative views of the relationship between the elder and Diotrephes are discussed.
2. Brown, *The Epistles of John,* 9.
3. Eusebius, *E.H.* 3.39.17. *Eusebius: The Ecclesiastical History,* trans. Kirsopp Lake, LCL (Cambridge, Mass.: Harvard University Press, 1926), 1:299.

4. Irenaeus, *Adv. Haer.* 1.16.3 (citing 2 John 10–11; *ANF* 1:342); 3.16.5 (citing 1 John 2:18–19, 21–22 as having been written by the same John who wrote the Gospel; *ANF* 1:442); and 3.16.8 (citing 2 John 7–8 and 1 John 4:1–2, 5:1; *ANF* 1:443). See also Brown, *The Epistles of John,* 9–10.

5. See *Stromata* 2:15 *(ANF* 2:362), and *Fragments from Cassiodorus* 4 *(ANF* 2:576); see below, p. 141.

6. See below, pp. 128–29.

7. See below, p. 144.

8. See below, p. 146.

9. See below, p. 153.

10. See below, pp. 163–64.

11. C. H. Turner, "Latin Lists of the Canonical Books. I. The Roman Council under Damasus, AD 382," *JTS* 1 (1900): 544–60; cited in Judith Lieu, *The Second and Third Epistles of John: History and Background,* ed. John Riches (Edinburgh: T. and T. Clark, 1986), 14 n. 31. See Lieu, *The Second and Third Epistles of John,* 5–36, and A. E. Brooke, *A Critical and Exegetical Commentary on the Johannine Epistles,* ICC (Edinburgh: T. and T. Clark, 1912), lii–lxii, for surveys of the reception of the Epistles.

12. Brown, *The Epistles of John,* 12.

13. H. J. Holtzmann, "Das Problem des ersten johanneischen Briefes in seinem Verhältnis zum Evangelium," *JPT* 7 (1881): 690–712; and *JPT* 8 (1882): 128–52, 316–42, 460–85. Holtzmann's list is reproduced in Brooke, *The Johannine Epistles,* xiii–xv.

14. Brooke, *The Johannine Epistles,* i–xix; R. H. Charles, *The Revelation of St. John,* ICC (Edinburgh: T. and T. Clark, 1920), 1:xxxiv–xxxvii.

15. Brooke, *The Johannine Epistles,* xviii.

16. C. H. Dodd, "The First Epistle of John and the Fourth Gospel," *BJRL* 21 (1937): 129–56.

17. See Brown, *The Epistles of John,* 23.

18. Dodd, "The First Epistle of John," 131.

19. Dodd, "The First Epistle of John," 156.

20. C. H. Dodd, *The Johannine Epistles,* MNTC (London: Hodder and Stoughton, 1946), lvi, lxxi.

21. W. F. Howard, "The Common Authorship of the Johannine Gospel and Epistles," *JTS* 48 (1947): 12–25. See also W. G. Wilson, "An Examination of the Linguistic Evidence Adduced against the Unity of Authorship of the First Epistle of John and the Fourth Gospel," *JTS* 49 (1948): 147–56; A. P. Salom, "Some Aspects of the Grammatical Style of I John," *JBL* 74 (1955): 96–102; Nigel Turner, *Style,* vol 4 of *Grammar of New Testament Greek,* by J. H. Moulton (Edinburgh: T. and T. Clark, 1976), 4:132–38.

22. Salom, "Some Aspects of the Grammatical Style of 1 John," 100–101.

23. Fernando F. Segovia reaches the conclusion that the redaction of the Gospel can be traced to the *Sitz im Leben* of 1 John; see *Love Relationships in the Johannine Tradition: Agape/Agapan in 1 John and the Fourth Gospel,* SBLDS 58 (Chico, Cal.: Scholars Press, 1982), 21–22, 213–19.

24. Brown, *The Epistles of John,* 24–25.
25. Brown, *The Epistles of John,* 30.
26. See Kenneth Grayston, *The Johannine Epistles,* NCB (Grand Rapids: Wm. B. Eerdmans, 1984), 6–14, 27–29; Georg Strecker, "Die Anfänge der johanneischen Schule," *NTS* 32 (1986): 31–47.
27. Strabo, *Geography* 10.5.13; *The Geography of Strabo,* trans. Horace Leonard Jones, LCL (Cambridge, Mass.: Harvard University Press, 1954), 5:173. Thucydides, *History of the Peloponnesian War* 3.33.3; *Thucydides,* trans. Charles Forster Smith, LCL (Cambridge, Mass.: Harvard University Press, 1953), 2:53.
28. Tacitus, *Annals* 4.30, 15.71; *Tacitus: The Annals,* trans. John Jackson, LCL (Cambridge, Mass.: Harvard University Press, 1937), 3:53; 4:329.
29. Tertullian, *On Prescription against Heretics* 36 (*ANF* 3:260); see below, p. 140.
30. G. B. Caird, *The Revelation of St. John the Divine,* BNTC (London: Adam and Charles Black, 1966), 21–22.
31. Shepherd of Hermas, *Visions* 2.2.7, refers to those who "endure the great persecution which is coming" (*Apostolic Fathers,* trans. Kirsopp Lake, LCL [Cambridge, Mass.: Harvard University Press, 1913], 2:21; see 4.2.5, 4.3.6, and Rev. 7:14. The texts relevant to the reception of the Apocalypse are cited and discussed in R. H. Charles, *The Revelation of St. John* 1:xcvii–ciii.
32. See below, p. 153.
33. See Charles, *The Revelation* 1:xcviii.
34. Tertullian, *Against Marcion* 4.5 (*ANF* 3:350).
35. Justin Martyr, *Dialogue with Trypho* 81 (*ANF* 1:240).
36. Attested in Eusebius, *E.H.* 4.26.2 (LCL 1:387), and in Jerome, *Lives of Illustrious Men* 9 (*NPNF,* 2d ser., 3:364–65).
37. See Eusebius, *E.H.* 3.28.1–2 (LCL 1:263). See below, p. 121.
38. See, e.g., Irenaeus, *Adv. Haer.* 3.11.1, 4.20.11 (*ANF* 1:426, 491). For a fuller discussion, see below, p. 124.
39. Eusebius, *E.H.* 4.24 (LCL 1:385), 5.18.14 (LCL 1:493).
40. See below, p. 129.
41. Tertullian, *Against Marcion* 3.14. (*ANF* 3:333); see also *On the Resurrection of the Flesh* 38 (*ANF* 3:573).
42. Clement of Alexandria, *Instructor* 2.11 (*ANF* 2:265); *Who Is the Rich Man That Shall Be Saved?* 42 (*ANF* 2:603).
43. See Eusebius, *E.H.* 6.25.9 (LCL 2:77); see below, p. 144.
44. Cited by Eusebius, *E.H.* 6.25.1 (LCL 2:197). See below, p. 145.
45. Eusebius, *E.H.* 3.39.6 (LCL 1:293); see below, p. 154.
46. Cyril of Jerusalem, *Catechesis* 4.36, in *The Works of Saint Cyril of Jerusalem,* trans. Leo P. McCauley and Anthony A. Stephenson, FC 61 (Washington, D.C.: Catholic University of America Press, 1969), 1:137.
47. Charles, *The Revelation* 1:ci–cii.
48. Charles, *The Revelation* 1:cii.
49. Martin Luther, "Preface to the Revelation of Saint John," quoted in Werner Georg Kümmel, *The New Testament: The History of the Investigation of Its Problems,*

trans. S. McLean Gilmour and Howard C. Kee (Nashville: Abingdon Press, 1972), p. 26.

50. This view has recently been defended by Stephen S. Smalley in "John's Revelation and John's Community," *BJRL* 69 (1987): 549–71, esp. 569–71.

51. Notable here is C. K. Barrett's hypothesis that John the apostle moved to Ephesus, where he gathered a number of pupils and wrote apocalyptic works. After his death, various of his pupils composed the Apocalypse, John 1–20, 1 John, 2 and 3 John, and eventually John 21. See *The Gospel According to St. John*, 2d ed. (Philadelphia: Westminster Press, 1978), 133–34.

52. Dionysius, quoted in Eusebius, *E.H.* 7.25.22 (LCL 2:207); see below, p. 146.

53. G. R. Beasley-Murray, *The Book of Revelation*, NCB (Greenwood, S.C.: Attic Press, 1974), 34. See also Otto Böcher, "Johanneisches in der Apokalypse des Johannes," *NTS* 27 (1981): 310–21.

54. From antiquity, however, there have been differing opinions as to the sequence of the writing of the Gospel and the Apocalypse. The so-called "anti-Marcionite," or monarchian, prologue to Luke, quoted below, p. 130, claims that John wrote the Apocalypse before the Gospel. Edgar Hennecke indicates that Hippolytus (*c. Noetus* 15; *ANF* 5:229) sets the writing of the Apocalypse after the writing of the Gospel, but the reference is questionable; see Edgar Hennecke, *New Testament Apocrypha*, ed. Wilhelm Schneemelcher, trans. R. McL. Wilson (Philadelphia: Westminster Press, 1965), 2:56

55. See Otto Böcher, "Das Verhältnis der Apokalypse des Johannes zum Evangelium des Johannes," in *L'Apocalypse johannique et l'Apocalyptique dans le Nouveau Testament*, BETL 53 (Louvain: Louvain University Press, 1980), 294. Böcher reassesses the similarities between the Gospel and the Apocalypse in the areas of Christology, pneumatology, angelology, satanology, ecclesiology, eschatology, and formal elements and concludes that since the two books were written at about the same date, they must be influenced by a common tradition.

56. Cited in Eusebius, *E.H.* 7.25.25 (LCL 2:207).

57. Charles, *The Revelation*, cxvii–clix.

58. Steven Thompson, in *The Apocalypse and Semitic Syntax*, SNTSMS 52 (Cambridge: Cambridge University Press, 1986), generally agrees with Charles and Nigel Turner that Revelation is written in "Jewish Greek," but the evidence for such a conclusion has been reassessed from a socio-linguistic perspective by Stanley E. Porter in "The Language of the Apocalypse in Recent Discussion," *NTS* 35 (1989): 582–603.

59. See further the data collected by Henry Barclay Swete in *The Apocalypse of St. John* (Grand Rapids: Wm. B. Eerdmans, 1954), cxx–cxxx; and, more recently, by Elisabeth Schüssler Fiorenza in *The Book of Revelation: Justice and Judgment* (Philadelphia: Fortress Press, 1985), 93–101.

60. Charles, *The Revelation*, xxxiii.

61. W. G. Kümmel, *Introduction to the New Testament*, 17th ed., trans. Howard Clark Kee (Nashville: Abingdon Press, 1975) says: "Thus concerning the author of Rev.

we know nothing more than that he was a Jewish-Christian prophet named John"
    (472).

62. Schüssler Fiorenza, *The Book of Revelation,* 94–95.
63. Schüssler Fiorenza's view that Revelation has traditionally been linked too closely
    and exclusively with the Johannine writings (the Gospel and the Epistles) has
    received a detailed response from Stephen S. Smalley, who examines the relation-
    ship between Revelation and the Gospel of John in five areas—ethos, theology,
    tradition, language, and structure—and concludes "that John's Revelation is in-
    deed closely bound up with the life of John's community" ("John's Revelation and
    John's Community," 568).
64. Schüssler Fiorenza, *The Book of Revelation,* 106. This interpretation has received
    significant confirmation through David E. Aune's thorough examination of the
    issues posed by Rev. 22:16; see Aune's "The Prophetic Circle of John of Patmos
    and the Exegesis of Revelation 22:16," *JSNT* 37 (1989): 103–16.
65. David E. Aune, "The Social Matrix of the Apocalypse of John," *BR* 26 (1981): 18–
    19, 27–29.
66. Aune, "The Prophetic Circle of John of Patmos and the Exegesis of Revelation
    22:16," 111.
67. Adela Yarbro Collins, *Crisis and Catharsis: The Power of the Apocalypse* (Phila-
    delphia: Westminster Press, 1984), 46.
68. Collins, *Crisis and Catharsis,* 47–49.

CHAPTER 5

Obscurity
The Apostle in the Second Century

The legends that grew up around the apostle in the second century challenge every interpreter with a baffling conundrum. Imagine going to a play in which there are numerous roles and an undetermined number of actors (one, two, or three); each actor is named John, and you are not told which actor plays which role. The playbill gives various identifications and interpretations, but informed critics have raised questions about the reliability of each explanation.

The title of the production is "The Traditions of the Fathers about the Apostle John and the Authorship of the Johannine Writings." There are an undetermined number of roles: Beloved Disciple; author(s) of the Gospel, the Epistles, and Revelation; early martyr, Ephesian teacher, aged apostle, elder. Some of these roles are almost certainly spurious. The others are played by one of the three actors named John: the seer/author of Revelation, the apostle, and the elder. The challenge before us is twofold: to determine which roles were played by each John, and to explain how the traditions about the various roles developed. The three roles may be one, two, or three persons. For example, the seer and the elder may be the same person; the seer and the apostle may be the same person; even the apostle and the elder may be one and the same. The problem is compounded in view of commonly held opinions that distinguish the Beloved Disciple, the evangelist, the redactor (or final editor, the "I" of John 21:25), the elder (the author of the Epistles; see 2 John 1 and 3 John 1), and the seer (Rev. 1:9). The theoretical possibilities are therefore almost endless, and virtually every conceivable theory has found a champion among New Testament scholars of the past two centuries.

A fresh assessment of the traditions of the church fathers is needed, along with a comprehensive compilation of the legends about the apostle. In an effort to trace the development of the traditions as well as to distinguish history from legend, we will examine the interpretations of the play in chronological order.

THE FIRST HALF OF THE SECOND CENTURY

The nearly complete absence of any explicit reference to the apostle or to the Gospel of John in the first half of the second century is surprising. After reviewing the evidence in his commentary, C. K. Barrett concludes: "There is no evidence for his [John's] residence in Ephesus in any orthodox Christian writer earlier than Irenaeus. It cannot but appear probable that if John had been alive in Ephesus (a great center of Christian life and letters) in or near A.D. 100 some trace of the fact would have survived from the literature of the first half of the second century."[1] We will not tarry over every possible echo of a verse from the Gospel. It is difficult to assess such references, since they may derive from oral traditions, tracts, or collections of sayings of Jesus which are no longer extant. Nevertheless, the evidence of Papyrus[52], Ignatius, Papias, and Justin Martyr must be considered.

Papyrus[52]

The earliest evidence of the Gospel of John is p[52] (Manchester, John Rylands Library, P. Ryl. Gr. 457), a scrap of papyrus with the text of John 18:31–33 and 18:37–38. This fragment was discovered in Egypt and published in 1935. Generally dated about 125, it is widely regarded as the earliest known manuscript of the New Testament. Barbara and Kurt Aland, internationally recognized authorities on the text of the New Testament, comment, "Although 'about 125' allows for a leeway of about twenty-five years on either side, the consensus has come in recent years to regard 125 as representing the later limit, so that p[52] must have been copied very soon after the Gospel of John was itself written in the early 90s A.D."[2] This early date has recently been called into question. Egerton Papyrus 2 has been dated around 200 rather than 150 as it once was, and a later date, about 150–175 has therefore been proposed for p[52].[3] If an early date for p[52] holds, it sets the upper limit of the date of the composition of the Gospel and, if the Gospel was not written in Alexandria, shows that it was disseminated and copied very quickly.

Ignatius of Antioch

Ignatius of Antioch, martyred not later than A.D. 117, wrote to the churches he had visited on his journey to Rome—among them being the church at Ephesus, to which he sent a letter he had written in Smyrna. In this letter, he mentions Paul but not John. The references to Paul occur in the context of references to his own martyrdom: he will be a "fellow-initiate" with Paul.[4] The absence of any reference to John may be explained on the assumption either that John the apostle had not worked in Ephesus or that Ignatius did not mention John because John had not been martyred. We will examine the tradition that John was martyred when it arises in later traditions.

Parenthetically, although Ignatius refers to Mary three times in this letter,[5] he says nothing about Mary's residence in Ephesus. In this case, the argument from silence is convincing. Had Ignatius known anything of the later reports of Mary's residence in Ephesus, he would certainly have made some reference to it. The question of whether Ignatius knew the Gospel of John is still open to debate. The closest "echoes" are found in *Romans* 7.2, *Magnesians* 8.2, and *Philadelphians* 7.1 and 9.1.[6] Here there is an occasional affinity with the language and thought of the Gospel of John, but no explicit reference. Even when writing to the church at Ephesus, Ignatius makes no reference to the Gospel of John. Neither does he mention the Book of Revelation, however, which speaks of the nearby Island of Patmos. Therefore, Ignatius's silence can hardly be turned into testimony that Ephesus was not the home of the Johannine tradition.

Papias

Sometime during the reign of Hadrian (117–138), probably around 130, Papias of Hierapolis wrote five books entitled *Interpretation of the Oracles of the Lord.* The five books have not survived, but a few excerpts are preserved in the writings of Eusebius of Caesarea (fourth century) and others. Irenaeus identifies Papias as "the hearer of John, who was a companion of Polycarp and one of the ancients." Eusebius, however, points out that Irenaeus was mistaken. Papias had not been "a hearer and eyewitness of the sacred Apostle." Instead, he taught what he had received from "those who had known them."[7]

The fragment of principal interest describes Papias's contacts with the bearers of the traditions of the Apostles:

> And I shall not hesitate to append to the interpretations all that I ever learnt well from the presbyters and remember well, for of their truth I am confident. For unlike most I did not rejoice in them who say much, but in them who teach the truth, nor in them who recount the commandments of others, but in them who repeated those given to the faith by the Lord and derived from the truth itself; but if anyone ever came who had followed the presbyters, I inquired into the words of the presbyters, what Andrew or Peter or Philip or Thomas or James or John or Matthew, or any other of the Lord's disciples, had said, and what Aristion and the presbyter John, the Lord's disciples, were saying. For I did not suppose that information from books would help me so much as the word of a living and surviving voice.[8]

The vagaries and "flexible Greek" of this passage have fostered vigorous debate over its meaning. Eusebius himself, by way of comment on this passage, points out that the name of John appears twice, once with the names of the other apostles, and once after Aristion, where John is identified as "the elder John." From this fact Eusebius reasoned that there were two authorities named John in Ephesus—a deduction which he took as confirmation of the report that there were "two tombs at Ephesus both still called John's."[9] That Papias refers to two Johns has been accepted generally but not universally.[10] Other uncertain references include Papias's use of the term "elder" or "presbyter" and his relationship to the elders and the apostles. "Elders" appears to be a general term of respect rather than a church office, but its meaning is uncertain. More specifically, does Papias refer to the apostles as elders or does he claim that he asked the elders what the apostles had said? The latter makes better sense of the passage. Also to be noted is the difference of tenses: "what the Lord's disciples *had said*" and "what Aristion and the elder John *were saying*." The apparent meaning, therefore, is that Papias had no direct contact with John or any other of the Lord's disciples. Neither was he in direct contact with Aristion and the Elder John, who were still living. Rather, Papias seized every opportunity to inquire of traveling Christians passing through Hierapolis—Christians who had followed the elders and could therefore tell him what Aristion and John were saying.

C. K. Barrett depicted the links in the chain as follows:[11]

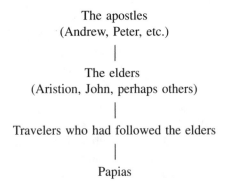

The apostles
(Andrew, Peter, etc.)

|

The elders
(Aristion, John, perhaps others)

|

Travelers who had followed the elders

|

Papias

The words of the apostles already lay in the past and were available to Papias only through the testimony of the elders, which was reported to Papias by traveling Christians.

Papias knew of books, which presumably contained words of the Lord, but he preferred the oral tradition. Did Papias know the Gospel of John but prefer the teaching of the Elder John? Unfortunately, we cannot answer that question. It should be noted further, however, that Papias does not associate either

John (apostle or elder) with the Gospel or any other writing. Neither does he associate either John with Ephesus.[12]

One other peculiar feature of this excerpt must be recognized. Papias uses the phrase "the Lord's disciples" twice in close proximity, once to describe the apostles and once to describe Aristion and the Elder John. Various interpretations are possible, and several emendations have been proposed. (1) Both the apostles and the elders had been eyewitnesses, disciples of the Lord. The span of about a century between Jesus and Papias makes this interpretation virtually impossible, even if one is willing to posit aged disciples about whom Papias had heard reports at a young age. (2) Papias was mistaken in calling Aristion (about whom nothing is known) and the Elder John "the Lord's disciples." The authority of the elders may have already attracted the claim that they too had been among "the Lord's disciples." (3) The epithet "the Lord's disciples" may mean nothing more than "Christians." Such a weak or reduced meaning, however, is inconceivable following a list of the apostles. The difficulty in accepting any of these three interpretations has led scholars to a fourth alternative. (4) The text is corrupt. Among the conjectural emendations, one finds "these disciples" (*hoi toutōn mathētai*), simply "the disciples" (*hoi mathētai*), and "the disciples of John." The latter requires the assumption that the abbreviation *tou Iōu mathētai* was mistaken for *tou ku mathētai*.[13] The latter is the most exciting hypothesis, and the one that affords the best sense for the use of the term "disciples," but it is also the most conjectural. If one is driven to emend the text, the simplest procedure is to treat the phrase as an example of diplography (writing a word or phrase twice) and to delete the second occurrence, following the two elders. The words "the Lord's disciples" are missing from the Syriac and the Rufinian Latin translation of Eusebius.[14]

Finally, the sequence of the names of the apostles in Papias's list is strikingly parallel to the sequence in John 1:40 and 21:2, and divergent from the sequence(s) in the synoptics and Acts.

Papias	John 1	John 21:2
Andrew	Andrew	
Peter	Peter	Peter
Philip	Philip	
Thomas		Thomas
	Nathanael	Nathanael
James		sons of Zebedee
John		
Matthew		
Aristion		two others
John		

These parallels can be taken to mean either that Papias followed the Johannine sequence in preference to Mark,[15] or that both John and Papias independently attest an Asian tradition of the list of disciples which diverged from the synoptic tradition's elevation of Peter.

From Papias, therefore, we have little more than a credible reference to John the Elder—no reference to the Johannine writings, and no link between either of the two Johns and Ephesus.[16] Had John the Elder been at Ephesus, not far from Hierapolis, one would have expected that Papias would not have relied on chance visits by Christian travelers but would have made the journey to Ephesus to question John in person. Eusebius tells us that Papias quoted from 1 John and 1 Peter,[17] and other fragments supply evidence that Papias knew the Apocalypse of John also. If so, Eusebius may have suppressed Papias's use of Revelation because it did not accord with his own estimate of that disputed writing.[18]

Later tradition, however, also elevates Papias's relationship to John to the point where he is named as John's amanuensis. Christoph Luthardt cites Corderius's *Catena* as the source for the following statement: "Last of these [of all the evangelists], John, called the son of thunder, being far advanced in years . . . dictated his gospel against the frightful heresies springing up at that time, to his disciple Papias, Eubiotos [read "bishop"] of Hierapolis."[19]

Justin Martyr

Justin fills the gap between Papias and Irenaeus. A Gentile, born in Samaria, Justin studied philosophy before his conversion, probably during his residence in Ephesus.[20] Later he taught in Rome, where he was martyred (about 165).

The witness of Justin is perplexing, justifying the observation that "quotations are absent in those places where we should most confidently look for them if the Fourth Gospel was composed in Ephesus about A.D. 100 by John the Apostle."[21] Nowhere does Justin explicitly refer to the Gospel of John or connect the apostle with it. On the other hand, Justin cites Revelation 20:4–5, attributing it to "a certain man with us, whose name was John, one of the apostles of Christ."[22] The earliest attestation of authorship claimed for the apostle John, therefore, relates him to Revelation but is silent about his relationship to the Gospel or the Epistles.

Justin uses the term "gospel" (*euangelion*) only three times, but repeatedly refers to the "Reminiscences [or Memoirs] of the Apostles," which he explains "are called Gospels."[23] Justin quotes or refers to the Gospels some 170 times.[24] Given the frequency of these references, Justin's lack of use of the Fourth Gospel becomes all the more striking. Edgar J. Goodspeed listed about forty echoes of the Fourth Gospel in Justin,[25] but James Drummond found only three quotations,[26] the clearest of which is in *Apology* 1.61.4: "For Christ also said, 'Except ye be born again, ye shall not enter into the kingdom of heaven.' Now, that it is impossible for those who have once been born to enter into their mothers' wombs is manifest to all." This obvious parallel to John 3:3 and Nicodemus's perplexed response occurs in the context of a discussion of baptism, "the washing with water."

As close a parallel as this is, it is not a direct quotation. John 3:3 contains the characteristically Johannine formula "Amen, amen, I say to you"; the ambiguous term "again," or "from above" (anōthen); the verbs "not able to see"; and the phrase "the kingdom of God." On the other hand, the statement in Justin lacks the introductory formula "Amen, amen, I say to you," contains a verb not found anywhere in John (anagennēthēte) but common in baptismal liturgies (1 Pet. 1:3, 23),[27] makes an emphatic reference to entering rather than seeing the kingdom, and uses the phrase "the kingdom of heaven" rather than "the kingdom of God." Differing as it does from John 3:3, the last half of the saying in Justin is a verbatim recitation of Matthew 18:3, "Amen, I say to you, unless you turn and become as children, you will not enter into the kingdom of heaven." The sentence which follows in Justin is likewise not a verbatim repetition of John 3:4.

If Justin knows the Fourth Gospel, he is not quoting it but reproducing the saying from memory while conflating it with Matthew 18:3. It is possible, however, that Justin and Matthew 18:3 preserve an earlier form of a traditional logion that has been adapted and altered by the Fourth Evangelist. The protest that one cannot literally be born again can be made any time such metaphorical language is used. Here too, Justin need not be citing John 3:3–5.

Critical opinion regarding the source of this allusion is divided. Is Justin citing the Fourth Gospel,[28] a collection of Gospel texts,[29] or an independent baptismal tradition?[30] In favor of the conclusion that Justin quotes from John, one may cite the following factors: Justin knows not only the logion but Nicodemus's response; Justin's logos Christology is "inconceivable without the prologue of John";[31] Justin does not cite the other Gospels by name; and he may not have made more extensive use of John because it had not been accepted by his Roman audience. The considerations which challenge the conclusion that Justin quoted from John as one of the "Memoirs of the Apostles" include: (1) Apology 61.3 does not reproduce John 3:3ff. verbatim, and in part is closer to Matthew 18:3; (2) Justin's references to John are very indirect; (3) Justin affirms the apostolic origin of Revelation but says nothing about the Fourth Gospel; (4) his Logos Christology draws from other sources, especially Philo.[32] On balance, the conclusion that accounts for the perplexing data best is that Justin knew the Fourth Gospel and was influenced by its theology but made only tentative use of it because its origin was suspect or because it had not gained widespread recognition as an apostolic writing.[33]

Even granting that Justin knew the Fourth Gospel, was influenced by it, and quoted from it on at least one occasion—which is more than many scholars would grant—it is still significant that Justin, who had been in Ephesus, says nothing about the apostolic origin of the Gospel, does not connect it with Ephesus, and uses it much less than the synoptics. What Justin does give us is the first claim that Revelation was written by the apostle; that is, Justin is the first witness for the identification of John the seer with John the apostle.

USE OF THE FOURTH GOSPEL IN THE LATTER HALF OF THE SECOND CENTURY

From the time of Justin on, there is ample evidence for the use of the Fourth Gospel among Gnostics, Montanists, and orthodox Christians. The contrast with the paucity of evidence from the first half of the second century is dramatic.

John among the Gnostics

Contemporary with Justin, the earliest certain and common use of the Gospel of John appears among the Gnostic teachers in the school of Valentinus. Even in the second- and early third-century Gnostic literature, however, common use of the Gospel of John is limited to the students of Valentinus. That Valentinus (ca. 100–175) knew or used the Gospel of John cannot be established, but since his pupils Ptolemy and Heracleon both wrote about the Gospel, and Theodotus used it, it seems likely that Valentinus came in contact with the Gospel, at least during the time of his residence in Rome.

Valentinus

Valentinus was born in the Egyptian delta and was educated in Alexandria, where he may have had direct contact with Basilides. Hippolytus's account of the teachings of Basilides contains two references which indicate use of the Gospel of John, but this material probably reflects the teachings of Basilides' successors rather than Basilides himself.[34]

A later report also claims that Valentinus had been taught by Theudas, whom Valentinus claimed was a student of the apostle Paul.[35] By 140, Valentinus had moved to Rome, where he was active as a teacher and leader in the Roman church. In Rome, Valentinus also came into sharp debate with both Marcion and Justin.[36] Unlike Marcion, Valentinus stayed within the community of the church and at one point hoped to be elected bishop of Rome. Justin, therefore, cited Matthew 24:11 as a condemnation of Valentinus:

> Beware of false prophets, who shall come to you clothed outwardly in sheep's clothing, but inwardly they are ravening wolves,

... there are many, my friends, who, coming forward in the name of Jesus, taught both to speak and to act impious and blasphemous things. . . . Yet they style themselves Christians. . . . Some are called Marcians, and some Valentinians, and some Basilideans, and some Saturnalians, and others by other names. . . . [37]

Valentinus founded a school in Rome, not unlike the philosophical schools, that was intent on raising Christian theology "to the level of pagan philosophical studies."[38] Although Justin condemned Valentinus, attempts to separate Valentinians from the church were ineffective prior to Irenaeus's attack on the Valentinians in his *Against Heresies*. Eventually, the Valentinians were condemned by the emperor Constantine (ca. A.D. 326),[39] but they continued to exist for several centuries.

The question of Valentinus's knowledge and use of the Fourth Gospel has four facets: (1) the fragments of Valentinus, (2) the testimony of Tertullian, (3) the evidence of the *Gospel of Truth*, and (4) the weight of the undisputed use of the Gospel by Valentinus's students. The fragments of Valentinus's work contain no clear evidence that he used the Gospel of John.[40]

Tertullian contrasts Valentinus with Marcion, saying:

One man perverts the Scriptures with his hand, another their meaning by his exposition. For although Valentinus seems to use the entire volume, he has none the less laid violent hands on the truth only with a more cunning mind and skill than Marcion. Marcion expressly and openly used the knife, not the pen, since he made such an excision of the Scriptures as suited his own subject-matter. Valentinus, however, abstained from such excision. . . . [41]

If Tertullian had any grounds for thinking that Valentinus did not know or use the Fourth Gospel, he would surely have condemned him for such an omission.[42]

Gospel of Truth

The *Gospel of Truth*, which derives its title from Irenaeus's report that the Valentinians read "a gospel of truth,"[43] contains echoes of the Fourth Gospel.[44] The origin and date of the Gospel of Truth are uncertain, but it clearly derives from the Valentinian school, and with varying degrees of confidence, scholars who have worked on this document suggest that the *Gospel of Truth* was composed by Valentinus himself around A.D. 150.[45]

If the assertion that the *Gospel of Truth* derives from Valentinus himself is dependable, and its echoes of the Fourth Gospel are based on a knowledge of the Gospel, then one obviously has a basis for asserting that Valentinus knew John. The parallels show affinities in language and thought between the *Gospel of Truth* and the Gospel of John which illustrate why the Valentinians made such extensive use of the latter. Whether there are direct quotations, however, is still doubted.[46] Even if one maintains a degree of skepticism regarding the attribution of the *Gospel of Truth* to Valentinus, its early date (ca. A.D. 150) and its affinities with the Gospel of John indicate either the use of John by Valentinus and his early disciples or the conditions that made Valentinians receptive to the Gospel shortly thereafter.

Ptolemy

Ptolemy, one of Valentinus's early students, wrote a commentary on the prologue of the Gospel of John. The section of commentary quoted by Irenaeus begins with the words, "John, the disciple of the Lord, wishing to set forth the origin of all things. . . ."[47] As in the fragment of Papias, John is called "the disciple of the Lord," not an apostle. There can be little doubt, however, that these words are the earliest attribution of the Gospel to the apostle John.[48] John is also mentioned twice later in the fragment. Ptolemy's *Epistle to Flora* contains an explicit reference to the prologue of John: "And, further, the apostle states that the craftsmanship of the world is his, and that 'all things were made through him, and without him was not anything made. . . . ' "[49]

Little is known about Ptolemy except that he is reported to have been one of Valentinus's early disciples and that he became a leader of the Valentinian school in Italy. Whether the author of these fragments should be identified with the Ptolemy who was martyred in Rome in A.D. 152 is debated.[50] Martyrdom in 152 would mean that Ptolemy died before Valentinus rather than succeeding him as the head of the school, but it would confirm what is already probable: Ptolemy was using John during the lifetime of Valentinus.

Heracleon

Heracleon, another Valentinian, wrote the first commentary on the Gospel about A.D. 170, and apparently did so independently of Ptolemy's work on the prologue of the Gospel. Fragments of commentary on the first eight chapters of the Gospel are preserved in Origen's *Commentary on John*.[51] Clement of Alexandria called Heracleon the most famous member of the Valentinian school,[52] and Origen introduced the first excerpt from Heracleon's commentary by identifying Heracleon as a disciple of Valentinus.[53]

The approximate date of Heracleon's commentary is established by the following chain of references. Origen wrote his *Commentary on John* about

A.D. 228. Clement quoted Heracleon on Luke about A.D. 193, and Irenaeus described Heracleon's heresy in lectures given not later than A.D. 177.[54] Heracleon is also mentioned on several occasions along with Ptolemy.[55] Unfortunately, the surviving fragments of Heracleon's commentary say nothing about the apostle John or the authorship of the Gospel. A comment on John 1:18 explains, "This was said not by the Baptist but by the disciple." Such a clarification would have been all the more necessary if, as is probable, Heracleon knew of the attribution of the Gospel to John, the disciple of Jesus.

Theodotus

Excerpts from a third Valentinian, Theodotus, survive in two manuscripts of the writings of Clement of Alexandria. The fragments have been dated to ca. A.D. 160–170[56] and contain interpretations not only of the prologue of the Gospel and the sayings of Jesus in John 14:6; 11:25; 10:9; 10:30 but also of other sections of the Gospel (4:24; 3:8; 10:11–12; and 19:36–37). Two sections can be distinguished and traced to different Valentinian schools.[57] On occasion, the author attributes words to "the apostle," indicating that he is quoting from the written Gospel and that its apostolic authorship was accepted by the Valentinians.[58] Points at which these quotations differ or agree with other manuscripts of the text of the Gospel supply valuable information for textual criticism of the prologue to John.

Apocryphon of John

Less direct evidence for the use of the Gospel can be found in a Naassene fragment preserved by Hippolytus[59] and in the *Apocryphon of John.* Both originated in the latter part of the second century, and at least the *Apocryphon of John* must be dated earlier than Irenaeus,[60] who apparently knew an early form of the document.[61] The *Apocryphon* purports to contain a dialogue of the risen Lord with "John the brother of James, one of the sons of Zebedee." While going up to the temple, John is challenged by a Pharisee named Arimanios: "Where is your teacher, the man that you used to follow?" John responds, "He has returned to the place from which he came." The Pharisee then charges: "That Nazarene has greatly misled you." When John becomes distressed, the heavens are opened, and in the light he sees three forms—a child, then an elderly person, then a young person—which say, "John, John, why do you have doubts, and why are you afraid?"[62] What follows is a classic exposition of the Gnostic myth, which in part takes the form of a dialogue about Genesis 1–4.

The narrative framework of the *Apocryphon* appears to draw on an already-established tradition regarding the apostle because it contains reports found also in the *Acts of John* (88–105). It has been proposed that this section of the *Acts of John* contains a document (chapters 94–102) that originated in a milieu close to the Valentinians.[63] Both report that John went to the Mount of Olives, where he had a vision of Christ (*Acts* 97). Both claim that John received and transmitted esoteric tradition. The thesis that the *Acts of John* drew on the framework of the *Apocryphon* is rendered unlikely by the observation that the material is more integral to the story in the *Acts* but more artificial in the *Apocryphon.* Hence, the alternative explanation has been advanced—that the *Apocryphon* drew on oral traditions reproduced independently in the *Acts of John.*[64]

What is of interest here is not literary dependence on the Gospel but the choice of John as the apostle with whom the risen Lord speaks. Granting that other Gnostic apocrypha feature Peter more frequently than John, the legend-making evident in the *Apocryphon of John* is further evidence of the importance of the apostle John (and, indirectly, evidence of the importance of the Gospel attributed to him) among the Gnostics who used this apocryphon.[65]

Prior to Irenaeus, therefore, the Gospel of John was quoted and used extensively by the Valentinians. Valentinus himself probably knew the Gospel. Ptolemy wrote a commentary on the prologue to the Gospel which attributes the Gospel to "John, the disciple of the Lord." Heracleon apparently wrote a commentary on the entire Gospel (though the extant fragments cover only the first eight chapters), a fact which suggests that Heracleon regarded the Gospel as scripture. Excerpts from Theodotus attribute verses from the Gospel to "the Apostle," and the *Apocryphon of John* shows that the figure of the apostle had already assumed a place of great importance among the Gnostics.

Apocryphon of James

Johannine allusions in the *Apocryphon of James* suggest that the author knew the Gospel of John. The clearest parallel is the repetition of the beatitude in John 20:29, which in the *Apocryphon of James* reads, "Blessed will be those who did not see but believed."[66] Although the origin of this document is uncertain, it was found in the Jung Codex, which contains other Valentinian documents. The *Apocryphon of James* seems to be a defense of Gnostic doctrine against charges like those raised by Irenaeus, and therefore a setting in Asia Minor early in the third century has been suggested.[67] On the other hand, the sayings of Jesus in this document may have been collected and composed prior to Irenaeus, during the first half of the second century.[68]

Is it an accident of history that the evidence for the knowledge and use of the Johannine writings is so scarce among the Apologists and "orthodox" Christian writers through the middle of the second century, while John's place among the Valentinian Gnostics is secured by quotations, allusions, commentaries, and an apocryphon bearing the name of John? Perhaps. Nevertheless, while the Johannine writings were used only tentatively by the church fathers before Irenaeus, the Gospel was treated as an authoritative writing by the Valentinian school in Rome. The contrast with Justin, who was in Rome about the same time, after having come from Ephesus, is particularly striking. Did Justin treat the Gospel with caution because of its popularity among the Valentinians? Unfortunately, Justin does not provide an answer to this question, but it is reasonable to assume that his reticence about using the Gospel was influenced by its popularity among the Gnostics.

The Church's Acceptance of the Johannine Writings

Eusebius reports that Papias "made use of the testimonies from the First Epistle of John."[69] The first clear citation of 1 John appears in Polycarp's *Letter to the Philippians,* which is dated no later than A.D. 140. Polycarp writes: "For everyone who does not confess that Jesus Christ has come in the flesh is an anti-Christ" (7.1), which appears to be a citation of 1 John 4:2–3 and/or 2 John 7.[70] A reference to being "of the devil" (1 John 3:8) follows in the next line, adding further weight to the probability that Polycarp knew 1 John.

Epistula Apostolorum

The *Epistula Apostolorum* is an anti-heretical polemic that has been dated to about 160–170 and traced to Asia Minor, Syria, or Egypt. It purports to give a special revelation from the risen Lord and opposes Simon and Cerinthus as false prophets. Yet the *Epistula Apostolorum* contains both orthodox features (e.g., insistence on the incarnation of the Logos) and Gnostic elements (mention of the Ogdoad, and a cosmology including eons).[71] Allusions to the Gospel of John include parallels to the prologue,[72] a reference to the new command,[73] a quotation of the beatitude in John 20:29,[74] and a reference to the wedding at Cana.[75] The *Epistula Apostolorum* is the earliest example of the genre of post-resurrection revelatory discourses that are found frequently in Gnostic materials. Its discourse form, however, has affinities with the Johannine discourses, especially the farewell discourse, so that the genre itself may have been influenced by the Gospel of John.[76] In the list of disciples in the *Epistula Apostolorum,* John is named first, followed by Thomas, Peter, Andrew, James, and six others. Epiphanius reports that John was also listed first among the apostles in the Gospel according to the Ebionites: "And coming to Capernaum he entered into the house of Simon surnamed Peter, and opened his mouth and said, 'Passing beside the Sea of

Tiberias I chose John and James, the sons of Zebedee, and Simon and Andrew. . . . ' "[77] The *Epistula Apostolorum* does not identify John as the writer of the Gospel, though it uses John more than any other Gospel.

The Quartodecimans

In the latter part of the second century, a controversy arose between Asia Minor and Rome regarding the date and character of the Easter celebration. The difference in practice surfaced during a visit of Polycarp, bishop of Smyrna, to Anicetus, bishop of Rome, in A.D. 154 or 155. Polycarp, following the chronology of the Gospel of John, maintained that Easter should be celebrated on the 14th day of the Jewish month of Nisan, the same day as the Passover. Eusebius quotes the following excerpt from Irenaeus:

> For neither was Anicetus able to persuade Polycarp not to observe it, inasmuch as he had always done so in company with John the disciple of our Lord and the other apostles with whom he had associated; nor did Polycarp persuade Anicetus to observe it, for he said that he ought to keep the custom of those who were presbyters before him.[78]

Adherents of this practice were called "Quartodecimans." The Roman church objected to this practice, maintaining that Easter should always be celebrated on Sunday.

This controversy takes us back to fragments from Apollinaris of Hierapolis and Melito of Sardis. Apollinaris cited "the Gospels" in his attack on Christians who claimed that according to Matthew, Jesus ate the Passover on Nisan 14 and died on the Great Day of unleavened bread.[79] Melito of Sardis, whose writings can be dated between 169 and 177,[80] makes extensive allusions to the Gospel of John in his Paschal homily.[81] Melito himself, moreover, is cited as a Quartodeciman by Polycrates of Ephesus.[82]

The Montanists and Gaius

The shadow of John's influence falls next on the Montanists, whose origins also predate Irenaeus or are contemporary with him. Around A.D. 170 or slightly earlier, in the region of Phrygia, Montanus began to proclaim that he was a prophet, the fulfillment of the promise of the Johannine Paraclete, who would "teach . . . all things" and "guide you into all truth" (John 14:26; 16:13). The New Prophecy, as its adherents called it, was a threat to the authority of the official leaders of the church and drew an immediate response from them. The Montanists appealed to the desire for fervor over order. The Paraclete, they asserted, also spoke through women, Priscilla and Maximilla.[83] Montanus taught that "God brought forth the Word."[84] The Montanists also revived the apocalyptic spirit of Revelation and Papias, claiming that the new Jerusalem would be established near Pepuza in Phrygia. The movement spread rapidly, even after the deaths of Montanus, Priscilla, and Maximilla (who died in A.D. 179). In North Africa, even Tertullian was drawn to the movement, but it was later repudiated by synods in Asia Minor and by Zephrinus, bishop of Rome (199–217).[85]

By about 170–180, the Montanist movement made its presence felt in Rome. Gaius, a presbyter and noted orthodox scholar, opposed Proclus, a Montanist, attacking Montanism as a heresy.[86] As one facet of his polemic, Gaius rejected both the Gospel of John and Revelation, and denied the apostolic authorship of both writings. The Gospel was the authority for the Montanist claims regarding the Paraclete and for their own prophetic enthusiasm; Revelation was the authority for their millennial views. Gaius sought to discredit the Gospel of John by carefully noting its historical discrepancies and its contradictions of the synoptic Gospels. He did not challenge it on theological grounds. Irenaeus, whose work is treated below, was apparently the first to respond to Gaius (about A.D. 185).[87] In the course of his defense of the fourfold Gospel, he condemns both those who take away from the four Gospels and those who add to them. He did not mention Gaius by name, however—probably because of Gaius's reputation in the church. If Irenaeus was responding to others besides Gaius, we have no knowledge of them. The supposition that Irenaeus was responding to the Alogoi mentioned by Epiphanius, or any activity of such a group in Asia Minor, is not supported by the primary sources. Gaius's standing as a leader of the church at Rome shows that the authority of John and its apostolic authorship were not so firmly established (at least in Rome, from which we have the most evidence for the use of the Gospel in the mid–second century) that it could not be challenged by one of the scholars of the church.

Some years later (ca. 202–203) Gaius wrote down his arguments against Montanism in the form of a *Dialogue with Proclus*. In this treatise Gaius explained his rejection of the Gospel and Revelation on literary-historical grounds, arguing from such a basis that they could not be apostolic and that even Cerinthus had appealed to Revelation to establish his chiliastic views.

Hippolytus, also of Rome, was incensed by Gaius's attack on the apostolic authority of the Gospel and any hint that Revelation contained Cerinthian heresy. He immediately (ca. 204–205) wrote a *Defense of the Gospel of John and Revelation*. Still debated, however, is the question of whether Hippolytus wrote more than one apologetic work. Origen, Dionysius of Alexandria, and

Eusebius knew of Gaius's work. Epiphanius (who wrote ca. 374–376), how-ever, was dependent on Hippolytus. Epiphanius, therefore, coined the term "Alogoi" for those who rejected the Logos:

> Therefore the Alogoi claim, for this is the epithet which I myself am applying to them. For from now on then so will they be designated and thus, Beloved, let us apply (this) name to them, that is Alogoi. For indeed the heresy which they held is appropri-ately so called because it rejected the books of John. Since therefore they do not accept the Logos preached by John, they shall be called Alogoi.[88]

Epiphanius, therefore, had no independent knowledge of a group, either in Asia Minor or in Rome, who had rejected the Gospel of John. Rather, he labeled as "Alogoi" the views of Gaius which he learned of through Hippo-lytus.[89] Recent scholarship has therefore dismissed the Alogoi from the stage of history. We have no evidence of such a group. The figure of Gaius has emerged with greater clarity, however, and shows us that the authority of the Gospel of John was still quite tenuous up to the time of Irenaeus.[90]

Tatian

Tatian was a Syrian who converted to Christianity while studying philoso-phy in Rome and who later studied with Justin Martyr. Tatian is best known for his *Oration against the Greeks* and the Diatessaron, a harmony of the four Gospels which uses John for its framework of the life of Jesus. Both were probably written in Syria after the death of Justin. Whereas the one reference in Justin that may show knowledge of the Gospel of John is open to debate (see above), Tatian's use of John is certain. *Oration* 13.1 cites John 1:5 using an introductory formula which suggests that he regarded it as scripture.[91] The Gospel of John may also have influenced Tatian's concept of the Logos. The contrast between Justin's silence and Tatian's acceptance of John can be explained on the assumption that Justin was reluctant to use the Gospel because of its popularity among the Valentinians, while Tatian, whether because of the influence of the Valentinians or the growing acceptance of the Gospel,[92] had no such reservations.

Theophilus of Antioch

One other figure must be noted before we turn to Irenaeus. The first orthodox writer to identify John as the author of the Gospel of John—and evidently the apostle John, though he does not say so—appears to have been

Theophilus, bishop of Antioch (168–181, or 188), who wrote: "And hence the holy writings teach us, and all the spirit-bearing [inspired] men, one of whom, John, says, 'In the beginning was the Word, and the Word was with God.' "[93] Theophilus certainly has a high regard for the Gospel of John, a fact which could mean that it was accepted as scripture in Antioch earlier than in Rome. It has been suggested that Theophilus stops short of calling John scripture,[94] saying only that John was a spirit-bearer, like one of the prophets. Such an interpretation, however, forces a nuance that is not called for by Theophilus. Parenthetically, Eusebius later reported that Theophilus "quoted the Apocalypse of John" in a work entitled *Against the Heresy of Hermogenes.*[95]

Irenaeus

Irenaeus (ca. 130–200) is the most important champion of the Fourth Gospel in the second century. After Irenaeus, neither the authority of the Gospel as scripture nor its apostolic authorship were debated until modern scholarship began to challenge the latter. Born in Asia Minor, Irenaeus migrated to the West, where he became bishop of the church at Lyon following the martyrdom of Pothinus in A.D. 177. In addition to letters, some of which are preserved in quotations in Eusebius, Irenaeus wrote the *Demonstration of the Apostolic Preaching* and, around A.D. 185, *Against Heresies,* a much longer work comprising five books. In his writings Irenaeus sought to refute the heresies of Marcion, the Gnostics, the Montanists, and probably Gaius, all of which he encountered in Rome. Drawing on scripture and tradition, Irenaeus gave the church a powerful anti-Gnostic theological synthesis that spoke to such vital issues as God as Creator, the union of flesh and spirit in humanity, the "recapitulation" of God's relationship to humanity in Christ, and a defense of the fourfold Gospel.

As we have seen, there is ample evidence of the growing use and influence of the Gospel and the Epistles of John from the middle of the second century, especially among the Valentinians, but also among the Montanists and orthodox writers. Nevertheless, Irenaeus is the first writer to offer a defense of the apostolic authorship of the Gospel and Epistles, the first to claim that the Gospel was written in Ephesus, and the first to report that the apostle John lived to an old age in Ephesus. Irenaeus further contended that John wrote the Gospel to answer the errors of Cerinthus and the Nicolaitans.[96]

The credibility of Irenaeus's testimony, however, is vigorously debated.[97] Much depends on one's estimate of Irenaeus's sources and the tradition he received from Polycarp (ca. 70–156). Irenaeus's testimony is as follows. In the course of arguing that Jesus was baptized when he was thirty but lived to be nearly fifty (see John 8:56–57), Irenaeus claims: "Those who were conversant in Asia with John, the disciple of the Lord, [affirm] that John conveyed to them that information. And he remained among them up to the times of Trajan. Some of them, moreover, saw not only John, but the other apostles also, and heard the very same account from them. . . ."[98]

Several points need to be noted. First, while Irenaeus continues the practice of referring to John as "the disciple of the Lord," which is his customary term for John, we can hardly doubt that Irenaeus regarded this John of Asia, who "lived up to the times of Trajan," as the apostle John. In the next sentence Irenaeus speaks of John and "the other apostles also."[99] Irenaeus may here have reference to the testimony of Papias, but he shows no knowledge of a John the Elder who was not John the apostle. Second, it is also clear that Irenaeus, in seeking to harmonize John with the synoptics, created a false chronology of Jesus' ministry, contending for a ministry of some ten to twenty years in duration, from age thirty to between forty and fifty. Moreover, Irenaeus appealed to those who "were conversant with John" as the source of this tradition. Here he may have the testimony of Papias in mind. If so, he may have justified his appeal to Papias on the logic that the following are all true: the Gospel of John supplies data for such a chronology; the Gospel was written by the apostle; and Papias or Polycarp bears witness to the truth of the teaching of John, "the disciple of the Lord." If Irenaeus is dependent on Papias, then Irenaeus stands four steps from the apostle: Irenaeus, Papias, travelers who have followed the elders, the elders, and finally the apostles.[100]

At the beginning of the third book of *Against Heresies,* Irenaeus lists the four Gospels in their present canonical order, saying that John wrote after the other three: "Afterwards, John the disciple of the Lord, who also had leaned upon His breast, did himself publish a Gospel during his residence at Ephesus in Asia."[101] This statement makes it clear that Irenaeus identified the evangelist with both the Beloved Disciple mentioned in the Gospel and with the apostle. Irenaeus also speaks of the author of 1 and 2 John and Revelation as "John, the Lord's disciple."[102] There is no place in Irenaeus's understanding of the authorship of the Gospel for John the Elder. If the Elder was the evangelist, Irenaeus has misunderstood the tradition he received about the apostle and the origin of the Gospel.

Irenaeus also reports that he had heard Polycarp, the bishop of Smyrna, who visited Rome in the time of bishop Anicetus and was later martyred (ca. A.D. 156). Irenaeus claims that Polycarp was "instructed by apostles" and that Irenaeus himself, "in my early youth," had seen Polycarp:

> And Polycarp also was not only instructed by apostles and conversed with many who had seen the Lord, but was also appointed bishop by apostles in Asia in the church in Smyrna. We also saw him in our childhood, for he lived a long time and in extreme old age passed from life, a splendid and glorious martyr. He con-

stantly taught those things which he had learnt from the apostles, which also are the tradition of the church, which alone are true. To these facts all the churches in Asia bear witness, and the present successors of Polycarp, and he is a far more trustworthy and reliable witness of the truth than Valentinus and Marcion and the others who hold wrong opinions.[103]

Irenaeus continues: "There are also those who heard from him that John, the disciple of the Lord, going to bathe at Ephesus, and perceiving Cerinthus within, rushed out of the bath-house without bathing, exclaiming, 'Let us fly, lest even the bath-house fall down, because Cerinthus, the enemy of the truth is within.' "[104] The chapter concludes: "Then, again, the church in Ephesus, founded by Paul, and having John remaining among them permanently until the times of Trajan, is a true witness of the tradition of the apostles."[105]

In a letter to Florinus, quoted by Eusebius, Irenaeus tells the story of his association with Polycarp:

These opinions, O Florinus, that I may speak sparingly, do not belong to sound doctrine. These opinions are inconsistent with the church, and bring those who believe in them into the greatest impiety. These opinions not even the heretics outside the church ever dared to proclaim. These opinions those who were presbyters before us, they who accompanied the apostles, did not hand on to you. For while I was still a boy I knew you in lower Asia in Polycarp's house when you were a man of rank in the royal hall and endeavoring to stand well with him. I remember the events of those days more clearly than those which happened recently, for what we learn as children grows up with the soul and is united to it, so that I can speak even of the place in which the blessed Polycarp sat and disputed, how he came in and went out, the character of his life, the appearance of his body, the discourses which he made to the people, how he reported his intercourse with John and with others who had seen the Lord, how he remembered their words, and what were the things concerning the Lord which he had heard from them, and about their miracles, and about their teaching, and how Polycarp had received from the eyewitnesses of the word of life, and reported all things in agreement with the Scriptures. I listened eagerly even then to these things through the mercy of God which was given me, and made notes of them, not on paper but in my heart, and ever by the grace of God do I truly ruminate on them.[106]

In this excerpt from the letter, Irenaeus reminds Florinus of their common experience, sitting at the feet of Polycarp. His point is to remind Florinus that he did not learn his Gnostic views from Polycarp. Since he appeals to Florinus's memory of their shared experience, it is most unlikely that Irenaeus would have fabricated any of this. Presumably, Florinus's memory was as clear as Irenaeus's. On the other hand, Irenaeus does not say that Polycarp taught that the apostle John was the author of the Fourth Gospel, the Epistles, or Revelation.[107]

The issue of Polycarp's direct contact with the apostle John, or John the Elder, moreover, is called into question by the following considerations.[108] First, Irenaeus also claims that Papias said John had reported Jesus had told them that in the coming days every vine would have ten thousand branches, and every branch ten thousand twigs, and each twig ten thousand shoots, and each shoot ten thousand clusters, and on every cluster ten thousand grapes, and every grape when pressed would give twenty-five *metretes* of wine. The wheat and other plants would be equally bountiful, and the animals would live in harmony.[109] This description is not found in the New Testament but does appear in a pseudepigraphical writing from the late first century (2 Baruch 29.5). Evidently, Irenaeus accepted a spurious report of Jesus' teaching on the authority of Papias, who attributed it to John. In this context, Irenaeus claims: "And these things are borne witness to in writing by Papias, the hearer of John, and a companion of Polycarp, in his fourth book; for there were five books compiled by him."[110] Eusebius quotes these words, but immediately points out that Papias had no direct contact with the apostle: "So says Irenaeus. Yet Papias himself, according to the preface of his treatises, makes plain that he had in no way been a hearer and eyewitness of the sacred apostles. . . ."[111] Eusebius then quotes the passage from Papias discussed above.[112] While Irenaeus does not claim to have had direct contact with Papias, as he had with Polycarp, his acceptance of a spurious tradition on the basis of Papias's contact with the apostle raises the question of whether his understanding of Polycarp's relationship with the apostle is similarly distorted.

We have little independent evidence regarding Polycarp on which to judge this issue. A later life of Polycarp, attributed to Pionius,[113] which praises him as a saint and martyr, says nothing of his association with the apostle John. Had the author of this life of Polycarp known anything of the claim that Polycarp had been a disciple of the apostle, he would surely have included it to add further luster to his praise of the bishop of Smyrna. On the other hand, one can hardly use this author's silence on this point as positive evidence that no such traditions existed. The most we can say is that they were not part of the common tradition about Polycarp.

Finally, Polycarp's *Letter to the Philippians* says nothing about the apostle

John or the Gospel. Twice, Polycarp mentions Paul—both times, however, in the context of an allusion to Paul's letter(s) to the Philippians.[114] The *Letter to the Philippians* is brief, and there are no references to the other evangelists. On the other hand, the letter (7.1) cites 1 John 4:2–3; and/or 2 John 7, but says nothing about the apostle.[115] Had Polycarp been a disciple of the author of these letters, we would expect him to make some reference to his association with John; but he makes no such claim.

Irenaeus's testimony, therefore, remains an enigma—credible but not certain, substantial but open to suspicion at crucial points. Given the uncertainty of the evidence, exaggerated claims—either that John was used only by the Valentinians and Montanists before Irenaeus or that the authority of the Gospel was clearly established before Irenaeus—are out of place. The use of John by the *Epistula Apostolorum*, the Quartodecimans, Melito of Sardis, Tatian, and Theophilus of Antioch, when taken together, show that the Gospel was used widely between 150 and 180. On the other hand, the lack of earlier attestation, its popularity among the Valentinians and the Montanists, the tentative nature of many of the early allusions, and the rejection of the Gospel and Revelation by Gaius, a leader in the Roman church, when taken together, show that the authority of the Gospel was by no means certain at the time Irenaeus wrote. The status of the fourfold Gospel was still fluid: Marcion accepted only an edited version of Luke, the Valentinians added the Gospel of Truth, Tatian wove the four Gospels into one, and Gaius rejected the Fourth Gospel.

With Irenaeus, however, the battle for the fourfold Gospel was won. The authority of the Gospel of John as scripture was never again in question.[116] The question remains, however: how secure is Irenaeus's report of the tradition of the apostolic authorship of the Gospel in Ephesus? On this point, the silence of the first three quarters of the second century and the slowness with which John was accepted by the church make it difficult to believe that the Gospel was composed so late (90–100), from a source so close to Jesus, in a cosmopolitan center so well connected with other churches. What we have instead is the story of the growing authority of a Gospel on the basis of its content. Accounts of its apostolic origin arose only after it was widely accepted as an authoritative writing. The claim of apostolic authorship is evidence that the Gospel's authority had been widely accepted, not vice versa. If not entirely original with Irenaeus, therefore, the coalescing of the traditional view that the Gospel of John was of apostolic authorship—written by the apostle John, who was also the Beloved Disciple, the elder, and the seer of the apocalypse—owes a great deal to Irenaeus's interpretation of the tradition he used in his defense of the Gospel of John as an orthodox, apostolic writing.

About the time of Irenaeus and shortly thereafter, the authority of the Gospel is widely attested. The Bodmer Papyrus p[66] contains the Gospel of

John in book form and is remarkably well preserved. Being dated about A.D. 200, it is the earliest manuscript to contain the superscription "Gospel according to John."[117] P[72] and p[75] (early third century) also contain the same superscription.[118]

Polycrates of Ephesus

Polycrates, bishop of Ephesus (189–198), reflects further developments in the legends about John in his letter to Pope Victor:

> For great luminaries sleep in Asia, and they will rise again at the last day of the advent of the Lord, when he shall come with glory from heaven and call back all the saints, such as was Philip, one of the twelve apostles, who sleeps at Hierapolis with his two daughters who grew old as virgins and his third daughter who lived in the Holy Spirit and rests in Ephesus. And there is also John, who leaned on the Lord's breast, who was a priest wearing the mitre [or sacerdotal plate, Greek *petalon;* cf. Exod. 28:15–30], and martyr and teacher, and he sleeps at Ephesus.[119]

This is the only report that John was a priest,[120] a curious note since the New Testament makes no such claim. Some have linked this tradition with John 18:15, suggesting that the other disciple, who was known to the family of the high priest, was John, the Beloved Disciple. Acts 4:6 mentions a priest by the name of John from the family of the high priest, but if this is the source of the tradition that John was priest, the tradition has no basis in history. The excerpt from Polycrates confuses Philip and his daughters (Acts 6:5; 8:5–40; 21:8–9) with the apostle Philip (Mark 3:18; John 1:43; 6:5ff.; 12:21–22; 14:8–9). Nevertheless, it is still noteworthy that Polycrates does not call John an apostle, that he mentions Philip the apostle first, and does not say that John wrote the Gospel. He does, however, identify John with the Beloved Disciple, so we may assume that he and Pope Victor connected John the apostle with the author of the Gospel.[121] We are now, after all, in the decade following Irenaeus.

Muratorian Canon

The *Muratorian Canon* (named after Muratori, who discovered it in 1740), was once generally accepted as a crude Latin translation of a Greek text that originated in Rome about 180–200. Now assigned by some scholars to the fourth century and an eastern provenance,[122] the *Muratorian Canon* reports that the Gospel was written by John, at the urging of his fellow-disciples, and that divine revelation directed that it should bear John's name:

The fourth of the Gospels, that of John, (one) of the disciples. When his fellow-disciples and bishops urged him, he said: Fast with me from today for three days, and what will be revealed to each one let us relate to one another. In the same night it was revealed to Andrew, one of the apostles, that whilst all were to go over (it), John in his own name should write everything down. And therefore, though various rudiments (or "tendencies"?) are taught in the several Gospel books, yet that matters nothing for the faith of believers, since by the one and guiding (original?) Spirit everything is declared in all.[123]

The *Muratorian Canon* also refers to the Epistles: "being thus always true to himself, [John] adduces particular points in his epistles also where he says of himself: What we have seen with our eyes and have heard with our ears and our hands handled, that have we written to you." Later, the *Muratorian Canon* claims two (not three) letters of John are accepted as scripture. John is also called Paul's predecessor and the author of Revelation, with its seven letters.

These references to John and the origin of the Gospel, which evidently respond to charges of discrepancies between John and the other Gospels, may well be calculated to respond to the criticism of Gaius.[124] The Gospel is to be accepted as the work of John the apostle, who wrote by divine revelation, and the Gospel was checked by the other disciples. The apologetic function of this legend could hardly be more clear.[125]

The Oldest Gospel Prologues

For reasons of convenience if not chronology, the witness of the oldest Gospel prologues may be considered at this point. The so-called "anti-Marcionite" prologue to John reads:

> The Gospel of John was revealed and given to the church by John while he was yet in the body as one Papias of Hierapolis, a dear disciple of John, has reported in the five books of his "exoterics" [that is, in the last ones]. Indeed, he took down the gospel word for word while John was dictating. But the heretic Marcion was cast out by John after having been disapproved by him because of his opposite opinions. Marcion had, however, carried to John writings or letters from the brethren who dwelt in Pontus.[126]

Some historical review is necessary in order to evaluate the significance of this text. In 1928, Donatien de Bruyne published a study of the Gospel prologues he had collected from various medieval manuscripts. The oldest manuscript to contain the prologue to John (quoted above) dates from the eighth century. Nevertheless, de Bruyne argued that both the prologue to John and the extant prologues to Mark and Luke were anti-Marcionite prologues to the four Gospels which were composed by the same hand, in Rome, during the second century.[127] His thesis attracted even more attention when it was endorsed by Adolf Harnack, the greatest living authority on Christian origins, who assigned them to the period of 160–180, maintaining that they predate Irenaeus.[128] On the basis of the thesis of de Bruyne and Harnack, we have a Roman text from 160–180 which affirms Papias's acknowledgment that he wrote down the Gospel as John had dictated it to him and that he, and subsequently John himself, had rejected Marcion, who carried letters (of commendation?) from the church in Pontus to John. The condemnation of Marcion is clearly anachronistic but may have been connected in some way with Tertullian's claim that Marcion had already been condemned in John's Gospel and letters.[129] In a corruption of a report that Marcion met with the elders of Asia, the Codex Toletanus—a late Spanish manuscript containing prologues to the Gospel of John—actually reports a meeting between Marcion and the apostle John![130]

J. B. Lightfoot had suggested in 1889 that "Papias may have quoted the Gospel 'delivered by John to the churches, which *they* wrote down from his lips' (*ho apegrapson apo tou stomatos autou*); and some later writer, mistaking the ambiguous *apegrapson* [which can mean either "they wrote" or "I wrote"], interpreted it, 'I wrote down,' thus making Papias himself the amanuensis."[131] And in one of the curious anomalies of scholarship, Robert Eisler later suggested that the original text read that John dictated the Gospel to Marcion![132]

More recent scholarship has challenged each of the main tenets of the thesis of de Bruyne and Harnack: (1) that the prologues came from a common hand, (2) that they are anti-Marcionite, (3) that they can be traced to the second century, and (4) that they furnish historically credible testimony to the origin of the Gospel of John and to the second-century tradition.[133] Had Papias made anything like these assertions, Irenaeus or Eusebius, who had his work, would surely have quoted them. The so-called "anti-Marcionite" prologue is now being assigned to the period between the fourth and the sixth centuries, and hence to a later stage in the development of the legends about John.

The prologue to Luke—which R. G. Heard assigns to the third century but allows that it may contain "earlier and very valuable biographical material"[134]—adds that after he wrote his Gospel, "Luke wrote the Acts of the Apostles; and later John the apostle of the Twelve wrote the Apocalypse in the island of Patmos and after this the Gospel."[135] This note affirms that Revelation is of apostolic authorship and that it was written before the Gospel, a view that many still find attractive.

CONCLUSION

One of the remarkable items in the history of the traditions about John is the nearly complete silence of the record during the crucial decades of the early second century. If one or more of the Johannine writings was authored by the apostle, or if they emerged from an influential school associated with a cluster of communities in Asia Minor, then why is there such a gap in the record so soon after the composition of these works?

In view of the sparsity of evidence, the role of Papias becomes all the more important. Did Papias have direct contact with either John the apostle or John the Elder in Asia Minor? Apparently not. In chapter 6, we will examine the evidence that Papias reported John had suffered martyrdom along with his brother, James.

Justin Martyr came to Rome from Ephesus and frequently refers to the Gospels, but if he used the Fourth Gospel at all, he did so without citing it directly. Justin may have known the Gospel, but he never refers to its authorship, never discusses the work of the apostle, does not link the Gospel with Ephesus, and evidently chose not to cite the Gospel in his writings. On the other hand, Justin does claim that the Apocalypse was written by the apostle John, thereby linking the apostle with Asia Minor.

The earliest use of the Gospel is found not among orthodox Christians but among the Valentinian Gnostics (Ptolemy, Heracleon, Theodotus). Not surprisingly, therefore, the first claim of apostolic authorship is also preserved in the writings of Ptolemy. The evidence suggests that the pivotal developments for the later tradition were related to the growing acceptance of the Gospel by orthodox Christians in Rome. Here the central figures in the drama are Valentinus and his followers, Justin, Tatian, Gaius, and finally Irenaeus.

Attribution of the Gospel to the apostle emerges from the data only when and where the Gospel itself is accepted. Sources that can be traced to the period of 150–180 indicate increasingly widespread acceptance of the Gospel during these decades (in the *Epistula Apostolorum* and by the Quartodecimans, Melito of Sardis, Tatian, and Theophilus). The claim of apostolic authorship, therefore, seems to have functioned as apologetic for the use of the Gospel where it had already found acceptance. With Irenaeus, this tradition took the decisive step toward the dominance it would enjoy in later church tradition. Irenaeus defended the fourfold Gospel and the apostolic authorship of the Gospel, 1 and 2 John, and Revelation as well.

Decisive moments in the growth of the tradition are the identification of John the seer as the apostle (Justin); the claim that the Gospel was written by the apostle John (Ptolemy, Theophilus, and Irenaeus); the acceptance of 1 and 2 John as apostolic (Irenaeus also), and finally identification of the elder of 2 and 3 John as the apostle (at least by the time of Jerome, and possibly as early as Origen).

By the end of the second century, therefore, the place of the apostle John as the author of the five canonical books that bear his name was well established. The claim of apostolic authorship not only established the authority of the Gospel, however; it also contributed to the authority of those who defended it. A lineage of legitimacy was created: the truth was passed from Jesus to the apostles, to the elders, to Papias, Polycarp, and Irenaeus. The credibility of the synthesis maintaining the direct apostolic authority of the five books was challenged in one respect or another by Gaius, Dionysius, and Eusebius, but it nevertheless prevailed and became the tradition of the church. Succeeding generations would embellish legends about the apostle and supply stories of the wonders that had occurred at his hands. To these fascinating stories we may now turn our attention.

NOTES

1. C. K. Barrett, *The Gospel According to St. John,* 2d ed. (Philadelphia: Westminster Press, 1978), 104.
2. Kurt Aland and Barbara Aland, *The Text of the New Testament,* trans. E. F. Rhodes (Grand Rapids: Wm. B. Eerdmans, 1987), 85. See also Leon Vaganay, *An Introduction to New Testament Textual Criticism,* 2d ed., rev. and ed. C.-B. Amphoux, trans. J. Heimerdinger (Cambridge: Cambridge University Press, 1991), 98.
3. For recent arguments regarding the dating of Papyrus Egerton 2 and p[52], see Helmut Koester, *Ancient Christian Gospels: Their History and Development* (Philadelphia: Trinity Press International, 1990), 205–7; Andreas Schmidt, "Zwei Anmerkungen zu P. Ryl. III 457," *Archiv für Papyrusforschung* 35 (1989): 11f.; Dieter Lührmann, "Das neue Fragment des PEgerton 2 (PKöln 255)," in *The Four Gospels 1992: Festschrift for Frans Neirynck,* ed. F. Van Segbroek et al. Bibliotheca ephemeridum theologicarum lovaniensium 100 (Leuven: University Press, 1992), 2239–55. Dieter Lührmann kindly supplied these references in a personal letter, May 5, 1992.
4. Ignatius, *Ephesians* 12.2; *Apostolic Fathers,* trans. Kirsopp Lake, LCL (Cambridge, Mass.: Harvard University Press, 1912), 1:187.
5. Ignatius, *Ephesians* 7.2, 18.2, 19.1; *Apostolic Fathers, LCL,* 1:181, 191–93.
6. See Christian Maurer, *Ignatius von Antiochien und das Johannesevangelium,* ATANT 18 (Zurich: Zwingli Verlag, 1949); Ernst Haenchen, *John,* trans. and ed. Robert W. Funk, Hermeneia (Philadelphia: Fortress Press, 1984), 1:7.
7. Irenaeus, *Adv. Haer.* 5.33.4 (*ANF* 1:563); Eusebius, *E.H.* 3.39.1 (*Eusebius: The Ecclesiastical History,* trans. Kirsopp Lake, LCL [Cambridge, Mass.: Harvard University Press, 1926], 1:291).
8. Eusebius, *E.H.* 3.39.3–4 (LCL 1:291–93).
9. Eusebius, *E.H.* 3.39.6 (LCL 1:293).
10. Stephen Smalley, for example, maintains that there was only one John; see *John:*

Evangelist and Interpreter (Greenwood, S.C.: Attic Press, 1978), 73–74. See also the extended discussion in François-Marie Braun, *Jean le théologien* (Paris: J. Gabalda, 1959), 1:357–64.

11. Barrett, *The Gospel According to St. John,* 107.

12. B. W. Bacon's insistence on this point is salutary even though there is little reason to follow him in identifying John the Elder with the John who appears in Hegesippus' list of fifteen "bishops of Jerusalem," as Bacon proposed; see "The Elder John in Jerusalem," *ZNW* 26 (1927): 194. Bacon's writings on the elder are numerous: "Date and Habitat of the Elders of Papias," *ZNW* 12 (1911): 176–87; "The Elder John, Papias, Irenaeus, Eusebius and the Syriac Translator," *JBL* 27 (1908): 1–23; "The Elder of Ephesus and the Elder John," *HibJ* 26 (1927): 112–34; *The Fourth Gospel in Research and Debate* (London: T. Fisher Unwin, 1910); "John and the Pseudo-Johns," *ZNW* 31 (1932): 132–50; "The Mythical 'Elder John' of Ephesus," *HibJ* 29 (1931): 312–26.

13. Wilhelm Larfeld, "Das Zeugnis des Papias über die beiden Johannes von Ephesus," in *Johannes und sein Evangelium,* ed. K. H. Rengstorf (Darmstadt: Wissenschaftliche Buchgesellschaft, 1973), 392.

14. G. H. Dix, "The Use and Abuse of Papias on the Fourth Gospel," *Theology* 24 (1932): 10.

15. Martin Hengel, *The Johannine Question,* trans. John Bowden (Philadelphia: Trinity Press International, 1989), 17–21.

16. Robert M. Grant (*Second-Century Christianity: A Collection of Fragments* [London: S.P.C.K., 1946], 65) accepts the reference to John 14:2 in Irenaeus, *Adv. Haer.* 5.36.1, 2 (*ANF* 1:567), as a quotation of the Gospel by Papias, but Irenaeus says only "as the presbyters say. . . . "

17. Eusebius, *E.H.* 3.39.17 (LCL 1:299).

18. Hengel, *The Johannine Question,* 16.

19. Corderius, Introduction to *Catena Patrum Graecorum in Sanctum Joannem ex Antiquissimo Graeco Codice MS. nunc primum in lucem edita* (Antwerp, 1630); cited in Christoph Ernst Luthardt, *St. John the Author of the Fourth Gospel,* rev. and trans. Caspar Rene Gregory (Edinburgh: T. and T. Clark, 1875), 73. Papias is also identified as John's scribe in the anti-Marcionite prologue, quoted above, p. 129.

20. Eusebius, *E.H.* 4.18.6 (LCL 1:371); cf. Justin Martyr, *Dialogue with Trypho* 2 (*ANF* 1:195).

21. T. W. Manson, "The Fourth Gospel," in *Studies in the Gospels and Epistles,* ed. M. Black (Manchester: The University Press, 1962), 111.

22. Justin Martyr, *Dial.* 81 (*ANF* 1:240); cf. Eusebius, *E.H.* 4.18.8 (LCL 1:371–73).

23. Justin Martyr, *First Apology* 66.3 (*ANF* 1:185).

24. James Drummond, *An Inquiry into the Character and Authorship of the Fourth Gospel* (London: Williams and Norgate, 1903), 100.

25. Edgar J. Goodspeed, *Die ältesten Apologeten* (Göttingen: Vandenhoeck and Ruprecht, 1914), 378.

26. Drummond, *An Inquiry,* 149.

27. See Helmut Koester, "History and Cult in the Gospel of John and in Ignatius," *JTC* 1 (1965): 118; and Koester, *Ancient Christian Gospels,* 361.

28. See Drummond, *An Inquiry,* 158–62; D. M. Davey, "Justin Martyr and the Fourth Gospel," *Scripture* 17 (1965): 117–22; J. N. Sanders, *The Fourth Gospel in the Early Church: Its Origin and Influence on Christian Theology up to Irenaeus* (Cambridge: Cambridge University Press, 1943), 31; L. W. Barnard, *Justin Martyr: His Life and Thought* (Cambridge: Cambridge University Press, 1967), 61–62; Hengel, *The Johannine Question,* 13.

29. See Ernestus Lippelt, *Quae Fuerint Justini Martyris Apomnemoneumata Quaque Ratione cum Forma Evangeliorum Syro-Latina Cohaeserint* (Halis Saxonum: E. Karras, 1901), p. 35; cited by A. J. Bellinzoni, *The Sayings of Jesus in the Writings of Justin Martyr,* NovTSup 17 (Leiden: E. J. Brill, 1967), p. 2 n.2.

30. See Melvyn R. Hillmer, "The Gospel of John in the Second Century" (Th.D. diss., Harvard Divinity School, 1966), 58; Bellinzoni, *The Sayings of Jesus in the Writings of Justin Martyr,* 136–37; Koester, *Ancient Christian Gospels,* 257–58; Leslie L. Kline, *The Sayings of Jesus in the Pseudo-Clementine Homilies,* SBLDS 14 (Missoula, Mont.: Scholars Press, 1975), 135–36; J. J. Gunther, "Early Identifications of Authorship of the Johannine Writings," *JEH* 31 (1980): 409. Cf. Eric F. Osborn, *Justin Martyr,* BHT 47 (Tübingen: J. C. B. Mohr, 1973), 137–38.

31. Hengel, *The Johannine Question,* 13.

32. See E. R. Goodenough, *The Theology of Justin Martyr* (Jena: Verlag Fromman-nsche Buchhandlung, 1923), 172–75.

33. J. N. Sanders asserts: "The most reasonable conclusion from this examination of the passages from the writings of Justin which appear to show traces of the influence of the Fourth Gospel seems to be that on the whole one may say that certain passages are most naturally explained as reminiscences of the Fourth Gospel, while there are few, if any, which can certainly be said to be dependent upon it. It is therefore going further than the evidence warrants to say that the theology of Justin is based upon the teaching of the Fourth Gospel. Justin's writings illustrate rather the first tentative use which was made of the Fourth Gospel by an orthodox writer, and this tentativeness makes it difficult to believe that Justin regarded the Fourth Gospel as Scripture or as the work of an apostle" (*The Fourth Gospel in the Early Church,* 31).

34. Hillmer, "The Gospel of John in the Second Century," 132–35.

35. Bentley Layton, *The Gnostic Scriptures* (Garden City: Doubleday, 1987), 217.

36. See Gerd Lüdemann, "Zur Geschichte des ältesten Christentums in Rom: I. Valentin und Marcion, II. Ptolemäus und Justin," *ZNW,* 70 (1979): 86–114.

37. Justin Martyr, *Dial.* 35 (*ANF* 1:212).

38. Layton, *The Gnostic Scriptures,* 267.

39. Layton, *The Gnostic Scriptures,* 272.

40. See Walther Völker, *Quellen zur Geschichte der christlichen Gnosis,* SAQ, n.F. 5 (Tübingen: J. C. B. Mohr, 1932), esp. fragments 4, 6, 7; see also Hengel, *The Johannine Question,* 146 n. 43.

41. Tertullian, *On Prescription against Heretics* 38 (*ANF* 3:262).

42. Drummond writes: "If, therefore, Tertullian was correctly informed, we must concede that Valentinus made use of the Fourth Gospel" (*An Inquiry,* 269).

43. Irenaeus, *Adv. Haer.* 3.11.9 (*ANF* 1:429).

44. See W. C. van Unnik, "The 'Gospel of Truth' and the New Testament," in *The Jung Codex: A Newly Recovered Gnostic Papyrus*, trans. and ed. F. L. Cross (London: A. R. Mowbray, 1955), esp. 115; Layton, *The Gnostic Scriptures*, 251; Harold W. Attridge and George W. MacRae, S.J., "The Gospel of Truth," in *Nag Hammadi Codex I (The Jung Codex)*, ed. H. W. Attridge, NHS 22 (Leiden: E. J. Brill, 1985), 80; Schnackenburg, *John* 1:146–48; Braun, *Jean le théologien*, 1: 113–33; see also C. K. Barrett, "The Theological Vocabulary of the Fourth Gospel and the Gospel of Truth," in *Current Issues in New Testament Interpretation: Essays in Honor of Otto A. Piper*, ed. W. Klassen and G. F. Snyder (New York: Harper and Row, 1962), 210–24.

45. Gilles Quispel, "The Jung Codex and Its Significance," in *The Jung Codex*, 50; Layton, *The Gnostic Scriptures*, 251; Harold W. Attridge and George W. MacRae, "The Gospel of Truth (I,3 and XII,2)," in *The Nag Hammadi Library*, 2d ed., ed. James M. Robinson (San Francisco: Harper and Row, 1988), 38; Attridge and MacRae, "The Gospel of Truth," *Nag Hammadi Codex I*, 79.

46. See the helpful list of parallels in Rudolf Schnackenburg, *The Gospel According to St. John*, trans. Kevin Smyth, HTCNT (New York: Herder and Herder, 1968), 1:194; and Barrett, *John*, 114.

47. Irenaeus, *Adv. Haer.* 1.8.5 (*ANF* 1:328). Epiphanius, *Panarion* 31.27.1, quotes this section of Irenaeus in his refutation of the Valentinians. For an informative discussion of Ptolemy's contribution to the development of the Valentinian interpretation of the Gospel of John, see Jean-Daniel Kaestli, "L'exégèse valentienne du quatrième évangile," in *La communauté johannique et son histoire*, ed. Jean-Daniel Kaestli, Jean-Michel Poffet, and Jean Zumstein, Le monde de la Bible (Geneva: Labor et Fides, 1990), 323–50.

48. For the text, see *ANF* 1:328. See also Werner Foerster, *Gnosis: A Selection of Gnostic Texts*, trans. and ed. R. McL. Wilson (Oxford: Clarendon Press, 1972), 1:144; and Layton, *The Gnostic Scriptures*, 300.

49. John 1:3; Epiphanius, *Panarion* 33.3.5; for the English translation see Layton, *The Gnostic Scriptures*, 308.

50. Justin Martyr, *Second Apology* 2 (*ANF* 1:189). This identification is accepted, for example, by Gerd Lüdemann in "Zur Geschichte des ältesten Christentums in Rom," 114.

51. See Heracleon, *The Fragments of Heracleon*, ed. A. E. Brooke, TextsS, vol. 1, no. 4 (Cambridge: Cambridge University Press, 1891); Robert M. Grant, *Gnosticism* (New York: Harper and Brothers, 1961), 195–208; Grant, *Second-Century Christianity*, 39–52; Elaine H. Pagels, *The Johannine Gospel in Gnostic Exegesis: Heracleon's Commentary on John*, SBLMS 17 (Nashville: Abingdon Press, 1973). For an assessment of the significance of Heracleon's work, see Kaestli, "L'exégèse valentienne du quatrième évangile," 349–50.

52. Clement of Alexandria, *Stromata* 4.9 (*ANF* 2:422).

53. Origen, *Commentary on John* 2.8 (*ANF* 10:331).

54. Heracleon, *The Fragments of Heracleon*, 33–34.

55. Irenaeus, *Adv. Haer.* 2.4.1 (*ANF* 1:363); Tertullian, *Against the Valentinians* 4 (*ANF* 3:505).

56. Hillmer, "The Gospel of John in the Second Century," 97; and François Sagnard, trans., *Clément d'Alexandrie, Extraits de Théodote* (Paris: Éditions du Cerf, 1948), 7.
57. Kaestli, "L'exégèse valentinienne du quatrième évangile," 340–41.
58. Hillmer, "The Gospel of John in the Second Century," 106.
59. *Refutation* 5.6.3–5.11.1, 10.9.1–3 (*ANF* 5.1.5). See also Foerster, *Gnosis* 1:263–82; and Grant, *Gnosticism,* 105–15.
60. Edgar Hennecke, *New Testament Apocrypha,* ed. Wilhelm Schneemelcher, trans. R. McL. Wilson (Philadelphia: Westminster Press, 1963), 1:330.
61. Irenaeus, *Adv. Haer.* 1.29.1–4 (*ANF* 1:353–54); for the English translation see also Layton, *The Gnostic Scriptures,* 166–69.
62. Layton, *The Gnostic Scriptures,* 28–29.
63. See Eric Junod and Jean-Daniel Kaestli, *Acta Iohannis,* CChr (Turnhout: Brepols: 1983), 2:581–677, esp. 627–32; and Jean-Daniel Kaestli, "Le mystère de la croix de lumière et le johannisme. Actes de Jean ch. 94–102," *Foi et Vie* 86 (1987): 35–46, esp. 45–46. On the *Acts of John,* see below, p. 187.
64. M. Hornschuh, "The Apostles as Bearers of the Tradition," in Hennecke, *New Testament Apocrypha* 2:81–82.
65. Hillmer, "The Gospel of John in the Second Century," 143–44.
66. See Hillmer, "The Gospel of John in the Second Century," 86–96.
67. Pheme Perkins, "Johannine Traditions in *Ap. Jas.* (NHC 1, 2)," *JBL* 101 (1982): 403–14.
68. Ron Cameron, *Sayings Traditions in the Apocryphon of James* (Philadelphia: Fortress, 1984), esp. 130.
69. Eusebius, *E.H.* 3.39.17 (LCL 1:299).
70. See Brown, *The Epistles of John,* 8–9.
71. For recent work on the traditions and setting of the *Epistula Apostolorum,* see Julian Hills, *Tradition and Composition in the Epistula Apostolorum,* HDR 24 (Minneapolis: Fortress Press, 1990).
72. *Epistula Apostolorum* 3/John 1:13, 14; *Ep. Ap.* 14, 39/John 1:14.
73. *Ep. Ap.* 18/John 13:34.
74. *Ep. Ap.* 29.
75. *Ep. Ap.* 5/John 2:1. See Hennecke, *New Testament Apocrypha* 1:189–227; and Hillmer, "The Gospel of John in the Second Century," 28–41.
76. Hillmer, "The Gospel of John in the Second Century," 41–46.
77. Epiphanius, *Panarion* 30.13.1, in Williams, *The Panarion,* 129. See also Hillmer, "The Gospel of John in the Second Century," 47–48.
78. Eusebius, *E.H.* 5.24.16 (LCL 1:511).
79. See Othmar Perler, *Méliton de Sardes: Sur la Pâque et fragments* (Paris: Éditions du Cerf, 1966), 244–47; Hengel, *The Johannine Question,* 4.
80. Stuart G. Hall, *Melito of Sardis: On Pascha and Fragments* (Oxford: Clarendon Press, 1979), xii.
81. See the list of parallels compiled in Hengel, *The Johannine Question,* 141 n. 16.
82. See below. Cf. Eusebius, *E.H.* 5.24.2–6 (LCL 1:505–7). See also Hall, *Melito,* xi and 43 n. 34.

83. Hippolytus, *Refutation of All Heresies* 8.12 (*ANF* 5:123); Eusebius, *E.H.* 5.16.17 (LCL 1:481).

84. Cited in Tertullian, *Adv. Prax.* 8 (*ANF* 3:603). See also Gunther, "Early Identifications," 410–11; Gunther's statement that "the creation of a Johannine Asian myth started with Montanism" is surely an exaggeration, but it is hardly to be doubted that along with the Valentinians the Montanists contributed to the attribution of the Johannine writings to the apostle John.

85. Williston Walker et al., *A History of the Christian Church,* 4th ed. (New York: Charles Scribner's Sons, 1985), 69–70.

86. In this area, I am guided by the definitive study by Joseph Daniel Smith, Jr., "Gaius and the Controversy over the Johannine Literature" (Ph.D. diss., Yale University, 1979).

87. Irenaeus, *Adv. Haer.* 3.11.9 (*ANF* 1:429).

88. Epiphanius, *Panarion* 51.3.1–3. See further Joseph Daniel Smith, "Gaius and the Controversy over the Johannine Literature," 217–18.

89. See Joseph Daniel Smith, "Gaius and the Controversy over the Johannine Literature," 206–62, esp. 259.

90. See Hengel, *The Johannine Question,* 2–6, who—apparently without access to Joseph Daniel Smith's dissertation—diminishes the significance of Irenaeus's defense of the Gospel.

91. See Hillmer, "The Gospel of John in the Second Century," 75–76.

92. See Irenaeus, *Adv. Haer.* 1.28 (*ANF* 1:353).

93. Theophilus, *Ad Autolycum* 2.22 (*ANF* 2:103).

94. Hillmer, "The Gospel of John in the Second Century," 82–84.

95. Eusebius, *E.H.* 4.24 (LCL 1:385).

96. Irenaeus, *Adv. Haer.* 3.11.1 (*ANF* 1:426).

97. Cf., for example, Barrett, *John,* 100–25, 132–33; and Hengel, *The Johannine Question,* 2–4.

98. Irenaeus, *Adv. Haer.* 2.22.5 (*ANF* 1:392).

99. Irenaeus, *Adv. Haer.* 1.9.2 (*ANF* 1:329).

100. See above, p. 110.

101. Irenaeus, *Adv. Haer.* 3.1.1 (*ANF* 1:414); cf. Eusebius, *E.H.* 5.8.4. (LCL 1:455).

102. Irenaeus, *Adv. Haer.* 1.16.3 (*ANF* 1:342), 4.20.11 (*ANF* 1:491).

103. Irenaeus, *Adv. Haer.* 3.3.4 (*ANF* 1:416); Eusebius, *E.H.* 4.14.3–4 (LCL 1:337).

104. Irenaeus, *Adv. Haer.* 3.3.4 (*ANF* 1:416); Eusebius, *E.H.* 3.28.6, 4.14.6 (LCL 1:265, 337).

105. Irenaeus, *Adv. Haer.* 3.3.4 (*ANF* 1:416); Eusebius, *E.H.* 3.23.4 (LCL 1:243).

106. Eusebius, *E.H.* 5.20.5–7 (LCL 1:497–99).

107. For Irenaeus's attribution of the Apocalypse to John, see *Adv. Haer.* 5.30.1 (*ANF* 1:558); and Eusebius, *E.H.* 5.8.5–6 (LCL 1:457).

108. See Barrett, *John,* 105.

109. Irenaeus, *Adv. Haer.* 5.33.3 (*ANF* 1:562).

110. Irenaeus, *Adv. Haer.* 5.33.4 (*ANF* 1:563).

111. Eusebius, *E.H.* 3.39.2 (LCL 1:291).

112. See above, p. 109.

113. See J. B. Lightfoot, *The Apostolic Fathers,* 2d ed. (London: Macmillan, 1889), 3:423–68 (introduction and Greek text); 488–506 (translation). See also Lightfoot's discussion of Polycarp, 433–75.

114. Polycarp, *Letter to the Philippians* 3.2; 11.3 (*Apostolic Fathers,* LCL, 1:287, 297).

115. See above, p. 92.

116. A group of "Alogoi" known to Epiphanius may have challenged the authority of the Gospel of John, but on this, see above, pp. 121–22.

117. See Aland and Aland, *The Text of the New Testament,* 87 and 89, plate 22.

118. Aland and Aland, *The Text of the New Testament,* 91, plate 24.

119. Cited in Eusebius, *E.H.* 3.31.3 (LCL 1:271) and 5.24.1–3 (LCL 1:505).

120. Robert Eisler, *The Enigma of the Fourth Gospel: Its Author and Its Writer* (London: Methuen, 1938), 55, cites Hippolytus's *Odes on All the Scriptures* in Parisian Codex Coislin 195, which calls John "a high priest at Ephesus and prophet." Eisler argues that the John of Ephesus to whom Polycrates refers was the John mentioned in Acts 4:6, who belonged to the priestly family (39–45).

121. See Hengel, *The Johannine Question,* 7.

122. See A. C. Sundberg, Jr., "Canon Muratori: A Fourth-Century List," *HTR* 66 (1973): 1–41; and Sundberg, "Muratorian Fragment," in *IDBSup* (Nashville: Abingdon, 1976), 609–10.

123. *Muratorian Canon,* in Hennecke, *New Testament Apocrypha* 1:43–45; and *ANF* 5:603.

124. See above, pp. 120–22.

125. See, however, Alexander Faure, "Das 4. Evangelium im muratorischen Fragment," *ZST* 19 (1942): 143–49.

126. Haenchen, *John* 1:17. See also Robert M. Grant, "The Oldest Gospel Prologues," *ATR* 23 (1941): 241–42; R. G. Heard, "The Oldest Gospel Prologues," *JTS* n.s. 6 (April 1955): 11.

127. Donatien de Bruyne, "Les plus anciens prologues latins des évangiles," *RBén* 40 (1928): 193–214.

128. Adolf von Harnack, "Die ältesten Evangelien-Prologe und die Bildung des Neuen Testaments," in *SPAW,* Philosophisch-historische Klasse 24 (Berlin: G. Reimer, 1928), 322–41, esp. 335.

129. Tertullian, *On the Flesh of Christ* 3 (*ANF* 3:523); *On Prescription against Heretics* 33 (*ANF* 3:259). See also W. F. Howard, "TheAnti-Marcionite Prologues to the Gospels," *ExpTim* 47 (1935–1936): 537.

130. B. W. Bacon, "Marcion, Papias, and 'the Elders,'" *JTS* 23 (1921–1922): 139–40.

131. J. B. Lightfoot, *Essays on Supernatural Religion* (1889), 214; cited in Howard, "The Anti-Marcionite Prologues," 537.

132. Eisler, *The Enigma of the Fourth Gospel,* 161–62.

133. See Heard, "The Oldest Gospel Prologues"; Jürgen Regul, *Die antimarcionitischen Evangelienprologue,* Vetus Latina, die Reste der altlateinischen Bibel: AGLB 6 (Freiburg: Verlag Herder, 1969); Haenchen, *John* 1:17.

134. Heard, "The Oldest Gospel Prologues," 11.

135. Cited by Heard, "The Oldest Gospel Prologues," 7.

CHAPTER 6

Saint
The Eagle Soars

Saints . . . die to the world only to rise to a more intense life. . . .

Lynn M. Poland, *"The New Criticism, Neoorthodoxy, and the New Testament"*

The "more intense life" of the apostle John is manifested in various forms through the scholars of the Western Church, the Greek Church, and Syrian Christianity. Inevitably, the legends about John took on a life and vitality of their own—a tangibility that is barely evident to us from the fragments that have survived. Here and there, we can hear snatches of the legends in passing references, purportedly historical traditions, martyrologies, allusions to earlier sources, later apocryphal documents, and collections of ancient lore. From each source, we hear parts of the story, but the threads that hold it together and that could provide continuity are missing. The effect, therefore, is that of viewing slides or stills rather than a motion picture. The evidence is there, and sometimes in vivid colors, but we are aware that we are seeing only a small fraction of the story and missing more of it than we are grasping.

This chapter follows a roughly chronological scheme, moving from the Western to the Greek Church, and then to the medieval sources, as we trace the life of the legend from the early church through the Middle Ages.

TERTULLIAN

Tertullian (ca. 150–ca. 225) is often called the "father of Latin theology." Trained in law and educated in philosophy and history in Rome, Tertullian returned to Carthage, probably shortly after he was converted to Christianity. After persecution swept through North Africa in A.D. 202, Tertullian embraced Montanism and wrote a seminal work on Logos Christology, *Against Praxeas,* which in some respects anticipated the later trinitarian formulation of the Council of Nicea.

In the course of praising the apostolic churches, Tertullian mentions Ephesus in passing but then cites the legend that John had been plunged into boiling oil in Rome before being banished to Patmos:

> Since you are able to cross to Asia, you get to Ephesus. Since, moreover, you are close upon Italy, you have Rome, from which there comes even into our own hands the very authority (of the apostles themselves). How happy is its church, on which apostles poured forth all their doctrine along with their blood! where Peter endures a passion like his Lord's! Paul wins his crown in a death like John's [the Baptist]! where the Apostle John was first plunged, unhurt, into boiling oil, and thence remitted to his island-exile![1]

In Rome the Church of San Giovanni in Olio marks the spot of John's escape.[2] From this brief report, it is clear that Tertullian identifies John the seer of Revelation with the apostle John.[3] Tertullian also identifies John the apostle as the evangelist[4] and the elder of the Epistles,[5] commenting that John opposed the Nicolaitans, whose heresy was replicated by the Gaians: "But in his epistle he especially designates those as 'Antichrists' who 'denied that Christ was come in the flesh,' and who refused to think that Jesus was the Son of God. The one dogma Marcion maintained; the other, Hebion."[6]

Tertullian, therefore, was apparently the first to turn the authority of John against the teachings of Marcion.[7] The authority of the apostles, moreover, was transmitted to those whom they appointed as bishops. Churches should therefore be able to demonstrate that their first bishop was appointed by an apostle: "For this is the manner in which the apostolic churches transmit their registers: as the church of Smyrna, which records that Polycarp was placed therein by John; as also the church of Rome, which makes Clement to have been ordained in like manner by Peter."[8] Finally, Tertullian cites John as an example of virtuous celibacy, "a noted voluntary celibate of Christ's."[9] Whether this John is the Baptist or the apostle is not clear, however.[10] Apart from the *Acts of John* 113, the virginity of John is rarely attested before the fourth century.

CLEMENT OF ALEXANDRIA

Clement of Alexandria (?–ca. 215), born in Athens and the first head of the Alexandrian School, provides us with fascinating views of the development of the legends about the apostle early in the third century. Like Tertullian, Clement attributed the Gospel, Epistles, and Apocalypse to John.[11] Particularly significant for the patristic evidence regarding the authorship of the Epistles are the indications that Clement knew and attributed 2 John to the apostle. In the *Stromata* he alludes to John's "larger Epistle,"[12] and the *Fragments from Cassiodorus* record Clement's explanation that "The second Epistle of John, which is written to Virgins, is very simple. It was written to a Babylonian lady, by name Electa, and indicates the election of the holy Church."[13] The *Fragments* also show that Clement had received traditions similar to those preserved in the *Acts of John.* Commenting on the phrase "and our hands have handled" (1 John 1:1), Clement reports concerning the nature of Christ's flesh that "It is accordingly related in traditions, that John, touching the outward body itself, sent his hand deep into it, and that the solidity of the flesh offered no obstacle, but gave way to the hand of the disciple."[14]

Fragments from the lost *Hypotyposes,* which consisted of expositions of each of the books of Scripture, show that legend was filling the gaps left in the biblical accounts of the lives of those around Jesus. A fragment from the fifth book reports the baptism of the apostles in an order that differs from any of the canonical lists of the Twelve: "Yes, truly the apostles were baptised, as Clement the Stromatist relates in the fifth book of the Hypotyposes. For in explaining the apostolic statement, 'I thank God that I baptised none of you,' he says, Christ is said to have baptised Peter alone, and Peter Andrew, and Andrew John, and they James and the rest."[15] The priority of Peter and Andrew follows the sequence of the list of the apostles in Matthew and Luke, but placing John third, following Peter and Andrew, is unique.

Fragments of the *Hypotyposes* preserved by Eusebius fill in details of the activities of the apostles after the resurrection: "Clement in the sixth book of the *Hypotyposes* adduces the following: 'For,' he says, 'Peter and James and John after the Ascension of the Saviour did not struggle for glory, because they had previously been given honour by the Saviour, but chose James the Just as bishop of Jerusalem.'"[16] Parenthetically, this fragment illustrates the way in which legends foster other legends. If, as suggested earlier, the prominence of the circle of the three disciples, Peter, James, and John, originated with Mark, then Clement's report represents a second stage of legend making: the three disciples closest to Jesus chose the leader of the Jerusalem church. The same group, with the addition of Paul, appears early in Clement's *Stromata,* following a reference to his teachers: "But these men preserved the true tradition of the blessed teaching directly from Peter and James and John and Paul, the holy apostles, son receiving it from father (but there were few like their fathers), and by the blessing of God they came down to us to deposit those ancestral and apostolic seeds."[17]

Eusebius also cites a fragment from the seventh book of the *Hypotyposes:*

"After the Resurrection the Lord gave the tradition of knowledge (*gnōsin*) to James the Just and John and Peter, these gave it to the other Apostles and the other Apostles to the seventy, of whom Barnabas also was one."[18] Here again, the sequence of the apostles is distinctive. The group of three is here the same as "pillars of the church" names in Galatians 2:9, but there the sequence is James, Cephas, and John, as it is in the sequence of the epistles attributed to these three in the New Testament: James; 1 and 2 Peter; 1, 2, and 3 John.

The most famous story preserved by Clement, however, presents John as one genuinely concerned about the life and spiritual well-being of a young man who became a robber captain. Eusebius comments that the narrative is "most acceptable to those who enjoy hearing what is fine and edifying":[19]

> Listen to a story which is not a story but a true tradition of John the Apostle preserved in memory. For after the death of the tyrant he passed from the island of Patmos to Ephesus, and used also to go, when he was asked, to the neighboring districts of the heathen, in some places to appoint bishops, in others to reconcile whole churches, and in others to ordain some one of those pointed out by the Spirit. He came to one of the cities which were near by (and some tell even its name) [Eusebius's note: "According to the *Chronicon Paschale* it was Smyrna."], and gave rest in general to the brethren; then, while looking before them all at the bishop who had been appointed, he saw a young man of strong body, beautiful appearance, and warm heart. "I commend this man," he said, "to you with all diligence in the face of the church, and with Christ as my witness." The bishop received him, and promised everything, and the same conversations and protestations were used. John then returned to Ephesus and the presbyter took to his house the young man entrusted to him, brought him up, looked after him, and finally baptized him. After this he relaxed his great care and watchfulness, because he had set upon him the seal of the Lord as the perfect safeguard. But some idle and dissolute youths, familiar with evil, corrupted him in his premature freedom. First they led him on by expensive feasts, then they started out at night for robbery and took him with them, then they urged him to greater crimes. He gradually became accustomed to this, and like an unbroken and powerful horse starting from the straight way and tearing at the bit, rushed all the more to the precipice because of his natural vigour. Finally he renounced salvation from God; and now he planned nothing small, but, having perpetrated some great crime, since he was ruined once for all, accepted the same lot as the others. He collected them and formed a band of brigands

and was himself a born chief, excelling in violence, in murder, and in cruelty. Time went on and some necessity arose to summon John. When he had arranged the rest of his mission John said, "Come now, bishop, pay me back the deposit which Christ and I left with you, with the church, over which you preside, as witness." The bishop was at first amazed, thinking that he was being blackmailed for money which he had not received. He could neither show his faithfulness in what he had never had, nor could he fail John. But when John said, "I ask back the young man and the soul of the brother," the old man groaned deeply and shedding tears, said, "He has died." "How and with what death?" "He has died to God," he said, "for he turned out wicked and abandoned and finally a brigand, and now instead of the church he has taken to the mountains with an armed band of men like himself." Then the apostle rent his garments and beat his head with great lamentation. "Well," he said, "it was a fine guardian whom I left for the soul of our brother. But let me have a horse, and some one to show me the way." So he rode, just as he was, straight from the church. When he came to the place he was seized by the sentinel of the brigands and neither fled nor made excuses, but called out, "This is why I am come; take me to your leader." The leader waited for him, armed as he was, but when he recognized John on his approach, he turned and fled in shame. But John pursued with all his might, forgetting his age and calling out, "Why do you run away from me, child, your own father, unarmed and old? Pity me, child, do not fear me! You have still hope of life. I will account to Christ for you. If it must be, I will willingly suffer your death, as the Lord suffered for us; for your life, I will give my own. Stay, believe; Christ sent me." When he heard this he first stood looking down, then he tore off his weapons, then he began to tremble and to weep bitterly. He embraced the old man when he came up, pleading for himself with lamentations as best he could, baptized a second time in his tears, but his right hand he kept back. But John assured him by pledges and protestations that he had found forgiveness for him with the Saviour, led him back, prayed and kneeled and kissed that right hand as though cleansed by his repentance. He brought him to the church, he prayed with many supplications, he joined with him in the struggle of continuous fasting, he worked on his mind by varied addresses and did not leave him, so they say, until he had restored him to the church, and thus gave a great example of true repentance and a great testimony of regeneration, the trophy of a visible resurrection.[20]

Clement's greatest contribution to the growing tradition about the apostle, however, is his comment that John composed "a spiritual Gospel": "But that John, last of all, conscious that the outward facts had been set forth in the Gospels, was urged on by his disciples, and, divinely moved by the Spirit, composed a spiritual Gospel."[21] This remarkable quotation indicates that Clement sought to explain the divergences between the Gospel of John and the synoptic Gospels by attributing a different purpose to John. It further claims that John knew the other Gospels and that he was surrounded by a community of disciples who prompted him to write his Gospel after the other Gospels. The inspiration of the Gospel is also affirmed by reference to the Spirit. The phrase, "a spiritual Gospel," has been used ever since as an explanation or tribute to the character of the Fourth Gospel.

ORIGEN

Origen followed the now well-established tradition that John wrote after the other three evangelists.[22] Origen attributed not only the Gospel but also the Apocalypse and 1 John to the apostle. While he knew of the two shorter epistles, however, he was vague about the number of them or their attribution to John:

> Why need I speak of him who leaned back on Jesus's breast, John, who has left behind one Gospel, confessing that he could write so many that even the world itself could not contain them; and he wrote also the Apocalypse, being ordered to keep silence and not to write the voices of the seven thunders? He has left also an epistle of a very few lines, and, it may be, a second and a third; for not all say that these are genuine. Only, the two of them together are not a hundred lines long.[23]

Eusebius quotes these lines from the fifth of Origen's *Expositions on the Gospel According to John,* which he says Origen composed while he was in Alexandria.[24]

DIONYSIUS

Along with Gregory, Dionysius (200–265) was one of Origen's greatest students. Born to wealthy pagan parents in Alexandria, Dionysius was guided from an early age by presbyters. He became a devoted pupil under Origen and, about A.D. 232, succeeded Heraclas as the head of the Alexandrian School, a position Dionysius held for about fifteen years. Then, following the death of

Heraclas, Dionysius was once again chosen to be his successor, this time as bishop of Alexandria.

Dionysius has achieved a place of distinction for Johannine scholars primarily because he was the first to apply critical argument to the issue of the authorship of the Apocalypse. First he notes that others had rejected both the attribution of the Apocalypse to John and its authority:

> Some indeed of those before our time rejected and altogether impugned the book, examining it chapter by chapter and declaring it to be unintelligible and illogical, and its title false. For they say that it is not John's, no, nor yet an apocalypse (unveiling), since it is veiled by its heavy, thick curtain of unintelligibility; and that the author of this book was not only not one of the apostles, nor even one of the saints or those belonging to the Church, but Cerinthus, the same who created the sect called "Cerinthian" after him, since he desired to affix to his own forgery a name worthy of credit.[25]

Dionysius's assessment of the authorship of the Apocalypse is much more reasoned, anticipating modern scholarship by 1600 years. He allows that the book was written by a "holy and inspired person" named John, but he contends that this John was not the apostle, the author of the Gospel and the Epistles. The basis for this conclusion, Dionysius explains, is the absence of the name John as the author's self-identification in the Gospel and the Epistles, the difference in the character of the Apocalypse, and the differences in language and style:

> Moreover, after closely examining the whole book of the Apocalypse and demonstrating that it cannot be understood in the literal sense, he [Dionysius] adds as follows: "After completing the whole, one might say, of this prophecy, the prophet calls those blessed who observe it, and indeed himself also; for he says: 'Blessed is he that keepeth the words of the prophecy of this book, and I John, he that saw and heard these things.' That, then, he was certainly named John and that this book is by one John, I will not gainsay; for I fully allow that it is the work of some holy and inspired person. But I should not readily agree that he was the apostle, the son of Zebedee, the brother of James, whose are the Gospel entitled According to John and the Catholic Epistle. For I form my judgement from the character of each and from the nature of the language and from what is known as the general construction of the book, that [the John therein mentioned] is not

the same. For the evangelist nowhere adds his name, nor yet proclaims himself, throughout either the Gospel or the Epistle.

". . . . Nay, not even in the second or third extant epistles of John, although they are short, is John set forth by name; but he has written 'the elder,' without giving his name. But this writer did not even consider it sufficient, having once mentioned his name, to narrate what follows, but he takes up his name again: 'I, John, your brother. . . .'

"That the writer of these words, therefore, was John, one must believe, since he says it. But what John, is not clear. For he did not say that he was, as is frequently said in the Gospel, the disciple loved by the Lord, nor he which leaned back on His breast, nor the brother of James, nor the eye-witness and hearer of the Lord. For he would have mentioned some one of these aforesaid epithets, had he wished to make himself clearly known. Yet he makes use of none of them, but speaks of himself as our brother and partaker with us, and a witness of Jesus, and blessed in seeing and hearing the revelations. I hold that there have been many persons of the same name as John the apostle, who for the love they bore him, and because they admired and esteemed him and wished to be loved, as he was, of the Lord, were glad to take also the same name after him; just as Paul, and for that matter Peter too, is a common name among boys of believing parents. . . . [Dionysius cites the occurrence of the name John Mark in the Book of Acts]. But I think that there was a certain other [John] among those that were in Asia, since it is said both that there were two tombs at Ephesus, and that each of the two is said to be John's.

"And from the conceptions too, and from the terms and their arrangement, one might assume that this writer was a different person from the other. . . . In a word, it is obvious that those who observe their character throughout will see at a glance that the Gospel and Epistle have one and the same complexion. But the Apocalypse is utterly different from, and foreign to, these writings; it has no connexion, no affinity, in any way with them; it scarcely, so to speak, has even a syllable in common with them. . . .

"And further, by means of the style one can estimate the difference between the Gospel and Epistle and the Apocalypse. For the former are not only written in faultless Greek but also show the greatest literary skill in their diction, their reasonings, and the constructions in which they are expressed. There is a complete absence of any barbarous word, or solecism, or any vulgarism whatever. . . . But I will not deny that the other writer had seen revelations and received knowledge and prophecy; nevertheless I observe his style and that his use of the Greek language is not accurate, but that he employs barbarous idioms, in some places committing downright solecisms. These there is no necessity to single out now. For I have not said these things in mockery (let no one think it), but merely to establish the dissimilarity of these writings."[26]

Dionysius's reference to the two tombs of John in Ephesus provides further evidence for the association of the apostle with Ephesus, but it also reintroduces the question of whether there were in fact two Christian writers in Ephesus, both named John. On the other hand, it is also plausible that the John of Ephesus was not the apostle but the Elder of Asia Minor, and that the apostle became associated with Ephesus only after the Johannine writings were accepted as canonical and apostolic.[27]

The contributions of the Alexandrian school to Johannine scholarship did not end with Dionysius, however. Later, Didymus the Blind, who led the school in the fourth century, also wrote commentary on the Gospel of John.[28]

EXCURSUS: THE TOMB OF JOHN

The quest for the tomb of John and the references to two tombs in Ephesus add intrigue to the tradition of John's residence in Ephesus. The *Acts of John* describe the burial of the apostle.[29] The earliest reference to the place of John's burial comes from Polycrates, bishop of Ephesus, about 190, who wrote, "For great luminaries sleep in Asia. . . . And there is also John, who leaned on the Lord's breast, who was a priest wearing the mitre, and martyr and teacher, and he sleeps at Ephesus."[30]

Dionysius reports that by the third century, there were two tombs of John in Ephesus: "But I think that there was a certain other [John] among those that were in Asia, since it is said both that there were two tombs at Ephesus, and that each of the two is said to be John's."[31] While assessing the significance of Papias's testimony, Eusebius adds another reference to the tombs: "This confirms the truth of the story of those who have said that there were two of the same name in Asia, and that there are two tombs at Ephesus both still called John's."[32]

One of the tombs lies under the ruins of the Basilica of St. John and can be traced back to the late second or early third century. The nearby town was named Ayasoluk, from the Greek *hagios theologos,* or "holy divine." On the hill of Ayasoluk lie the impressive marble remains of the Basilica of St. John erected by the emperor Justinian (527–565). There is no way of knowing how long a chapel may have stood at this site. During the late third or early fourth century, a simple square church, the cross-vault of which was supported by four slender columns, was built over a system of underground vaults, one of which lay directly beneath the altar. This church may have been built by Theodosius I or even by Constantine the Great. Although at one time the vaults could be entered by a steep passage way, the entrance was later blocked up. The catacombs beneath the church are laid out in roughly the form of a cross, a fact which may have given rise to the legend—in the "Wanderings of John" (or the *Acts of John*) and attributed to Prochoros—that John ordered his tomb to be excavated in the shape of the cross.[33]

At some point, the access to the tomb was blocked off. The Syrian bishops at the council of Ephesus (A.D. 431) complained that "although they had travelled such a distance, [they were] unable to worship according to their desire at the tombs of the holy martyrs, especially that of the thrice-blessed John the Divine and Evangelist who had lived in such intimacy with the Lord."[34] The Council also described itself as meeting "in the [city] of the Ephesians, where John the divine and the holy Virgin Mary, the *Theotokos*," had been.[35] The obstacles preventing the Syrian bishops from worshiping at the tomb of John may have been political or ecclesiastical rather than physical, however.

The presence of two tombs of John in Ephesus has been explained in various ways. Jerome wrote that "some think that the two memorials at Ephesus are both in honor of John the evangelist."[36] Writing in the nineteenth century, James Stalker reported that "Zahn tries to prove that these two memorials were churches, one on the site of the house where John had lived inside the walls of the city, and he has succeeded in making this seem very probable."[37] Robert Eisler conjectures that the second tomb of John, referred to by Dionysius of Alexandria, was the original tomb of the Ephesian John before his remains were transferred to the catacombs under the Square Church. The moving of the saint's remains, Eisler suggests, may have spurred the development of the legend which reports that "on the morning after [John's inhumation], all came with prayers to lift his body so that it should be put to rest in the big church. But when we opened the grave we found nothing."[38]

September 26 was celebrated as the date of the martyrdom of John and others in a world-renowned religious feast at Justinian's Basilica of St. John until its destruction by the Seljuk Turks in A.D. 1090. Eisler supposes, therefore, that the remains of all these martyrs may have been collected in the catacombs beneath the square church.[39] Local Christians may have continued to worship at the original tomb. In more recent times, until the expulsion of the Greek inhabitants from the area in 1920, Greek Christians decorated with wreaths and lamps a simple arcosol-tomb cut into the rock a little east of the ancient stadium, identifying it as the grave of St. John.[40] If Eisler's theory of the movement of the remains from a simple tomb to the catacombs is correct, the remains were moved before Dionysius wrote in A.D. 262. Whether or not the Square Church had been built by this date, its location would have been connected with John's tomb by this time. Legends concerning the tomb of John include reports of manna or miraculous dust rising from the tomb, which had healing powers. Recounting a legend of apparently separate origins, Augustine says that the ground rose and fell over the tomb as though the apostle were sleeping.[41]

In the sixth century, Emperor Justinian ordered the construction of the Basilica of St. John. Procopius of Caesarea, a Greek historian who describes Justinian's buildings (ca. 553–555), writes:

> On that site the natives had set up a church in early times to the Apostle John; this Apostle has been named "the Theologian," because the nature of God was described by him in a manner beyond the unaided power of man. This church, which was small and in a ruined condition because of its great age, the Emperor Justinian tore down to the ground and replaced by a church so large and beautiful, that, to speak briefly, it resembles very closely in all respects, and is a rival to, the shrine which he dedicated to all the Apostles in the imperial city [Constantinople].[42]

Because the ruins of the temple of Artemis (destroyed in A.D. 263 by the Gotts) lay nearby, it is likely that the ruins were quarried for materials for the building of the Basilica of St. John.

Built in the Latin-cross style, the magnificent building was 380 feet long, 90 feet high, and had 6 domes. During the Turkish period, the Basilica may have been used as a mosque before the Mosque of Isa Bey was constructed. A visitor would move successively through the exonarthex to the narthex and the nave. The nave was separated from the aisles on both sides by columns and pillars. At the end of the nave was the site of the grave of St. John. On the north side of the Basilica was a baptistry and a chapel. The apse of this chapel was decorated with frescoes from the eleventh or twelfth century which depict St. John and Jesus.[43] In his *Secret History,* Procopius comments that it was "the most sacred shrine in Ephesus and one held in special honour."[44] Dallmann adds the following description of the splendor of the Basilica: "The columns were erected out of solid rock, with white marble shafts. The capitals of the principal nave were covered with gold and decorated with the monograms of the Emperor Justinian and Theodora. For a thousand years it was one of the greatest sanctuaries of the Christian Orient."[45]

More detailed descriptions of the Basilica of St. John are available in the excavation reports. The site was first excavated by the Greek archaeologist G.

A. Sotiriu in 1921–1922, then by Austrian archaeologists J. Keil and H. Hörmann in 1927 and following years.[46] Of these excavations, Dallmann wrote in 1932:

> In August, 1922, Prof. Georgius Sotiriu found the ruins of Justinian's Church of John. In 1926 the Ephesus Excavations Board of Trustees was organized at Berlin, financed in part by John D. Rockefeller, Jr. Since then Prof. Josef Keil of Greifswald has been uncovering the Basilica of St. John on Ayasolouk Hill, over which soar the eagles as they soared in the days of Heraclitus and Alexander, and Paul and John.[47]

Hörmann observed in favor of the authenticity of the site that the span of time between the death of the apostle and the earliest attested veneration of the site is too brief to allow for the tradition of the site of the tomb to have been lost entirely. The fact that there were no remains in the tomb is hardly surprising in view of the practice from the time of Constantine on of opening tombs to recover relics of the saints and in view of the reckless plundering of such sites by the Moslems.[48]

VICTORINUS OF PETAU

Victorinus, the bishop of Petau who flourished at the end of the third century and was martyred in the persecution of A.D. 304, left a commentary on the Apocalypse. Writing on the Gospels, he identifies Mark with the lion, Matthew with the man, Luke with the calf, and John with the eagle: "John the evangelist, like to an eagle hastening on uplifted wings to greater heights, argues about the Word of God."[49] In a later section, he supplies further detail about John's forced labor on Patmos and the sequence of the Apocalypse and the Gospel:

> He says this, because when John said these things he was in the island of Patmos, condemned to the labour of the mines by Caesar Domitian. There, therefore, he saw the Apocalypse; and when grown old, he thought that he should at length receive his quittance by suffering, Domitian being killed, all his judgments were discharged. And John being dismissed from the mines, thus subsequently delivered the same Apocalypse which he had received from God. . . . A reed was shown like to a rod. This itself is the Apocalypse which he subsequently exhibited to the churches; for the Gospel of the complete faith he subsequently wrote for the sake of our salvation. For when Valentinus, and Cerinthus, and

Ebion, and others of the school of Satan, were scattered abroad throughout the world, there assembled together to him from the neighboring provinces all the bishops, and compelled him himself also to draw up his testimony.[50]

EUSEBIUS

The life of Eusebius, the leading historian of the early church, spanned the years from approximately 260 to 340. He was known early on as "Eusebius of Pamphilus" for his close relationship with Pamphilus, who had a large library in Caesarea. Along with the library of bishop Alexander at Jerusalem, it was Eusebius's major resource for his writings. Eusebius's career gained him places of prominence at historic events. Imprisoned during the persecution in Caesarea during the years 309 and 313, he was shortly thereafter made bishop of Caesarea. At the Council of Nicea (A.D. 325), Eusebius sat at the right hand of Emperor Constantine and served as his theological adviser. Eusebius advocated a moderate position, inclined toward tolerance for Arian, but finally voted with the majority. After the Council he was an opponent of Athanasius. Later, Eusebius attended the Council of Antioch in A.D. 331, and was offered the bishopric of Antioch but declined it. He also attended the Synod of Jerusalem and the Synod of Constantinople during the same year. At the latter he was chosen to be the orator for the celebration of the thirtieth year of the reign of Constantine. Although Eusebius's works are numerous, he is best known for his *Ecclesiastical History,* which traces the history of the church up to his time.[51]

Eusebius vouches for the tradition that John was exiled on Patmos and lived to the time of Trajan. In his *Chronicle,* Eusebius places John 2114 years after Abraham and says that Papias and Polycarp were his students.[52] Ephesus was John's appointment, apparently assigned by lot: "Such was the condition of things among the Jews, but the holy Apostles and disciples of our Saviour were scattered throughout the whole world. Thomas, as tradition relates, obtained by lot Parthia, Andrew Scythia, John Asia (and he stayed there and died in Ephesus). . . ."[53] For his knowledge that John lived to the time of Domitian, Eusebius was dependent upon Irenaeus:

At this time [Domitian], the story goes, the Apostle and Evangelist John was still alive, and was condemned to live in the island of Patmos for his witness to the divine word. At any rate Irenaeus, writing about the number of the name ascribed to the anti-Christ in the so-called Apocalypse of John, states this about John in so many words in the fifth book against Heresies. "But if it had been necessary to announce his name plainly at the present times, it would have been spoken by him who saw the apocalypse. For it was not seen long ago but almost in our own time, at the end of the reign of Domitian."[54]

After his release from Patmos, John settled in Ephesus:

> After Domitian had reigned fifteen years, Nerva succeeded [Sept. 18, A.D. 96]. The sentences of Domitian were annulled, and the Roman Senate decreed the return of those who had been unjustly banished and the restoration of their property. Those who committed the story of those times to writing relate it. At that time, too, the story of the ancient Christians relates that the Apostle John, after his banishment to the island, took up his abode at Ephesus.[55]

For this chronology of the apostle's life, Eusebius cites Irenaeus and the story of the robber captain from Clement of Alexandria:

> At this time [the reign of Trajan, A.D. 98] that very disciple whom Jesus loved, John, at once Apostle and Evangelist, still remained alive in Asia and administered the churches there, for after the death of Domitian, he had returned from his banishment on the island. And that he remained alive until this time may fully be confirmed by two witnesses, and these ought to be trustworthy for they represent the orthodoxy of the church, no less persons than Irenaeus and Clement of Alexandria. The former of these writes in one place in the second of his books *Against the Heresies,* as follows: "And all the presbyters who had been associated with John, the disciple of the Lord, bear witness to his tradition, for he remained with them until the times of Trajan."[56] And in the third book of the same work he makes the same statement as follows: "Now the church at Ephesus was founded by Paul, but John stayed there until the times of Trajan, and it is a true witness of the tradition of the Apostles."[57]
>
> Clement indicates the same time, and in the treatise to which he gave the title *Who is the rich man that is saved,* adds a narrative most acceptable to those who enjoy hearing what is fine and edifying. Take and read here what he wrote. . . . [See above, pp. 142–43.] These remarks of Clement may be quoted both for the sake of the narrative and the edification of those who shall read them.[58]

At this point, Eusebius takes up the issue of the writings attributed to John and explains that John wrote only after a long period of passing on his teachings orally. John therefore knew the other Gospels and wrote to supplement them.[59] Recognizing the differences between John and the synoptics, Eusebius advances the simplistic solution that whereas the synoptic evangelists wrote about the period following the arrest of John the Baptist, John wrote about the earlier period:

> But come, let us indicate the undoubted writings of this apostle. Let the Gospel according to him be first recognized, for it is read in all the churches under heaven. Moreover, that it was reasonable for the ancients to reckon it in the fourth place after the other three may be explained thus. Those inspired and venerable ancients, I mean Christ's Apostles, had completely purified their life and adorned their souls with every virtue, yet were but simple men in speech. . . . Yet nevertheless of all those who had been with the Lord only Matthew and John have left us their recollections, and tradition says that they took to writing perforce. . . . John, it is said, used all the time a message which was not written down, and at last took to writing for the following cause. The three gospels which had been written down before were distributed to all including himself; it is said that he welcomed them and testified to their truth but said that there was only lacking to the narrative the account of what was done by Jesus at first and at the beginning of the preaching. The story is surely true. It is at least possible to see that the three evangelists related only what the Saviour did during the one year after John the Baptist had been put in prison and that they started this at the beginning of their narrative. . . . John was asked to relate in his own gospel the period passed over in silence by the former evangelists and the things done during it by the Saviour (that is to say, the events before the imprisonment of the Baptist. . . . Thus John in the course of his gospel relates what Christ did before the Baptist had been thrown into prison, but the other three evangelists narrate the events after the imprisonment of the Baptist. If this be understood the gospels no longer appear to disagree. . . . [60]

Eusebius then notes that questions of how many epistles should be attributed to the apostle and whether the author of Revelation was also John the apostle were still debated: "Of the writings of John in addition to the gospel the first of his epistles has been accepted without controversy by ancients and moderns alike but the other two are disputed, and as to the Revelation there have been many advocates of either opinion up to the present."[61]

On the side of apostolic authorship for the Book of Revelation, Eusebius cites Justin Martyr,[62] but he himself attributes the book to John the Elder.[63]

Some, however, rejected the Revelation and attributed it to Cerinthus.[64] Cerinthus interpreted the prophecy of Revelation as a promise of an earthly, carnal kingdom, for which Eusebius and others condemned his teaching roundly:

> Dionysius said this and Irenaeus in his first book *Against Heresies* quoted some of his [Cerinthus's] more abominable errors, and in the third book has committed to writing a narrative, which deserves not to be forgotten, stating how, according to the tradition of Polycarp, the apostle John once went into a bathhouse to wash, but when he knew that Cerinthus was within leapt out of the place and fled from the door, for he did not endure to be even under the same roof with him, and enjoined on those who were with him to do the same, saying, "Let us flee, lest the bathhouse fall in, for Cerinthus, the enemy of the truth, is within."[65]

When Eusebius reports the tradition of the apostle's death and burial in Ephesus, he cites as his authority a letter from Polycrates to Victor, bishop of Rome, in which Polycrates names Philip but confuses Philip the apostle with Philip the deacon, who is mentioned in Acts (6:5; 8:5–13, 26–40; 21:8–9). Surprisingly, Eusebius passes along this confusion without noting or correcting it, an oversight indicating how tenuous the line of tradition had become:

> The date of the death of John has been already mentioned [3.23.4, where Irenaeus, *Haer.* 2.22.5, is quoted to show that John lived until the reign of Trajan], and the place of his body is shown by a letter of Polycrates (he was bishop of the diocese of Ephesus) which he wrote to Victor, bishop of Rome. In this he mentions both John, Philip the Apostle, and Philip's daughters as follows: . . . [the letter of Polycrates which follows is quoted above, p. 128].[66]

Eusebius cites the same letter of Polycrates again later.[67]

One of the cruxes of unraveling the traditions about John is how one interprets Eusebius's comments regarding Papias. In the following passage, Eusebius quotes from the preface to Papias's five-volume work for the purpose of correcting Irenaeus's contention that Papias had direct contact with the apostle John. Eusebius interprets Papias as meaning that there were two Johns and that Papias had actually heard John the Elder rather than the apostle John. Nevertheless, Eusebius assigns the Book of Revelation to John the Elder and supposes that the presence of both Johns in Ephesus gave rise to the tradition that there were two tombs of John in that city:

These [Papias's five treatises] are also mentioned by Irenaeus as though his only writing, for he says in one place, "To these things also Papias, the hearer of John, who was a companion of Polycarp and one of the ancients, bears witness in writing in the fourth of his books, for five books were composed by him." So says Irenaeus. Yet Papias himself, according to the preface of his treatises, makes plain that he had in no way been a hearer and eyewitness of the sacred Apostles, but he teaches that he had received the articles of the faith from those who had known them, for he speaks as follows: . . . [the excerpt from Papias is quoted and discussed above, p. 109].

It is here worth noting that he twice counts the name of John, and reckons the first John with Peter and James and Matthew and the other Apostles, clearly meaning the evangelist, but by changing his statement places the second with the others outside the number of the Apostles, putting Aristion before him and clearly calling him a presbyter. This confirms the truth of the story of those who have said that there were two of the same name in Asia, and that there are two tombs at Ephesus both still called John's. This calls for attention: for it is probable that the second (unless anyone prefer the former) saw the revelation which passes under the name John. The Papias whom we are now treating confesses that he had received the words of the Apostles from their followers, but says that he had actually heard Aristion and the presbyter John. He often quotes them by name and gives their traditions in his writings. Let this suffice to good purpose.[68]

Questions still remain. A fragment attributed to the second book of Papias contains a report of the martyrdom of John.[69] Did Eusebius know all five books of Papias? If so, why does Eusebius not mention John's martyrdom? Did he interpret the report in such a way that it did not conflict with the tradition of John's long life and residence in Ephesus? Or did he suppress the report in favor of the tradition that the apostle wrote the Fourth Gospel? The latter is difficult to accept since Eusebius assumes the five books of Papias are still available and does not hesitate to challenge Irenaeus on the link between Papias and John.

Unfortunately, Eusebius gives us no further information on John the Elder: "In the same writing he [Papias] also quotes other interpretations of the words of the Lord given by the Aristion mentioned above and traditions of John the presbyter. To them we may dismiss the studious. . . ."[70] Eusebius's confusion regarding Philip and Irenaeus's confusion regarding Papias raises the issue of whether a similar confusion prevailed regarding Polycarp's association with

John. For the link between John and Polycarp, Eusebius is again dependent on Irenaeus and provides no independent evidence.[71]

Eusebius cites Irenaeus once again in the context of wrestling with the identity of the Antichrist, noting that the name of the Antichrist was not meant to be known at that time:

> Now since this is so, and since this number [of the Antichrist] is found in all the good and ancient copies and since those who have seen John face to face testify. . . . For if it had been necessary for his name to have been announced clearly at the present time, it would have been spoken by him who also saw the Revelation; for it was not even seen a long time ago, but almost in our own generation towards the end of the reign of Domitian.[72]

Referring to Apollonius, who wrote to refute the Montanists forty years after the outbreak of that heresy, Eusebius notes one of the legends of John's raising the dead: "He also makes quotations from the Apocalypse of John and tells how by divine power a dead man was raised by John himself at Ephesus."[73] Eusebius also collected traditions about John that are known to us from their primary sources. Since these are discussed in the present study in connection with their original sources, they will not be repeated here. Among these is Eusebius's extended quotation from Dionysius.[74]

In sum, Eusebius provides little new information in the history of tradition. His primary contribution lies in collecting and passing on tradition from Papias, Irenaeus, Polycrates, Apollonius, Clement, Origen, and Dionysius. Eusebius did, however, begin the process of reflecting critically on this tradition. He recognized the ambiguity in Papias's statement and pressed Irenaeus for misconstruing the relationship between the apostle John and Papias. He also recognized the uncertainty of the authorship of the two shorter Epistles and the Book of Revelation. Eusebius lists the second and third Epistles with the "disputed books," along with James, Jude, and 2 Peter. Revelation is listed both with the "recognized books" and with those that are "spurious" or "not genuine."[75] The *Acts of John,* however, are condemned as belonging to those "writings which are put forward by heretics under the name of the apostles. . . . To none of these has any who belonged to the orthodox ever thought it right to refer in his writings. . . . they are the forgeries of heretics . . . . shunned as altogether wicked and impious."[76] Eusebius, therefore, represents a major step in the canonization of tradition. Aspects of the legends about John were recognized and endorsed as apostolic, canonical, or historical, while other strands in the tradition were pushed further to the periphery and labeled as heresy, forgery, and falsehood.

EPHRAEM THE SYRIAN

Ephraem the Syrian (ca. 306–373) produced an extensive corpus of exegetical, dogmatic, and hymnic compositions. A fragment attached to two
Armenian translations of Ephraem's commentary on the Diatessaron attests to
a curious departure from the tradition that John worked in Ephesus. The
manuscripts date from 1195, but the translation comes from the fifth century.
The fragment describes the origins of the Gospels. The sentence on John
reads: "John wrote that Gospel in Greek at Antioch, for he remained in the
country until the time of Trajan."[77]

EPIPHANIUS

Most of what is known about the life of Epiphanius comes from his own
writings. He was born around 310–320 and reared by Christian parents in
Palestine, near Gaza. He was educated by monks, and the ascetic Hilarion
became his mentor and friend. After studying in Egypt, Epiphanius returned to
Palestine and founded a monastery at Eleutheropolis. About A.D. 367, he was
invited to Cyprus to become bishop of Salamis, where he continued to foster
the monastic movement. In A.D. 382, Epiphanius traveled to Rome with
Jerome and boarded with the wealthy widow Paula, who later became the
foundress of a convent at Bethlehem. Epiphanius was a defender of Nicene
Christianity and an opponent of Origenism. He died returning from a trip to
Constantinople in 402 or 403.[78]

In the *Panarion*, Epiphanius records the following variation on the story of
John and Cerinthus that is found in Irenaeus:[79]

> Again, while St. John was preaching in Asia, it was reported that
> he did an extraordinary thing as an example of the truth. Though
> his way of life was most admirable and appropriate to his apos-
> tolic rank, and he never bathed, he was compelled by the Holy
> Spirit to go to the bath, and said, "Look what is at the bath!" To
> his companions' surprise he actually went to the bathing-room,
> approached the attendant who took the bathers' clothes, and asked
> who was in the bathing-room inside. And the attendant stationed
> there to watch the clothes—some people do this for a living in the
> gymnasia—told St. John that Ebion was inside. But John under-
> stood at once why the Holy Spirit's guidance had impelled him, as
> I said, to come to the bath for the record, to bequeath to us the
> essence of the truth—who Christ's servants and apostles are, and
> the sons of that same truth; but what the evil one's vessels are, and
> the gates of hell. Though these cannot prevail against the rock,

and God's holy church which is founded on it. John immediately became disturbed and cried out in anguish; and as a testimony in proof of uncontaminated teaching he said, in an aside audible to all, "Brothers, let us get away from here quickly! Or the bath may fall and bury us with Ebion, in the bathing-room inside, because of his impiety."

And no one need be surprised to hear that Ebion met John. The blessed John had a very long life, and survived till the reign of Trajan.[80]

Like other stories, therefore, this one could be adapted to condemn not only Cerinthus but Ebion or presumably any other whose teachings one wished to discredit. According to Epiphanius, not only Cerinthus and Ebion but also Merinthus, Cleobius or Cleobulus, Claudius, Demas, Hermogenes, and others "were opposed by St. John and his associates, Leucius and many others."[81]

Various other traditions about the apostle John and the Gospel that bore his name can be gleaned from different sections of the *Panarion*. For example, Epiphanius reports that John was long reluctant to write a Gospel: "Therefore the Holy Spirit later compelled John, who did not want to write a gospel because of his piety and humility, to expound the gospel in his old age when he was over ninety years old, after his return from Patmos in the time of Claudius Caesar and after he had spent many years in Asia."[82] Notable here is the report that John was exiled to Patmos under Claudius rather than Domitian or Nero, and the compensating detail that he wrote the Gospel many years later, when he was over ninety. Elsewhere Epiphanius reports that John lived "until Trajan's time"[83] and, more precisely (though the number may be corrupt), until the nineteenth year of Trajan's reign.[84]

According to Epiphanius, the Gospel itself had an interesting history: "Some people have also said that the Gospel of John was even translated from Greek into Hebrew and is kept in the Jewish repositories, those that is in Tiberias, and is stored away in secret, as some of the faithful converted from Judaism have related to us in detail."[85] Not only John but also Acts had been so translated, and some of the Jews had come to believe in Christ by reading these documents.

Following the tradition that John remained a virgin, Epiphanius adds this explanation as a part of his interpretation of the statement in Matthew 19:2 that "There are Eunuchs who have made themselves such for the kingdom of heaven": "Who then are these if not the noble apostles and the virgins and monks who come after? John and James, Zebedee's sons, remained virgins and neither cut off their members with their own hands nor married. . . ."[86] Later, Epiphanius comments that James the brother of the Lord died a virgin at the age of ninety-six (contrary to the reports of his martyrdom in Jerusalem):

"For it was John and James and James, these three, who practiced this way of life: the two sons of Zebedee and James the son of Joseph and brother of the Lord on account of being reared and fostered with him, on account of the sole relationship which Joseph had with Mary: that she was pledged to him."[87] Epiphanius insists, no human being was to be worshiped—neither Elijah, nor John, nor even Mary. At this point in the *Panarion,* Epiphanius indicates his familiarity with the story of John's instruction that a grave should be dug for him, and of the prayer he gave before lying down in the grave:[88] "nor is John to be worshiped, even though by his prayer he had produced his own astonishing death, or rather received this favor from God. . . ."[89]

For Epiphanius, therefore, John was a model of piety and opposition to heresy. He lived to an old age, maintained his virginity, suffered exile, wrote the Gospel at the direction of the Holy Spirit, and opposed the teachings of Cerinthus, Ebion, and others.

CHRYSOSTOM

John—who was given the name Chrysostom, "golden-mouthed," after his death—was the most outstanding preacher of the Antiochian school. Born to well-to-do parents around 345–347, he was baptized about 370 and became a hermit shortly thereafter. Because of ill health he returned to Antioch, where he was ordained a deacon (ca. 381) and then a priest (386). For twelve years he moved Christians in Antioch with eloquent, exegetical sermons that spoke to the burning social issues of the day. In 398, he accepted the bishopric of Constantinople, where he made enemies and offended the powerful with his direct attacks on the excesses of wealth. Consequently, in A.D. 403, he was deposed. After having been recalled, he was then banished to small town on the edge of Armenia. From there, in A.D. 407, he was sent to an even more obscure town but died before he reached it.

In his *Homilies on the Gospel of John,* Chrysostom exalts the magnificence of the Gospel of John by describing John's humble origins:

> Of this [Galilee] he was, and his father a poor fisherman, so poor that he took his sons to the same employment. Now you all know that no workman will choose to bring up his son to succeed him in his trade, unless poverty press him very hard, especially where the trade is a mean one. But nothing can be poorer, meaner, no not more ignorant, than fishermen. Yet even among them there are some greater, some less; and even there our Apostle occupied the lower rank, for he did not take his prey from the sea, but passed his time on a certain little lake. And as he was engaged by it with his father and his brother James, and they mending their broken

nets, a thing which of itself marked extreme poverty, so Christ called him.

As for worldly instruction, we may learn from these facts that he had none at all of it. Besides, Luke testifies this when he writes not only that he was ignorant, but that he was absolutely unlettered. (Acts iv. 13). As was likely. For one who was so poor, never coming into the public assemblies, nor falling in with men of respectability, but as it were nailed to his fishing, or even if he ever did meet any one, conversing with fishmongers and cooks, how, I say, was he likely to be in a state better than that of the irrational animals? How could he help imitating the very dumbness of his fishes?

No wonder the people flocked to hear Chrysostom! After further deprecating the apostle's origins, the golden-mouthed preacher makes his point:

For the more barbarous his nation seems to them [the Greeks], and the more he seems removed from Grecian discipline, so much the brighter does what we have with us appear. For when a barbarian and an untaught person utters things which no man on earth ever knew, and does not only utter, (though if this were the only thing it were a great marvel,) but besides this, affords another and a stronger proof that what he says is divinely inspired, namely, the convincing all his hearers through all time; who will not wonder at the power that dwells in him?[90]

Chrysostom proceeds to elevate John's Gospel over all the works of the Greek philosophers, which pale by comparison.

The golden-mouthed preacher of Antioch also knew the tradition that John was a "native of Bethsaida."[91] In *The Gospel of Matthew*—in a passing remark that anticipates the debate over the date of the Gospel of John in recent literature—Chrysostom explains why John makes no reference to the destruction of Jerusalem, as do the synoptics, "lest he should seem to write from the very history of things done (for indeed he lived a long time after the taking of the city)."[92] Chrysostom also repeats in *Letters to the Fallen Theodore* the story of John and the robber captain (found in Clement of Alexandria) and assumes that the tale is common knowledge.[93] In the *Homilies on St. John,* Chrysostom writes at length about the special love between John and Jesus.[94] He emphasizes, moreover, that John took care to be exact and not allow any misinterpretation,[95] that he omitted from the Gospel many events which took place between the Jewish festivals because he could not include everything, and that he emphasized those things which might give an answer to the fault-finding of the Jews.[96] John referred to himself as the "Beloved Disciple," Chrysostom explains, out of modesty,[97] and the same modesty kept him from identifying himself in John 18:15,[98] or boasting of his role at the cross[99] or at the empty tomb.[100]

THEODORE OF MOPSUESTIA

If Chrysostom was the outstanding preacher of the school at Antioch, then Theodore of Mopsuestia (d. A.D. 428) was its most accomplished exegete and theologian. Among the works he left is a commentary on the Gospel of John. In the introduction to this commentary, Theodore explains that after the other Gospels had been published, the faithful at Ephesus, judging that John was the most worthy to be a witness to the gospel, brought the books to John to ask him which was the most glorious. John praised those who had written of the truth, but said that they had left some things out, especially concerning the wonders Jesus had performed. The brethren then urged John to write the things which he judged especially necessary for the truth to be known, and which the others had left out. And this was the occasion for the writing of the Gospel according to John.[101]

JEROME

Jerome was the leading Bible scholar of his day. Born about 340, Jerome studied in Rome and Constantinople, traveled in Gaul, and lived as a hermit near Antioch. After a severe illness, he turned from the classics to the study of the scriptures, and learned Hebrew while living as a hermit. After returning to Rome, he preached the merits of the monastic life and gained the favor of Pope Damascus (366–384), after whose death Jerome returned to Antioch and, in A.D. 386, settled in Bethlehem, where he remained as head of the monastery until his death in A.D. 420. It was there that he completed his greatest work, the translation of the Latin Vulgate. The New Testament was completed by A.D. 388, and for the translation of the Old Testament, he used the Hebrew texts rather than the Septuagint.

Jerome also wrote a biographical dictionary of Christian writers, the *Lives of Illustrious Men*. In this document he gives the following account of the life of John and the reasons for the differences between his Gospel and the synoptics:

> John, the apostle whom Jesus most loved, the son of Zebedee and brother of James, the apostle whom Herod, after our Lord's passion, beheaded, most recently of all the evangelists wrote a

Gospel, at the request of the bishops of Asia, against Cerinthus and other heretics and especially against the then growing dogma of the Ebionites, who assert that Christ did not exist before Mary. On this account he was compelled to maintain His divine nativity. But there is said to be yet another reason for this work, in that when he had read Matthew, Mark and Luke, he approved indeed the substance of the history and declared that the things they said were true, but that they had given the history of only one year, the one, that is, which follows the imprisonment of John and in which he was put to death. So passing by this year, the events of which had been set forth by these, he related the events of the earlier period before John was shut up in prison, so that it might be manifest to those who should diligently read the volumes of the four Evangelists. This also takes away the discrepancy which there seems to be between John and the others. He wrote also one *Epistle* which begins as follows "That which was from the beginning, that which we have heard, that which we have seen with our eyes and our hands handled concerning the word of life" which is esteemed of by all men who are interested in the church or in learning. The other two of which the first is "The elder to the elect lady and her children" and the other "The elder unto Gaius the beloved whom I love in truth," are said to be the work of John the presbyter to the memory of whom another sepulchre is shown at Ephesus to the present day, though some think that there are two memorials of this same John the evangelist. We shall treat this matter in its turn when we come to Papias his disciple. In the fourteenth year then after Nero, Domitian having raised a second persecution, he was banished to the island of Patmos, and wrote the *Apocalypse,* on which Justin Martyr and Irenaeus afterwards wrote commentaries. But Domitian having been put to death and his acts, on account of his excessive cruelty, having been annulled by the senate, he returned to Ephesus under Nerva Pertinax and continuing there until the time of the emperor Trajan, founded and built churches throughout all Asia, and, worn out by old age, died in the sixty-eighth year after our Lord's passion and was buried near the same city.[102]

For this account Jerome depended upon Eusebius. The phrase "the sixty-eighth year" proves that Jerome's calculation is based on Eusebius's *Chronicle,* which places the death of Jesus in the year 32 and that of John in the third year of the reign of Trajan, or A.D. 100 (100 − 32 = 68).[103] The claim that John lived sixty-eight years after the crucifixion may be compared with the following accounts of the age of John: (a) Epiphanius's report that John lived past the age of ninety,[104] (b) Jacobus de Voragine's claim that John was ninety-nine when he died,[105] (c) the *Acts of John by Prochorus* which makes John a hundred years old at his death,[106] and (d) the claim of the *Homily of pseudo-Chrysostom,* the catalogue of apostles of pseudo-Epiphanius, and the *Suidas* that John lived to be a hundred and twenty (the same age as Moses).[107]

Like many later writers, Jerome connected the name *Boanerges* with the incident in Samaria: "He [Jesus] is not received by a Samaritan city because His face was set for Jerusalem. James and John, who were truly the sons of thunder, and Phinees and Elias, burning with ardent desire, wish to bring down fire from heaven and they are rebuked by the Lord."[108] Although Jerome was well aware of the charge that Peter and John were untaught, he defended the apostle vigorously: "Was John a mere fisherman, rude and untaught? If so, whence did he get the words 'In the beginning was the word, and the word was with God and the word was God'?"[109] Jerome also knew the tradition that John never married: "And yet John, one of the disciples, who according to tradition was the least [smallest, youngest?] of the apostles, and whom trust in Christ found to be a virgin, remained a virgin, and moreover he is loved more by the Lord and reclines on Jesus' breast."[110]

Passages from chapters 5 and 17 of *Lives of Illustrious Men* connect John with Paul and with Polycarp:

> As Sergius Paulus Proconsul of Cyprus was the first to believe on his preaching, he [Paul] took his name from him because he had subdued him to faith in Christ, and having been joined by Barnabas, after traversing many cities, he returned to Jerusalem and was ordained apostle to the Gentiles by Peter, James and John.[111]

> Polycarp disciple of the apostle John and by him ordained bishop of Smyrna was chief of all Asia, where he saw and had as teachers some of the Apostles and those who had seen the Lord.[112]

Jerome knew the tradition transmitted by Papias (for which he may have again been dependent on Eusebius) and used it to support his judgment that the two shorter epistles were the work of John the Elder rather than the apostle John:

> Papias, the pupil of John, bishop of Hierapolis in Asia, wrote only five volumes, which he entitled *Exposition of the Words of Our Lord,* in which, when he had asserted in his preface that he did not follow various opinions but had the apostles for authority, he said "I considered what Andrew and Peter said, what Philip, what Thomas, what James, what John, what Matthew or any one else among the disciples of our Lord, what also Aristion and the elder John, disciples of the Lord had said, not so much that I have their

books to read, as that their living voice is heard until the present day in the authors themselves." It appears through this catalogue of names that the John who is placed among the disciples is not the same as the elder John whom he places after Aristion in his enumeration. This we say moreover because of the opinion mentioned above, where we record that it is declared by many that the last two epistles of John are the work not of the apostle but of the presbyter.[113]

In a letter to Paulinus, however, Jerome attributed the letters to the apostle John.[114]

Elsewhere, Jerome identified Irenaeus as "a disciple of Papias the hearer of the evangelist John,"[115] and from the preface to his *Commentary on Matthew,* we gain this detailed account of the events that led to the writing of the Gospel:

> The last [of the Gospel writers] is John, the apostle and evangelist, whom Jesus loved most, who, reclining on the Lord's bosom, drank the purest streams of doctrine. . . . When he was in Asia, at the time when the seeds of heresy were springing up (I refer to Cerinthus, Ebion, and the rest who say that Christ has not come in the flesh, whom he in his own epistle calls Antichrists, and whom the apostle Paul frequently assails), he was urged by almost all the bishops in Asia then living, and by deputations from many Churches, to write more profoundly concerning the divinity of the Saviour, and to break through all obstacles so as to attain to the very Word of God (if I may so speak) with a boldness as successful as it appears audacious. Ecclesiastical history relates that, when he was urged by the brethren to write, he replied that he would do so if a general fast were proclaimed and all would offer up prayer to God; and when the fast was over, the narrative goes on to say, being filled with revelation [*revelatione saturatus,* "having been saturated with revelation"], he burst into the heaven-sent Preface, "In the beginning was the Word, and the Word was with God, and the Word was God: this was in the beginning with God."[116]

The role of the bishops and the call for a fast in this account are distinctly reminiscent of the *Muratorian Canon.*[117] Jerome recognized the difficulty posed by Jesus' warning that the sons of Zebedee would drink the cup that he was about to drink, but Jerome explained that John qualified as a martyr by having been delivered from death:

> He asked how the sons of Zebedee, James and John, of course, would drink the cup of martyrdom, since scripture tells how

James was the only apostle beheaded by Herod (Acts 12). John, however, ended his life with his own (voluntary) death. If we read the ecclesiastical histories, we will see that John did not lack the spirit of martyrdom and drank the cup of confession which the three children in the fiery furnace drank (Dan. 3), although a persecutor did not shed his blood, for they note that he was placed in a vat of burning oil to be martyred and thence proceeded to receive the crown of a Christian athlete and immediately was dispatched to the isle of Patmos.[118]

In this account, Jerome is dependent on Tertullian, whose report of the burning oil Jerome cites explicitly elsewhere.[119] The most famous legend reported by Jerome, however, concerns the words John repeated over and over again as an old man:

The blessed evangelist John, when he delayed at Ephesus up to the highest old age and could scarcely be carried to church in the hands of disciples and was not able to put together a statement of several words, used to offer in different sayings nothing but: "Little children, love one another." At last the disciples and brethren who were present, tired of the fact that they always heard the same thing, said, "Teacher, why do you always say this?" John made a worthy response: "Because it was the Lord's precept, and if it alone is done, it is enough."[120]

HILARY OF POITIERS

Hilary of Poitiers (300?–367), the learned bishop of Gaul, wrote vividly of John the fisherman at the beginning of an exposition of the prologue to the Gospel and then rode the image relentlessly by referring to the apostle repeatedly as a "fisherman": "There stands by my side, to guide me through the difficulties which I have enunciated, a poor fisherman, ignorant, unedu- cated, fishing-lines in hand, clothes dripping, muddy feet, every inch a sailor."[121]

AMBROSE

From Ambrose (337/340–397), the great preacher of Milan, we have the suggestion that John was younger than Peter: "Often, too, those who were alike in virtue, but unlike in years were greatly rejoiced at their union, as Peter and John were. We read in the Gospel that John was a young man, even in his own words, though he was behind none of the elders in merits and wisdom."[122] Ambrose also supposed that the young man in the garden, who had fled naked at Jesus' arrest, was the apostle John.[123]

AUGUSTINE

Born in A.D. 354, in Tagaste, Algeria, Augustine was to become the primary shaper of much of Western Christianity. His life reflects both the worldly character of his father and the Christian devotion of his mother. He studied rhetoric in Carthage, began living with a concubine at the age of seventeen, and shortly thereafter had a son. He credited the study of Cicero's now-lost work *Hortensius* with turning his devotion to the Lord at the age of nineteen. When the study of the scriptures did not live up to his expectations, he turned to Manichaeism. He prayed: "Grant me chastity and continency, but not yet."[124] Eventually, however, Augustine also became disillusioned with Manichaeism. In A.D. 383, he moved to Rome and within a year secured a post as a teacher of rhetoric in Milan, where he heard the preaching of Ambrose. It was a chaotic period. He broke relations with his concubine, began a relationship with another, and was betrothed to a woman fit for his social position. Abandoning the dualism of Manichaeism, he embraced the worldview of Neoplatonism. He became painfully disturbed by the gulf between his sensuous pursuits and his lofty ideals. In A.D. 386, while reading Romans 13:13–14 in a garden, Augustine experienced a dramatic conversion. Subsequently, he resigned his professorship and began to prepare for baptism. For the next several years, he lived at Cassisacum, Rome, Tegaste, and then Hippo, where he founded a monastery. He died in A.D. 430, when Hippo was under attack by the Vandals.[125]

Among the voluminous writings of Augustine are his sermons on New Testament lessons and 124 tractates on the Gospel of John. From these, we get a clear indication of his high regard for the Gospel of John and some hints at interesting developments in the legends about the apostle. Many can identify with Augustine's observation that "The Gospel of John exercises our minds, refines and uncarnalizes them, that of God we may think not after a carnal but a spiritual manner."[126] Augustine never tired of citing the account of the Beloved Disciple's reclining on the breast of Jesus as the source of John's inspiration:

> For this beginning of the Gospel of St. John poured forth, for that he drank it in from the Lord's Breast. For ye remember, that it has been very lately read to you, how that this St. John the Evangelist lay in the Lord's Bosom. And wishing to explain this clearly, he says, "On the Lord's Breast;" that we might understand what he meant, by "in the Lord's bosom." For what, think we, did he drink

in who was lying on the Lord's Breast? Nay, let us not think, but drink, for we too just now heard what we may drink in.[127]

Augustine continues in the same vein in his next sermon:

> He saw the Word from the beginning and drank It in. He saw above every creature, he drank in from the Lord's breast. For this same St. John the Evangelist is he whom Jesus specially loved; inasmuch that he lay on His Breast at supper. There was this secret, that therefrom might be drunk in, what in the Gospel was to be poured forth.[128]

In a subsequent sermon, this imagery is developed one step further: "If he said the truth, truth cannot flow from the fountain of falsehood. Who is the Fountain? Christ: let John be the stream."[129] Augustine explains the differences between the Gospel of John and the synoptics by saying that although John recorded fewer of Christ's deeds, he recorded them "with greater carefulness" and recorded the words he spoke "with larger wealth of detail."[130]

It is not surprising, therefore, that Augustine felt it was more appropriate to assign the image of the eagle to John than to Mark:

> For these reasons, it also appears to me, that of the various parties who have interpreted the living creatures in the Apocalypse as significant of the four evangelists, those who have taken the lion to point to Matthew, the man to Mark, the calf to Luke, and the eagle to John, have made a more reasonable explanation of the figures than those who have assigned the man to Matthew, the eagle to Mark, and the lion to John.[131]

The following chart reflects the variety of interpretations to which Augustine refers:[132]

Revelation 4:7	Irenaeus	Augustine	Jerome
Lion	John	Matthew	Mark
Calf	Luke	Luke	Luke
Man	Matthew	Mark	Matthew
Eagle	Mark	John	John

Jerome's interpretation prevailed, however, and has since been repeatedly reflected in artists' images of the four evangelists.

In Tractate 36, Augustine appeals to legend to enhance the image of John as the eagle:

> There remains the eagle; this is John, the preacher of sublime truths, and a contemplator with steady gaze of the inner and eternal light. It is said, indeed, that the young eagles are tested by the parent birds in this way: the young one is suspended from the talons of the male parent and directly exposed to the rays of the sun; if it looks steadily at the sun, it is recognized as a true brood; if its eye quivers, it is allowed to drop off, as a spurious brood. Now, therefore, consider how sublime are the things he ought to speak who is compared to the eagle. . . . [133]

This image too is one Augustine is fond of repeating. He begins an earlier Tractate with the words: "It is nothing new to your ears, beloved, that the Evangelist John, like an eagle, takes a loftier flight, and soars above the dark mist of earth to gaze with steadier eyes upon the light of truth."[134] Praise for the sublime character of the Gospel breaks out repeatedly, as in the following passage:

> Those three evangelists occupy themselves chiefly with the things which Christ did in the flesh, and with the precepts which he delivered to men, who also bear the burden of the flesh, for their instruction in the rightful exercise of this mortal life. Whereas John, on the other hand, soars like an eagle above the clouds of human infirmity, and gazes upon the light of the unchangeable truth with those keenest and steadiest eyes of the heart.[135]

Augustine's further characterization of the apostle includes an observation on John's reticence to speak of himself,[136] as well as a description that contrasts him with Peter in allegorical terms:

> There are two states in life, therefore, . . . one is in faith, the other in sight; one in the temporal sojourn in a foreign land, the other in the eternity of the [heavenly] abode; one in labor, the other in repose; one on the way, the other in the fatherland; one in active work, the other in the wages of contemplation. . . . The one was signified by the Apostle Peter, that other by John.[137]

Augustine knew the tradition of John's chastity and celibacy, but points out that it is not based in scripture:

> There are some who have entertained the idea—and those, too, who are no contemptible handlers of sacred eloquence—that the

Apostle John was more loved by Christ on the ground that he never married a wife, and lived in perfect chastity from early boyhood. There is, indeed, no distinct evidence of this in the canonical Scriptures: nevertheless it is an idea that contributes not a little to the suitableness of the opinion expressed above, namely, that that life was signified by him, where there will be no marriage.[138]

On the basis of the account in Acts that the early Christians held all things in common, Augustine interprets the report in John 19:27 that the Beloved Disciple took the mother of Jesus to "his own" to mean that John took Mary "not unto his own lands, for he had none of his own; but to his own dutiful services."[139]

Augustine's knowledge of the tradition of John's chastity may also explain his curious references to 1 John as St. John's "Epistle to the Parthians."[140] There is no variant in the texts which have this superscription, but Augustine never explained the reference, and there is no prior tradition of John's work among the Parthians. According to the Venerable Bede, "Many ecclesiastical authors, and among them St. Athanasius, Bishop of the Church of Alexandria, witness that the first Epistle of St. John was written *Ad Parthos*."[141] But there is no evidence elsewhere that Athanasius knew of this superscription. It is an attractive suggestion that this curious superscription—which in Greek reads *pros parthous*—is a corruption of *pros parthenous,* "to the Virgins," or *tou parthenou,* "of the Virgin." The superscription known to Augustine, "The Epistle of John to the Parthians," is probably a corruption of an earlier superscription which read either "The Epistle of John to the Virgins" (cf. 2 John 1) or "The Epistle of John the Virgin."

Probably the most famous legend about the apostle recorded by Augustine is the report that the ground rose and fell above John's tomb, a phenomenon some took as evidence that John was not dead but asleep: "Let him employ as an argument the current report that there the earth is in sensible commotion, and presents a kind of heaving appearance, and assert . . . that this is occasioned by his breathing. . . ."[142] After referring to the story of John's burial,[143] Augustine goes on to refute the notion that John

was actually buried when asleep, and that he will so remain till the coming of Christ, making known meanwhile the fact of his life by the bubbling up of the dust, which is believed to be forced by the breath of the sleeper to ascend from the depths to the surface of the grave. I think it quite superfluous to contend with such an opinion. For those may see for themselves who know the locality whether the ground there does or suffers what is said regarding it, because, in truth, we too have heard of it from those who are not altogether unreliable witnesses.[144]

The preface to the tractates, written by an unknown author, adds that John "preached the word of the Lord, orally, with no writing to assist him" for sixty-five years, down to the final days of Domitian.[145]

PSEUDO-HILARIUS

The following introduction to John is found in Vatican Codex 4222 (fol. 46) under the title "Tractatus Sti. Hilarii episcopi," which is inserted between various works by Augustine in this ninth-century manuscript:

> John the most holy evangelist was the youngest among all the apostles, Him the Lord held (in his arms) when the apostles discussed who among them was greatest and when He said: He who is not converted as this boy, will not enter the kingdom of heaven. It is he who reclined against the Lord's breast. It is he whom Jesus loved more than the others and to whom he gave his mother Mary, and whom he gave as a son to Mary.[146]

This tradition is noteworthy because it identifies John both as the youngest of the apostles and as the child Jesus blessed (see Matt. 18:1–4).

PETER CHRYSOLOGUS

St. Peter Chrysologus (ca. 406–450), Archbishop of Ravenna, was not an outstanding theologian but an able pastor, administrator, and bishop remembered for his homilies. He also worked to promote the construction and decoration of ecclesiastical buildings. In fulfillment of a vow made during a storm, the Church of St. John the Evangelist was constructed and consecrated by Peter sometime before A.D. 439. The epithet *Chrysologus,* "Golden Worded" or "the Golden Orator," which was probably invented to give the Western Church a preacher of stature equal to John Chrysostom, first appears in the *Life* of Peter written by Agnellus (ninth century).[147] Peter preserves one further element of the legends about John, namely that he was the young man mentioned by Mark (14:51–52) who fled naked from the garden, leaving his linen cloth behind.[148]

PHILIP OF SIDE AND GEORGE THE SINNER

As his name indicates, Philip was a native of Side in Pamphylia. After he was ordained as a deacon at Constantinople by John Chrysostom, they became close friends. Between 434 and 439, Philip produced his greatest work, the thirty-six-volume *Christian History*. Unfortunately, only fragments of this work have survived—and these, only in the excerpts from a seventh-century collection preserved in Codex Baroccianus 142 (fourteenth or fifteenth century). The most celebrated and contested excerpt asserts that Papias wrote that John was martyred along with James by the Jews:

> Papias, bishop of Hierapolis, a disciple of John the Theologian and friend of Polycarp, wrote *The Lord's Gospel* in five books. There he gave a list of the Apostles and, after enumerating Peter and John, Philip and Thomas and Matthew, recorded as "disciples of the Lord" Aristion and another John, whom he also called "presbyter." As a result, some believe that (this) John is the author of the two short Catholic Epistles, which circulate under the name of John, their reason being that the men of the primitive age accepted the First Epistle only. Some have also erroneously believed the Apocalypse to be this man's work. Papias, too, is in error about the Millennium, and so is, in consequence, Irenaeus. Papias says in the second book that John the Evangelist and his brother James were slain by the Jews. The aforesaid Papias related, alleging as his source of information the daughters of Philip, that Barsabas, the same Justus that passed the scrutiny, was forced by the unbelievers to drink snake poison, but was in the name of Christ preserved unharmed. He relates still other marvelous events, in particular the rising of Manaemus's mother from the dead. Regarding those who were raised from the dead by Christ, he says that they survived till Hadrian's time.[149]

A similar report of the death of John at the hands of the Jews appears in one manuscript of the *Chronicle* of George the Sinner (ca. A.D. 840), which says: "John has been deemed worthy of martyrdom. For Papias, the Bishop of Hierapolis, having been an eyewitness of him (*or* of it?), says in the second book of his 'Dominical Oracles,' that he was killed by Jews, having evidently fulfilled, with his brother the prediction of Christ concerning them."[150] George maintains that Origen corroborated this report in his *Commentary on Matthew*, but concerning Matthew 20:23, Origen says only that Herod killed James and that John was sent into exile by the emperor. If it were not for the testimony of Philip of Side, one would be tempted to think that since George mistakenly cites Origen, he was also mistaken about Papias.

J. H. Bernard notes that the title "theologian" is not attested for John until the fourth century.[151] Moreover, James was not killed by the Jews but by Herod (to please certain Jews). On the other hand, Eusebius, Jerome, and

Hegesippus emphasize that James the brother of Jesus was killed by Jews. Bernard, therefore, conjectures that a corruption in the text of Papias led to the confusion of James the brother of Jesus and James the son of Zebedee, and that the corruption was then read as a reference to the death of James *and* John. Bernard's judgment that Philip of Side and George the Sinner are not reliable historians has continued to be the position of most Johannine scholars, but others—notably B. W. Bacon and, more recently, Martin Hengel— have maintained the credibility of these references to Papias.[152]

References in early Christian calendars, martyrologies, and homilies provide scattered but questionable support for the early martyrdom of John. The *Manichaean Psalm-Book,* for example, which has been traced to the fourth century and appears to derive from Syrian origins, contains the following reference to John in a tribute to the apostolic martyrs: "The two sons of Zebedee were made to drink the cup of the . . . / John the Virgin, he also was made to drink the cup, / fourteen days imprisoned that he might die of hunger. / And James also, he was stoned and killed."[153] These lines follow descriptions of the martyrdom of Peter and Andrew, preserving the sequence of a traditional list of the twelve apostles, but say only that John was imprisoned for fourteen days. They do not speak of a "red martyrdom."

The Calendar of Carthage, compiled about A.D. 505, places the commemoration of "St. John the Baptist and James the apostle, whom Herod murdered" on December 27, between the observance of the death of Stephen (December 26) and the slaughter of the innocents (December 28). The Western calendars all evidently depend on the Hieronymian Martyrology (early sixth century), which posits the death of John the Evangelist and the ordination of James the Just on December 27: "The Assumption of St John the Evangelist at Ephesus and the ordination to the episcopate of St James, our Lord's brother, who was the first of the Jews to be ordained by the apostles bishop of Jerusalem and gained the crown of martyrdom at the time of the pasch."[154] In the East, the earliest Syrian martyrology, which dates from A.D. 411 in Edessa, depends on a martyrology compiled in Greek at Nicomedia about A.D. 360. The Syrian martyrology commemorates the death of Stephen on December 26, the martyrdom of "the apostles John and James at Jerusalem" on December 27, and the deaths of Paul and Simon Peter in Rome on December 28.[155]

The death of St. John is celebrated in the Greek church (Byzantine) on September 26, and the miracle of the manna coming from his tomb is commemorated on May 8:

> For indeed annually on the eighth day of the month of May the
> tomb—in which the great apostle and evangelist John was buried
> when he was about to be changed—suddenly boiling over and

issuing forth elevates by the Holy Spirit holy dust (which the inhabitants called manna). Those who take it, use it for the redemption of all who suffer, for healing persons, for delivering bodies, praising God and venerating the Theologian who served Him.[156]

Syrian and Armenian Christians commemorated the feast of John on December 27 and 28 with the observances for James. In the West, the feast of St. John is observed on December 27 and May 6. The May 6 date can be traced to the eighth century and was apparently the anniversary of a church near the Porta Latina that was dedicated in his honor.[157] At times, John's feast was confused with that of St. John the Baptist, and during the Middle Ages, the Latins fixed the day of his death as June 24. Consequently, the martyrologies for that date announced the "Assumption of S. John." At Hertogenbosch, Holland, for example, the following feast dates were celebrated: feast of his exile, September 27; return from exile, December 3; feast of his death, June 26.[158] By one count, 181 ancient churches were dedicated to St. John.[159]

An argument from silence for the early martyrdom of John may be based on a quotation from Heracleon in Clement of Alexandria which says that "Matthew, Philip, Thomas, Levi, and many others" did not die a martyr's death— that is, they were not among those who "confessed with the confession made by the voice and departed."[160] Since John is not expressly mentioned among those who did not die a martyr's death, some have argued that Heracleon counted him among the early martyrs. A homily (A.D. 343 or 344) from the Syrian church father Aphraates, who was bishop of the Monastery of Mar Mathai and Metropolitan of Nineveh, claims: "Great and excellent is the martyrdom of Jesus . . . to him followed the faithful martyr Stephen whom the Jews stoned. Simon also and Paul were perfect martyrs. James and John trod in the footsteps of their Master Christ. Also other of the Apostles thereafter in divers places confessed, and proved themselves true martyrs."[161]

The evidence for the early martyrdom of John is scattered, therefore, and can hardly be traced to a common source unless it is Jesus' prediction in Mark 10:39 and Matthew 20:23.[162] Several issues must be dealt with, however. If Papias indeed had tradition of the death of John as well as James, was it independent of these Gospel references? Would Mark have made reference to the death of John along with his brother had John not already suffered martyrdom? If one reads these verses as evidence that Mark knew of John's death, then the time of John's death must be fixed between Paul's meeting with the three "pillar" apostles (Gal. 2:9) and the writing of Mark (about 70). The location would presumably be either Judea or Samaria. Indeed, it has been suggested that there was confusion in the traditions concerning the deaths of John the Baptist and the apostle John, and that the apostle was put to death in Sebaste and buried in the tomb of Nabi Jahja.[163] On the other hand, if one accepts the early martyrdom of John, then one must also account for both the suppression of John's martyrdom in later sources (after Irenaeus) and the silence throughout early Christian sources regarding the death of a prominent apostle who was martyred about the same time as James the Just, Peter, and Paul, whose martyrdoms are much more widely attested.

The cumulative weight of the references just considered has been enough to keep alive the possibility of the early martyrdom of John but not sufficient to override the tradition of his long residence in Ephesus. As the tradition of the Ephesian residence becomes more suspect there has naturally been renewed interest in the testimonies to John's early martyrdom. It is not necessarily an either/or choice, however, between the traditions of a long residence in Ephesus or an early martyrdom in Jerusalem. Both may be legendary, and the circumstances of the death of John may simply be unknown, as are the circumstances of the death of most of the other apostles.

HIPPOLYTUS OF THEBES

The fragments of Hippolytus (ca. A.D. 980) fill in details of already established legends. John is referred to as the one "whom Christ loved" and as the virgin and the evangelist. He remained in Jerusalem, and the "mother ŏf the church" stayed in his house. Zebedee, John's father, was first among the distinguished men of Galilee and owned his own boat. After his father's death, John sold the property in Galilee, gave a portion of the proceeds to the high priest, and bought land in Jerusalem—thus making himself known to the high priest.[164] John received the most holy mother of God in his home until her assumption and, after this, preached the word and was himself taken up.[165] According to one of the fragments, the Virgin—who lived to be fifty-six— stayed in John's house for eleven years. It was to John's house that the apostles fled in fear of the Jews, and the risen Lord appeared to them there.[166] Another fragment records a tradition that John's mother was Salome and that she was the daughter of Joseph, who had four sons and three daughters. Since Salome was the wife of Zebedee, John was the grandson of Joseph, the husband of Mary.[167]

EPIPHANIUS THE MONK

In his *Life of the Virgin,* Epiphanius the Monk (ca. A.D. 1015) embellishes several pericopes from the Gospels and connects them with John. Jesus, his mother, and the disciples came to Zebedee and ate with him. Jesus called James and John to be his disciples. Their mother thought he was announcing an earthly kingdom, so she asked that her sons might sit on his left and right hands in the kingdom (Matt. 20:20–21). Later, Zebedee died, and James asked to go and bury his father, but the Lord would not let him go (Luke 9:59–60). After a little while, though, Jesus allowed the two brothers, James and John, to bury Zebedee. They also brought their mother to Jesus, and she stayed with Jesus' mother the rest of her life. Because their possessions were many, James and John sold them, came to Jerusalem, and bought Zion.[168] Caiaphas stayed there, and hence John became known to the high priest. When Jesus sent two disciples into Jerusalem to prepare the Passover meal, they did so at John's house (Mark 14:12–16). John said, "Come to the dinner," and there, the Last Supper was eaten. After the resurrection, the disciples remained at John's house because John had taken Jesus' mother to his home, and it was there that the Lord appeared to them behind locked doors (John 20:19).[169]

SUIDAS

The *Suidas* is a historical and literary encyclopedia compiled about the end of the tenth century. Although it is a valuable source of ancient scholarship, it nevertheless often depends on abridgements and has suffered corruptions and interpolations. The reference to Chrysostom in the entry on John suggests that Chrysostom may have been the source for Suidas at this point, but 2 and 3 John are not used in any of the extant writings of Chrysostom. The entry reads: "John: A divine name. Because John the Theologian and Evangelist, having returned from the exile on Patmos, composed the Gospel, being 100 years old, enduring until 120, passing on and writing down the theology. And Chrysostom receives also his three letters and the Apocalypse."[170] The age of John given here can be compared with the ages recorded by Epiphanius, Eusebius, Jerome, and the *Legenda aurea*.[171]

JACOBUS DE VORAGINE, *LEGENDA AUREA*

By far the most popular and influential medieval compilation of the legends of the saints was the *Legenda aurea* (Golden Legend), written by the Dominican friar Jacobus de Voragine (ca. 1229–1298) about 1260. For his material on John, the author was largely dependent on a version of Pseudo-Melitus, which had been interpolated with the story of the boiling oil.[172] Pseudo-Melitus was abridged by Isidore of Seville, whose work Jacobus may also have known. Sherry L. Reames, who has written a monograph on the influence of the Golden Legend, says it was "not just a popular book in our sense; it was almost a cultural institution."[173] During the century and a half before the invention of the printing press, the *Legenda aurea* was probably copied as much as any other non-biblical manuscript. With the dawn of the print era, Caxton's English translation went through nine editions between 1483 and 1527, and on the continent, 156 editions of Jacobus's work appeared between 1470 and 1507.[174]

According to the Golden Legend, John was granted four privileges: the noble love of Jesus Christ, virginity, the revelation of the secrets of the Lord (e.g., the divinity of the Son of God and the end of the world), and keeping of "the mother of God."[175] John was the son of Zebedee, who had married the third sister of Mary, the mother of Jesus. In reference to John's virginity, Jacobus adds the following rather enigmatic observation: "our Lord kept to him his virginity like as S. Jerome saith, for he was at his wedding, and he abode a clean virgin."[176] Is this a reference to the tradition that John was the groom at the wedding at Cana, or does Jacobus assume—anachronistically—that Jerome was present at that event?

Following the ascension of Jesus, John worked in Greece and founded many churches there. Domitian brought John to Rome and cast him into a vat of hot oil in the presence of the senators. When this ordeal did not hurt John but left him "more pure and more fair" than before, Domitian sent the apostle into exile on Patmos. There, John was visited by angels "and governed," and wrote the Apocalypse. In the same year that Domitian was put to death, his decrees were overturned by the senate, and John was brought to Ephesus with great honor: "And all the people of Ephesus came against him singing and saying: Blessed be he that cometh in the name of our Lord."[177]

Drusiana loved John, kept his commandments, and longed for his return from exile. When she died just before that event, her friends brought her body to John, who commanded that they should set down the bier, unbind, and remove the clothes from her. Calling upon God, John raised her from the dead and sent her into her house to prepare for him "some refection." For three hours the people cried out, praising God.[178] (Note how closely this story parallels the synoptic account of the raising of the Widow of Nain's son, Luke 7:11–17).

The story of Crato and the sticks and pebbles, which is found in Pseudo-Abdias and Pseudo-Melitus,[179] follows at this point in the Golden Legend. Just as in Pseudo-Abdias, the account in the Golden Legend continues with the story of the destruction of the temple of Diana and Aristodemus's challenge to John to drink the cup of poison.[180] This popular story was no doubt given even more currency by its inclusion in the Golden Legend. Other well-known stories follow: that of John and the robber captain, from Clement of Alexandria,[181] that of John's fleeing from the bath when he learned that Cerinthus was inside,[182] and that of the partridge, told by Cassian.[183]

Jacobus adds that according to the Venerable Bede, John wrote his Gospel after the other evangelists, sixty-six years after the ascension. John asked the bishops around Ephesus to fast and pray for three days that he might write his Gospel truly. Jacobus also repeats Jerome's story of the elderly John repeating the charge that his disciples should love one another.[184] Sixty-eight years after the ascension, John, who was thirty-one at the time, died at the old age of ninety-nine. Jacobus repeats the story of John's departure,[185] apparently again depending on Pseudo-Melitus as abridged by Isidore. The Lord and his disciples summoned John: "Come my friend to me, for it is time that thou come, eat and be fed at my table with thy brethren."[186] John replied that he had long looked forward to this time, and the Lord told John that John would come to him on the next Sunday. The people all assembled in the church in Ephesus that had been built in John's honor. After the mass, John instructed the people to dig a pit in front of the altar (note the difference from the *Acts of John,* which reports that they went out of the city).[187] John descended into the pit, held his hands up to heaven, and prayed:

> Sweet Lord Jesu Christ, I yield me unto thy desire, and thank thee that thou hast vouchsafed to call me to thee, if it please thee, receive me for to be with my brethren, with whom thou hast summoned me, open to me the gate of the life permanable, and lead me to the feast of thy well and best dressed meats. Thou art Christ the son of the living God, which by the commandment of the father hast saved the world, to thee I render and yield grace and thankings, world without end, thou knowest well that I have desired thee with all my heart. After that he made his prayer much amorously and piteously, anon came upon him great clearness and light, and so great brightness that none might see him, and when this light and brightness was gone and departed, there was nothing found in the pit or grave but manna, which came springing from under upward, like as sand in a fountain or springing well, where much people have been delivered of many diseases and sicknesses by the merits and prayers of this glorious saint. Some say and affirm that he died without pain of death, and that he was in that clearness borne into heaven body and soul, whereof God knoweth the certainty. And we that be yet here beneath in this misery, ought to pray devoutly to him that he would impetre and get to us the grace of our Lord which is blessed in secula secolorum. Amen.[188]

Jacobus closes his compilation of the legends about John with the story of King Edward's meeting John.[189] From the Golden Legend, therefore, we see the form and content of the legends about John as they were popularly known and disseminated during the late Middle Ages.

NICEPHORUS CALLISTUS

The church history written by Nicephorus (ca. 1256–ca. 1335) chronicles events from the birth of Christ to the death of Emperor Phocas (A.D. 610) in eighteen books, drawing directly or indirectly on earlier histories. In a passing reference included in his account of the activities of the apostles following the ascension, Nicephorus says that John stayed in Jerusalem and cared for Mary at his house on Mount Zion until the day of her death.[190] Nicephorus also devotes a section of his history to "the holy apostle and evangelist John the Theologian."[191] John then preached the Gospel in Asia and was exiled on Patmos by Emperor Domitian. While on Patmos, he wrote both the Gospel and Revelation. After Domitian's death, John returned to preach in the churches of Asia. At this point, Nicephorus repeats the story of the robber captain, citing Clement of Alexandria. John died sixty-eight years after the crucifixion, a figure which shows his dependence on Jerome or Eusebius.[192]

CONCLUSION

This chapter has chronicled the various forms in which the legends about John circulated from the early centuries through the Middle Ages. Eusebius perpetuated the orthodox view that the Gospel of John was written by the aged apostle of Ephesus, but following Dionysius, he refused to attribute the Apocalypse to the apostle. Instead, he assigned it to John the Elder, who, in his view, also resided in Ephesus. Eusebius, therefore, took a major step in establishing the role of John the Elder in the history of debates concerning the role of the apostle and the authorship of the Johannine writings (as will become evident in chapter 10). For Epiphanius, John was a model of piety and opposition to heresy. Jerome reported the story of John's addressing the church in Ephesus when he was so aged that all he could say was "Little children, love one another." Jerome also attested to the acceptance of the two shorter epistles as apostolic writings and perpetuated the tradition that John never married. The story that the ground rose and fell above John's tomb, as though he were still breathing, can be traced to Augustine. Pseudo-Hilarius added to the tradition the report that John was the youngest of the apostles and that he was the child Jesus took in his arms and blessed. Peter Chrysologus further identified the young man who fled naked from the garden as the apostle John. Philip of Side and George the Sinner hold important places in the history of the tradition because of their reports that Papias had recorded the martyrdom of John at the hands of the Jews.

Ironically, however, the line between the emergence of ecclesiastical traditions about John as one of the church's saints and the apocryphal stories that feature John as an apostolic hero can hardly be drawn. Differences in the degree of freedom granted to the stories about the apostle or the prominence and authority of the communities which perpetuated them are difficult to document, so we turn to the apocryphal acts with no pretence that there is any clear distinction in historicity or veneration between the apocryphal acts and the authorized ecclesiastical traditions.

NOTES

1. Tertullian, *On Prescription against Heretics* 36 (*ANF* 3:260).
2. Other references to the boiling in oil appear in Jerome (*Against Jovinian* 1.26; Migne, *PL* 23:259b), Bede, and Pseudo-Augustine. For a full discussion of these texts and the alternative location in Ephesus rather than Rome, see Eric Junod and Jean-Daniel Kaestli, *Acta Iohannis,* CChr (Turnhout: Brepols, 1983), 2:775–80.
3. Tertullian, *Against Marcion* 3.14, 24; 4.5 (*ANF* 3:333, 342, 350).
4. Tertullian, *Against Marcion* 4.2 (*ANF* 3:347).
5. Tertullian, *Against Marcion* 5.16 (*ANF* 3:464).
6. Tertullian, *On Prescription against Heretics* 33 (*ANF* 3:259).
7. See Tertullian, *On the Flesh of Christ* 3 (*ANF* 3:523).
8. Tertullian, *On Prescription against Heretics* 32 (*ANF* 3:258). See also Tertullian, *Against Marcion* 4.5 (*ANF* 3:350), for another reference to John's churches, apparently the seven churches of the Apocalypse.
9. Tertullian, *On Monogamy* 17 (*ANF* 4:72).
10. Martin Hengel accepts Tertullian's list as a reference to the evangelist and suggests the tradition may have arisen either from John's taking Jesus' mother (John 19:26–27) or from the reference to the 144,000 elect's being chaste men (Rev. 14:4); see *The Johannine Question* (Philadelphia: Trinity Press International, 1989), 166 n. 33. Eric Junod, in a detailed examination of the tradition of John's virginity, ties that tradition to the interpretation of John 13:23–25, but dismisses the reference in Tertullian as a reference to John the Baptist; see "La virginité de l'apôtre Jean: rechereche sur les origines scripturaires et patristiques de cette tradition," in *Lectures anciennes de la Bible,* Cahiers de Biblia Patristica 1 (Strasbourg: Centre d'analyse et de documentation patristiques, 1987), 113–36.
11. Clement of Alexandria, *Paedagogus* 1.6, 9 (*ANF* 2:219, 229); *Stromata* 2.15, 6.13 (*ANF* 2:362, 504).
12. Clement of Alexandria, *Stromata* 2.15 (*ANF* 2:362).
13. Clement of Alexandria, *Fragments from Cassiodorus* 4 (*ANF* 2:576).
14. Clement of Alexandria, *Fragments from Cassiodorus* 3 (*ANF* 2:574).
15. Moschus, *Spiritual Meadow* 5.176 (*ANF* 2:578).
16. Eusebius, *E.H.* 2.1.3 (LCL 1:105).
17. Clement of Alexandria, *Stromata* 1.1 (*ANF* 2:301); the translation quoted is in Eusebius, *E.H.* 5.11.5 (LCL 1:465).
18. Eusebius, *E.H.* 2.1.4 (LCL 1;105).
19. Eusebius, *E.H.* 3.23.4 (LCL 1:243).
20. Clement of Alexandria, *Who Is the Rich Man That Shall Be Saved?* 42 (*ANF* 2:603); quoted in Eusebius, *E.H.* 3.23.6–19 (LCL 1:243–49).

21. Eusebius, *E.H.* 6.14.7 (LCL 2:49), quoting Clement of Alexandria, *Hypotyposes* 6 (*ANF* 2:580).

22. Origen, *Commentary on the Gospel According to Matthew* 1 (*ANF* 10:412); quoted in Eusebius, *E.H.* 6.25.6 (LCL 2:75).

23. Origen, *Exposition on the Gospel According to John* 5.3 (*ANF* 10:346–47); quoted in Eusebius, *E.H.* 6.25.9–10 (LCL 2:77).

24. Eusebius, *E.H.* 6.24.1 (LCL 2:71).

25. Dionysius, quoted in Eusebius, *E.H.* 7.25.1–2 (LCL 2:197).

26. Dionysius, quoted in Eusebius, *E.H.* 7.25.6–27 (LCL 2:199–209).

27. This solution has been argued with great erudition by Hengel in *The Johannine Question.*

28. Johannes Quasten, *Patrology* (Westminster, Maryland: Newman Press, 1960), 3:85, 91.

29. See below, p. 201.

30. Quoted in Eusebius, *E.H.* 3.31.3 (LCL 1:271). See the discussion of Polycrates above, p. 128.

31. Quoted in Eusebius, *E.H.* 7.25.16 (LCL 2:203). See above, p. 146.

32. Eusebius, *E.H.* 3.39.6 (LCL 1:292–93).

33. See Theodor Zahn, "Die Wanderungen des Apostels Johannes," *NKZ* 10 (1899): 191–218; and Robert Eisler, *The Enigma of the Fourth Gospel: Its Author and Its Writer* (London: Methuen, 1938), 121. See also the excavation reports cited below, n. 46.

34. Eduard Schwarz, ed., *Acta Conciliorum Oecumenicorum,* 1.5 (Berlin, 1927), 128, cited in Eisler, *The Enigma of the Fourth Gospel,* 124; and F. F. Bruce, *Peter, Stephen, James, and John: Studies in Early Non-Pauline Christianity* (Grand Rapids: Wm. B. Eerdmans, 1980), 124 n. 9.

35. Schwarz, ed., *Acta Conciliorum Oecumenicorum,* 1.2, 70; cited in Bruce, *Peter, Stephen, James, and John,* 124 n. 9.

36. Jerome, *Lives of Illustrious Men* 9 (*NPNF,* 2d. ser., 3:364–65).

37. James Stalker, *The Two St. Johns of the New Testament* (New York: American Tract Society, 1895), 140.

38. This legend is found in the Manuscript of Paris, gr. 1468, a revision of the *Acts of John by Prochorus,* and of a secondary form of the *Acts of John;* see Junod and Kaestli, *Acta Iohannis* 1:145–48. For the Greek text, see *Acta Iohannis* 1:375, or Zahn, *Acta Joannis* (Erlangen: Verlag von Andreas Deichert, 1880), 192. An English translation in which the first-person references are changed to third person is given by Eisler, *The Enigma of the Fourth Gospel,* 125–26.

39. Eisler, *The Enigma of the Fourth Gospel,* 126.

40. Eisler, *The Enigma of the Fourth Gospel,* 126.

41. See above, p. 169. See also Eric Junod and Jean-Daniel Kaestli, *L'histoire des actes apocryphes des apôtres du IIIe au IXe siècle: le cas des Actes de Jean,* Cahiers de la Revue de théologie et de philosophie 7 (Geneva: Revue de théologie et de philosophie, 1982), 85 n. 168, 116 n. 20; and Jean-Daniel Kaestli, "Le rapport entre les deux Vies latines de l'apôtre Jean," in *Apocrypha* 3 (1992).

42. Procopius of Caesarea, *Buildings* 5.1.6; *Procopius,* trans. H. B. Dewing and

Glanville Downey, LCL (Cambridge, Mass.: Harvard University Press, 1954), 7:317–19.

43. Musa Baran, *Ephesus and Its Surroundings,* trans. Hulya Terzioglu (Izmir: Molay Matbaacilik, n.d.), 17.

44. Procopius of Caesarea, *Secret History* 3.3; *Procopius,* trans. H. B. Dewing, LCL (Cambridge, Mass.: Harvard University Press, 1959), 6:33–35.

45. William Dallmann, *John: Disciple, Evangelist, Apostle* (St. Louis: Concordia, 1932), 107.

46. G. A. Sotiriu, J. Keil, and H. Hörmann, "Die Johanneskirche," pt. 3 of *Forschungen in Ephesos,* 4 (Vienna: Verlag des österreichischen archäologischen Institut, 1951); J. Keil, "XIII Vorläufiger Bericht über die Ausgrabungen in Ephesus," *Jahreshefte des österreichischen archäologischen Instituts in Wien* 24 (1929), Beiblatt, cols. 8–67 (esp. 52–67); "XIV Vorläufiger Bericht über die Ausgrabungen in Ephesus," *JhOAI* 25 (1929), Beiblatt, cols. 5–52 (esp. 5–21); "Die Wiederauffindung des Johannesgrabes in Ephesus," *Bib* 13 (1932): 121ff. François-Marie Braun, *Jean le théologien et son évangile dans l'église ancienne* (Paris: J. Gabalda, 1959), 1:365–74. See further Richard Krautheimer, *Early Christian and Byzantine Architecture* (Harmondsworth: Penguin Books, 1979), 112f.; and Clive Foss, *Ephesos after Antiquity* (Cambridge: Cambridge University Press, 1979), 87–94.

47. Dallmann, *John,* 107.

48. Hörmann, "Die Johanneskirche," 185.

49. Victorinus of Petau, *Commentary on the Apocalypse,* on Revelation 4:7–10 (*ANF* 7:348).

50. *Commentary on the Apocalypse,* on Revelation 10:11 and 11:1 (*ANF* 7:353–54). Note the similarity of this account and the description of the composition of the Gospel in the *Muratorian Canon* quoted above, p. 000.

51. For the life of Eusebius, see "Introduction" to Eusebius of Caesarea, *Ecclesiastical History,* trans. Kirsopp Lake, LCL (Cambridge: Harvard University Press, 1926), 1:ix–xvii; and "Introduction," *NPNF,* 2d ser., 1:1–26.

52. Eusebius, *Chronicle* 850, in *Eusebius Werke,* 5: *Die Chronik,* ed. Josef Karst, GCS (Leipzig: J. C. Hinrichs'sche Buchhandlung, 1911), 218.

53. Eusebius, *E.H.* 3.1.1 (LCL 1:191).

54. Eusebius, *E.H.* 3.18.1–3 (LCL 1:235–37); quoting Irenaeus, *Adv. Haer.* 5.30.3 (*ANF* 1:559–60).

55. Eusebius, *E.H.* 3.20.8–9 (LCL 1:241).

56. Irenaeus, *Adv. Haer.* 2.22.5 (*ANF* 1:392).

57. Irenaeus, *Adv. Haer.* 3.3.4 (*ANF* 1:416).

58. Eusebius, *E.H.* 3.23.1–19 (LCL 1:241–49); Clement of Alexandria, *Who Is the Rich Man That Shall Be Saved?* 42 (*ANF* 2:603–4).

59. Reports that John knew the synoptics and wrote to supplement them also appear in the *Acts of Timothy* (see H. Usener, ed., *Bonner Universitätsprogramm* [Bonn: Caroli Georgi, 1877]), in Theodore of Mopsuestia (see above, p. 161), and in Jerome (see above, p. 162).

60. Eusebius, *E.H.* 3.24.1–13 (LCL 1:249–55).

182   John, the Son of Zebedee

61. Eusebius, *E.H.* 3.24.17–18 (LCL 1:255–57).
62. Justin Martyr, *Dialogue with Trypho* 81 (*ANF* 1:240); Eusebius, *E.H.* 4.18.8 (LCL 1:371–73).
63. See below; and Eusebius, *E.H.* 3.39.1–7 (LCL 1:291–95).
64. Eusebius, *E.H.* 7.25.2 (LCL 2:197).
65. Eusebius, *E.H.* 3.28.6 (LCL 1:265–67); cf. *E.H.* 4.14.6 (LCL 1:337); and Irenaeus, *Adv. Haer.* 3.3.4. (*ANF* 1:416, quoted above, p. 125).
66. Eusebius, *E.H.* 3.31.2–3 (LCL 1:269–71).
67. Eusebius, *E.H.* 5.24.1–7 (LCL 1:505–7).
68. Eusebius, *E.H.* 3.39.1–7 (LCL 1:291–93). See the discussion of Papias above, pp. 109–12.
69. Josef Kürzinger, *Papias von Hierapolis und die Evangelien des Neuen Testaments,* Eichstätter Materialien, 4 (Regensburg: Verlag Friedrich Pustet, 1983), 116, fragment 16.
70. Eusebius, *E.H.* 3.39.14 (LCL 1:297).
71. Eusebius, *E.H.* 4.14.1–6 (LCL 1:335–37), 5.20.4–7 (LCL 1:497–99). See above, pp. 125–27.
72. Eusebius, *E.H.* 5.8.5–6 (LCL 1:457); quoting Irenaeus, *Adv. Haer.* 5.30.1, 3 (*ANF* 1:558, 559).
73. Eusebius, *E.H.* 5.18.12–14 (LCL 1:493).
74. Eusebius, *E.H.* 7.25.1–26.3 (LCL 2:197–209); see above, pp. 145–47.
75. Eusebius, *E.H.* 3.24.17 (LCL 1:255), 3.25.2–3 (LCL 1:256).
76. Eusebius, *E.H.* 3.25.6–7 (LCL 1:259).
77. Ephraem the Syrian, cited in Fred C. Conybeare, "Ein Zeugnis Ephräms über das Fehlen von c. 1 und 2 im Texte des Lucas," *ZNW* 3 (1902): 193; also cited in Charles H. Talbert, *Reading John: A Literary and Theological Commentary on the Fourth Gospel and the Johannine Epistles* (New York: Crossroad, 1992), 61.
78. See *The Panarion of Epiphanius of Salamis,* trans. Frank Williams, NHS 35 (Leiden: E. J. Brill, 1987), xi–xvi. For the Greek text, see Karl Holl, *Epiphanius (Ancoratus und Panarion),* GCS (Leipzig: J. C. Hinrischs'sche Buchhandlung, 1933).
79. See Irenaeus, *Adv. Haer.* 3.3.4 (*ANF* 1:416); see above, pp. 125, 154.
80. Epiphanius, *Panarion* 24.1–6; trans. Williams, 139–40. Cf. *The Panarion of St. Epiphanius, Bishop of Salamis: Selected Passages,* trans. Philip R. Amidon, S.J. (New York: Oxford University Press, 1990), 106.
81. Epiphanius, *Panarion* 51.6.9; trans. Amidon, 178.
82. Epiphanius, *Panarion* 51.12.2; trans. Amidon, 180.
83. Epiphanius, *Panarion* 66.19.7; trans. Amidon, 229.
84. Epiphanius, *Panarion* 66.20.1; trans. Amidon, 229.
85. Epiphanius, *Panarion* 30.3.8; trans. Amidon, 95.
86. Epiphanius, *Panarion* 58.4.5–6; trans. Amidon, 203.
87. Epiphanius, *Panarion* 78.13.4; trans. Amidon, 350.
88. See below, pp. 200–201.
89. Epiphanius, *Panarion* 79.5.3. This translation was suggested by Jean-Daniel Kaestli in a personal letter. He argues that this text alludes to the prayer in *Acts of John* 112–14 and 115, by which the apostle produces his own death.

90. Chrysostom, *Homilies on St. John* 2.1, 4 (*NPNF,* lst ser., 14:4–5).
91. Chrysostom, *Homilies on St. John* 2.4 (*NPNF,* 1st ser., 14:5).
92. Chrysostom, *The Gospel of Matthew,* Homily 76.2 (*NPNF,* 1st ser., 10:458).
93. Chrysostom, *Letters to the Fallen Theodore* 1.17 (*NPNF,* 1st ser., 9:109).
94. Chrysostom, *Homilies on St. John* 33.3 (*NPNF,* 1st ser., 14:117).
95. Chrysostom, *Homilies on St. John* 42.2, 43.1 (*NPNF,* 1st ser., 14:152, 156).
96. Chrysostom, *Homilies on St. John* 48.1 (*NPNF,* 1st ser., 14:173).
97. Chrysostom, *Homilies on St. John* 72.2 (*NPNF,* 1st ser., 14:264).
98. Chrysostom, *Homilies on St. John* 83.2 (*NPNF,* 1st ser., 14:308).
99. Chrysostom, *Homilies on St. John* 85.2 (*NPNF,* 1st ser., 14:318).
100. Chrysostom, *Homilies on St. John* 85.4 (*NPNF,* 1st ser., 14:321).
101. For the Greek text, see Robert Devreesse, *Essai sur Théodore de Mopsueste,* ST 141 (Città del Vaticano: Biblioteca Apostolica Vaticana, 1948), 305–7.
102. Jerome, *Lives of Illustrious Men* 9 (*NPNF,* 2d ser., 3:364–65).
103. Rudolf Helm, *Eusebius Werke, 7: Die Chronik des Hieronymous,* GCS 47 (Berlin: Akademie-Verlag, 1956), 192–93. See also above, n. 52.
104. See above, p. 158.
105. See above, p. 177.
106. See below, p. 221.
107. For the catalogue of the apostles from Pseudo-Epiphanius, see Theodor Schermann, *Propheten- und Apostellegenden nebst Jüngerkatalogen des Dorotheus und verwandter Texte,* TU 31,3 (Leipzig: J. C. Hinrichs'sche Buchhandlung, 1907), 257, 265. For the *Homily of Pseudo-Chrysostom* and the *Suidas,* see pp. 236 and 175. See also Jean-Daniel Kaestli, "Le rôle des textes bibliques dans la genèse et le développement des légendes apocryphes: Le cas du sort final de l'apôtre Jean," *Augustinianum* 23, nos. 1–2 (1983): 326–27.
108. Jerome, "Against the Pelagians," in *Saint Jerome: Dogmatic and Polemical Works* 2.15; trans. John N. Hritzu, FC 53 (Washington, D.C.: Catholic University of America Press, 1965), 318.
109. Jerome, *Letters* 53, "To Paulinus" (*NPNF,* 2d ser., 6:98).
110. Jerome, *Against Jovinian* 1.26; (Migne, *PL* 23:258); trans. E. Glenn Hinson.
111. Jerome, *Lives of Illustrious Men* 45 (*NPNF,* 2d ser., 3:362).
112. Jerome, *Lives of Illustrious Men* 17 (*NPNF,* 2d ser., 3:367).
113. Jerome, *Lives of Illustrious Men* 18 (*NPNF,* 2d ser., 3:367).
114. See Jerome, *Letters* 53.8 (Migne, *PL* 22:548); cited in Brown, *The Epistles of John,* 11.
115. Jerome, *Letters* 75.3, "To Theodora" (*NPNF,* 2d ser., 6:156).
116. Jerome, "Preface," *Commentary on Matthew* (*NPNF,* 2d ser., 6:495).
117. Quoted above, p. 129. Note also the role of fasting in Eusebius, *E. H.* 3.24.1–13 (LCL 1:249–55).
118. Jerome, *Commentary on Matthew* 20.23; in *S. Hieronymi Presbyteri Opera,* CChr, Series Latina 77 (Turnhout: Brepols, 1969), 178; trans. E. Glenn Hinson.
119. Jerome, *Against Jovinian* 1.26 (Migne, *PL* 23:259B).
120. Jerome, *Commentary on Galatians* 6.10 (Migne, *PL* 26:462); trans. E. Glenn Hinson.
121. St. Hilary of Poitiers, *On the Trinity* 2.13 (*NPNF,* 2d ser., 9:56).

122. Ambrose, *Duties of the Clergy* 2.20.101 (*NPNF,* 2d ser., 10:59).

123. Ambrose, *Exposition of Ps. 36.* See also Peter Chrysologus, *Sermons* 78, 150, 170 (Migne *PL* 52:421, 600, 645). These references are cited by B. W. Bacon in "John and the Pseudo-Johns," *ZNW* 31 (1932): 146. Bacon also cites a reference in Epiphanius stating the opinion that the master of the house in Matthew 26:18 was the apostle John. Ambrose refers twice to the question of John's final parting (*Exposition of the Gospel of Luke* 7.4). See Gabriel Tissot, *Traité sur l'évangile de s. Luc,* Sources Chrétiennes (Paris: Éditions du Cerf, 1958), 9–10; and *Exposition of the Psalms* 118.20.12 (CSEL 62, p. 451, 2–6).

124. Augustine, *Confessions* 8.7 (*NPNF,* 1st ser., 1:124).

125. Williston Walker et al., *A History of the Christian Church,* 4th ed. (New York: Charles Scribner's Sons, 1985), 160–62.

126. Augustine, Sermon 90 (*NPNF,* 1st ser., 6:530–31).

127. Augustine, Sermon 69 (*NPNF,* 1st ser., 6:466).

128. Augustine, Sermon 70 (*NPNF,* 1st ser., 6:467). For similar references in Augustine to John's reclining in the Lord's bosom, see Tractates 1.7, 20.1, 124.7 (*NPNF,* 1st ser., 7:137, 208, 268).

129. Augustine, Sermon 83 (*NPNF,* 1st ser., 6:508).

130. Augustine, "The Harmony of the Gospels" 1.5 (*NPNF,* 1st ser., 6:80).

131. Augustine, "The Harmony of the Gospels" 1.6 (*NPNF,* 1st ser., 6:80).

132. See Irenaeus, *Adv. Haer.* 3.11.8 (*ANF* 1:428); and Jerome, Homily 75, in *The Homilies of Saint Jerome,* trans. Marie Liguori Ewald, FC 57 (Washington, D.C.: Catholic University of America, 1966), 121.

133. Augustine, "Lectures or Tractates on the Gospel of John," Tractate 36.5 (*NPNF,* 1st ser., 7:210).

134. Augustine, "Lectures or Tractates on the Gospel of John," Tractate 15.1 (*NPNF,* 1st ser., 7:99).

135. Augustine, "The Harmony of the Gospels" 1.6 (*NPNF,* 1st ser., 6:81). See also "Lectures or Tractates on the Gospel of John," Tractates 20.13, 36.1, 48.6 (*NPNF,* 1st ser., 7:137, 208, 268).

136. Augustine, " Lectures or Tractates on the Gospel of John," Tractate 61.4 (*NPNF,* 1st ser., 7:311).

137. Augustine, "Lectures or Tractates on the Gospel of John," Tractate 124.5 (*NPNF,* 1st ser., 7:450).

138. Augustine, "Lectures or Tractates on the Gospel of John," Tractate 124.7 (*NPNF,* 1st ser., 7:452).

139. Augustine, "Lectures or Tractates on the Gospel of John," Tractate 119.3 (*NPNF,* 1st ser., 7:433).

140. Augustine, "Ten Homilies on the Epistle of John to the Parthians," trans. H. Browne, ed. Joseph H. Myers (*NPNF,* 1st ser., 7:459). See also the editor's comments, 459 n. 1.

141. *NPNF,* 1st ser., 459 n. 1

142. Augustine, "Lectures or Tractates on the Gospel of John," Tractate 124.2 (*NPNF,* 1st ser., 7:448).

143. See below, the story of the burial of John in the *Acts of John,* pp. 200–201.

144. Augustine, "Lectures or Tractates on the Gospel of John," Tractate 124.2 (*NPNF,* 1st ser., 7:448). See the detailed discussion of Augustine's testimony in Junod and Kaestli, *L'histoire des actes apocryphes des apôtres du IIIe au IXe siècle,* 81–86; and in Kaestli, "Le rôle des textes bibliques dans la genèse et le développement des légendes apocryphes," 325–26.

145. *St. Augustine: Tractates on the Gospel of John 1–10,* trans. John W. Retting, FC 78 (Washington, D.C.: Catholic University of America Press, 1988), 37.

146. Cited in Eisler, *The Enigma of the Fourth Gospel,* 47.

147. See Peter Chrysologus, *Saint Peter Chrysologus, Selected Sermons, and Saint Valerians, Homilies,* trans. George E. Ganss, S.J., FC (New York: Fathers of the Church, Inc., 1953), 5–6.

148. Peter Chrysologus, *Saint Peter Chrysologus, Selected Sermons,* Sermons 78, 150, 170 (Migne *PL* 52:421, 600, 645). In Sermon 170, Chrysologus states: "He sent them two by two that no one of them, being abandoned and alone, might fall into a denial, like Peter, or flee, like John" (*Saint Peter Chrysologus,* 280). Corroborating this point, B. W. Bacon also cites Ambrose on Psalm 36 and Epiphanius, *Panarion* 78.13; see "John and the Pseudo-Johns," *ZNW* 31 (1932): 146.

149. Quasten, *Patrology* 3:530. For the Greek text, see C. de Boor, "Neue Fragmente des Papias, Hegesippus und Pierius in bisher unbekannten Excerpten aus der Kirchengeschichte des Philippus Sidetes," *TU* 5 (1888): 165–84.

150. The translation is from J. H. Bernard, "The Traditions as to the Death of John, the Son of Zebedee," in *Studia Sacra* (London: Hodder and Stoughton, 1917), 267.

151. Bernard, "The Traditions as to the Death of John, the Son of Zebedee," 270.

152. See below, chap. 10, for discussion of Bacon and Hengel. The references to the report of John's death in Papias's second book are compiled in Hengel, *The Johannine Question,* 158 n. 121.

153. C. R. C. Allberry, ed., *Manichaean Psalm-Book,* Manichaean Manuscripts in the Chester Beatty Collection (Stuttgart: W. Kohlhammer, 1938), 2:142.

154. Herbert Thurston and Donald Attwater, ed., *Butler's Lives of the Saints* (New York: P. J. Kenedy and Sons, 1956), 4:622.

155. L. Duchesne, *Christian Worship, Its Origin and Evolution: A Study of the Latin Liturgy up to the Time of Charlemagne,* trans. M. L. McClure, 5th ed. (London: Society for Promoting Christian Knowledge, 1949), 265b–66; C. L. Feltoe, "St John and St James in Western 'Non-Roman' Calendars," *JTS* 10 (1909): 589–92.

156. *Menologio Basilii* 88 for May 8 (Migne, *PG* 117, 441); my translation. See below, p. 201 and p. 249n.292.

157. Duchesne, *Christian Worship,* 281–82.

158. David Hugh Farmer, *The Oxford Dictionary of Saints,* 2d ed. (Oxford and New York: Oxford University Press, 1987), 229; Frederick George Holweck, *A Biographical Dictionary of the Saints* (St. Louis: B. Herder Book Co., 1924), 549.

159. Farmer, *The Oxford Dictionary of Saints,* 228.

160. Clement of Alexandria, *Stromata* 4.9 (*ANF* 2:422).

161. Aphraates, *De Persecutione* 23; quoted by H. Latimer Jackson, *The Problem of the Fourth Gospel* (Cambridge: At the University Press, 1918), 147. See Hengel, *The Johannine Question,* 158 n. 121; Bernard, "The Traditions as to the Death of

John, the Son of Zebedee," 279; and Edgar Hennecke, *New Testament Apocrypha,* ed. Wilhelm Schneemelcher, trans. R. McL. Wilson (Philadelphia: Westminster Press, 1965), 2:53.

162. Kaestli contends that if anything is certain, it is that Mark 10:38–39 did not give rise to any apocryphal tradition by which John died a violent death ("Le rôle des textes bibliques dans la genèse et le développement des légendes apocryphes," 321).

163. See C. Erbes, "Der Apostel Johannes und der Jünger, welcher an der Brust des Herrn lag," *ZKG* 33 (1912): 217.

164. Hippolytus of Thebes, "Syntagmate chronologico" (Migne, *PG* 117:1032, 1052).

165. Hippolytus of Thebes, "Syntagmate chronologico" (Migne, *PG* 117, 1032).

166. Hippolytus of Thebes, "Syntagmate chronologico" (Migne, *PG* 117:1037; cf. col. 1049).

167. Hippolytus of Thebes, "Syntagmate chronologico" (Migne, *PG* 117:1033).

168. Epiphanius the Monk, *The Life of the Virgin* 18 (Migne, *PG* 120:208).

169. Epiphanius the Monk, *The Life of the Virgin* 20 (Migne, *PG* 120:209).

170. Ada Adler, ed., *Lexicographi Graeci,* vol. 1: *Suidae Lexicon,* Sammlung wissenschaftlicher Commentare (Stuttgart: Verlag B. G. Teubner, 1967), 647; my translation.

171. See above, pp. 162–63.

172. See Junod and Kaestli, *Acta Iohannis* 2:789 n. 1.

173. Sherry L. Reames, *The Legenda aurea: A Reexamination of Its Paradoxical History* (Madison: University of Wisconsin Press, 1985), 3.

174. Reames, *The Legenda aurea,* 4.

175. The following summary of the section of the Golden Legend related to John the Evangelist draws upon F. S. Ellis, ed., *The Golden Legend or Lives of the Saints as Englished by William Caxton* (London: J. M. Dent and Sons, 1900) 2:161–76.

176. Ellis, ed., *The Golden Legend* 2:162.

177. Ellis, ed., *The Golden Legend* 2:163.

178. This form of the story of Drusiana is typical of the *Passio Iohannis* of Pseudo-Melitus (see Migne, *PG* 5:1241–42).

179. See below, pp. 202–3.

180. See below, pp. 203–4.

181. See above, pp. 142–43.

182. See above, pp. 125, 154; cf. pp. 157–58.

183. See below, pp. 196–97.

184. See above, p. 165.

185. See below, pp. 199–201.

186. Ellis, ed., *The Golden Legend* 2:173.

187. See below, p. 200.

188. Ellis, ed., *The Golden Legend* 2:174–75.

189. See below, pp. 257–58.

190. Nicephorus Callistus, *Ecclesiastical History* 2.1 (Migne, *PG* 2145:751–54).

191. Nicephorus Callistus, *Ecclesiastical History* 2.42 (Migne, *PG* 145:869–74).

192. See above, p. 162.

CHAPTER 7

Hero
The Acts of the Apostle

By the beginning of the third century, it was widely accepted that John was the evangelist of the Gospel, the elder of the Epistles, and the seer of Revelation. Stories of miracles John had performed and reports of his later life and martyrdom were already beginning to circulate, however. This chapter will trace the legends that gathered around the apostle from the second century into the Middle Ages, especially the material in the apocryphal *Acts of John* and the later additions to this work.

Apollonius, a Christian writer about whom little is known except that he opposed the Montanists at the end of the second century, signaled the direction of things to come. Eusebius reports that Apollonius quoted from the Apocalypse "and tells how by divine power a dead man was raised by John himself at Ephesus."[1]

ACTS OF JOHN

The earliest explicit reference to the *Acts of John* appears in Eusebius, who lists it among "the writings which are put forward by heretics under the name of the apostles." These, Eusebius continues, have never been referred to by any orthodox writer. They belong, rather, to the "forgeries of heretics" and should be shunned as "wicked and impious."[2] The *Acts of John* are also referred to in the *Manichean Psalm-Book,* ca. A.D. 340.[3]

The tradition cited by Clement of Alexandria is often used as still earlier evidence of the *Acts of John,* but the indirectness of Clement's reference and the differences between the two accounts suggest rather that Clement knows of a tradition that was also contained in the *Acts.* Clement's comment on 1 John 1:1 reads: "It is accordingly related in traditions, that John, touching the outward body itself, sent his hand deep into it, and that the solidity of the flesh offered no obstacle, but gave way to the hand of the disciple."[4] *Acts of John* 93 reads: "sometimes when I meant to touch him I encountered a material, solid body; but at other times again when I felt him, his substance was immaterial and incorporeal, and as if it did not exit at all." Obviously, Clement does not quote the *Acts of John* but reports the same tradition.[5] Nevertheless, the *Acts of John* have been dated to the latter half of the second century (A.D. 150–200) in the authoritative introduction, translation, and commentary by Eric Junod and Jean-Daniel Kaestli. As considerations that point to an early date, they cite the peculiar Christology of the work, its silence regarding Scripture, its distance from the ecclesiastical institution and rites, and the likelihood that the *Acts of John* were used by the writers of the *Acts of Thomas, Acts of Peter,* and *Acts of Paul.*[6]

While the locus of other Johannine traditions in Asia Minor has led to the hypothesis that the *Acts of John* also originated there, the author's lack of clarity about the topography of the area or the importance of the temple of Artemis in Ephesus militates against an Asian or Ephesian provenance. Since chapters 94–102 probably originated in Syria, there is reason to believe that the whole work derives from that locale, but Junod and Kaestli favor an Alexandrian provenance. The rationale for this hypothesis is built around (1) the common emphasis on the polymorphic nature of Christ in both the *Acts* and other texts which can be traced to Egypt, (2) the origin or at least the popularity of the ancient novels in Egypt, (3) the common tradition cited by Clement of Alexandria (quoted above), (4) the similarity of the emphasis on the spiritual nature of Christ and the miracles in Clement, Origen, and the *Acts of John,* (5) the fact that the Greek substantive *dikrossion* is attested elsewhere only in an anonymous account of a voyage in the area of the Red Sea (*Periplus maris Erytraei*), and (6) the possibility that the motif of the serpent of justice (*Acts of John* 71) which inflicts a mortal wound on the wicked (Fortunatus) while only immobilizing the righteous (Callimachus) may have been suggested to our author by a similar Egyptian tradition.[7] The case for an Egyptian provenance for the *Acts of John* is therefore strong but not conclusive. The theory of an origin in Egypt late in the second century or early in the third century may serve well as a working hypothesis, but it cannot be confirmed on the basis of our present documents.

Epiphanius reports that the Encratites used "the writings called *Acts of Andrew, of John and of Thomas.*"[8] They were apparently adopted from them by the Manicheans. The *Acts of John* are attested from the end of the fourth century by Latin writers (Philaster of Brescia, Faustus of Mileve, Augustine, Evodius of Uzala, pseudo-Titus, Innocent I, and Turribius of Astorga).[9] From about the fifth century, the *Acts of John* were ascribed to Leucius, who was eventually identified as an associate of the apostle John and the author of the collection of the five Acts of the Apostles, which the Manicheans used in place of the canonical Acts.[10] Photius—the ninth-century Byzantine scholar and Patriarch of Constantinople whose *Bibliotheca* contains a critical account of 280 prose works—wrote of the collection of five apocryphal Acts: "a book, the so-called journeyings of the Apostles, in which are contained the Acts of Peter, John, Andrew, Thomas, Paul. These were written, as the book makes clear, by Leucius Charinus."[11] Prior to Photius, however, the name of Leucius was primarily associated with the *Acts of John*. Turribus of Astorga (first half of the fifth century) says that Leucius wrote the *Acts of John,* and Innocent I attributes both the *Acts of John* and the *Acts of Peter* to Leucius. Augustine refers to Leucius (which he spells "Leutius) in an ambiguous reference to apocryphal Acts of the Apostles which has been interpreted as a reference to the Manichean Acts as a whole.

The pseudonymous attribution of the *Acts of John* to Leucius may ultimately derive from the document itself. Since it purports to provide first-person, eyewitness testimony, it may have begun by identifying the narrator as Leucius, a disciple of the apostle. A tantalizing reference to Leucius survives in Epiphanius's account of the Alogoi, in which he reports that "St. John and his companions, Leucius and many others"[12] frequently attacked a whole series of heretics. Such a reference preserves the tradition that one of John's disciples was named Leucius, inviting the later attribution of the apocryphal *Acts of John* to this shadowy figure.

The *Acts of John* achieved enduring notoriety when it was condemned during the fifth session of the Second Council of Nicea in A.D. 787. The *Acts,* which had also been condemned at the Iconoclastic Council of 754, were criticized by Amphilochius of Iconium. Parts of the *Acts* were read as evidence of falsehood and iconoclastic sympathies, and the Council issued the following decree: "No one is to copy (this book): not only so, but we consider that it deserves to be consigned to the fire."[13] In light of this decree, and the similar condemnation of all the apocryphal works of the apostles by Leo the Great three centuries earlier, it is amazing that so much of the *Acts of John* has survived. The Stichometry of Nicephorus (ninth century) indicates that the work encompassed 2,500 lines, the same as the Gospel of Matthew. On the basis of this record, we can calculate that seventy percent of the work has survived in various sections. Sections of the *Acts* were included in the "ecclesiastical" *Acts of John of pseudo-Prochorus* (fifth century), were copied by others as late as 1324, and continued to influence Christian art and literature.[14] The fifth book of the *Apostolic History of Abdias,* composed in the sixth or seventh century, contains several of the stories from the earlier *Acts* (*Acts of John* 62–86, 106–115): the caldron of oil at Ephesus; the exile to Patmos and the recall; the robber (ultimately from Clement of Alexandria); the death of Drusiana; the conversion of Atticus and Eugenius; the destruction of the temple of Artemis; the poison; and the assumption of John.[15] Official condemnation, it is evident therefore, failed to extinguish the fires of pious imagination that were fueled by these apocryphal stories.

Because of the repeated condemnations of the apocryphal acts, it is hardly surprising that the text has come down to us in a fragmentary state. Recovering the text of the *Acts of John* requires that one compile fragments and versions preserved in various sources and then attempt to piece together a continuous account, recognize the remaining lacunae, and reconstruct the history of transmission, redaction, and expansion of the text. The details of such work need not concern us here, but it is important to recognize that we are dealing not with a single apocryphal account but with a history of apocryphal traditions.[16]

The chapter numbers of the *Acts of John* were assigned to the various sections by Maximilianus Bonnet in his definitive edition of the text, first published in 1897.[17] Bonnet's arrangement of the text was subsequently adapted by Knut Schäferdiek.[18] The recent comprehensive edition of the text by Junod and Kaestli follows the sequence proposed by Schäferdiek, but locates and numbers the lacunae as indicated in the following summary.[19]

Lacuna I: the beginning of the account, the journey from Miletus to Ephesus, and first events of the stay in Ephesus (chaps. 18–36). Lacuna II: John's preaching of the gospel (chaps. 87–105). Lacuna III: the concluding events of the stay in Ephesus, and summons to Smyrna (chaps. 37–55). Lacuna IV: the healing of Antipatros's sons in Smyrna (chaps. 56–57). Lacuna V: the journey from Laodicea to Ephesus (chaps. 58–61); the second sojourn in Ephesus—Drusiana and Callimachus (chaps. 62–86); and the departure (chaps. 106–15). The origin and setting of two episodes cannot be identified with any certainty: the defiance of the demons at the arrival of John (the second "citation" from Pseudo-Titus), and John's discourse against marriage (the third "citation" from Pseudo-Titus). The story line of the *Acts of John* is summarized below according to this reconstruction, with the chapter numbers indicated to permit easy reference to one of the published translations.

Lacuna I

Junod and Kaestli propose two possible beginnings for the *Acts of John*. The first suggestion is that the opening chapters reported a meeting of the disciples in Jerusalem before they set out on mission. They divided the regions and assigned Asia to John. Alternatively, these chapters may have reported John's conversion to a life of virginity after various interventions by the risen Christ. Either of these openings would have been followed by an account of John's voyage to Miletus, which was probably the setting for several scenes: the conversion of Demonicus and Aristodemus, the introduction of Cleobius, and a story perhaps telling how Marcellus and his wife began to practice sexual abstinence after hearing John's preaching. The account of a vision ordering John to travel to Ephesus supplied the transition to chapter 18, where the extant text begins.[20]

Acts of John 18–36

Chapters 18–25 contain the story of the raising of Cleopatra and Lycomedes. Chapter 18 recounts that John, prompted by a vision, was on his way to Ephesus. Demonicus, Aristodemus, a wealthy man named Cleobius, and the wife of Marcellus prevailed on John to spend a day in Miletus. The next morning, they set out for Ephesus. About four miles out of Miletus, a voice from heaven that was heard by all of them announced to John that he would give glory to his Lord in Ephesus. John responded: "Lord, behold I go according to thy will. Thy will be done."[21] In the next chapter, as John and his companions approached Ephesus, they were met by Lycomedes, who told them that his wife, Cleopatra, was paralyzed and failing rapidly. God had sent a messenger to Lycomedes, telling him that he was sending from Miletus a man named John who would restore her to health. Echoing the words of John's vision on the road, Lycomedes entreated John, "Glorify your God by healing her."

When they arrived at the house, Lycomedes lamented Cleopatra's condition, questioned what use his piety had been, and threatened to take his own life if she should die. John intervened, urging Lycomedes to cease his lamentation. He promised, further, that if Lycomedes would awaken and open his soul to God, Cleopatra would be cured. Lycomedes, however, fell on the ground, consumed with lamentation. John then complained to God that he had been cast in this situation, and that the crowd would not let him leave the house alive if Cleopatra was not restored. In prayer, John urged God to heal Cleopatra, to save her and Lycomedes, and by this miracle to convert those who had gathered at the house. Touching Cleopatra's face, he commanded, "Rise and be not an excuse for many who wish to disbelieve," at which Cleopatra arose and asked God to save her. When Cleopatra asked about her husband, John reassured her that if she would be steadfast in her faith, he too would be restored through the power of God. When John saw the composure of Cleopatra as she saw her dead husband, he again petitioned the Lord to restore Lycomedes' life so that Cleopatra might not die of her grief. Following John's instructions, Cleopatra took the hand of her husband and said, "Rise up and glorify the name of God, since to the dead he gives (back) the dead." Immediately, Lycomedes arose and began to kiss John's feet, but John directed his praise toward God. Lycomedes then compelled John and his companions to stay with them.

Chapters 26–29 describe the portrait of John. When a crowd gathered to hear John, Lycomedes ran to a friend who was a painter and asked him to paint a portrait of John without his knowing it. By the next day the painter had finished the colored portrait and given it to Lycomedes, who put it in his bedroom and put garlands on it and set lamps before it. When John saw the portrait, he challenged him: "Lycomedes, what is it that you (have done) with this portrait? Is it one of your gods that is painted here? Why, I see you are still living as a pagan!" Lycomedes responded that his faith was in God alone but that one might call his earthly benefactors gods, since it was a portrait of John himself. John had never seen his own face, however, and did not recognize himself. So Lycomedes brought him a mirror, and John compared his reflection with the portrait. John acknowledged that the portrait was like him, but that he only liked his image in the flesh. If Lycomedes wanted a portrait of him, John contended, he would need the right colors, the colors that Jesus would give him: "faith in God, knowledge, reverence, kindness, fellowship, mildness, goodness, brotherly love, purity, sincerity, tranquility, fearlessness, cheerfulness, dignity, and the whole band of colors which portray your soul." John then reproached Lycomedes: "But what you have now done is childish and imperfect; you have drawn a dead likeness of what is dead."

Chapters 30–36 recount the healing of the old women. John commanded Verus, one of his companions, to bring the old women of Ephesus to him, while he, Cleopatra, and Lycomedes made preparations to care for them. Verus reported, however, that only four of the women over sixty were in good health. After a period of silence, John ordered that the women be gathered in the theater so that he could heal them and perhaps convert others through the healing. The next day, when the crowds gathered in the theater, the proconsul came too, and Andronicus, a praetor, challenged John to appear naked and work the impossible cures he had promised, holding nothing in his hands and not pronouncing the magical name he was known to use. John commanded that the women be brought before him in the theater anyway. He then addressed the crowd, stating the purpose of his visit to the city and explaining that he would raise the sick and invalid women to convert even their praetor. John preached to the crowd in the theater, encouraging the poor and warning the wicked to turn from their sinfulness. A summary statement reports that John "healed all (their) diseases through the power of God."

Lacuna II

A considerable section of the narrative seems to be missing at this point. From the preceding section, we may infer that it contained an account of the healing of the old women. Similarly, from the following section, it appears that Drusiana and Andronicus have already been introduced. Since Andronicus has become a disciple of John between his introduction in chapter 31 and the next extant reference to him (in chapter 37), we may suppose that his conversion has been narrated in this lost section. From other indications in the narrative, it has also been suggested that the lost section told of how Andronicus imprisoned Drusiana in hopes of forcing her to abandon her vow of continence, and how the Christ had appeared to her. The account of John's imprisonment for fourteen days, which is reported in the *Manichean Psalm-Book,* may also have stood at this point in the narrative. The section apparently closed with a report of the miraculous deliverance of both the apostle and Drusiana from prison.

Acts of John 87–105: John's Preaching of the Gospel

First, John described the various forms in which the Lord appeared. Those who were gathered, apparently at the house of Andronicus, were perplexed by Drusiana's report that the Christ had appeared to her both in the form of John and as a young man. John, therefore, began to teach them the things they could hear. When the Lord called the fishermen, James saw him as a child, while to John he appeared as a handsome, cheerful man. When they got to land, Jesus appeared to John as a bald-headed man with a thick beard but to James as a young man whose beard was just beginning. His eyes were never closed, but always open. When John reclined at table with him, his breast sometimes felt smooth and soft and at other times like a rock. Once, when Jesus had taken Peter, James, and John to the mountain where he prayed, they saw a light on him; his feet were whiter than snow, and his head stretched to heaven. John was frightened, but the Lord caught hold of his beard and said, "Do not be faithless but believing and not inquisitive" (cf. John 20:27), and for days, John's beard hurt. Peter and James asked whom the Lord had been speaking with, but John replied that they would have to learn this from the Lord himself. On a later occasion, while they were sleeping in a house at Gennesaret, John saw another form like Jesus come down to him and say that the disciples still disbelieved him. John further reported that sometimes he was able to touch the form of Jesus, but sometimes he was not able to do so: "at other times again when I felt him, his substance was immaterial and incorporeal, and as if it did not exist at all." When they ate with the Pharisees, Jesus would bless his loaf and distribute it to each, and they would all have enough. Often John looked for his footprint, but never saw it.

Chapters 94–96 recall the hymn of Christ. Before he was arrested, Jesus told the disciples to form a circle, holding hands. Standing in the center of the circle, the Lord sang, and the disciples responded at intervals with "Amen." In the course of the hymn, the Lord sings (chap. 96, vv. 31–34, 38–39):

> You who dance, consider
>   what I do, for yours is
> This passion of Man
>   which I am to suffer.
> For you could by no means
>   have understood what you suffer
> unless to you as Logos
>   I had been sent by the Father.
>
> . . . .
>
> Who I am, you shall know
>   when I go forth.
> What I now am seen to be,
>   that I am not.

In chapters 97–102, following the hymn, John described the mystery of the cross. After the dance, the disciples were confused and fled. John went to the Mount of Olives and wept. At the sixth hour, while Jesus hung on the cross and there was darkness over all the land, the Lord stood in a cave and spoke to him. The Lord showed John a cross of light, and the Lord was above the cross and spoke with the voice of God. "This Cross of Light," he said, "is sometimes called Logos," but is also called mind, Jesus, Christ, a door, a way, bread, and other names. The cross is what has united all things, but the cross, John was warned, was not the wooden cross he would see when he went down from the mountain, nor was the Lord the man he would see on the cross. When human nature is transformed and those who obey his voice are joined with the Lord, those who understand the mystery will be separated from the others and will be as the Lord is now. Actually, the Lord did not suffer any of the things that would be reported. He suffered, but he did not suffer. He was pierced, but he was not wounded. The blood flowed from him, but it did not flow. John must understand that this happened to the Logos, for he is Logos, Lord, and man. Having said these things, the Lord was taken up, but no one else saw him ascend.

Chapters 103–105 report John's concluding admonitions. He called those assembled to worship, knowing that the Lord was now present everywhere, with all who call upon him, just as John and Drusiana had called upon him from prison. John called upon all to worship God, and then he and Andronicus went out to walk .

Lacuna III

Following John's preaching of the gospel, Junod and Kaestli suggest, there was a third lacuna. The lost section apparently contained other episodes from

John's first sojourn in Ephesus, perhaps an account of the history of Zeuxis, a confrontation with a demon-possessed soldier (preserved in Oxyrhynchus Papyrus 850 and the Irish *Life of John the Evangelist*), and the miracle of changing hay into gold.

Acts of John 37–55

This section reports the destruction of the Temple of Artemis, the resurrection of the priest of Artemis, the resurrection of a father killed by his son, and John's departure from Ephesus.

Believers from Miletus urged John to come to their city, but he replied that he wanted to go to the temple of Artemis first. Two days later, John appeared at a festival in the temple wearing black, while everyone else was dressed in white. They seized John, but he ascended a high platform to address the crowd. John rebuked the people for worshiping the idol after all the miracles and cures he had done among them. John therefore challenged them all to pray to the idol that he and he alone would die, and if they could not, then he would pray to his God that they would all die. Immediately, the people began to plead with John not to do this because they had seen him raise the dead. John replied that either they must turn from their idolatry or their idol must kill him. John then prayed that the demon that dwelt in that temple would be put to flight, and that God would show mercy on those who had assembled there. While he was still speaking, the altar was split in pieces. Half of the temple fell in, and a priest was killed. Immediately, the people began to confess God, the God of John, and to ask for mercy. John called upon the people to rise up and pray to God. Artemis has no power, he said, or she would have protected her temple and her priest. The people responded by sacking the rest of the temple, crying out, "The God of John is the only God we know; from now on we worship him, since he has had mercy upon us!" When John descended from the platform, the crowd surrounded him and began to plead with him to help them.

John therefore remained with them a while longer, and the crowd congregated at the house of Andronicus. One of them laid the body of the priest at the door of the house without telling anyone. John went to the man, a kinsman of the priest, and assured him that the Lord would raise the priest from death. Indeed, he instructed the man to go to the body of the priest and say, "John, the servant of God, says to you, Arise!" When he had done so, the kinsman came back bringing the priest with him. John then challenged the priest to believe that he might have life for all eternity.

Responding to what he had seen in a dream, John walked down a road outside the city until he came upon a young man who was being warned by his father not to take another man's wife. The young man, however, kicked his father and killed him. The young man then drew a sickle from his belt and began running toward his house. John stopped him, and the guilt-stricken man confessed that he had been planning to kill the woman, her husband, and last of all, himself. John replied that he could not leave the man in this condition, but offered to raise his father if he would never see the woman again. When they had returned to the body of the young man's father, John prayed that God would raise him and spare the young man who had not spared even his own father. The father sat up, but complained because he felt that in death he had been released from a terrible life with a rebellious son. John assured him that he had been called back to a better life. When the young man saw what had happened, he took his sickle and castrated himself, ran to the house of the adulteress, and threw his private parts down in front of her, denounced her, and then told John what he had done. John responded, however, that it was not his sexual organs that had made him do this, but Satan. He should therefore put out of his mind every temptation and rely on God's help. The people of Smyrna then sent to John and urged him to come and preach among them.

Lacuna IV

At this point, another lacuna is evident. The missing section apparently reported a scene of leave taking and John's journey to Smyrna.

Acts of John 56–57

The Manuscript of Paris, Gr. 1468 (eleventh century) moves straight from the story of the parricide to that of the partridge. Accordingly, Bonnet, followed by Edgar Hennecke and M. R. James, located the incident of the partridge at this point in the narrative and numbered it chapters 56 and 57. Both Knut Schäferdiek and Junod and Kaestli place the healing of Antipatros's sons at this point, however, identifying that episode as comprising these two chapters.[22] They conclude that the story of the partridge was not originally a part of the *Acts of John*. For the sake of completeness, we will summarize both at this point.

The story of John and the partridge is of unknown origin, but seems to have been attached to the *Acts of John* by the eleventh century. John Cassian (360–435) transmitted to the West the ascetic wisdom of the desert fathers from the East. In his *Collationes* (24.21), he reports an early version of the story. John was stroking a partridge when a hunter appeared and expressed surprise that the great apostle was amusing himself in this way. John asked the hunter why he did not keep his bow strung all the time, and the hunter answered that if he did so, it would soon be weakened from the constant strain. John replied that just in the same way, the mind needs to relax from time to time.[23]

Manuscript Q contains a different version of the story. While John watched a partridge playing in the dust before him, a priest took offense, saying to himself, "Can such a man, at his age, take pleasure in a partridge playing in the dust?"[24] John knew what he was thinking, however, and replied that the partridge, which was defiled, was the priest's soul and that it would be better for the priest to be watching a partridge play than to defile himself with shameful practices. The priest realized that the apostle knew what was in his heart and responded: "Now I know that God dwells in you, blessed John! How happy is the man who has not tempted God in you; for the man who tempts you tempts the untemptable."

Junod and Kaestli, after a thorough assessment of the manuscript tradition, place the healing of the sons of Antipatros at this point.[25] When John arrived in Smyrna, Antipatros, one of the leading citizens, offered John ten thousand pieces of gold if he would heal his thirty-four-year-old twins, who had been tormented by a demon since their birth. John replied that his physician did not seek payment in gold. Rather, he sought the reconciliation of the souls of those whom he healed. When Antipatros pleaded that no one had been able to help, John prayed that God would take the unclean spirits from Antipatros's sons, and immediately they came out of the sons. In gratitude, Antipatros praised God and gave John money for those in need.

Lacuna V

A final gap occurs at this point. The missing material probably reported the end of John's sojourn in Smyrna "and the other cities" and his journey to Laodicea. Zahn proposed that the other cities were the seven cities of the Apocalypse.[26] Prior to John's return to Ephesus from Laodicea in chapter 58, there must have been an account of the journey to Laodicea and the events that occurred there. One possibility is that the lost section reported episodes with Aristobula and her husband Tertullus, Aristippus and Xenophon, and "the virtuous prostitute"—all of whom are mentioned in the next section.

Acts of John 58–61: Journey from Laodicea to Ephesus

Chapter 58 records that after some days, John announced that he was returning to Ephesus. The brethren in Laodicea were grieved, but John reassured them that "Christ is with you always" and that he first loves those who love him (cf. 1 John 4:19). The next chapter names John's traveling companions (see above, *Lacuna V*), including Andronicus and Drusiana, whose story will be reported shortly.

The next two chapters recount the story of the obedient bugs. The first night, at a lonely inn, they spread cloaks over a bed for John, while the others prepared to sleep on the floor. John was troubled by insects, however, so about midnight, in the hearing of his companions, he said, "I tell you, you bugs, to behave yourselves, one and all; you must leave your home for tonight and be quiet in one place and keep your distance from the servants of God."[27] The others laughed and talked, while John went on to sleep. The next morning his companions saw a mass of insects collected by the door. When John awoke, they pointed to the bugs, and John addressed them, "Since you have behaved yourselves and listened to my correction, go (back) to your own place."[28] Immediately they raced to the bed, climbed the legs, and disappeared into its joints. Seeing this, John replied that the creatures had heard a man's voice and were obedient, but they who had heard God's commands refused to obey.

Acts of John 62–86: Drusiana and Callimachus

When John arrived in Ephesus, the brethren greeted him at the house of Andronicus. A certain man, Callimachus, prompted by Satan, fell in love with Drusiana, the wife of Andronicus. The others discouraged him, reminding him that she had some time ago separated from her husband because of her piety. He had locked her in a sepulchre and forced her to choose either death or union with him. When she had chosen to die rather than compromise her piety, he gave in. Even so, the man's friends could not dissuade him. He sent to Drusiana, but she learned of his intentions and made herself sick, and eventually died, with remorse that she had been the source of his temptation. Andronicus was deeply grieved, but John reassured him that Drusiana had gone to a better life. John was grieved also when Andronicus told him the cause of Drusiana's death—that is, Callimachus's love for her and the mortal chagrin it provoked in her. At the funeral John spoke, using various metaphors of victory in contests. The genuineness of faith is likewise demonstrated by its triumph through endurance. The person of faith, therefore, must take thought as to how his or her life will end, despising the temporal and prizing the eternal. While John was speaking, the evil man, prompted by the "many-formed Satan" bribed the steward and entered Drusiana's tomb with the intention of fulfilling his lust with her corpse. While they were stripping the clothes from her body, though, a serpent appeared and killed the steward with a single bite. The serpent then wound itself around the man's feet, and when he fell, it coiled itself on top of him. The next day, the third day after Drusiana had died, John, Andronicus, and the others went to the tomb, but they could not find the keys. John assured them, however, that Drusiana was not there and that the doors would open of their own accord. The doors did open, and a beautiful young man greeted them and related that he had come for the sake of Drusiana, "for (only) for a short time did I receive her as mine."[29] He then instructed John to raise her up. Having said this, the beautiful young man ascended to heaven. John turned and saw the evil man, Callimachus, with the serpent sleeping upon him, and the dead steward, whose name was Fortunatus. When Andronicus saw Drusiana, unclothed except for her vest, he realized what had happened, and asked John to raise Callimachus first—even though he did not deserve to live—so that he could confirm what had taken place there. John commanded the serpent to leave, prayed, and at once Callimachus arose. When he had returned to his senses, Callimachus reported that while he was preparing to do his vile deed, he had seen a beautiful young man covering Drusiana with his cloak. Rays of light shown from the young man's face, and he told Callimachus, "You must die in order to live."[30] Callimachus then pleaded for mercy and confessed that he had indeed died and now wished to live in purity and faith. Overcome with gladness, John praised God for his compassion and mercy and took Callimachus and kissed him. Andronicus then urged John to raise Drusiana also, so John took Drusiana's hand and prayed to God to restore her to life now that there was no cause for her to be distressed. When Drusiana arose, she was perplexed that she was wearing only a vest, but when Andronicus told her all that had happened, she too praised God. When Drusiana saw Fortunatus, still dead, she pleaded with John to raise him also, but Callimachus stopped her, saying that the beautiful young man had said nothing about Fortunatus. John intervened, however, reminding Callimachus that though they had done much evil, God had not held it against them. John then replied that if Callimachus would not have him raise Fortunatus, then it was a task for Drusiana. Drusiana immediately prayed to God, thanking God for restoring her to life through his servant John, and entreating God to raise Fortunatus also, even though he had conspired against her. She then took Fortunatus's hand and raised him up, but when he saw John, Andronicus, and the others, he exclaimed that he wished he were still dead so that he would not have to see them. Then he ran from the tomb. Seeing his unrepentant spirit, John denounced him and reminded the others of all the blessings this one would not know. John then took bread and broke it and thanked God for the grace that they had received. When he had concluded this prayer, they celebrated the Lord's Eucharist and then returned to Andronicus's house. John reported that a spirit had told him that Fortunatus would soon turn black and die from the serpent's bite. One of them ran, then, and found Fortunatus already dead, with the blackness spreading to his heart.

Acts of John 106–115: The Departure

Chapters 106–110 recall John's last act of worship. The next day, Sunday, John reminded the brethren of all that God had done through him and encouraged them to be steadfast in their faith. Exhorting the brethren to be chaste, John warned them: "If, then, you sin no longer, he forgives you what you did in ignorance; but if when you have known him and found mercy with him you resort again to such (deeds), then both your former (sins) will be laid to your charge, and you shall have no part nor mercy in his presence."[31] John then prayed, acknowledging God's mercy and protection. Then he took bread and gave thanks, recalling that Jesus was the door, the resurrection, and the way. Distributing the bread, John prayed over each of the brethren and partook himself, saying "May there be for me also a part with you," and "Peace be with you, my beloved."[32]

Finally, chapters 111–115 describe the death of John.[33] After the Eucharist, John instructed Verus[34] to take some men with baskets and shovels and follow him. He then led them outside the gates to where a brother was buried and told them to start digging. While they worked, he spoke the word of God to them. When they had dug the trench to his satisfaction, John laid his outer garments in the bottom and began to pray, praising God and asking him to receive his soul. In the course of his prayer, John recalled how God had prevented him from marrying:

> Thou who hast kept me also till this present hour pure for thyself and untouched by union with a woman; who when I wished to marry in my youth didst appear to me and say to me, "John, I need thee"; who didst prepare for me also an infirmity of the body; who on the third occasion when I wished to marry didst prevent me at once, and then at the third hour of the day didst say to me upon the sea, "John, if thou wert not mine, I should have allowed thee to marry"; who didst blind me for two years, letting me be grieved and entreat thee; who in the third year didst open the eyes of my understanding and didst give me (back) my eyes that are seen; who when I regained my sight didst disclose to me the repugnance of even looking closely at a woman. . . . [35]

John concluded his prayer, asking God to count him worthy of God's rest, shatter the rulers, vanquish Satan, and grant to him (John) what God had promised to those who live purely and love God alone. Then he lay down in the trench, said farewell to the brethren, and gave up his spirit.[36]

Manuscripts from recension γ add that the next day his body could not be found. Still other accounts add that when the brethren returned the next day, all they could find were his sandals, with dust pouring from them. They remembered John 21:22 (which could be taken as a promise that John would remain until the Lord returned), and they praised God. The conclusion of the Arabic version, a secondary compilation, reports the disappearance of this body in the following way:

And when we had heard this from him, we kissed his hands and his feet; and we wept bitter tears; and we left him in the hole, and went away to the city. And we told the brethren what had happened; and they went forth with us in haste to that place; and we did not find the holy John; but we found his clothes, and his shoes, and the earth had filled up the place, and the hole which we had dug. We did not recognize it, and we returned to the city, and we gave thanks to the Lord. . . . [37]

Augustine reported the tradition that John lay in the grave but was asleep, not dead, and that the earth was shaken by his breathing.[38] According to pseudo-Abdias, the empty tomb produced manna, and according to Ephraim of Antioch, the dust that poured out was a holy substance.[39]

Material preserved in an eighth-century Latin manuscript entitled "The Apocryphal Epistle of Titus" contains three speeches attributed to John that may have derived from the *Acts of John*.[40] The first fragment is a shortened version of John's prayer from the Departure (*Acts of John* 113): "Hearken to the thanksgiving of John, the disciple of the Lord, how in the prayer at his passing he said: 'Lord, who hast kept me from my infancy until this time untouched by woman, who hast separated my body from them, so that it was offensive to me (even) to see a woman'" (ll. 437–40).[41] The other two fragments have no parallel in the extant texts of the *Acts of John* and cannot be located in the plan of the work with any confidence.

Pseudo-Titus: Defiance of the Demons at the Arrival of John

The demons confessed to a deacon, Dyrus (a name which may be a variation of "Verus," found in *Acts of John* 30, 61, 111): "Many will come to us in the làst times to drive us out of our vessels [viz. the demoniacs], saying that they are clean and undefiled by women, and not possessed by desire for them. If we wished we would gain possession of them also" (ll. 446–49).[42] Junod and Kaestli conjecture that this fragment may have been part of Lacuna I or V.[43]

Pseudo-Titus: John's Discourse against Marriage

The third fragment contains an appeal to abstain from marriage. It is uncertain whether this fragment derives from the *Acts of John* or was a later accretion to the tradition:

Take also to heart the warnings of blessed John, who when he was called to a marriage went there only for the sake of chastity. And what did he say?

"Children, while your flesh is still clean and you have a body
that is untouched, and you are not caught in corruption nor soiled
by Satan, that most adverse and shame⟨less⟩ (enemy) to chastity,
know now more fully the mystery of conjugal union: it is a device
of the serpent, a disregard of the teaching, an injury to the seed, a
gift of death, a work of destruction, a teaching of division, a work
of corruption, a lingering . . . a second sowing of the enemy, an
ambush of Satan, a device of the jealous one, an unclean fruit of
parturition, a shedding of blood, a passion in the mind, a falling
from reason, a token of punishment, an instruction of pain, an
operation of fire, a sign of the enemy, the deadly malice of envy,
the embrace of deceit, an union with bitterness, a morbid humour
of the mind, an invention of ruin, the desire of a phantom, a
converse with matter, a comedy of the devil, hatred of life, a fetter
of darkness, an intoxication . . . a derision of the enemy, a hin-
drance of life, that separates from the Lord, the beginning of
disobedience, the end and death of life. Hearing this, my children,
bind yourselves each one of you in an indivisible, true and holy
matrimony, waiting for the one incomparable and true bridegroom
from heaven, even Christ, who is a bridegroom for ever." (ll. 460–
77)[44]

A number of other fragments and versions of uncertain origin and uncertain
relationship to the *Acts of John* have survived in various sources. The *Passion
of John,* wrongly attributed to Bishop Melitus of Laodicea and thus known as
Pseudo-Melitus, and the *Virtutes Johannis,* otherwise known as Pseudo-
Abdias, represent two parallel compilations of accounts of John's marvelous
works.[45] Both depend on an earlier Greek text which contained accounts
drawn from the *Acts of John*.[46] The text of Pseudo-Melitus dates from
Ephesus or its environs, late in the fifth century. This locale is suggested by
the way Pseudo-Melitus describes the burial of John in the church at
Ephesus.[47] The redactor of Pseudo-Abdias followed Pseudo-Melitus for sections of his account.[48]

The story of Craton appears in Pseudo-Abdias (not before the end of the
sixth century). Preceding the story of John's death, Pseudo-Abdias recalls that
a philosopher by the name of Craton denounced riches in the forum in
Ephesus. Following his exhortations, two brothers—the richest in the city—
sold their inheritance, and each bought a jewel and then destroyed the jewels
as a public rejection of riches. John denounced the performance and quoted
Jesus' words to the rich young man (Mark 10:21). Responding to a challenge
by Craton, John then restored the jewels, and Craton and his followers were

converted and began to preach Christ. The brothers sold the jewels and gave the proceeds to the poor.

Two leading Ephesians followed their example and joined the group around the apostle, but when they saw their own slaves in Pergamum prosperous and well-dressed, they regretted what they had done. Knowing what they were thinking, John challenged them to gather sticks and pebbles. Then he changed the sticks and pebbles into gold and jewels. Goldsmiths and jewelers verified that the result was the purest gold and the finest jewels they had ever seen. In a lengthy speech, John turned away those who had desired to regain their wealth, saying that they had the material wealth they desired but they had lost their eternal treasure. In the speech, John quoted the parable of Lazarus and the rich man (Luke 16:19–31) with an apocryphal addition that describes the raising of a dead man. Just then, a widow burying her son, Stacteus, who had been married only a month, pleaded with the apostle to raise him. When Stacteus was returned to life, he dramatically and vividly reported to the two who had turned back to their riches that their only hope of eternal life was that they too should be raised from their spiritual death:

> I beheld your angels weeping, and the angels of Satan rejoicing at your overthrow. For now in a little time ye have lost the kingdom that was prepared for you, and the dwelling-places builded of shining stones, full of joy, of feasting and delights, full of ever-lasting life and eternal light: and have gotten yourselves places of darkness, full of dragons, of roaring flames, of torments, and punishments unsurpassable, of pains and anguish, fear and horri-ble trembling. Ye have lost the places full of unfading flowers, shining, full of the sounds of instruments of music (organs), and have gotten on the other hand places wherein roaring and howling and mourning ceaseth not day nor night.[49]

Not surprisingly after such a graphic appeal, the two, whose names were Atticus and Eugenius, pleaded for John's help. He instructed them to do penance for thirty days and then to pray that their gold and jewels should be turned back into sticks and pebbles. When they were not able to accomplish this transformation, they again appealed to John for his intercession. The story ends with the gold and jewels returned to their former state, and Atticus and Eugenius returned to the grace of God.[50]

Pseudo-Abdias continues with an account of the destruction of the Temple at Ephesus and a second narrative which has been traced to the *Acts of John*. When Aristodemus, the chief priest in Ephesus, stirred up the people to violence, John challenged him, asking what he could do that would take away his anger. Aristodemus responded with the challenge that John should undergo an ordeal by a poisoned cup (cf. Mark 16:18).[51] Aristodemus first secured two men whom the proconsul had condemned to death and forced them to drink the poison, whereupon they died immediately. John then took the cup, made the sign of the cross, and drank it without fear. When, after three hours John was not harmed by the poison, the people began to cry out, "He is the one true God whom John worshippeth."[52] Even so, Aristodemus did not believe but demanded that John raise the two men who had died of the poison. The people were incensed, but John quietened the crowd and counseled patience with unbelievers. He then called Aristodemus, gave him his coat, and instructed him to spread it upon the bodies of the dead men and say that the Lord's apostle had sent him to do this so that they might rise again. When Aristodemus had carried out these instructions, the men were returned to life, and the chief priest ran to the proconsul and reported to him all that had happened. The two of them then came to the apostle, who received their confession, assigned them to fast for a week, and at the end of the week, baptized them in the name of the Trinity. They then destroyed their idols and built a church in the name of John.[53]

The Greek Oxyrhynchus Papyrus No. 850 preserves fragments of two other episodes, which Hennecke assigned to the beginning of *Acts of John* 37.[54] Both the location of these episodes and their sequence is debated, however. The recto contains the name Andronicus, with an uncertain reference to his wife. When John went to cross a bridge over a river, a demon appeared disguised as a soldier. John rebuked him and then prepared to lead the brethren in prayer. In the text on the verso Zeuxis has tried to hang himself, but his efforts to take his life have been defeated. At a service of thanksgiving, the proconsul brought letters from the emperor. The significance of this reference is that it may have reported that John's exile or the attempts to execute him were carried out with the authority of the emperor.

The *Acts of John,* in retrospect, provide us not only with a further illustration of the development of legends around the figure of the apostle but also with fascinating reflections of how that legend was conscripted by various ideologies in the course of its development. If we could sort out the stages of composition and redaction of the *Acts* more clearly, we would no doubt be able to assign tendencies to various groups. In any case, several ideological, theological, and ethical emphases do stand out clearly. The body of Christ is described in "John's Preaching of the Gospel" (chaps. 87–105) as polymorphous—appearing variously as a handsome, fair man, a bald-headed man, and a young man whose beard was just beginning (chap. 89). Once, while Jesus was praying on a mountain, his head stretched up to heaven (chap. 90), and on another occasion, John reached out to touch Jesus, but he was immaterial, as if he did not exist at all. Often John looked for Jesus' footprint in the earth, but never saw it (chap. 93). Such descriptions could be expressions of a docetic Christology—the belief that because the flesh is inherently evil, Jesus could not actually have become flesh.[55] Hence, he only appeared to be human.

In particular, the incarnate logos did not die on the cross. While the form of Jesus appeared to be on the cross, he appeared to John in a cave (chap. 97). The Christ declared to John: "Nor am I the (man) who is on the Cross, (I) whom now you do not see but only hear (my) voice. I was taken to be what I am not, I who am not what for many others I was; but what they will say of me is mean and unworthy of me" (chap. 99).[56] By implication, the confession that the word became flesh is an unworthy confession. In an intriguing way, the *Acts of John* continue the kind of Christological interpretation that 1 and 2 John (cf. 1 John 4:2; 2 John 7) and the prologue to the Gospel of John (1:14) opposed.[57] The variety of Christ's manifestations, therefore, is a narrative expression of this Christological perspective, which carried with it a world-rejecting stance toward society and material possessions.

That posture is further manifested in the rejection of wealth (especially in the stories of Craton, and Atticus and Eugenius in Pseudo-Abdias), in the adoption of an ascetic life-style (evident especially in the story of John and the partridge), and in the rejection of sexual relations even within marriage. The latter emphasis recurs in the story of the parricide (chaps. 48–55), the bizarre story of Drusiana and Callimachus (chaps. 63–86), in John's farewell speech, in which he says that three times he was kept from marrying (chap. 113), and in John's declarations against marriage in Pseudo-Titus.

Although these references come from different manuscripts, composed in different times and contexts, the cumulative evidence that the legends about John were employed to promote the ideal of a world-rejecting, ascetic, and celibate life is inescapable. The fascinating variety of the functions of the legends about the apostle continues to unfold.

ACTS OF JOHN AT ROME

The *Acts of John at Rome* is the title that Junod and Kaestli give to the accounts of a group of manuscripts that originated independently of the *Acts of John*. Bonnet printed these accounts as chapters 1–17 at the beginning of the *Acts of John*, but these chapters are attested only by two Greek recensions and were not part of the ancient *Acts of John*. One of the recensions is primitive. The other is a secondary revision designed to insert the *Acts of John at Rome* into the *Acts* attributed to Prochorus. These accounts report that Domitian, who persecuted the Jews and later, at the instigation the Jews, persecuted Christians, summoned John to Rome after hearing of his teaching in Ephesus. John's ascetic diet of dates impressed those who accompanied him to Rome. In the presence of the emperor, John drank a cup of poison but was not harmed. The potency of the poison was demonstrated, however, when a condemned man who drank the dregs died. John revived the dead man, and by one account also revived one of the royal chambermaids whose life was taken suddenly by an unclean spirit. Although he was impressed by John's miracles, Domitian exiled John to Patmos. When Domitian died, however, John returned to Ephesus. One of the accounts adds that he floated on a piece of cork to Miletus after being shipwrecked. A chapel was built to John in Miletus, and from there, he proceeded on to Ephesus. This story is clearly not the original introduction to the *Acts of John,* since chapters 18 and following describe John's first arrival in Ephesus. Neither was it composed as an introduction to the Departure of John (*Acts* 106–115).[58]

ACTS OF THE HOLY APOSTLE AND EVANGELIST JOHN THE THEOLOGIAN, WRITTEN BY HIS DISCIPLE PROCHORUS

Commonly referred to as the *Acts of John by Prochorus,* this document is dated variously between the fourth and the seventh centuries but was probably written in the fifth century.[59] The document is attributed to Prochorus, one of the seven named in Acts 6:5, and survives in Greek, Latin, Arabic, and other versions.[60] Local traditions at Patmos derive from this document, which provides a lengthy account of John's exploits in Ephesus and of his writing the Gospel on Patmos.

While this legend is similar to the Syriac *History of John,*[61] it presents a distinctly different version of the story. Both begin with Peter's address to the apostles in Jerusalem and their assignment to different territories. Both report John's arrival in Ephesus and his finding a job at a bathhouse, but in the fifth-century account, the keeper of the bathhouse is an imposing woman rather than a man, as in the Syriac. Both record the death and resurrection of a young man, but the details differ. Both also tell of the death of John.[62] There the similarities stop, however, and the *Acts of John by Prochorus,* summarized below, contains rich developments that differ from the Syriac history.

The story opens with Peter's addressing the gathered disciples at Gethsemane following the death of Jesus' mother, challenging them to carry out the commission that the Lord had given them.[63] When it fell John's lot to go to Asia, he groaned three times and wept. Peter responded: "We all regard you as a father, and your endurance is a source of strength for all of us, so why do you do this and trouble our hearts?" (6, ll. 2–5). John then explained that he had premonitions of distress at sea and asked them to pray for him. The seventy sent Prochorus to accompany John (3–7).

Together they went down to Joppa, stayed three days with Tabitha, and then boarded a ship from Egypt headed west. John warned Prochorus of his premonitions and told him that if they were separated, Prochorus should go on to Ephesus and wait there three months. If at the end of three months John had not come, Prochorus should return to Jerusalem. Mighty winds shook the boat, and each man clung to planks in the sea, but God spared all of them. The next day all forty-six of them were washed up on shore in Seleucia, not far from Antioch. The sailors then began to charge that John was a wizard and threatened to have Prochorus put to death if he did not turn John over to them. Good to their word, they had Prochorus arrested (7–10).

The next day the governor of the city accused Prochorus of being a wizard and conspiring with John to sink the ship and steal its cargo. When Prochorus had recounted his experience, however, a secretary from Antioch spoke on his behalf, and Prochorus was released (10–13).

Traveling on to Ephesus, Prochorus stopped to rest along the way at a place called Marmareon. There, a huge wave threw John up on the shore. After a joyful reunion, Prochorus and John thanked God for bringing them together again. John related how he had spent forty days and nights being carried by the waves of the sea (14, ll. 7–8)—a period exceeding even Jonah's experience, on which the story is evidently patterned.[64]

When Prochorus and John entered Ephesus, they sat down at the place of Artemis, near a bathhouse owned by Dioscorides, the chief magistrate of the city. Romana—a barren woman, with a manly body, yet like a mule—offered John a job as a stoker and employed Prochorus as an attendant (14–17). On the fourth day, when John was overcome by the work, she beat him mercilessly and challenged him to render good service. Prochorus was grieved at the way John had been beaten, but John said it was nothing compared to what they had already been through or the sufferings that their Lord had endured. He further pledged to Romana that he would get better at his craft (17–20).

After she had left, the Devil appeared to John in the form of Romana, threatened him again, and told him to leave the city. John perceived that it was the demon, however, and calling upon the name of God, drove him away. The next day Romana said she had been warned about John by a certain man, threatened to tear John apart if he did not discharge his duty, and made him pledge that he and Prochorus were her servants (20–21). She even asked a lawyer to write a deed of servitude, making John and Prochorus her slaves. John encouraged Prochorus not to resist her plan but to use it as a means of making her realize who they were. When Romana took them to the temple of Artemis, they therefore complied, swearing before witnesses that they were her slaves (21–24).

That bathhouse was possessed by a demon, however, because when it was built, a young man or young woman had been buried under the foundation (24, ll. 5–11).[65] Three times each year, the demon strangled a young man or woman in the bathhouse. Since these days were known to Dioscorides, the owner of the bath, he had them written down and would not allow his eighteen-year-old son, Domnos, to bathe. Domnos entered the bath, however, and the demon strangled him. His servants began to wail, and Romana tore her hair. In desperation she appealed to Artemis to bring Domnos back to life, but the young man was not raised (24–26).

When John asked what all of the wailing was about, Romana accused him of driving her god from her. John, though, went into the bath, rebuked the spirit, and then led Domnos out, alive and well. When Romana saw the boy alive, she was filled with shame and remorse and began to ask for forgiveness. John sealed her three times and then said: "I am neither God nor the son of God, but John the disciple of Jesus Christ the son of God, who reclined on his chest and heard divine mysteries from him, which I announce to you. And if you will believe in him, you will be his servant as I too am his servant" (28–29). Romana vowed that she believed whatever she heard from his mouth.

While John was instructing her, one of the servants of Dioscorides came, saying that his master had fainted and fallen dead when he had heard of the death of his son. Domnos ran and found his father dead and then returned, asking John to have mercy on his father also. When John had raised Dioscorides, the chief magistrate offered John all that he had. John replied that he had no need of the magistrate's goods, that he had left everything to follow his God. He then related how Jesus had been crucified and raised from Hades after three days, having freed all who were being held in Hades (32, l. 1). Dioscorides fell at John's feet and asked John to baptize him and his son. Romana came, bringing the deed of servitude as a written confession of her sin. John took the deed, wiped it clean, and baptized her. Then he returned to the bathhouse to drive out the evil spirit. That night they stayed with Dioscorides (29–32).

The next day was a great feast of Artemis, and all the city gathered at the idol. When they saw John there, dressed in his working clothes, they took up stones against him; but their stones shattered the idol, and they were all the more angry with John. John prayed that they might believe, and immediately the earth shook violently and 800 fell dead. When the people urged John to restore them also, John prayed again and the 800 were raised from the dead. That day John baptized the 800. At a place in the city called Tyche ("by Fate" or "Fortunate"), John healed a man who for twelve years had been unable to stand on his feet (32–36).

When the demon who dwelt in Artemis saw the signs John did, he took the form of one of the officers of the magistrate and sat in a conspicuous place, weeping and clutching some papers. Two officers stopped and asked why he was weeping. He told them he was overcome by his distress and asked for their pledge of loyalty to him, which they gave him. He then showed them a bag of gold and promised to give it to them if they would help him. When they agreed, he explained that he was a poor wretch from Caesarea and that two men from Jerusalem named John and Prochorus had escaped from him while the ruler was hearing their case. Now, his own life depended on catching the two. He pled that the money was for expenses and showed them his deceptive papers. Leaving his wife and child, he had come to Ephesus because he heard reports that the two were there. The demon then persuaded the two officers to seize John and Prochorus and kill them, and they made a pact with him to do so (36–38).

John knew by the Spirit what the demon had done, however, and warned Prochorus to be strong. Just then, the two officers approached them—at a time when Dioscorides was not with them—and accused them of practicing evil magic. John protested: "You cannot seize us unless you have our accusers present" (39, l. 14). The two beat John and took the apostle and Prochorus to a house so that they could kill them. When Romana alerted Dioscorides to what had happened, he rescued them and demanded due process of law for John and Prochorus. The officers agreed, but their search for the one who had appeared to them as an officer was fruitless until the demon appeared to them in disguise again. When the two told the demon what had happened, he walked with them, weeping, until a crowd had gathered—most of whom were Jews (40, l. 23);[66] and he told them all the same deceptive story he had told the two officers. Aroused, the crowd demanded that Dioscorides turn over John and Prochorus to them or they would burn his house, plunder his goods, and kill him and his son. Even so, Dioscorides assured John that he would allow this to happen before he would betray them to the crowd. John insisted, however, that Dioscorides deliver them to the crowd so that all could see the glory of God (38–41).

When they came near to the temple of Artemis, John asked them whose it was and then prayed that the temple would fall down without taking the life of any in the crowd. Immediately, it fell. John then challenged the demon that dwelt in the temple: "'How many years have you dwelt in this place?' The demon said to him: '249 years.' And John said to him: 'Are you the one who set the officers against us?' And the demon said: 'Yes.' And John said to him: 'I command you in the name of Jesus Christ, the Nazarene, not to dwell in this place from now on'" (42, ll. 15–20). Immediately, the demon fled. When a crowd assembled, a Jew by the name of Mareon stirred them up to kill John and Prochorus, but others said they should be taken to the magistrates. Mareon told the magistrates that an officer from their country had come seeking the two men. In turn, the magistrates agreed to hold the two in prison until the officer came to testify against them. For three days, they all searched but could not find the man, so the magistrates released John and Prochorus and sent them out of the city. When they reached Marmareon, where John had been delivered from the sea, the Lord appeared to John in a vision and instructed him to go back to Ephesus because after three months he would be sent to an island in exile. When they returned to Ephesus, they converted the rest of the priests so there was no longer a temple in Ephesus (42–44).

The citizens of Ephesus petitioned Trajan for help, saying that John and Prochorus, men of Judea, were preaching a new teaching and had destroyed their temples by the practice of magic. Trajan sent back an order exiling John and Prochorus to the island of Patmos for insulting the gods, disdaining the law, and not honoring the king (44–46). When the proclamation had been read in Ephesus, they seized John and Prochorus. John was bound in irons, Prochorus was beaten, and they were taken by a hundred men to a ship. For the journey they were given rations of bread, water, and cheap wine (46–48).

On the third day, while the soldiers were entertaining themselves, a young soldier fell overboard. His father, who was on the ship, was so distraught that he wanted to throw himself into the sea also. One of the members of the guard asked John to help them if he could. John asked each of them what gods they worshiped and why their gods could not help them. Then he broke the irons and commanded the sea to give up the boy unharmed. Immediately, there was a great swelling and commotion, and a wave on the right side of the boat dropped the boy at John's feet. The soldiers all fell before John, confessing his God, and released John and Prochorus from their bonds (48–50). After the soldiers took a brief shore leave at Katoikia, they encountered a storm at sea. In fear that they would all perish, the ten members of the imperial guard again asked John to intercede for them. The apostle told them all to be calm. When the storm grew worse, they again appealed to John. The apostle assured them that no one would perish. Then he prayed, and the sea grew calm (50–51).

After sailing three days and three nights, they put in at a place called Epikouros. The Jew named Mareon who had stirred up the crowd at Ephesus was there. When he saw John and Prochorus on the ship, he inquired of the guards who they were and began to revile them. The guards ordered them off the ship, but Mareon, who was very rich, called together the residents of Epikouros and began to incite them to burn the ship and its passengers. When the imperial officers read the emperor's order, Mareon invited them to eat with him and persuaded them that John and Prochorus were evil and dangerous men. As a result, the guards again bound John in irons (51–53).

Two days later, they came to Myreon. One of the imperial officers was gravely ill, so they remained there seven days. On the eighth day, however, some were saying that they should sail on because they were carrying out an imperial order. Seeing their contentiousness, John sent Prochorus to bid the sick officer to come to him in the name of Jesus Christ. When he came, no longer ill, John told him to go and tell the others they could depart now (53–54). At Lophos they stayed for six days because of a storm at sea, but there was no water there. When many on the ship were in danger of dying of thirst, John instructed Prochorus to fill the water jug from the sea and then to fill all the jugs from it. When Prochorus had finished, and had filled the jug again from the sea, the water in all the jugs became sweet, and they all drank and slaked their thirst. Amazed at what John had done, the officers freed him from the irons. They even offered to let John go wherever he wanted, while they would return home, but John responded that since his joy was doing what his Lord commanded, they should carry out their orders and then return home in peace. John then interpreted the scriptures to them and taught them about the Son of God. That day, he baptized the ten officers (54–56).

When they reached the city of Phora on the island of Patmos, they handed John and Prochorus over to the authorities as they had been commanded. They wanted to remain with John, but he told them to return to their homes. So, after spending ten days being instructed by John, they departed in peace (56–57). At Phora, John and Prochorus were invited to stay in the home of Myro with his wife, Phone, and their three sons, who were advocates. The evil spirit Pythonos ("spirit of divination") dwelt in the eldest son, and immediately it drove the son away to another village. Myro blamed John and Prochorus for his son's flight from home, and began to plan to seek vengeance on them (57–59).

Just then, a letter arrived from the son, Apollonides, which related that John had sent into him the spirit that had driven him away. Apollonides had gone to the esteemed Kynopos, who told him that unless John fought wild beasts and was killed, Apollonides would never be able to return home (59–60). When Myro had read the letter, he took it to the governor (who was his son-in-law). The governor—being especially disturbed when he saw the name Kynopos, since all of the inhabitants of Patmos held Kynopos to be a god because of his magic—ordered that John should be made to fight wild beasts. The governor ordered John to give an account of himself, charging that although he had been spared by the emperor for what he had done in Ephesus, John had done even worse things on Patmos. John told how he had been sent out to preach in the name of Christ, and challenged the governor to let him send Prochorus to bring Apollonides so that he could bring charges against him in person. The governor agreed, and further allowed John to be released from his irons so that he could write a letter to Apollonides. John addressed the spirit that had taken control of him and commanded it in the name of Jesus Christ to leave Apollonides and not to enter anyone else but to dwell in a waterless place. Prochorus took the letter with him, traveled about sixty miles to the village where Apollonides was, and inquired after him. When he approached Apollonides, the spirit left him, and Apollonides asked him what had happened. Prochorus told him that he had come to restore him to his right mind and return him to his family. Immediately they prepared for the journey back to Phora (60–64).

When they arrived, they went directly to the prison, where John was bound by two chains. The jailor was amazed when he saw Apollonides and, at his request, released the apostle. Then they went to the home of Apollonides. After a joyful reunion, Apollonides explained that these things had come upon them because of the sin in their house and because they had not recognized God's apostle when he came to them. When John asked Apollonides to explain how the demon had come upon him, he said:

> I was three years old, and when I lay upon the bed, something came and shook me violently and woke me. And I saw it, and its eyes were as burning torches, and its face was darkened by soot. And it said to me, "Open your mouth," and I opened it, and it entered through my mouth and filled my stomach, and from that day it informed me about good and evil and about all who were in my house. (66, ll. 13–20)

Therefore, when John came to the house, the spirit had driven Apollonides away, lest it be cast out by the apostle. When Apollonides had finished relating his experience, John asked Prochorus to produce the letter the apostle had written. Apollonides then took them all to the governor. When the governor had heard everything that had transpired, he loved John. They returned once more to the home of Myro, and John taught them from scriptures and then baptized Myro and his whole house (60–68).

When Chrysippe, the daughter of Myro and the wife of the governor, Laurentios, heard that her father's house had been baptized, she urged Laurentios that they be baptized also. The governor reminded her that Christianity was despised by the people and that if they embraced the preaching of John, there would be dissension and they would lose everything. Instead, he sent her to her father's home to be instructed by John. He would not be baptized, but would nevertheless protect the Christians. Chrysippe returned to her father's house and explained what her husband had said. The apostle was gladdened by the news and baptized Chysippe and her son. Her father, however, offered her money and encouraged her to stay in his house. John intervened, saying that God did not intend to separate husband and wife or father and daughter. Chrysippe then returned to her home, and her father gave his gift to help those who had need (68–74).

Basileios, another rich man in the town, had a wife Charis, who was barren. He went to Rodon, Myro's cousin, and asked him what had taken place at Myro's house and what was the teaching of the stranger who was there. Rodon said he did not know his teaching but others reported that what he said never failed to take place. Basileios, the military tribune, went immediately to Myro's house and asked to meet John so that he could ask that his wife might bear a child. John exhorted him not to test God and all the requests of his heart would be fulfilled. Basileios brought his wife to John, and John baptized both of them. They wanted John to come and stay with them, but he blessed their house and then returned to the home of Myro. Basileios's wife later conceived and bore a son, whom they named John. Even before the birth, they brought goods to John, but he told them to give them to those who had need and they would have treasure in heaven (74–77).

When two years had passed, the time for the succession of the governor came, and he went to the house of Myro and asked John to enlighten him and cleanse him from his transgressions. After teaching him from the scriptures, and after the governor had confessed faith in the crucified, John baptized him in the name of the Father, the Son, and the Holy Spirit. Chrysos and Selene, another couple who lived in Phora, had a son possessed by an unclean spirit. Chrysos was a politarch. When he heard the things John had done, he took his son to the home of Myro. John warned Chrysos about taking bribes and showing partiality. Then, at the father's request, John took the son, made the sign of the cross over him three times and drove out the spirit. When John had further instructed Chrysos, he confessed Christ. Then Chrysos returned to his house and brought his wife and many goods and asked John to baptize him. And when John had baptized Chrysos and his wife, John instructed them to give their goods to the poor and receive the grace of God (77–80).

They remained three years in the home of Myro while John taught those who believed in Christ. Then John took Prochorus and went to a temple of Apollo, where a great crowd gathered. The priests of Apollo, however, ordered the crowd not to listen to this one who had been exiled for his evil magic. In response, John called for the temple to be left desolate, and immediately it fell down so that there was not one stone on another. The priests reported to the governor what John had done. Grieved, he ordered that they be held in prison. When Myro and Apollonides heard, they went to the governor, Akylas, who had succeeded Myro's son-in-law. Although this governor was from Sinope of Pontus and venerated Apollo, he agreed to their request to release John and Prochorus to their custody when Myro pledged with his life that John would not run away. Myro urged John to stay in his house because of the evil and violent men in the city, but John said that he had been sent to such men and was prepared to be persecuted and even to die (80–84).

Then John took Prochorus to a place called Tychios. A paralytic called out to John, explaining that he was a foreigner and that his parents had bound him and paralyzed him. And he invited John and Prochorus to share his bread and butter. When they had gone, an old woman met them, asking where the temple of Apollo was. She explained that she had a son who had been possessed by an unclean spirit for thirty-three days, that she was from the country and was seeking deliverance for her son. John told her to return home, that her son had been cleansed in the name of Jesus Christ. Believing that he was a priest of Apollo, she went home and found her son delivered from the unclean spirit. When John and Prochorus returned to Tychios to eat with the paralytic, he told them that he had no servant to serve them, so John invoked the name of Jesus Christ, took him by the hand, and lifted him up. After they had eaten with the paralytic, they returned to the home of Myro, where they met and subsequently baptized Rodonos, Myro's cousin. The next day the paralytic they had healed came and asked to be baptized also (84–87).

The following day, they went to a place called Proclos, where there was a tanning pit. One of the tanners was a Jew named Karos. When Karos instructed John from the books of Moses, John opened the scriptures to him, especially the prophets, and told him of the incarnation, death, resurrection, ascension, and coming of Christ. Karos was contentious and called John's teaching blasphemy. Immediately, John commanded him to be silent and unable to speak. The others were amazed, and one of them, a philosopher by the name of Mareotes, said to John, "Teacher, honey does not know bitterness, and milk does not have malice (*kakian*)," and he asked John to open Karos's mouth once more. At John's word, Karos was again able to speak, so they were all amazed. From there, they went to the home of Rodonos. The next day, Karos came, and at his request, John instructed him in the faith and baptized him (87–89).

A magician by the name of Kynops lived on the Island of Patmos in a cave where unclean spirits dwelt. Some said he had been there sixteen years. Seeing that John had suffered nothing from the governor for destroying their temple, the priests of Apollo went to Kynops to ask for his help. They told him that John had destroyed the temple of Apollo and corrupted the officials by his magic and that no one remembered his name any longer. Kynops was irritated that they had disturbed him with this matter and refused to enter the city because of a square little man. He, Kynops, would send an evil angel to take John's soul and deliver it to eternal judgment. When the evil angel approached, however, John forbade it to enter unless it told John why it had come. When John questioned him, the angel explained that Kynops had the power of Satanael, and that he had an arrangement with all the rulers. John then commanded the unclean spirit never again to go out to harm anyone but to leave the island (90–94).

Seeing that the spirit was delayed in returning to him, Kynops sent another. But John sent it away also. This time, Kynops sent two rulers of the spirits, instructing them that one should remain outside the house to hear what was said and to see what happened. When one entered the house and was sent away by John, the second returned to Kynops and told him what had happened. Being filled with anger, Kynops did not send another demon but summoned the multitude of the demons and led them into the city. All the city gathered, and Kynops granted their requests. John encouraged Prochorus and taught all the brethren for ten days. When they exhorted John not to go out because of the commotion in the city, he replied that those who were gathered and amazed at Kynops would be equally amazed at his destruction (94–97).

After the ten days, John took Prochorus to a place called Botrys and began teaching a great crowd. When Kynops heard, he was filled with anger. He came to the place where the crowd was and challenged John, saying that John was deceiving the people, but that if John would do what Kynops said, he would believe the things John said and did. Then, Kynops picked a young man out of the crowd and asked him if his father was alive or not. The young man explained that his father was dead. He had been a sailor; his ship was crushed at sea, and he had drowned. Kynops then challenged John, if he taught truly, to lead the young man's father up out of the sea and present him to his son alive. John replied that he had not been sent to raise the dead but to teach those who had been led astray. Kynops again asserted that John was a magician deceiving the people with his magic, and told the crowd to seize John while he (Kynops) raised the boy's father. When they had led John and Prochorus to the shore of the sea, Kynops clapped his hands loudly and disappeared from them. They all cried out saying, "Kynops, you are great, and there is none other like you." Suddenly, he came up out of the sea with the young man's father. Kynops asked the young man if this was his father. When he replied that he was, the crowd all worshiped Kynops and sought to kill John, but Kynops forbade them, saying that after John had seen greater things than these, then he (Kynops) would be avenged. Then Kynops called another man and said to him, "Do you have a son?" He replied that he had a son but that someone had killed him. Kynops assured him that his son would be raised. Kynops called by name both the son and his killer, and suddenly both stood before him. When John responded that he was not amazed by these signs and that the signs would soon be destroyed with him, the people fell on John like wild animals and bit him with their teeth until he was dead. Kynops told them not to bury him but to leave him for the birds and the animals, that they might devour his flesh, and then they would see if the Christ whom he preached raised him from the dead. Being certain that John was dead, they all went back to their homes (97–101).

After the others had left, Prochorus remained, watching intently. About the second hour of the night, there was a great calm, and John spoke to him and told him to go to the home of Myro and tell the brothers not to mourn, that he was alive. When Prochorus came to them, they would not open the door at first because they thought it was some people from the town, but first one servant and then another affirmed that it was Prochorus, so they opened the door (cf. Acts 12:12–17). When they heard that John was alive, immediately they went to him and found him praying. When he had finished praying, he instructed them to beware of Kynops and not be deceived by him. Then they all greeted him and departed (101–3).

When some came and saw them at a place called Lithou Bole, they went and told Kynops that John was alive. Kynops called the demon through whom he performed necromancy, found John, and instructed the demon to bring John to the shore once more so that he might see even greater magic before Kynops delivered the apostle to eternal judgment. There were demons in Lithou Bole, who Kynops said were men. Then Kynops clapped his hands, cast himself into the sea, and disappeared from sight, and they all cried out, "You are great, Kynops, and there is none but you." Then John charged the two demons to stand where they were until Kynops was destroyed, and, stretching out his hand like Moses defeating the Amalekites, John called upon the Lord to lead Kynops down into the depths of the sea so that he would no longer be seen. Immediately there was a sound, and where Kynops went in, the water began to spin, and he was drawn down by the sea. John then ordered the demons to leave the region (103–5).[67]

When the crowd saw what John had done, they were displeased—especially those whose fathers and sons had become demons—and they sought to kill him. Others encouraged them to wait for Kynops to return and send John to judgment. So they waited three days and nights, fasting. Many became weak, and three died. Seeing what was happening, John interceded for them, raised the three from the dead, and sent them to their homes to eat and refresh themselves. John and Prochorus remained at the house of Myro. The next day, the whole city gathered at Myro's house, calling for John. Myro thought that they wanted to deceive John and kill him, but John reassured him and went out to meet the people. When they began to worship him as their benefactor and god, John tore his clothes, put dirt on his head, and went up on the roof to teach them. When he had finished, he went into the house again, but they urged him to give them the seal of Christ. After he had taught them further, John baptized 300 men (105–10).

The next day, they all followed John to a hippodrome, where a Jew by the name of Philo began to challenge John from the Law and the prophets. John responded, interpreting by the Spirit, saying, "Philo, Philo, the divine writings do not need many words [of explanation] but a clean heart and right faith" (110, ll. 16–17). Later, they met someone who had been thrown down on the ground with a fever, and a young man sitting near him who called for John to have mercy on this one. In the name of Jesus Christ, John healed the man and sent him to his home. When Philo saw what John had done, he asked John, "What is love?" John answered, "God is love, and the one who has love has God" (cf. 1 John 4:16). Then, Philo invited John to come to his home and eat with him. Philo's wife, having heard John's teaching, asked him to baptize her, for she had leprosy. Immediately she was cleansed of her leprosy, and Philo, who had been contentious, fell at John's feet and asked for mercy. John baptized him also and remained with him that day (110–12).

The following day they met one of the priests of Apollo, who tested John. He asked John to heal his lame son, claiming that he would believe in the crucified one if his son were made whole. John challenged him to believe first. When the priest reasserted his demand that his son be healed first, John made the priest lame. Then he sent Prochorus to heal the son and bring him to John. When the priest saw that his son had been healed, he pleaded for mercy. John sealed him (with the sign of the cross) three times. Immediately his legs were restored, and John baptized him (112–14).

The next day they went to the stoa called Dometia, where John taught a great crowd. A man who had suffered from dropsy for sixteen years, and could neither walk nor talk, motioned for some writing materials and wrote to John, asking that he have mercy on him. In return, John wrote him a note, sending his weakness away from him in the name of the Father, the Son, and the Holy Spirit. As soon as the man had read the note, he was healed. Immediately he asked for the seal of Christ, and John baptized him (114–15).

As they went from there, a man sent by the governor approached John and told him that the governor had called for him because the governor's wife was due to have a child but had not yet given birth. As John entered the governor's house, the child was born. When the governor professed his faith, John baptized him. But when his wife asked also to be baptized, John told her that she could not be baptized until she had fulfilled the forty days. The governor offered him many gifts, but John instructed him instead to give it all to the poor and his house would be blessed. After three days, they returned to Myro's house, where again John taught the crowds (115–16).

They remained in Phora for three years, then went to Myrinousa, which was fifty miles from Phora. It was a small town encircled by a river and filled with idols. They arrived there at the beginning of the month of Loos. When they came to a place called Piasterios, John saw twelve children bound and lying on the ground before the leaders of the city. He was told that at the beginning of each month, twelve children were sacrificed to the god Lykos ("wolf"). He asked a man there to take him to see the god and offered him a priceless pearl. Gladly the man took him to the place, and while they were talking, the demon arose from the river. In response to John's questioning, the demon said it had been there for sixty years. John then ordered the spirit to leave the island, and immediately it disappeared from their sight. When the man saw this, he begged John for mercy and asked to know who he was that he could command the gods in this way. John told him that he was a disciple of Jesus Christ but that this one they called Lykos was an evil spirit who was destroying the souls of men. After John had taught the man from the scriptures, he baptized him in the river and told him that he had received the pearl of great value. Just then, the priests with the twelve bound children came. Their custom was to wait for the appearance of the demon and then sacrifice the children. John told them that he had driven the demon away in the name of Christ and commanded them to release the children. The priests were amazed to hear John speaking boldly because no one dared to speak at that time. When they still did not answer, John released the children from their bonds and sent them to their homes, for none of their families were there. Then he took the swords from the hands of the priests, and no one opposed him (117–22).

When they entered the town, John was teaching the people at a small stoa called Thyra, but the priests held back from him. One of the priests of Dio had a son named Moka. When Moka entered a bathhouse, the demon that John had driven from the bathhouse in Ephesus, who had killed Domnos, strangled Moka also. When the priest saw his son dead, he ran to John and asked him to raise him, professing his faith in the one preached by John. The apostle went to the bathhouse, took the boy by the hand, and raised him in the name of Jesus Christ. Moka told John that while he was bathing, a man named Aithiops arose from the bath and strangled him. John, knowing that it was a demon, entered the bathhouse. The demon cried out, however, identifying himself as the demon who had strangled Domnos. The apostle had driven him out six years before. He ordered John and his Lord to leave him alone, but John sent him out from there to a desolate place and forbade him to come around people again. The priest then invited John to his home, where he and his household were baptized. And they remained there three days while everyone gave thanks for the wonders God had done through John (122–25).

On the fourth day, they went to a place called Phlogios, and while John was teaching the people, a woman ran up to him and begged for him to help her. Her husband had abandoned her son, and she had reared him, though with much hardship. An unclean spirit had seized him, and although she had spent all her money, no one could help her. John sent her to bring her son to him, but when she told her son that she was taking him to the apostle, the unclean spirit left him. She took her son to the apostle nevertheless, and asked him to baptize her and her son. They went to her house, therefore, and after John had baptized them, they remained there for three days (125–27).

After that time, they came to a place where there was a temple of Dionysius. A great crowd was entering the polluted temple, eating and drinking. After eating and drinking they closed the doors, and "in uncivilized fashion, like horses mad for females, they mounted the women in an irregular mixture" (127, ll. 13–15). Their festival fell on the day that John was teaching there. When John denounced the festival and called for them all to leave the place, twelve priests beat him, bound him, and then went into the temple. Lying upon the ground, John called upon the Lord to destroy their temple. Immediately, it collapsed, killing the twelve priests (127–28).

In that city lived a man named Noetianos and his wife, Phora, and their two sons, Rox and Polycarp. Noetianos, who was a devotee of the magical arts, was furious when he saw that the temple had been destroyed and that the people now worshiped John. He challenged John to raise the twelve priests from the dead, but John responded that if they had been worthy to be raised, they would not have perished in the destruction of the temple. Noetianos therefore walked through the ruins and summoned twelve demons in the likeness of the twelve priests. The demons refused to go near John, however, so Noetianos returned alone and rallied the crowd to come and see that he had raised the priests just as he had said he would. John and Prochorus went by another route, and when they approached, the demons vanished. John and Prochorus then hid in a cave. When Noetianos came, he summoned the demons in vain. After four hours, John led Prochorus to the crowd, who were now reviling Noetianos for separating them from the apostle. Some wanted to kill Noetianos, but they brought him to John, agreeing to do as he instructed. John would not let them kill him, saying they should now walk in the light. Many asked John to baptize them, but since it was late, he sent them to their homes. The next day, they came again asking to be baptized. When John led them to the river and taught them, Noetianos turned the river to blood, and they were all amazed. At John's command, however, the water was made clean and Noetianos was blinded. That day, John baptized 200. Noetianos cried out for mercy, so John led him to the river, taught him, and baptized him. Immediately, Noetianos regained his sight and led them to his house, where John baptized his wife, sons, and the whole household. They remained there for ten days and then went to Karos, a town about thirteen miles from Myrinousa, where a Jew by the name of Phaustos taught and baptized, and they remained there for some time (129–35).

The governor had been succeeded by a proconsul named Makrinos, a Greek who had no compassion on Christians. He too was visiting Karos. Prokliane, a rich widow, had a twenty-four-year-old son, Sosipatros, who was handsome and had the discretion of Joseph. Prodded by unclean spirits, Prokliane proposed that she be as a wife to her son and that he be as a husband to her. While John was teaching in that city, Sosipatros heard him. Calling Sosipatros to him, John told him a riddle about a woman named Deceit and her son named Not Deceived. An enemy deceived Deceit to kill her son, but the son was not deceived. Which is worthy of praise? When Sosipatros saw through the riddle, John charged him to relate to his mother as a mother. Sosipatros then invited John to his house. Prokliane was angry that Sosipatros had invited two men to their house and, rather than eating with them, hid where she could hear what was said. Knowing her intent, however, John said nothing while they were eating. Then he invited Sosipatros to go outside with them. Prokliane stopped Sosipatros at the door and forbade him to follow John, but he knew his mother's evil intent and tore himself from her hands to follow John and Prochorus. On the fourth day, a demonic passion seized Prokliane, and she left the house to search for Sosipatros. Seeing him not far from where John was teaching, she took hold of his garment and held him fiercely. By chance, the proconsul was passing by, and Prokliane called out for his help, tearing out her hair. She then explained, weeping, that she was a widow and had spent much rearing her son. Now he annoyed her, asking her to sleep with him. The proconsul commanded that Sosipatros be seized and wrapped in the skins of serpents and vipers so that they might kill him. John ran and cried out in Sosipatros's defense, but Prokliane accused the apostle of teaching her son his unnatural ways. When the proconsul ordered that John also be seized and held in animal skins, the apostle looked into heaven and called upon the Lord for deliverance. Immediately, the earth shook, the proconsul's hand was para-lyzed, Prokliane also was paralyzed, and the others fell dead. The proconsul called on the apostle to restore his hand, professing faith in the one John preached. Again John prayed, and the earth stopped shaking, the proconsul's hand and Prokliane's body were restored, and the others were raised (135–46).

At the proconsul's invitation, John accompanied him to his home, baptized his family, and remained with him that day. The next day, he proposed to Sosipatros that they go to his home, to his mother. Sosipatros refused, but John assured him that they would find his mother penitent and delivered from the demons that had troubled her. When they reached the house, Prokliane fell at the apostle's feet and confessed her sin. After instructing them, John baptized Prokliane and her son; and she devoted herself to fasting, prayer, and giving her goods to those who had need. Through John's words, everyone on the island of Patmos believed. Then, there arose another king who did not forbid the teaching of Christ. When others had told him about John, he wrote releasing John from his exile. After reading the order, John wanted to return to Ephesus, but the people of the island urged him to remain with them. When they saw that they could not persuade him to stay, they asked that he write something for them, since he had seen the signs of the Son of God and heard his words, so that they might be steadfast and not again fall under the power of the Devil. John invited them to hear about the signs Jesus had done, but when they saw that they had not convinced John to write for them an exposition of all that Christ had done, they pleaded with him until he agreed (146–53).

After sending the crowd to their homes, John led Prochorus outside the city to a place called Katastasis, where there was a small mountain. After praying and fasting for three days, John sent Prochorus into the city to procure papyrus and ink. When Prochorus returned, John sent him back to the city for two days. When Prochorus returned this time, John told him to take the papyrus and write what he told him. There was thunder and lightning, and the whole mountain shook. Prochorus fell dead, but John raised him, and after praying again, John said: "In the beginning was the Word, and the Word was with God, and the Word was God," and he continued with all the rest of the exposition, standing while Prochorus sat and wrote. They stayed there two days and six hours. When they had finished, they returned to the house of Sosipatros and Prokliane. The next day, John sent Sosipatros to find some good parchments for the transcription of the Gospel, and with great care, Prochorus transcribed the Gospel. When Prochorus had finished, John commanded that the people be gathered and that Prochorus read the Gospel to them. When he had finished reading, they all rejoiced and glorified God. John instructed them to copy the Gospel for all the churches, to keep the parchments on Patmos but to send the papyri to Ephesus (154–58).

John and Prochorus then spent six months visiting the other villages. In one of the villages lived a priest of Dios named Euchares, who had a blind son. The son heard John teach and asked that John restore his sight so that he could see the apostle's face. When Euchares saw that his son could see, he invited John to his home, where John baptized them. The next day, John gathered a crowd and exhorted them to hold fast to the traditions they had received from him and to guard the commandments of Christ, for John was on his way to Ephesus. Again, they urged him to remain with them, but John and Prochorus boarded a ship crossing to Asia and, after ten days, put in ten miles from Ephesus. When the brethren heard, they came to them, and Domnos took John and Prochorus to his house. They remained in Ephesus twenty-six years after returning from exile. They were on Patmos for fifteen years, and before the exile, they were in Ephesus nine years. John was fifty years and seven months old when they had come from Jerusalem (and, therefore, a hundred when he died), and Prochorus was thirty years and three months old (158–62).

The death of John is reported as follows:

> And having completed twenty-six years after we came from Patmos to Ephesus, John went out of the house of Domnos and took along seven of his disciples, me—Prochorus—and six others, and he said to us, "Take implements for digging in your hands and follow me." And we took implements for digging in our hands and followed him, and we went to a certain place, and he said to us, "Sit here." And we sat in that place. And it was just before daybreak, for it was night. And he went from us about a stone's throw, and he prayed that the place might be quiet and that no one might pass by that place except the seven of us. And after he had prayed, he came to us and said to us, "Dig with the

implement the length of my stature like a cross." And after we dug, just as he told us, he prayed and after the prayer he placed himself in the hole we had dug, and he said to me, "Prochorus, my child, go to Jerusalem because it is necessary for you to die there." And having taught us, he bade us farewell and said to us, "Draw earth, my mother, and cover me." And we bade him farewell and having drawn earth we covered him to the knees. And again he bade us farewell and said to us, "Draw earth and cover me to the neck." And we bade him farewell and drawing earth we covered him to the neck. And he said to us, "Bring a linen cloth and place it over my face and bid me farewell mightily because you will not see me any longer in this life." And we again bade him farewell weeping, and drawing earth we covered him. And the sun rose, and he handed over the spirit. And when we had entered into the city, the brothers said to us, "Where is our teacher?" And we told them the things that had happened, but they compelled us to show them the place. And when we had gone to the place, we dug but found nothing, and we wept violently. And we stood in prayer, and after the prayer, we bade one another farewell and went into the city, glorifying the Father and the Son and the Holy Spirit, to whom be glory and power now and forever to the endless ages of the ages. Amen. (162–65; my translation)

Many of the motifs of this legend are by now easily recognizable as standard fare in the corpus of the apocryphal Acts of John. Indeed, the succession of confrontations, healings, or raisings from the dead, and destruction of pagan temples becomes monotonous for the reader. Several features of this history attributed to Prochorus stand out, however: the power of the gospel over pagan magic, the story of the Devil's taking on a human form so as to deceive, the frequent identification of John's opponents as Jews, and the careful repetition of the report that John preached the gospel to converts before he baptized them. The allusion to the pagan practice of burying a live girl under the foundation stone of a building and the obvious parallel between the shipwreck and the story of Jonah show that stories about one hero readily borrowed from current practices and the remembered motifs of other legends. One can easily detect parallels to the stories of Joseph and Potiphar's wife, the story of Jonah, Jesus' healing and nature miracles, and miracles performed by the apostles in the Book of Acts, especially Paul's adventures at sea. Similarly, the account of the apostle's death, digging the grave in the shape of a cross, and covering the apostle bit by bit while bidding him farewell represents an expansion of the "Departure of John" in the *Acts of John* attributed to Leucius.

JOHN IN SYRIAN CHRISTIANITY

Two Syriac documents published by William Wright in 1871 provide evidence of the important place John occupied in the lore of the Syrian Church. One of the Syriac documents is a version of the "Departure of John" drawn from the *Acts of John*.[68] The other, *The History of John,* is taken from two vellum manuscripts, one from the sixth century, which is in the Imperial Public Library of St. Petersburg, and one from the ninth century, which is located in the British Museum (Add. 17, 192). A note in the former indicates that it once belonged to the convent of St. Mary Deipara in the desert of Scete. The latter was conveyed to the convent of St. Mary Deipara by the abbot Moses Nisibis in A.D. 932. Wright maintained that *The History of John* was "obviously translated from Greek,"[69] but it has subsequently been shown that it was actually composed in Syriac, probably by the end of the fourth century, and that the author used the Diatessaron for the text of the Gospel.[70]

This Syriac document records the legend of John's conversion of the city of Ephesus, his triumph over the cult of Artemis, and the events that led up to his writing the Gospel of John in one hour. It is a wonderful example of the way in which legend builds on legend. The acceptance of the twin pillars of orthodoxy regarding the Gospel of John, that the apostle John lived and worked in Ephesus and that he wrote the Gospel attributed to him, gave rise in Syrian Christianity to this detailed story of the way in which these events occurred.

The History of John, the Son of Zebedee, the Apostle and Evangelist

This Syriac *History of John,* sometimes called the *History of St. John at Ephesus,* purports to be composed by Eusebius of Caesarea, who found it in a Greek book. Some days after Pentecost, each of the disciples departed to a separate country to preach the gospel. The Spirit led John, the "holy virgin" (5), to go to Ephesus. On the third day of his journey from Jerusalem to Ephesus, John erected a cross in the east and prayed that wherever the gospel was preached, people would believe and the devils of Satan would wail. John confessed that "there was not (a time) when the Father was without Thee, or Thee without Him . . . and Thou didst enter by the ear of the Virgin, and didst dwell in her nine months, and didst come forth from her" (6–7). The Lord assured John that he would be with him and give him what he was to say: "But when thou hast converted this city and this country from error, another band too of the disciples, which is labouring in the Gospel, is destined to come and see all that I shall do by thy hands" (8). As he traveled, dressed in the fashion of Palestine, John preached and baptized about 200 converts. He ate only "bread and herbs with a mess of boiled lentils" (8), which he carried with him, and he drank only water. He kept to himself so that he did not associate with the heathen. The author professes that he has found this account recorded in books "in the archives of Nero, the wicked emperor" (9).

John approached the city of Ephesus at the time of a pagan festival. Smoke from the sacrifices veiled the sun. As John approached the southern gate of the city, he saw the image of Artemis over the gate, her lips painted with gold and her face covered with a veil of fine linen. John wept and went around to another gate and found that all the gates had a similar image of the goddess. At the eastern gate he met an old woman worshiping the idol. When John chastised her, she stooped down and threw dust and gravel in his eyes. Again, John prayed—this time, that he might be allowed to destroy this wicked people, that God would dash Satan and convert the godless. He prayed that God would let him enter the city with the sign of the cross and guide his path to a place where he could earn a living until the city confessed the Lord's name.

When he entered the city, John went to a bathhouse and met the owner, Secundus, who agreed to John's request for a job. John worked for Secundus for forty days, carrying bundles of firewood. Secundus noticed that John was spending none of his wages, not even for shoes or a coat. When he asked John about it, John responded that his master had forbidden him to possess gold, silver, or two coats. Secundus became anxious that John's master might be angry with him for harboring John, but John began to explain that his master was in heaven, the Creator. After summarizing the events of the Fall and the Flood, John described the means of the incarnation: finally, God had sent his beloved Son, who "entered by the ear of the woman, and dwelt in her nine months. . . . And when the nine months were fulfilled, He came forth from the woman, the Word that became flesh, and her virginity remained immaculate for ever" (14). Jesus lived sinless, began his ministry at the age of thirty, and was crucified in his thirty-third year. At his death, the dead came forth from the tombs and worshiped him while he hung on the cross.

When John had finished relating the wonders of Jesus' death and resurrection, he pressed Secundus to believe, even offering to take him back to Galilee to show him some of those who had been healed by Jesus. Secundus responded that he believed. For years he had worshiped Artemis, but she had not given sight to his blind son. Nevertheless, he insisted that they should keep the matter quiet lest it become known that John did not worship Artemis. He also made John the manager of the bath with responsibility for oversight of the servants and management of the receipts. During the next twenty-two days, the receipts increased dramatically. When Secundus asked what it would take for John to make him his associate, John said he would allow it only after Secundus's son had received his sight and been baptized.

On the twenty-fifth day, Menelaus, the son of the procurator, Tyrannus, came at the end of the day and bathed with a harlot. When John learned what he had done, he confronted him and told him that if he ever came again, he would not leave the bath alive. Two days later, however, Menelaus came again and bathed with the harlot. John had been out with those who were gathering wood to stoke the fires. When he returned and saw Menelaus and the harlot, he invoked an oath to God, and Menelaus was struck dead on the spot. It was dinner time. The harlot ran out in the street wailing, and when others saw that the son of the procurator was dead, a tumult of wailing erupted. The procurator seized John, stripped him, and found a wooden cross hanging around his neck. When they tried to take it from him, four tongues of fire came from it and burned their hands.

As they were dragging John off to prison, he protested that the boy was not dead. But they verified that he was indeed dead. John responded that he would raise him from the dead. Meanwhile, Secundus was weeping for John, but the procurator thought he was weeping for his son. John quieted the crowd and then commanded the youth to rise in the name of Jesus. The youth then fell at John's feet and subsequently related to the crowd all that had happened. He also reported that when the angel of the Lord had smitten him, the angel carried off his soul and he had seen the glory of God and other sights which he could not report unless the holy man beside him allowed him to do so.

The father urged John to allow his son to speak. When John agreed, Menelaus said that he had seen the chariot of the cherubim, seraphim without number, twelve men in one band, and another band of seventy-two. The voice of the Son of God sent them forth to preach. When he looked upon the twelve, he saw John standing there in white robes beside an old man whose name was Simon. John reported to Simon that he was weeping for Ephesus because its people worshiped devils who dwelled in idols. A gentle voice told John to go, that his prayers had been answered. While Menelaus was marveling at these things, his soul heard John's voice, and came, and was made alive again. Menelaus thereupon urged them all to turn from their idols and believe in the Trinity. After John had also addressed the crowd, about 36,706 believed, while others said that Artemis ought to be worshiped. The procurator dismissed the crowd, urging them all to pray that evening and to assemble again in the theater the next morning.

That evening the priests of Artemis blew horns, lighted lamps, and opened the gates of the temple. All the people of Ephesus ran to the temple, as was their custom. The procurator wanted to massacre the crowd for assembling without his order, but John interceded for them. Some of the nobles gave orders and brought 150 papyrus lamps, saying that they should not leave the city that night lest it be burned by the followers of Artemis, who would say that fire had fallen on the houses of those who had turned away from her. The multitude took John on their shoulders and assembled in the theater, crying out with joy. The procurator ordered that the throne be taken away, saying it was no longer a proper place for him to sit. After dark, they sent a thousand men to walk around the perimeter of the city, to keep watch over it, and if they caught anyone, they were to say, "There are two watches in the city, one made by Satan in the temple of Artemis, and one made by our Lord Jesus in the theatre; to whichsoever thou choosest to go, go" (31).

The procurator then called for silence, brought John to highest row of seats, and asked him to speak the word of life. The nobles sat at John's feet, but the procurator stood so that he could rouse any who got sleepy. Finally, however, he too sat down. John sprang up, took out the cross, and with his right hand, made the sign over them all. When they asked John what he had done, he told them that he had made the cross a defense for them so that Satan might not prey upon them or make them drowsy. Led by the procurator, they all lay prostrate before the cross and professed their faith in God. At their continued urging, John taught them from the Torah and the prophets. Again he told of the process of the incarnation and affirmed the perpetual virginity of Mary. When Jesus had turned water to wine at the wedding, John himself drank of it along with the others. After relating to the crowd the events recorded in the Gospels, John said that if they truly believed, he would do what was commanded. He would intercede for them, anoint their knees—which they had bent before idols—with oil, make the sign for them with the cross, and place a seal on their foreheads to drive Satan away. He would also give them living bread, "the body of God, and . . . the blood of the Son of God . . . and His body and His blood remain in your flesh, and He will raise you up and ye shall arise" (38–39).

The crowd urged John to proceed. Following John's instruction, the procurator sent for stone cutters, who set to work that hour making a cistern in one corner of the theater. The cistern was spacious, twelve cubits by twelve cubits, and two-and-a-half cubits deep, and they filled it with the water pipe that ran into the theater. Then they brought seventy pints of fine oil, which John consecrated, praying and making the sign of the cross over it. Immediately, fire blazed forth from the oil, but it did not catch fire because two angels spread their wings over it, crying, "Holy, holy, holy, Lord Almighty" (39). John consecrated the water in the same manner, and again the angels repeated, "Holy, holy, holy, Father and Son and Spirit of holiness" after him (39).

Having instructed the procurator to strip, John took oil, made the sign of the cross on his forehead, anointed his body, and then told the procurator to descend into the water. The procurator confessed, "I believe in the Father and in the Son and in the Spirit of holiness" (40), and then leaped into the font. John then dipped him three times, in the name of the Father, the Son, and the Holy Spirit. Then he clothed the procurator in white garments and greeted him with the kiss of peace. The crowd became agitated and started pushing forward, each vying to be the next to be baptized, lest the oil or the water give out. But John quietened the crowd and seated the procurator in a place of honor. The procurator addressed the crowd and reported that the first time he went down into the water, he saw that he was not going down but up. The second time, he saw a hand writing, and the third time he heard a voice saying, "The sinner, the sheep which was lost, is found; let him come in" (42).

Immediately, John fell before the cross, praising God, and then took the nobles and baptized them, and then the whole crowd, baptizing from the eighth hour of the night until the sun rose. In the morning, the people ran and brought their children, so that by the fifth hour of the day, John had baptized a total of 39,205 people. John stayed with the procurator for the next three days. He had intended to go up into the mountains, but the people prevailed on him to remain in Ephesus. When he agreed, the procurator led him around the city to find a suitable dwelling place. John asked to see the temple of Artemis. Others wanted to slay the priests there, but John spared them, saying they too would believe. He then spotted a prominent hill overlooking the temple. The procurator offered to build him a palace, but John would not accept anything more than a common hut. From there, he watched the temple, received converts and believers, and administered the Eucharist.

Three months and ten days later, the priests of Artemis assembled the people for a festival. The crowd urged the priests to find out why the goddess was angry with them. Then Legion, the sister of the demon who had gone into the sea with the herd of swine (Mark 5:1–20), spoke through the idol. First, they heard humming like a swarm of bees. The priests put their ears to the mouth of the idol. Legion warned the priests not to fight with John because his master had defeated their master, and she was afraid that John's master would destroy her in the same manner. When the people asked who John's master was, the demon responded that he was the Son of God, who had come to earth in human form so that their master did not recognize him but thought he was a mere man. But he rose from the grave and was making war on them from heaven.

The priests were amazed to hear that the apostle's common hut would destroy their temple. When they told the people what they had heard, the crowd began to complain that they had consumed all their possessions in sacrifices to no avail. So the priests and the whole crowd ran to the hut of the apostle and fell on their faces. Some of the crowd put ropes around the idol and dragged it down, chanting, "Thou destroyer of our lives, arise, deliver thyself! Not from heaven didst thou descend; artisans made thee in a furnace" (46). Without speaking a word, John directed them to pray, and he knelt among them, praying toward the east. When those who had been baptized saw the crowd, they greeted them, inviting them to believe and be of one spirit with them. Likewise, when the procurator saw what was happening, he urged John to baptize the new crowd also because otherwise they would perish from crying out, for there were old men among them wet with tears.

John arose and signed them with the cross, and they all fell on their faces, confessing that they had sinned and done wrong, but had not known it until that day. The people rose up, praising God, and thanking God for sending John to them. If John was powerful, they said, John's master must be even more powerful. Immediately there was a low thundering from a cloud over the city, and once again, the crowd cried out in praise to God. John instructed them from the Law and the prophets and taught them about Jesus. After they had received the faith, the crowd urged John to baptize them. The procurator suggested that criers be sent throughout the city inviting all who would to come for baptism. John agreed, so the procurator addressed the people, telling them to go to the theater for baptism and, as they were going, to chant, "Glory to the Father and to the Son and to the Spirit of holiness! Lord have mercy upon us" (49). The procession into the city was more than five miles long.

In the theater, they all fell on their faces, praying to the east, saying, "Lord, have pity upon us" (50). Last of all, the priests came in sackcloth and ashes, lamenting and calling out to God to have mercy on them. When John saw their repentance, he was moved and thus interceded for them. The priests confessed their faith but said they were unworthy to stand in the midst of the crowd with the procurator. The apostle, however, commanded that water be brought into the font and that tables be prepared for a feast, saying that God, who had fed the multitude, would feed them also. Menelaus, the son of the procurator, took ten men and began to make preparations. John then took the hand of the chief priest, Apollo, and of another, named Dionysius, but they begged that the others not be punished. Wasting no time, John consecrated the oil and water, praying that the nations of the earth might hear that Ephesus was the first to receive the gospel and that Ephesus had thus become a second sister to Urhai (Edessa) of the Parthians. Fire blazed over the oil, and angels spread their wings over it. The whole crowd chanted, "Holy, holy, holy, Lord Almighty, of whose praises Heaven and earth are full" (54).

When once again, the priests confessed their faith, John washed the soot off of them, anointed them with oil, and baptized them in the name of the Trinity. Then John sent them to prepare "fine white bread" (54) and wine while the others were being baptized. When the others had been baptized, the priests said they now bore the sign of the cross and asked why images of Artemis should stand over the gates. So they pulled down the images and erected crosses over each entrance to the city. Then they found a suitable place for a church, erected a cross, and celebrated the Eucharist there each Sunday.

Nero, "The unclean and impure and wicked king" (55), soon heard about all that had happened in Ephesus. In retaliation, he imprisoned the procurator, sent John into exile, and declared that the city should be laid waste. The leaders of the city assembled and decided to offer Nero a bribe. Three hundred pounds of gold were collected, and ten men were dispatched to offer the bribe to Nero in return for the release of the apostle. When the men arrived in Rome, God sent an angel to appear to Nero at night. Ordering the emperor to send John back to Ephesus, the angel told Nero he would smite him that very night if he did not obey God's demand. As a warning, the angel took away Nero's speech so that he howled like a dog. When the servants found Nero, he made a sign and wrote that they should immediately, that same day, find John and let him return to Ephesus. He also sent to Ephesus to release all who had been imprisoned there. Men in arms went on board ships and found John, at prayer, and returned him to Ephesus. When those who had been sent to bribe Nero heard what had happened, they returned to Ephesus praising God. The people took the gold and with it built two churches for the worship of the Lord. Meanwhile, John returned to his hut and was teaching people who had gathered from all across the province of Asia. It was this same Nero who later slew Paul and Peter, "but he did not dare again to give orders regarding the province of Asia" (57).

When the apostles heard all that had happened, they were amazed: "And Paul was asking and inquiring of the Apostles, that he might hear the history of S. John; and every day and every hour he was supplicating before God, that he might be deemed worthy to see him" (58). The Spirit directed Matthew, and then Mark, and then Luke to write a Gospel. Then the three evangelists sent word to John that he should write a Gospel also, but he did not wish to do so. When the apostles had spread the gospel over the four quarters of the earth, Simon Peter arose and took Paul with him, and traveled to Ephesus to see John: "Peter and Paul entered Ephesus on a Monday, and for five days they were persuading him, whilst rejoicing, to compose an Evangel, but he was not willing, saying to them, 'When the Spirit of holiness wills it, I will write'" (59).

On Sunday, at night, while the apostles slept, at the very hour of the Lord's resurrection, the Spirit descended, and the whole house in which they were sleeping was aflame: "And John took paper and wrote his Evangel in one hour, and gave it to Paul and to Peter. And when the sun rose, they went down to the house of prayer, and read it before the whole city, and prayed, and partook of the body and blood of our Lord Jesus" (59). After thirty days, they returned to Jerusalem to see James the brother of Jesus, and then went on to Antioch. John sat in his hut, summer and winter, until he was 120, "and there his Master buried him in that place, as Moses was buried on Mount Nebo. . . . Here ends the Doctrine of John the son of Zebedee, who leaned on the breast of our Lord Jesus at the supper, and instructed and taught and baptized in the city of Ephesus" (59–60).[71]

This legend also survives in an Arabic recension, somewhat abbreviated.[72] For example, it omits the scene in the theater, compresses the exchange with the emperor, and does not mention Nero by name. The number of converts is placed at 39,005—200 fewer than in the Syriac version, and the Arabic account reports that John wrote the Gospel in one night, rather than in one hour as in the Syriac version. The importance of the hut has led to the suggestion that the account must have been written prior to the building of the great Basilica of St. John by Justinian (A.D. 527–565), hence prior to the sixth century.[73]

Mingana Syriac 540

In 1930, Alphonse Mingana, Keeper of Oriental Manuscripts in the John Rylands Library in Manchester, published statements from a Syriac manuscript that relate to the authorship of the Gospel of John.[74] The manuscript, called Mingana Syriac 540, contains the Peshitta New Testament. While it dates from 1749, Mingana concluded that it was a faithful copy of an original from about A.D. 750. Before the text of the Gospel of John, the following statement appears: "The holy Gospel of our Lord Jesus Christ (according to) the preaching of John *the younger.*" At the end of the Gospel, the following colophon appears: "Here ends the writing of the holy Gospel (according to) the preaching of John who spoke in Greek in Bithynia." These statements are found in no other Syriac manuscripts, which customarily read "Ephesus" rather than "Bithynia." The reference to John the Younger may be taken as an effort to distinguish this figure another John, hence John the Elder.

Mingana also published another excerpt from the same manuscript: a treatise in a different hand attributed to Eusebius of Caesarea, which presents a short account of each of the twelve apostles and the seventy disciples who were sent out by twos:

> John the Evangelist was also from Bethsaida. He was of the tribe of Zebulun. He preached in Asia first, and afterwards was banished by Tiberius Caesar to the isle of Patmos. Then he went to Ephesus and built up the church in it. Three of his disciples went thither with him, and there he died and was buried. [These three were] Ignatius, who was afterwards bishop in Antioch and was thrown to the beasts at Rome; Polycarp, who was afterwards bishop in Smyrna and was crowned [as a martyr] in the fire; John, to whom he committed the priesthood and the episcopal see after him. He then [the evangelist], having lived a long time, died and was buried in Ephesus, in which he had been bishop. He was buried by his disciple John, who was bishop in Ephesus [after

him]; and their two graves are in Ephesus—one concealed, namely the Evangelist's; the other being that of John his disciple, who wrote the revelations, for he said that he heard all that he wrote from the mouth of the Evangelist.[75]

The reference to Tiberius Caesar is clearly erroneous, but the statement provides further evidence for the vigor of the legends about John in Syrian Christianity. John is associated with Ignatius and Polycarp, both martyrs, and with a disciple also named John. The two tombs in Ephesus are traced to these two martyrs, but the evangelist's tomb was concealed. This may be a reference to the rock tomb discussed by Robert Eisler.[76]

APOCALYPSE OF JOHN THE THEOLOGIAN

The oldest reference to the apocryphal *Apocalypse of John the Theologian* appears in the scholia to the *Grammar* of Dionysius the Thracian, which has been traced to the ninth century. After the ascription of the Apocalypse of Paul to Paul of Samosata in Dionysius's work, the following statement appears: "And there is another called the Apocalypse of John the Theologian. We do not speak of that in the island of Patmos, God forbid, for it is most true; but of a suppositious and spurious one."[77] Assemani found the *Apocalypse of John the Theologian* in three Arabic manuscripts. It was first edited in 1804 from a Vatican manuscript and collated with a manuscript from Vienna. Constantin Tischendorf collated five manuscripts dating from the fourteenth to the sixteenth centuries, and an English translation was published in the *Ante-Nicene Fathers.*[78]

The *Apocalypse* opens with John speaking in the first person, relating that after the ascension he was alone on Mount Tabor, at the location of the transfiguration. For seven days, John prayed that the Lord would teach him about his coming. After this, a cloud of light caught him up from the mountain, and a voice addressed him, "Behold, righteous John." Then he saw a book, with the thickness of seven mountains and an incomprehensible length, in which were described "the things in the heaven, and the things in the earth, and the things in the abyss, and the judgments and righteousness of all the human race." The rest of the *Apocalypse* reports the conversation between John and the Lord in which the Lord described for John the appearance of the Antichrist, the death of the human race, and the succeeding events.

In the resurrection, all people will appear "Just as the bees are, and differ not one from another, but are all of one appearance and one size, so also shall every man be in the resurrection. There is neither fair, nor ruddy, nor black, neither Ethiopian nor different countenances; but they shall all arise of one appearance and one stature."[79] The righteous shall recognize one another, but the sinners shall not be able to recognize others. There will be no recollection of things here, as David said (Pss. 103:14–16 and 146:4 LXX). All honorable, precious, and holy things will be lifted off the earth. The earth will then be burned by the angels and be cleansed from sin. Then the angels will bring down to the earth Jerusalem, "robed like a bride," and the entire human race and every evil spirit will be set before the Lord naked and chained by the neck. The seven seals will be opened. The unclean spirits and the adversary will be judged first. The nations, Greeks, and idolaters will be judged, and the sinners will be thrown into Hades, where "death shall be their shepherd." The race of the Hebrews "who nailed me to the tree like a malefactor" will likewise perish. Christians who have received baptism will shine as stars of light. The whole world will be a paradise for the righteous, and there will be no pain or grief, no Devil and no death. John was then instructed to deliver these words to the faithful, and the cloud brought John down and put him again on Mount Tabor.

JOHN'S ROLE IN THE ACCOUNTS OF THE ASSUMPTION OF MARY

The manuscript traditions of the various accounts of the assumption of Mary are rich and complicated.[80] Since the accounts differ in detail, we will focus here on the Greek narrative of *The Book of John concerning the Falling Asleep of Mary*.[81] Tischendorf dated the composition of this text not later than the fourth century. The Coptic versions represent a separate tradition. In particular, one Sahidic text attributed to Cyril of Jerusalem reports that after the resurrection, according to Josephus and Irenaeus, John and Mary lived together in Jerusalem for ten years.[82] In the seventh century, John Archbishop of Thessalonica wrote a discourse on the falling asleep of Mary which drew from the Greek narrative. In some manuscripts, his discourse is attributed to the apostle John.[83]

Book of John concerning the Falling Asleep of Mary

This Greek narrative describes the assembling of the apostles and the sign that accompanied the death of Mary. Because Mary went to the tomb of Jesus each day to burn incense, the chief priests placed guards at the site to prevent anyone from approaching the sepulchre, but they were kept from seeing Mary (chap. 2). One day while she was praying at the tomb, Gabriel came to her and announced that her prayer had been heard: it was time for her to go to the heavenly places—to her Son and to everlasting life (chap. 3).

Mary therefore returned to Bethlehem and prayed that the Lord Jesus would send the apostle John and the other apostles to her (chap. 5). Immediately, her prayer was answered: "And while she was praying, I John came, the Holy

Spirit having snatched me up by a cloud from Ephesus, and set me in the place where the mother of my Lord was lying" (chap. 6).[84] John remembered the words of Jesus, "Behold thy mother, and Behold thy son" (John 19:26–27), and prayed for Mary (chaps. 7–9). The mother of Jesus gave thanks that John had come, saying that the Jews had sworn to burn her body when she died (chap. 10). The Holy Spirit spoke to John, telling him that the other apostles were coming: "Peter from Rome, Paul from Tiberia, Thomas from Hither India, James from Jerusalem, Andrew, Peter's brother, and Philip. Luke, and Simon the Cananaean, and Thaddaeus who had fallen asleep, were raised by the Holy Spirit out of their tombs" (chaps. 13–14).[85]

Mark also came from Alexandria (chap. 14), and at Peter's suggestion, each apostle reported what he had been doing before he was transported to Bethlehem (chap. 16). John said: "Just as I was going in to the holy altar in Ephesus to perform divine service, the Holy Spirit says to me, The time of the departure of the mother of thy Lord is at hand; go to Bethlehem to salute her. And a cloud of light snatched me up, and set me down in the door where thou art lying" (chap. 17).[86]

Each of those assembled gave similar reports of what they had been doing before they were summoned (chaps. 18–24). Then Mary prayed again and gave thanks. An assembly of first-born saints stood around the house, and many signs came to pass, "the blind seeing, the deaf hearing, the lame walking, lepers cleansed, and those possessed by unclean spirits cured" (chap. 27).[87] The priests of the Jews determined to intervene in these events, but they were stopped by a frightful vision (chap. 29). Frustrated, they complained to the procurator (chap. 30), but at the Holy Spirit's direction, the apostles carried Mary to Jerusalem (chaps. 31–32). When the procurator found them at Mary's house in Jerusalem, the people and the priests started to burn the house, but "when the people of the Jews came to the door of the house, behold, suddenly a power of fire coming forth from within, by means of an angel, burnt up a great multitude of the Jews" (chap. 35).[88] After further prayer and praise (chaps. 37–43), the Lord instructed Peter to begin singing the hymn. The face of Mary shone brighter than light (chap. 44). She blessed each of the apostles, and they wrapped her feet and laid her on a couch (chap. 45).

A certain "well-born Hebrew, Jephonia by name" touched the couch, and an angel with a sword of fire cut off his two hands (chap. 46). The Jews cried out that the one born of Mary was indeed the true God. Following Peter's orders, Jephonias cried out to Mary for mercy, so Peter commanded that his hands be fixed again on Jephonias (chap. 47). Then the apostles laid Mary in a new tomb in Gethsemane. For three days, angels were heard glorifying Christ. When the body of Mary was transferred to paradise, the apostles departed praising God for what had happened (chaps. 49–50).

In this account, the legends about the apostles are combined with Mariology and anti-Jewish invective. John is given a certain prominence based on John 19:26–27, but the document is primarily of interest as a sample of how legends propelled by popular piety, imagination, and bigotry can be combined and reissued in new forms.

Assumption of Mary: Latin Narrative of Pseudo-Melito

The Latin *Assumption of Mary*—falsely attributed to Melito, bishop of the church at Sardis—enlarges the role attributed to John in these events. The following excerpts do not attempt to convey the full story or compare it with the Greek narrative. Only those sections featuring John are summarized.[89]

Melito begins by condemning Leucius, who after he had been "a companion of the apostles, with alienated sense and rash mind departed from the way of righteousness and put into his books many things concerning the acts of the apostles" (chap. 1).[90] Melito, therefore, agrees to write the things he had heard from the apostle John. He explains that Jesus loved John more than the other apostles "because he alone of them was a virgin in body" (210, chap. 2). From the hour of Jesus' death, the "holy mother of God" continued in John's care until her death: "She abode in the house of his parents beside the Mount of Olivet" (210, chap. 2). In the second year after the Lord's resurrection, an angel appeared to her and presented her with a palm-branch brought from paradise (chap. 3).

Suddenly, "While Saint John was preaching at Ephesus, on the Lord's day, at the third hour, there was a great earthquake, and a cloud raised him up and took him out of the sight of all and brought him before the door of the house where Mary was" (211, chap. 4). After greeting John, she "took him into the secret part of the house and showed him her grave-clothes and that palm of light which she had received from the angel, and charged him to cause it to be borne before her bed when she should go the tomb" (211, chap. 4). When John asked how he alone could prepare for her burial, God commanded that all the apostles should be lifted up on a cloud and brought to where they were. Later, John contended that Peter should carry the palm-branch, but Peter answered that John was the only virgin, the one who had reclined on the Lord's breast, and the one to whom the Lord had committed his mother. John, therefore, carried the palm of light before the bier (chap. 11).

Other References to John and Mary

The story that after the ascension Mary lived with John until her death can be traced back at least to the time of the Council at Ephesus in A.D. 431.[91]

The *Menologium Graecorum,* written in Constantinople about A.D. 980, contains the following notice under September 26:

> The great apostle and evangelist John, after the ascension of the Lord and the death of the Mother of God, went to Ephesus preaching the Christ. And having been charged by Domitian the Roman king, he was banished to Patmos, the island, where also the saint wrote the Gospel. But after the death of Domitian, having been called back again, he returned to Ephesus. And after having taught the multitude and having led them to Christ through baptism, he foresaw his death. And when the Lord's day came, when he had taught the brethren the great things of God, and having charged them to keep all that he had taught them, he ordered his disciple to take men, secure the implements needed for digging, and follow him. And when they had come to the place, he commanded them to dig a deep trench in the shape of a cross. And after he had prayed and said, "Peace be with you, brothers," he reclined in the trench. Then, when the disciples had covered him, they withdrew. And after this, when they came to see him, they could not find him.[92]

Later, the legend is reported by a Jacobite, Denys Bar Salibi (d. A.D. 1171), an account that is reproduced in an appendix to the *Chronique,* by Michael the Syrian, Patriarch of Antioch (1166–1199):

> John preached at Antioch; he went away to Ephesus and the mother of our Lord accompanied him. Immediately, they were exiled to the island of Patmos. On returning from exile, he preached at Ephesus and built a church. Ignatius and Polycarp served him. He buried the blessed Mary. He lived 73 years and died after all the other apostles; he was buried at Ephesus.[93]

Here legend is reported with brevity and confidence as historical fact. The challenge of sorting one from the other did not arise until the beginning of the modern period (see below, chapter 9).

BOOK OF JOHN THE EVANGELIST

The genre of books that contain questions to the Lord and answers from him reaches back to the Gnostic materials. Irenaeus knew such a work. While some have been lost, late Greek examples of this genre have survived. The *Book of John the Evangelist,* the *Apocalypse of John the Theologian,* and the

Arabic Gospel of John fall into this category.[94] The former was found among the Albigensian heretics in Southern France. The Latin translation is no older than the twelfth century.[95]

Among the questions which John asks the Lord are several that concern Satan: "Lord, before Satan fell, in what Glory abode he with thy Father?" "When Satan fell, in what place dwelt he?" "How long shall be the reign of Satan?" and "What shall be in that time?" The document begins with an allegedly autobiographical reference to the Beloved Disciple reclining on the breast of Jesus and asking Jesus about the identity of the betrayer. John, therefore, served in later legends as a suitable figure to ask questions of the Lord regarding matters of popular curiosity—and to become the mediator of secret knowledge in these legends.

HOMILY OF PSEUDO-CHRYSOSTOM

An encomium of Saint John the Theologian, transmitted under the name of Chrysostom and known as the *Homily of Pseudo-Chrysostom,* is preserved in Greek and Arabic versions.[96] Both the date and provenance of this document are uncertain, but Junod and Kaestli conclude that it was written a little earlier than the earliest exemplar (which has been dated in the ninth or tenth century) and that it originated in Egypt.[97] Junod and Kaestli also propose that, for the sake of discussion, the text be divided into seven parts:

I. The Exordium;
II. The final destiny of John and its conformity with John 21:22;
III. The study of the relics and the apparition of John to Constantine;
IV. The miraculous dust spouting from the tomb on the day of the feast of the apostle;
V. The destruction of the temple of Artemis;
VI. The resurrection of the brother of the priest;
VII. Conclusion: John, revealer of the divine mysteries.

I. From Our Father [who is] among the Saints, John Chrysostom, Archbishop of Constantinople, a Word for the Holy John the Theologian

John the evangelist assembled this spiritual festal assembly for us today. John the fisherman, the friend, the one chosen by Christ—for thus also the Gospel testifies that this one is "the disciple whom Jesus loved"—John who threw the net and caught the gospel, John who threw the pen and transcribed the word, John the catcher of dumb fish [who is] more educated than the masters of eloquence. Therefore you all have gathered today to hear the encomiums of John the Theologian and to learn what sort of friend Christ procured, who proceeded from the bosom of the Father.

And who will dare to grapple with the achievements of that one? But now for a little while put up with the poverty of my words. I speak with all truth the things which I saw when I recently went to the places [where they occurred] and which I learned and from the fathers. For this is also what the prophet does and is not ashamed saying, "Pay attention, my people, to my teaching; incline your ears to the words of my mouth! I will open my mouth in parables; I will utter ancient riddles, things that we have heard and known, that our fathers have related to us" [Ps. 78:1–3]. Hence also receive with gladness the things which we have seen and which we have learned [being] in their places.

II. Christ said to Peter just as you heard a moment ago concerning John: "If I will that he remains until I come, what is that you?" [John 21:22] But this one, having lived a long time in the body and having attained a divine old age, on that very day which is being honored by the whole world, ordered his own disciples to dig a hole and to make a place like a tomb. When this was done, when he had entered [it] and laid down, he ordered his own disciples to cover [him] and depart, which they did. But when the disciples had gone, after seven days, they wished to investigate whether he had left this [worldly] life so that they might deliver his body to a perfect tomb, having honored it with the funeral rites. But when they stripped it bare, they found nothing. For indeed that apostle had departed in an inexpressible manner to the intimate friend.

And this also happened to Moses. God said to Moses, "Go up on the mountain and die." And when he had died, the body was sought by the sons of Israel, and to this day it has not been found. This also happened to the savior, for after the burial, from the cross, the angels rolled back the stone from the tomb, and at the resurrection the disciples found nothing when they entered into the tomb except the wrapping lying there and the face cloth folded up in one place.

Then the disciples of John, having built a church [lit. "a house"] at that place, had a place for prayer.

III. After a sufficient time, a pious emperor named Constantine desired to transfer his remains into the city which he was building. And having sent some of those who were held in honor, he ordered the place to be excavated and any part of his remains to be brought back to himself. But when they had come to the places, having labored and searched for many days, they found nothing.

But the blessed John appeared to Emperor Constantine and said, "Why are you searching, devout emperor? Why are you laboring at vain things on this earth, even if you have a pious intent? You will not find me in the earth. For I stand above with Christ who also gave you the empire, and who received me also with Elijah to the heavens. You have seen the meaning of the word which says, "If I will that he remains until I come, what is that to you?" [John 21:22]

IV. On that day a festal assembly, brighter than the stars, is held for this one at those places, and a great crowd as numerous as the stars of the heavens arrives at Ephesus. But into that same grave which was made by his disciples a fine dust sprang up for the healing of the believers. [This dust] is distributed by a multitude of servants during all the night vigil and during all the [following] day to a large number of people, but it is not exhausted by the multitude. On the contrary, the more all receive, the more it springs up. And just as the sea is not spent by being dipped out bit by bit, so neither is that dust spent by being distributed to the multitude. Then does such a great sign appear small to you? But if anyone should wish for the whipped demons and the healings that occurred there to be described in detail, he will never be strong enough for the word. For I judge that to speak the wonders of this place exceeds even the tongue of the angels.

V. And if these things can be named after the resurrection, since the scripture itself knows death, saying, "precious before the Lord is the death of his saints" [Ps. 116:15], who is able to speak, in a way worthy of him, the marvels which he did while he was in the world? The things of theology I pass by now lest by my poor words I insult that voice which has sanctified the whole world and all the creation in heaven and on earth and under the earth. But now, by bringing to the fore only one of his achievements, I shall demonstrate through the works themselves that I am not equal to the speech.

The greatest temple of Artemis was situated near the city, which had such honor among the idol worshipers, such as not even Serapis, the great god of the Egyptians, had in Egypt. But celebrating a special day in honor of this Artemis, they assembled in this place, coming from every place and region, as many as the innumerable sand of the sea.

But when the blessed John saw all that river of people being swept away by error, he entered with the multitude on that very day into the remarkable festival. And what did he do? When he had sought out a high place, rising over the multitude, he climbed on it. Then, when he had motioned with his hand and silenced the crowd, he said to them:

"Men of Ephesus, why do you go astray in vain, considering as goddess one who has never lived? Why do you provoke God in vain, worshiping the stone? She is some mute piece of wood that is not able to care for herself. If you wish to receive the proof of this, behold two things I lay before all of you: either you all pray to your god, if it is able to send only me to death, or I will pray to my God and I will deliver all of you to death."

But being greatly frightened by this—for many of them knew his power and from each hour the wonders that had come about through him—they urged him, saying: "John, servant of the most high God, spare our lives."

When John saw this change and imitated his own Lord, who did not desire the death of the sinner over his returning and living [Ezek. 33:11], he ordered them to withdraw far from the temple. And what did he do? He lifted his hands to heaven and began to call upon God, and the temple began to be thrown down. And as long as John stretched out his hands, so long the temple with Artemis [inside] fell down. He imitated Moses when he stretched out his hands to heaven and turned back Amalek [Exod. 17:11–13]. So also John lifted his hands to heaven and threw down the temple which stood for the destruction of souls.

And having seen these things happen, all of like mind cried out, saying, "Great is the God of John." Such a great salvation of souls occurred on that very day [the day] of their remarkable festival. [Cf. *Acts of John* 38–44.]

VI. But also it is necessary to relate what transpired on that very day and hour. When the temple fell down and souls were awakened, that building which stood in vain, having been shaken in an inexpressible manner, knocked down the brother of the priest of Artemis and killed him.

At this, the priest was grieved not a little because of the death of his brother. Then, having taken the dead one and having quickly acquired much faith, he brought him to the feet of John. And what did he say to him?

"Servant of the most high God, who has freed us from the great error; who has led our eyes to the heavens so that we might no longer pray to the stones, but taught us [to pray] to God; who ransomed these myriads of souls from death, do not disregard my prayer; who turned such great crowds to good cheer, and I alone grieve, I too will be glad with all and have the benefit of well doing; who quelled such a great error, light up the soul of the one outstretched; who put to sleep such a great deception, awaken the dead one; who made alive so many souls, give this one life."

John saw the faith of the priest and did not throw his head back in refusal; he did not set himself above him, but only prayed and the dead one he raised up living. He saw the faith of the one who brought [the dead man] to him, and quicker than the sleeping [awake] he awakened the dead. He received faith and gave life, since also Christ received faith on the cross from the thief and displayed a citizen of paradise. [Cf. *Acts of John* 46–47.]

VII. So also to us the blessed John, when he had spoken the heavenly teachings, sanctified the world. Thus to us the blessed John, having mediated the Father and the Son and the Holy Spirit, he also revealed to all the ineffable mysteries and said, "In the beginning was the word, and the word was with God and the word was God" [John 1:1] To Him be glory forever. Amen.

This pseudonymous text is particularly interesting because it illustrates some of the dynamics of the growth of legends. The death of John is related to the death of Elijah—both were received into heaven. The story of the dust that sprang up in the apostle's tomb has now been interpreted and embroidered further:[98] the dust had healing power and was inexhaustible, no matter how much of it was given out to the faithful. Moreover, the absence of physical remains of the apostle has now produced an account of a resurrection appearance to no less a figure than the emperor Constantine. Finally, we may note how a legend can pick up material from other stories. Here, John's stretching out his arms is compared to the story of Moses' vanquishing Amalek as long as he held out his arms (see Exod. 17:11–13). Legend easily grows by borrowing, interpreting, and embroidering other legends.

LIFE OF JOHN THE EVANGELIST

The texts of Pseudo-Melitus and Pseudo-Abdias and other traditions circulated with other apocryphal texts in the rich tradition of the Irish biblical Apocrypha.[99] Two fragments of what may have been an account of the life and death of the apostle are preserved in *Liber Flavus Fergusiorum* (fifteenth century). A colophon reports that Uighisdin Mac Raighin (O.S.A.; d. 1405), who was a member of the Canons Regular of St. Augustine in Holy Island, Lough Ree, translated the *Life of John the Evangelist* from Latin into Irish. The work is a composite of several earlier traditions, but it is uncertain whether these had already been compiled in the Latin or whether the compilation was the work of Mac Raighin.

The fragment of episodes from the life of John begins with John's prayer before he drank the poisoned cup—a beautiful golden cup in this account. Even after others had drunk from the cup and died, Aristodemus persisted in his unbelief. John instructed him to place John's tunic over the bodies of the dead and say, "The apostle of Christ sent me to you with his own tunic, to say to you: 'Arise from the dead, in order that all may understand that death and life are in my power, and in the power of the Lord whom I reverence and entreat, Jesus Christ, son of the living God.'"[100] The dead rose immediately and described the city of heaven and the monsters and beasts of hell. Aristodemus reported these events to the proconsul, and together they begged John for forgiveness. The apostle first instructed them to spend a week meditating on the matter and then baptized them along with many others. In their enthusiasm, the new converts smashed the idols they had worshiped, destroyed their temples, and built a beautiful church in honor of John.

Some time later, John entered the church for the Mass, which was celebrated by a handsome priest named Seusisp. When John perceived that the priest had a hidden sin, John immediately fell to the ground and began to beg for God's mercy and to intercede for Seusisp, who fled from the church and began to confess his sins before God. After John had sent the deacon Birro to bring Seusisp, the sinful priest knelt before the apostle and addressed him with these words:

> Disciple of the Lord,
> ever-angelic John,
> a goodly, handsome-haired man,
> with bright blue eyes,
> red-cheeked and fair of face,
> with gleaming teeth and dark brows,
> red-lipped, white throated,
> skilful and dexterous,

with supple lithe fingers,
fair-sided, light-footed,
noble, slender, and serene,
distinguished, bright with holiness,
friend of Christians,
expeller of the dark devil,
God's fine disciple.[101]

The next episode concerns the grumbling of the nuns, widows, and others who followed John and listened to his splendid sermons. Since they depended on alms for their livelihood, they began to complain that although John received ample and substantial gifts and lived well, their share was meager. The rest of this episode should be read in its entirety:

John heard this, yet he did not react with an angry outburst or uncontrolled rage, but went on with calmness and composure, until one day he chanced to be on a great wide bridge, where patient asses were drawing home hay. John drew out a good handful of the hay, and said: "O God whom I trust and follow, turn all of this into gold without delay." And John said to his companions: "Count all the gold." This was done, and there was found to be a hundred smooth rods of beautiful burnished gold. John said: "Beloved children, take the gold to the smelters." They took it to the nearest craftsman, and it was put over the fire to smelt it and refine it. They said that they had never found finer gold. Then the gold was handed to John, who dropped it into the deep waters and swift-flowing stream beneath the bridge. Everyone was astonished at this. John said: "If I had wanted unlimited gold and riches, I would have received them from the Lord himself. But I freely prefer to be poor and lowly, for the kingdom of heaven belongs to the poor in spirit, as the Creator has said. And tell the hypocritical widows that the only thing I do with what I receive is to give it to them, and to other poor people. For the garment which I put on when I became an apostle of my Lord is none the worse yet, as far as its sheen and material and border is concerned, nor are the shoes any the worse, nor will they be, as long as I live. Moreover, Christ granted to us a knowledge of the seventy-two existing languages, so that we understand them as well as we do our mother-tongue."[102]

On another occasion, while he was traveling, John was met by a fully armed soldier who threatened to kill him. John replied by asking God to extinguish both the soldier's threat and his life. Immediately the soldier vanished because it was the Devil, who had come to do battle with John because he had converted so many to Christianity.

The second fragment, which actually precedes the first in the *Liber Flavus Fergusiorum,* records the death of John. The first part of the fragment contains the conclusion of an apocalypse narrated by the Beloved Disciple, who tells how Michael will vanquish the Antichrist. The familiar story of the digging of the grave and the departure of the apostle is given new flourishes in this account. John instructed that the grave be dug in front of the altar. He then delivered a long prayer of consecration and farewell, giving thanks that he had been granted the ability to deliver eloquent sermons and had been filled with the sevenfold Spirit. At the end of his prayer, "a great brightness" came upon them all for an hour, while they threw themselves upon the ground, and the place was filled with "perfume of angelic incense." When they looked where John had been, "They found nothing there in place of the valiant priest, the eloquent judge, the devout helper, the wise preacher, the splendid confessor, the merciful dispenser of forgiveness, red-cheeked and blue-eyed, namely John, the beloved apostle."[103] When thereafter the sick and afflicted gathered at the site, they were cured.

> As for the body of John, it is in a beautiful golden tomb, and at the end of each year, the best youth, who is without defilement or sin, is chosen, and he goes to cut John's hair and pare his nails, and when he has completed that task, he partakes of the body and sacrifice of Christ, and he himself ascends to heaven on that day. Thus John's body remains without putrefaction or corruption. Indeed, it is as if he were in a deep sleep, and it will be thus until Doomsday.[104]

Again, it is evident that while the Irish tradition depends on earlier accounts, it embellishes them with delightful and imaginative additions to the basic stories.

CONCLUSION

The stories summarized in this chapter span several centuries of development. The earliest stages of the apocryphal *Acts* of the apostle have been traced to the second century, while other episodes and expansions continued to be added for the next five or six hundred years at least. From the earliest echoes of this stream of tradition in Clement through the medieval interpolations, we see the elastic character of the apocryphal *Acts.* At points the *Acts of John* seem to reflect on Johannine tradition or promote views not markedly different from those of the opponents in 1 John. In other passages, Gnostic and Manichean tenets emerge. The *Acts,* popular as folklore, became a ready vehicle for a variety of theological and ascetic teachings. As a result, they were opposed and suppressed by orthodox ecclesiastical leaders, but without success.

Documents which circulated among Syrian Christians, however, gave detailed accounts of John's conversion of the city of Ephesus. A Syriac document published by Mingana adds to the lore that John was from the tribe of Zebulun and that he was buried in Ephesus by three of his disciples: Ignatius, Polycarp, and John (the author of Revelation). The Coptic texts of *The Book of John concerning the Falling Asleep of Mary* add (interpreting John 19:27) that Mary lived with John for ten years in Jerusalem. Other accounts add that John then went to Ephesus, or that he was carried back to Jerusalem from Ephesus on the clouds at Mary's death. In *The Homily of Pseudo-Chrysostom* one learns that like Elijah, John was received into heaven at his death. The dust from his tomb, moreover, had healing power and was inexhaustible. Following the pattern of accounts of appearances of the risen Lord in the Gospels, *The Homily* also reports that John appeared after his death to the emperor Constantine.

The Irish *Life of John the Evangelist* collected legends from a variety of sources and fueled the incandescence of pious imagination during the late Middle Ages. Popular imagination, piety, bigotry, asceticism, and theological precepts were all encouraged, defended, and disseminated by these legends. Stories that had once been told to defend the authority of the canonical writings had now taken on a life of their own and could therefore be used as vehicles for other interests and purposes. In a sense, the apostle had become incidental to the other interests served by the legends about him. On the other hand, the figure of the apostle so fired imagination and speculation that curiosity about his later life was never satisfied, no matter how many episodes and details were added to the traditions.

The legends were also taken up in other media we have not yet considered, however—especially in art and poetry. The hero and saint had also become an icon.

NOTES

1. Eusebius, *E.H.* 5.18.14 (LCL 1:493).
2. Eusebius, *E.H.* 3.25.6 (LCL 1:259).
3. Edgar Hennecke, *New Testament Apocrypha,* ed. Wilhelm Schneemelcher, trans. R. McL. Wilson (Philadelphia: Westminster Press, 1965), 2:179–80, 190.
4. Clement of Alexandria, Fragments from Cassiodorus, "Comments on the First Epistle of John [1:1]," in *ANF* 2:574.

5. For a detailed comparison of the account in Clement with that in the *Acts of John,* see Eric Junod and Jean-Daniel Kaestli, *L'histoire des actes apocryphes des apôtres du IIIe au IXe siècle: le cas des Actes de Jean,* CRTP 7 (Geneva: Revue de théologie et de philosophie, 1982), 13–16.

6. Eric Junod and Jean-Daniel Kaestli, *Acta Iohannis,* CChr (Turnhout: Brepols, 1983), 2:694–700. See also Knut Schäferdiek, "Johannesakten," in *Neutestamentliche Apokryphen,* ed. Wilhelm Schneelmelcher, 5th ed. (Tübingen: J. C. B. Mohr, 1989), 2:155.

7. Junod and Kaestli, *Acta Iohannis,* 692–94.

8. Epiphanius, *Panarion* 47.1.5, in *The Panarion of St. Epiphanius, Bishop of Salamis: Selected Passages,* trans. and ed. Philip R. Amidon (New York: Oxford University Press, 1990), 168.

9. For details, see Hennecke, *New Testament Apocrypha* 2:189–93; and Junod and Kaestli, *L'histoire des actes apocryphes des apôtres.*

10. M. S. Enslin, "John, Acts of," in *IDB* (Nashville: Abingdon Press, 1962), 2:930–31.

11. Photius, *Bibliotheca;* cited in Hennecke, *New Testament Apocrypha* 2:178.

12. Epiphanius, *Panarion* 51.6.9.; cited in Hennecke, *New Testament Apocrypha* 2:186.

13. Mansi 13:176A; cited in Hennecke, *New Testament Apocrypha* 2:193.

14. See Hennecke, *New Testament Apocrypha* 2:192–93. The Prochorus text was published by Theodor Zahn in *Acta Joannis* (Erlangen: Verlag von Andreas Deichert, 1880).

15. See Junod and Kaestli, *Acta Iohannis* 2:750–834, for an introduction and critical edition of *Virtutes Iohannis* (also called Pseudo-Abdias); see also M. R. James, *The Apocryphal New Testament* (Oxford: Clarendon Press, 1953), 438, 464.

16. See Rosa Söder, *Die apokryphen Apostelgeschichten und die romanhafte Literatur der Antike* (Stuttgart: W. Kohlhammer Verlag, 1969); Gerlinde Sirker-Wicklaus, *Untersuchungen zu den Johannes-Akten,* BzR 2 (Witterschlick: Verlag M. Wehle, 1988); François Bovon et al., *Les actes apocryphes des apôtres: Christianisme et monde païen* (Geneva: Labor et Fides, 1981).

17. Maximilianus Bonnet, *Acta Apostolorum Apocrypha* (Hildesheim: Georg Olms Verlagsbuchhandlung, 1959), 151–216.

18. See Hennecke, *New Testament Apocrypha* 2:194.

19. Junod and Kaestli, *Acta Iohannis* 1:76–100.

20. Junod and Kaestli, *Acta Iohannis* 1:76–86.

21. This and the following quotations are taken from Hennecke, *New Testament Apocrypha.* An English translation is also available in James, *The Apocryphal New Testament,* 228–70. For the Greek text and a French translation, see Junod and Kaestli, *Acta Iohannis* 1:160–343.

22. See Junod and Kaestli, *Acta Iohannis* 1:25, 239–43; Schäferdiek, "Johannesakten," 2:151, 176–77.

23. For this version of the story see James, *The Apocryphal New Testament,* 241.

24. Hennecke, *New Testament Apocrypha* 2:242.

25. Junod and Kaestli, *Acta Iohannis* 1:7–8, 75, 93, 145–58, 238–43.

26. Theodor Zahn, "Die Wanderungen des Apostels Johannes," *Neue kirchliche Zeitschrift* 10 (1899): 198; cf. Junod and Kaestli, *Acta Iohannis* 1:93–94.
27. Hennecke, *New Testament Apocrypha* 2:244.
28. Hennecke, *New Testament Apocrypha* 2:244.
29. Junod and Kaestli, *Acta Iohannis* 1:268 n. 3. Bonnet conjectured that the text read "who had nearly been violated."
30. Junod and Kaestli, *Acta Iohannis* 1:250.
31. Hennecke, *New Testament Apocrypha* 2:255.
32. Hennecke, *New Testament Apocrypha* 2:256.
33. For English translations of the Arabic versions of the death of John, see Agnes Smith Lewis, *The Mythological Acts of the Apostles,* Horae Semiticae 4 (London: C. J. Clay and Sons, 1904), 54–59, 168–71. For English translations of other ancient versions of the "Departure," see: (Syriac) William Wright, *Apocryphal Acts of the Apostles* (1871; Reprint, Amsterdam: Philo Press, 1968), 2:61–68; (Coptic) Ernest A. Wallis Budge, *Coptic Apocrypha in the Dialect of Upper Egypt* (London: British Museum, 1913), 233–40 [N.B.: the latter translation is frequently defective]; (Ethiopic) Budge, *The Contendings of the Apostles* (Amsterdam: Apa-Philo Press, 1976), 2:253–63.
34. One Arabic version says "Prochorus," and the account switches to first-person narration; the other has the name "Byrrhus." See Lewis, *The Mythological Acts of the Apostles,* xxxiv–xxxv, 57, 169; and Budge, *The Contendings of the Apostles* 2:217. Theodor Zahn points out that an Ephesian deacon by the name of "Byrrhus" or "Burrhus" is mentioned by Ignatius (*Eph.* 2, *Philad.* 11, *Smyrn.* 12); see *Acta Joannis* (Erlangen: Verlag von Andreas Deichert, 1880), clii. Other late witnesses identify the grave digger as Eutychus, but this name, like Prochorus, is a secondary modification.
35. Hennecke, *New Testament Apocrypha* 2:257. There are two Arabic versions of "The Death of Saint John" (see n. 33 above). The one attributed to Prochorus does not contain this account of how John was kept from marrying. The other, which follows the Syriac *History of John,* does contain this motif. Cf. Agnes Smith Lewis, *The Mythological Acts of the Apostles,* 58 and 170.
36. A translation of the Syriac version of "The Decease of Saint John" is preserved in Wright, *Apocryphal Acts of the Apostles* 2:61–68. The translation was made from a vellum manuscript in the British Museum (Add. 12,174), dated A.D. 1197.
37. Cited in Agnes Smith Lewis, *The Mythological Acts of the Apostles,* 59.
38. Augustine, Tractate 124.2 (*NPNF,* 1st ser., 7:448). Junod and Kaestli contend that this is a clear instance of Augustine's use of the *Acts of John.* See *L'histoire des actes apocryphes des apôtres,* 81–86; and Kaestli, "Le rôle des textes bibliques dans la genèse et le développement des légendes apocryphes: Le cas du sort final de l'apôtre Jean," *Augustinianum* 23, nos. 1–2 (1983): 325–26.
39. Hennecke, *New Testament Apocrypha* 2:258–59. For Pseudo-Abdias, see Junod and Kaestli, *Acta Iohannis* 2:831–32. For Ephraim of Antioch, see Junod and Kaestli, *L'histoire des actes apocryphes des apôtres,* 115–16.
40. Hennecke, *New Testament Apocrypha* 2:141–43, 209.
41. Hennecke, *New Testament Apocrypha* 2:209.

42. Hennecke, *New Testament Apocrypha* 2:209.

43. Junod and Kaestli, *Acta Iohannis* 1:96–98.

44. Hennecke, *New Testament Apocrypha* 2:209–10.

45. The Greek text of Pseudo-Melitus is most accessible through Migne (*PG* 5:1239–50). For a critical text of the "Virtutes," see Junod and Kaestli, *Acta Iohannis* 2:798–834. The best interpretation of the relationships between these documents and their relationship to the *Acts of John* is Knut Schäferdiek, "Die 'Passio Johannis' des Melito von Laodikeia und die 'Virtutes Johannis,'" *AnBoll* 103 (1985): 367–82.

46. See Junod and Kaestli, *Acta Iohannis* 2:770–90; and Schäferdiek, "Die 'Passio Johannis' des Melito von Laodikeia und die 'Virtutes Johannis,'" 373.

47. Schäferdiek, "Die 'Passio Johannis' des Melito von Laodikeia und die 'Virtutes Johannis,'" 380.

48. Schäferdiek, "Die 'Passio Johannis' des Melito von Laodikeia und die 'Virtutes Johannis,'" 375.

49. James, *The Apocryphal New Testament,* 261.

50. See Hennecke, *New Testament Apocrypha* 2:204–205.

51. For the relationship to Mark 16:18, see Junod and Kaestli, *Acta Iohannis* 2:852.

52. James, *The Apocryphal New Testament,* 263.

53. See Hennecke, *New Testament Apocrypha* 2:205–6; and Schäferdiek, "Die 'Passio Johannis' des Melito von Laodikeia und die 'Virtutes Johannis,'" 374–75.

54. For a translation of the fragments, see Hennecke, *New Testament Apocrypha* 2:207–8; and James, *The Apocryphal New Testament,* 264–65. The Irish *Life of John the Evangelist* also contains parallels to episodes in the papyrus; see Junod and Kaestli, *Acta Iohannis* 1:109–36, esp. the English translation of three episodes, 113–16. See also Ruairí ó hUiginn, "Beatha Eoin Bruinne," *Neutestamentliche Apokryphen,* ed. Wilhelm Schneelmelcher, 5th ed. (Tübingen: J. C. B. Mohr, 1989), 2:191–93. Regarding the Irish *Life of John the Evangelist,* see above, p. 241.

55. Junod and Kaestli do not consider the discourse on the polymorphous nature of Christ to be docetic (*Acta Iohannis* 2:490–93). On the other hand, chapters 94–102, which have an independent origin, reflect a docetic Christology like that of the oriental Valentinians (*Acta Iohannis* 2:600–606, 629–30).

56. Hennecke, *New Testament Apocrypha* 2:233.

57. The argument that there is a connection between the *Acts of John* and the views opposed in the prologue of John and the Johannine Epistles is defended by Jean-Daniel Kaestli in "Le mystère de la croix de lumière et le johannisme. Actes de Jean ch. 94–102," *Foi et Vie* 86 (1987): 35–46; and by Richard I. Pervo in "Johannine Trajectories in the *Acts of John,*" *Apocrypha* 3 (1992): 47–68, esp. p. 62.

58. See Junod and Kaestli, *Acta Iohannis* 2:835–86, esp. 840–44; Hennecke, *New Testament Apocrypha* 2:195–96; James, *The Apocryphal New Testament,* 228–29; and *ANF* 8:560–64.

59. Junod and Kaestli, *Acta Iohannis* 2:748–49.

60. For the Greek text, see Zahn, *Acta Joannis,* 3–165. I have not found an English translation of the Greek text. For an introduction and analysis, see Junod and Kaestli, *Acta Iohannis* 2:718–49; and Aurelio de Santos Otero, "Jüngere Apostelakten," in *Neutestamentliche Apokryphen,* ed. W. Schneemelcher, 5th ed. (1989), 2:385–91. For an introduction and English translation of the Ethiopic version, see Budge, *The Contendings of the Apostles* 2:186–220. For an English translation of the Arabic version, see Agnes Smith Lewis, *The Mythological Acts of the Apostles,* xxi, 37–53. For a French translation of the Armenian version, see Louis Leloir, *Écrits apocryphes sur les apôtres: Traduction de l'édition arménienne de Venise,* CChr 3 (Turnhout: Brepols, 1986), 289–407. For the Old Slavonic version, see Aurelio de Santos Otero, *Die handschriftliche Überlieferung der altslavischen Apokryphen* (New York: De Gruyter, 1978), 1:97–123. See further Junod and Kaestli, *Acta Iohannis* 2:718 n. 1; and Hennecke, *New Testament Apocrypha* 2:575–76.

61. See the summary of Wright's translation of the Syriac *History of John* above, pp. 223–30.

62. For comparisons of the different accounts of the death of John, see pp. 170–74, 177, 325.

63. The page and line numbers refer to Zahn, *Acta Joannis.* My translations.

64. See Junod and Kaestli, *Acta Iohannis* 2:740 n. 1.

65. For discussion of this ancient practice, see Agnes Smith Lewis, *The Mythological Acts of the Apostles,* xxii–xxiv.

66. This comment is absent from some manuscripts, but the anti-Jewish motif is accented in the Arabic version.

67. William Steuart McBirnie reports that local legend identifies Kynops with a distinctive rock formation: "Fishermen will point out Kynops petrified in rock from beneath the calm water of the bay of Scala, and monks will show you the frescoes illustrating this scene in the outer narthex of the big monastery of St. John the Theologian at Chora," the principal site on Patmos; see *The Search for the Twelve Apostles* (Wheaton, Ill.: Tyndale House, 1973), 111.

68. See above, p. 199–201.

69. Wright, *Apocryphal Acts of the Apostles* 2:vii–ix. The quotations in the summary in the next section are taken from this text and are annotated by page numbers in parentheses. See Junod and Kaestli, *Acta Iohannis* 2:705–17, for discussion of the theological and literary character of the document.

70. R. H. Connolly, "The Original Language of the Syriac Acts of John" and "The Diatessaron in the Syriac Acts of John," *Journal of Theological Studies* 8 (1906–1907): 249–61, 571–81. See also Junod and Kaestli, *Acta Iohannis* 2:705–17.

71. Regarding the assimilation of the tradition of John's death to that of Moses, especially in Syrian traditions, see Kaestli, "Le rôle des textes bibliques dans la genèse et le développement des légendes apocryphes," 326–28.

72. For an English translation, see Agnes Smith Lewis, *The Mythological Acts of the Apostles,* 157–67.

73. Agnes Smith Lewis, *The Mythological Acts of the Apostles,* xxxiii—an argument attributed to Lipsius.

74. Alphonse Mingana, "The Authorship of the Fourth Gospel," *BJRL* 14 (1930): 333–39.

75. Trans. F. F. Bruce, cited in Bruce, "St. John at Ephesus," *BJRL* 60 (1978): 356–57; see also Bruce, *Peter, Stephen, James and John: Studies in Non-Pauline Christianity* (Grand Rapids: Wm. B. Eerdmans, 1979), 146.

76. See above, pp. 148–149.

77. *ANF* 8:359.

78. See *ANF* 8:582–86.

79. *ANF* 8:583.

80. On the complicated issue of the different versions of the assumption of Mary, see Maurice Geerard, *Clavis Apocryphorum* (Turnhout: Brepols, 1992), which identifies and inventories each text. For English translations of various versions, see *ANF* 8:359, 587–91; and James, *The Apocryphal New Testament*, 194–227.

81. See *ANF* 8:587–91. See also James, *The Apocryphal New Testament*, 201–9. Chapter references in the summary that follows come from James; quotations are taken from the translation in *ANF*.

82. James, *The Apocryphal New Testament*, 197.

83. See *ANF* 8:359.

84. *ANF* 8:587.

85. *ANF* 8:588.

86. *ANF* 8:588.

87. *ANF* 8:589.

88. *ANF* 8:590.

89. For an English translation of the *Assumption of Mary,* see James, *The Apocryphal New Testament*, 209–16; and *ANF* 8:595–98.

90. *Assumption of Mary,* in James, *The Apocryphal New Testament*, 210. Page and chapter references in the summary that follows refer to this translation.

91. François-Marie Braun, *Jean le théologien et son évangile dans l'église ancienne* (Paris: J. Gabalda, 1959), 1:327.

92. *Menologium Graecorum* 1:70; my translation. This text is often designated as the *Menologium of Basil;* it is reproduced in Migne, *PG* 117:73B–C, and is edited by H. Delehaye in *Synaxarium Ecclesiae Constantinopolitanae* (Brussels, 1902), 79–82. The *Menologium* depends on the *Acts of John:* the Gospel is written at Patmos, and the tomb is dug in the form of a cross.

93. Cited in J.-B. Chabot, *Chronique de Michel le Syrien Patriarche Jacobite d'Antioche (1166–1199)* (Brussels: Culture et Civilisation, 1963), 1:148; my translation.

94. For the Arabic Gospel of John, see J. Galbiati, ed., *Iohannis Evangelium apocryphorum arabice*, 2 vols. (Milan: In aedious Mondadorianis, 1957).

95. James, *The Apocryphal New Testament*, 187. An English translation follows, 187–93.

96. See Junod and Kaestli, *Acta Iohannis* 1:402–19, for an introduction to, and the Greek text of, the *Homily of Pseudo-Chrysostom.* An English translation of the Arabic version has been published by Agnes Smith Lewis in *The Mythological*

Acts of the Apostles, 171–74. The following translation is from the Greek text and is my own.

97. Junod and Kaestli, *Acta Iohannis* 1:411.

98. See Junod and Kaestli, *Acta Iohannis* 1:410 n. 2.

99. See Martin McNamara, M.S.C., *The Apocrypha in the Irish Church* (Dublin: Dublin Institute for Advanced Studies, 1975), 95–99; and Máire Herbert and Martin McNamara, M.S.C., ed., *Irish Biblical Apocrypha: Selected Texts in Translation* (Edinburgh: T. and T. Clark, 1989), 89–98, 180–81. See also Junod and Kaestli, *Acta Iohannis* 1:109–33.

100. Herbert and McNamara, *Irish Biblical Apocrypha,* 90.

101. Herbert and McNamara, *Irish Biblical Apocrypha,* 92.

102. Herbert and McNamara, *Irish Biblical Apocrypha,* 93. For an English translation of the story of John and Seusisp, see Junod and Kaestli, *Acta Iohannis* 1:113–16.

103. Herbert and McNamara, *Irish Biblical Apocrypha,* 97.

104. Herbert and McNamara, *Irish Biblical Apocrypha,* 98.

CHAPTER 8

Icon
The Apostle in Art and Literature

Although a discussion of the representations of John in medieval art and in poetry, primarily from the nineteenth century, may hang together topically, it really encompasses two distinct periods in the development of the Johannine legend. The paintings and stained glasses of the late Middle Ages often depict scenes from the *Acts of John* and related stories. In this respect, the poetry of Adam of St. Victor and even that of Henry Wadsworth Longfellow, though different in medium, is not so different from the representation of the legends in graphic art. Robert Browning's "A Death in the Desert," however, represents a dramatic departure from previous expressions of the legend. With the impact of modern historical and critical consciousness, the freedom to create legends and stir imaginations with them was severely curtailed.

In the next chapter, we will review the works of the early questers for the "historical John." Browning responded to the advent of higher criticism by meeting it on its own ground and creating a dramatic monologue purportedly handed down by tradition and contained in a manuscript that had been revised and interpolated. "A Death in the Desert" tells the story of John's death and final words, but it does not purport to be historical fact. Browning is far more nuanced, responding to skepticism regarding the apostle by setting forth what the poet held to be truth, but fashioning it in a story that is self-evidently fiction. First, however, let us look at examples of the expression of the legends about John in visual media.

JOHN IN CHRISTIAN ART

John is the patron saint of theologians, writers, and all whose vocation is the production of books. Each episode of his life and tradition has been the subject of artistic representation. A worthy study of the impact of legend on the

251

artistic representations of John would comprise another book, however.[1] What follows is a cursory treatment of the subject, at best.

John is represented in three roles: as evangelist, apostle, and prophet.[2] In Greek art, he is always depicted as an old man with white hair and a venerable beard. In the works of the later Latin painters, however, John appears as a youthful apostle, beardless, with curly hair, and usually with a pen, his book, and the eagle nearby. When John is depicted as the prophet or seer, he is usually an old man, seated in rocky, arid terrain with the sea in the distance, representing John on Patmos. In some prints of the apostle writing his Gospel, his eyes are turned toward a vision of the Virgin and the infant Christ. Anna Jameson also reports seeing a work in which the Devil appears behind the apostle, intercepting the message and overturning the ink on the evangelist's pages.[3] In works of the early Siena school, Jameson reports, John carries a radiant circle inscribed with the words "*In primo est verbum,*" and within the circle is an eagle with outstretched wings.[4]

The clearest evidence of the influence of the legends about John on artistic representations can be seen in the depictions of John as apostle with a cup with a viper in it, recalling the story that Aristodemus, the high priest of Diana at Ephesus—or in other versions, the emperor Domitian—challenged John to drink a poisoned cup. Others interpret the cup as a depiction of the cup of suffering referred to in Mark 10:38–39. Jameson was especially impressed with the rendering in the Brera at Milan,

> where St. John bends on one knee at the foot of the throne of the Madonna and Child, his pen in one hand, the other pressed to his bosom, and looking up to them with an air of ecstatic inspiration. Two little angels, or rather *amoretti,* are in attendance: one has his arms around the neck of the eagle, sporting with it; the other holds up the cup and the serpent. Every detail is composed and painted to admiration; but this is the artistic and picturesque, not the religious, version of the subject.[5]

Albrecht Dürer's painting of John and Peter together contrasts Peter's sturdy, rugged appearance with John's refinement and grace. John is holding the open Gospel for Peter to read it, and Jameson suggests that since this painting was done after Dürer became a Protestant, he may have intended the implication that the apostle is making Peter study the Gospel of John.[6]

The bronze bas-relief on the tomb of Henry VII in Westminster Abbey depicts John the apostle and John the Baptist together. Here again, there is a fine contrast between the characters: "the dark, emaciated, hairy prophet of the wilderness, and the graceful dignity of the youthful apostle."[7] At times, the two Johns are even depicted together as infants. John often appears in

St. John the Evangelist by El Greco (1541–1614); print 2444, Museo del Prado, Madrid, Spain; reproduced by permission.

St. John the Evangelist by Juan Ribalta (1597–1628); print 3044, Museo del Prado, Madrid, Spain; reproduced by permission.

paintings with the Madonna because of his testimony to the Incarnation. When John appears in scenes with the other disciples, he is usually distinguished by his youth, beauty, and nearness to Christ.

As a result of the youthful depictions of John, the notion of his perpetual youth entered the stream of tradition—a notion nurtured also by the reports that the apostle would not die before the Lord's return. James M. MacDonald reported the story of the discovery in Constantinople of "an antique agate intaglio, representing a young man with a cornucopia, and an eagle and figure of Victory placing a crown on his head. They [the monks] maintained it was a portrait of John, sent to their hands by miraculous preservation. It proved to be a representation of the apotheosis of Germanicus."[8]

Unfortunately, the hostility toward "the Jews" that is often evident in the Gospel of John has been depicted in religious art also. Without identifying specific works, Jameson cites "examples in which St. John is seen trampling a Jew under his feet; on the other side [of the cross] the Virgin tramples on a veiled woman, signifying the old law, the synagogue, as opposed to the Christian Church, of which the Virgin was the received symbol."[9] Among the early painters, there are scenes of the descent from the Cross, in which John usually holds the head of Christ. In a work by Zurbaran at Munich, John supports the Virgin Mary as together they make their way from the crucifixion.[10]

In a variation of the theme of John writing his Gospel, a painting in the Church of Haghia Aikaterina that dates from the mid-sixteenth century portrays John dictating the Gospel to Prochoros.[11] The two sit in the cave on Patmos. John is seated on the left on a square stool, dictating to a young Prochoros, who sits facing him on a similar stool with an open book on his knees. The beginning of the Gospel is visible on its pages. Between the two figures is a tall, elaborate book stand supporting an open codex on which one can read 1 John 4:12. The posture of the apostle is distinctive: his head is turned back sharply to the right, towards the blessing hand of God that reaches from above him.

Jameson describes ten subjects drawn from the later legends about John.[12] John is depicted teaching his disciples at Ephesus in a work by Israel von Meckenen. The apostle and five disciples sit in a Gothic church, while the apostle interprets the Scriptures. In the background, there is a large chest full of money, apparently a reflection of the description in Acts 4:37 of the believers laying money at the disciples' feet.

The scene of John's drinking from the poisoned chalice is portrayed in a painting in the Vatican Museum. Others look on in awe, and a man falls dead at John's feet. Jameson comments that among the relics at the church of S. Croce in Rome is "the cup in which St. John, the apostle and evangelist, by command of Domitian the emperor, rank poison without receiving injury;

which afterwards being tasted by his attendants, on the instant they fell dead."[13] In depictions of this scene in medieval art, John is usually represented as a beautiful youth with a cup in his hand, out of which a serpent is escaping—an image reflecting the notion that the poison drew itself out of the cup in the form of a serpent. This legend also gave rise to the folk custom of the "Johannes-Minne," drinking from the loving cup in honor of John, which is especially common in Germany. Medieval ritualia preserve a number of blessings which were supposed to render the drink potent for warding off dangers to health and assuring one's entry into heaven.[14]

Clement of Alexandria's story of John and the robber captain is the subject of some old engravings. John is embracing the robber, who has thrown away his weapons and is weeping on John's neck. The story of the two young men who sold everything to follow John and then regretted their decision[15] is the represented on one of the windows of the Cathedral at Bourges. The apostle instructed the two to collect pebbles and then changed these into gold. In the scene, the two men stand before John with a pile of gold on one side and a heap of stones on the other. The story of the raising of Drusiana[16] is portrayed in a fresco by Filippo Lippi on a wall of the Strozzi Chapel in Florence.

The story of John and the partridge[17] has not been a subject chosen by painters, but a partridge does appear in a number of works from the Venetian School. Works entitled the *Martyrdom of St. John* portray his immersion in a caldron of boiling oil.[18] The chapel of San Giovanni in Olio stands over the place where this event is supposed to have happened, and the scene is depicted in a fresco on the chapel's walls. It is also the subject of one of Albrecht Dürer's woodcuts, of Rubens's altar piece at Malines depicting John, and of Padvanino's work for the San Pietro at Venice.[19] Because of his martyrdom, John is occasionally portrayed bearing a palm. The story of John's descending into the grave and lying down to sleep[20] was treated only rarely, but can be seen in the *Menologium Graecum* (Vatican MSS, tenth century), where the grave is in the shape of a cross.[21] Other works depict the Virgin, Peter, Paul, and the ascension of John to Christ. According to a late version of the Greek legend, John died without pain or change, and immediately rose again in bodily form. A small painting at the Vatican Christian Museum in Rome depicts a crypt that looks somewhat like the Xanthian tombs; one end is open, and John is seen issuing from it.

Jameson's account of two late legends about the apostle are quoted here in full because they are rarely found in other sources.

When the Empress Galla Placidia was returning from Constantinople to Ravenna with her two children (A.D. 425) she encountered a terrible storm. In her fear and anguish she vowed a vow to St. John the Evangelist, and being landed in safety, she dedicated to his honor a magnificent church. When the edifice was finished, she was extremely desirous of procuring some relics of the Evangelist, wherewith to consecrate his sanctuary; but as it was not the manner of those days to exhume, and buy and sell, still less to steal, the bodies of holy men and martyrs, the desire of the pious empress remained unsatisfied. However, as it is related, St. John himself took pity upon her; for one night, as she prayed earnestly, he appeared to her in a vision; and when she threw herself at his feet to embrace and kiss them, he disappeared, leaving one of his slippers or sandals in her hand, which sandal was long preserved.

The antique church of Galla Placidia still exists at Ravenna, to keep alive, after the lapse of fourteen centuries, the memory of her dream, and the condescension of the blessed apostle.[22]

Various aspects of this legend are represented inside the church of Galla Placidia.

From Johannis Brompton's *Cronicon,* Jameson quotes the legend of John and Edward the Confessor:

King Edward the Confessor had, after Christ and the Virgin Mary, a special veneration for St. John the Evangelist. One day, returning from his church at Westminster, where he had been hearing mass in honor of the evangelist, he was accosted by a pilgrim, who asked him for an alms for the love of God and St. John. The king, who was ever merciful to the poor, immediately drew from his finger a ring, and, unknown to any one, delivered it to the beggar. When the king had reigned twenty-four years, it came to pass that two Englishmen, pilgrims, returning from the Holy Land to their own country, were met by one in the habit of a pilgrim, who asked of them concerning their country; and being told they were of England, he said to them, "When ye shall have arrived in your own country, go to King Edward, and salute him in my name; say to him, that I thank him for the alms bestowed on me in a certain street in Westminster; for there, on a certain day, as I begged of him an alms, he bestowed on me this ring, which till now I have preserved, and ye shall carry it back to him, saying that in six months from this time he shall quit the world, and come and remain with me for ever." And the pilgrims, being astonished, said, "Who art thou, and where is thy dwelling-place?" And he answered, saying, "I am John the Evangelist. Edward your king is my friend, and for the sanctity of his life I hold him dear. Go now, therefore, deliver to him this message and this ring; and I will pray to God that ye may arrive safely in your own country." When St. John had spoken thus, he delivered to them the ring, and vanished out of their sight. The pilgrims, praising and thanking the Lord for this glorious vision, went on their journey; and being arrived in England, they repaired to King Edward, and saluted him, and delivered the ring and the message, relating all truly. And the king received the news joyfully, and feasted the messengers royally. Then he set himself to prepare for his departure from this world. On the eve of the Nativity, in the year of our Lord 1066, he fell sick, and on the eve of the Epiphany following he died. The ring he gave to the Abbot of Westminster, to be forever preserved among the relics there.

"According to one account," Jameson says, "the pilgrims met the king near his palace at Waltham, at a place since called *Havering*." As Brompton continued: "In allusion to this story, King Edward II. offered at his coronation a pound of gold made in the figure of a king holding a ring, and a mark of gold (8 oz.) made like a pilgrim putting forth his hand to receive the ring."[23]

According to the *Golden Legend*,[24] however, the pilgrims were miraculously transported back to England after talking with John:

> And anon as he was gone they had great lust to sleep, and laid them down and slept, and this was in the Holy Land, and when they awoke they looked about them and knew not where they were. And they saw flocks of sheep and shepherds keeping them, to whom they went to know the way, and to demand where they were, and when they asked them they spake English and said that they were in England, in Kent on Barham Down.[25]

This legend is represented in three compartments along the top of the screen of Edward the Confessor's chapel. It was also painted on one of the windows of the Romford Church in Essex. John was often represented on rood-screens in the Middle Ages. Scenes from his life are portrayed in medieval apocalypses, and in the West, he is often represented with John the Baptist, as on the stole of Cuthbert, embroidered at Winchester during the ninth century.[26]

Celtic Christianity frequently appealed to the authority of St. John. For example, Celtic monks shaved the front half of their heads from ear to ear, claiming the authority of John for this practice.[27] Moreover, in A.D. 664, Bishop Colman defended their date for the celebration of Easter with these words:

> Our fathers and their predecessors, plainly inspired by the Holy Spirit as was Columba, ordained the celebration of Easter on the

fourteenth day of the moon, if it was a Sunday, following the
example of the Apostle and Evangelist John "who leaned on the
breast of the Lord at supper" and was called the friend of the Lord.
He celebrated Easter on the fourteenth day of the moon and we,
like his disciples Polycarp and others, celebrate it on his authority. . . . [28]

An illustrated manuscript of the fourteenth century reports the legend that
the unnamed groom at the wedding at Cana (John 2:1–11) was John the son of
Zebedee and that the wedding was taking place under the direction of Mary,
the mother of Jesus. According to this legend, Jesus did not allow John to
consummate the marriage, but called him as soon as the wedding was over:
"Leave this wife of yours and follow me, for I shall lead you to a higher
wedding." The author of the *Meditations* explains the reason for this disap-
pointing conclusion to the story of the wedding: "The wedding shows that he
approved carnal marriage as instituted by God, but since he called John from
the wedding, you must clearly understand that spiritual marriage is much more
meritorious than carnal."[29]

Another version of this legend, which had been traced back as early as
Bede, identifies the matrimonial couple as John and Mary Magdalen. Jesus
was present at the wedding because he and his mother had been invited by
Salome, the groom's mother. Jesus called John after the wedding—"Leave thy
wife and follow me"—and John followed him, choosing celibacy over marriage.[30] This legend too has left its legacy in art. In the choir enclave of Notre
Dame in Paris, one of the betrothed wears a nimbus, which was given only to
saints in medieval iconography—a fact leading to the conclusion that this
figure represents John. The later legends about John were so popular in the
Middle Ages that some of the windows dedicated to him (for example, those
at Chartres and Bourges) do not contain a single feature drawn from the New
Testament.[31]

JOHN IN POETRY

The story of the apostle's role in poetry has never been adequately
chronicled, and indeed merits a fuller and more competent treatment than can
be given here. Nevertheless, one can see a marked development from the plain
medieval poetry of Adam of Saint Victor to the sophisticated verse of Robert
Browning. Of particular interest is the survival and perpetuation of elements
of the early legends—as in Herder's retelling of the story of the partridge. The
following selection of verse on John, though limited, illustrates an important
facet of the relationship between legend, art, and poetry.

Adam of Saint Victor

Recognized as the greatest Latin poet of the Middle Ages, Adam of Saint Victor (ca. 1172) wrote two poems about the four evangelists. In one of them, "Jocundare plebs fidelis," we find these lines:

> John, the eagle's feature having,
> Earth on love's twain pinions leaving,
> Soars aloft, God's truth perceiving
> In light's purer atmosphere.[32]

This passage repeats the common image of the eagle and is reminiscent of Augustine's fondness for praising the sublime character of the Gospel by describing the soaring flight of the eagle.[33]

Johann Gottfried Herder

The story of the partridge can be traced back to the fourth or fifth century, and was attached to the *Acts of John* by the eleventh century.[34] In it, Herder (1744–1803) found inspiration for his "Saint John," a winsome verse with witty good sense. The following translation reproduces the sense of the poem, but does not pretend to capture its poetic qualities:

> Do you want to strive long,
> Don't strive all the time!
> Otherwise, your faint soul will fail
> Alternate rest and work so that the work
> May be faithful to you and quicken your soul.

> Saint John, now in old age,
> Lived at Ephesus and rested
> After and between the stresses of his office.
> So he played with a tame partridge
> To which he daily gave food and drink,
> Which slept in his bosom. He stroked
> Its feathers affectionately, spoke to it,
> And it listened to him, chirped thanks to him cheerfully.

> Once a strange hunter stepped out of the forest
> Bloody of countenance. Over his shoulder
> Hung his quiver, on his arm hung
> The unstrung bow. For a long time he had wanted

To see this holy man, and he saw him—
Playing with a partridge. Greatly surprised
He stood before him, called finally, exasperated:
"Blessed John! Having come far
To see a saintly man, I see
A man who fritters away the time."

And the old man answered him in this way, gently:
"Kind stranger, why is it that your bow
Hangs there unstrung?" "Unstrung," he answered,
"Because it serves if I now stretch it
Purposefully. Can the string of the bow
Always be taut, so that it never relaxes?"
John answered: "Can the string of life
Always be taut, so that it never relaxes?"[35]

Friedrich Gottlieb Klopstock

Klopstock (1724–1803) has been called the founder of German free verse, the reformer of German literature, the first modern German poet, and the forerunner of Goethe. As a student he was deeply impressed with Milton and resolved to write a great religious epic. The first three cantos of Klopstock's *The Messiah* were published anonymously in 1748. The last five appeared in 1773. Writing the epic in classical hexameters, and throwing off the fetters of earlier conventions, Klopstock intermingled imaginative fictions with inter-pretation and retelling of the events of Jesus' death and resurrection.

In Klopstock's epic verse, John's intimacy with Jesus is given much greater play than in the Gospels. The Beloved Disciple is given the visionary powers of John the seer. One interpreter has even commented that in *The Messiah* "the visionary apostle John [is] the most prominent and vivid person—perhaps the only person—in the poem . . . as Jesus is the merciful mediator between God and man, so John is the merciful mediator between the Son of God and man. . . . It is precisely his humanity that makes him the beloved of Christ and opens to him the visionary experiences denied to the other apostles."[36] The rationale for this epic interpretation of John appears to be that because his humanity is confirmed, his visions can be extravagant but still credible.

The following summary focuses exclusively on the passages in which John plays a role, so the story line is abridged and John may seem to have more prominence in the epic than is actually the case. The epic begins with Jesus ascending the Mount of Olives to pray. John, the Beloved Disciple, follows but remains among the tombs (I.5).[37] When the Messiah awakes in the morning, he perceives the presence of Raphael, John's guardian angel, who tells him that John is lamenting over a demoniac that is lying among the tombs (II.28). Jesus casts out the demon and banishes Satan, who returns to Hell and plots Jesus' death. Still among the tombs, John is allowed to see the seraph Eloa (III.59), while the rest of the disciples are searching for Jesus. Judas hates John because Judas knows of Jesus' love for John and imagines that John will collect the heavenly treasure that otherwise he himself might receive (III.71). Ithuriel, Judas's guardian angel, goes to warn Jesus.

John, we are told, has two guardian angels, Raphael and a young seraph named Salem (III.73), who reassure the other angels with the following tribute to John:

Ye seraphs, compose your minds, said he; there with Jesus in the tombs, is John, the most amiable of all the disciples. Cast your eyes on him, and you will no longer think of Judas. Devout as a seraph, he lives with the Messiah as one of the immortals. To him the Redeemer opens his heart; and him has he chosen his chief confident. As the friendship of Gabriel and the exalted Eloa, or as the affection Abdiel once felt for Abbadona, while living with him in native innocence, is the friendship that subsists between John and his divine Master. Of this he is worthy: for of all the souls of men, the Creator never formed one more pure and heavenly than that of John. I was present when the immortal essence came forth, and beheld a resplendent rank of young celestial spirits, thus, in flowing numbers, hail their companion:

We salute thee, holy offspring of the breath divine! Beauteous and loving art thou as Salem, as Raphael heavenly and sublime. From these pure sentiments will flow as dew from the purple clouds of the morning, and thy humane heart—thy heart, filled with tender sensations, shall melt, as the eyes of the seraphim, enraptured at the sight of virtue, overflow with sweetest transports. Fair daughter of the breath divine, faithful sister of the soul which once, in its unspotted youth, animated the first of men, we will not conduct thee to the body, thy companion, which smiling nature moulds for thee in proportions just and lovely. It will be beautiful, like the body of the Messiah, which soon the Divine Spirit will form, and which, in manly grace, shall exceed all the sons of Adam. In this thy tender and amiable frame, thy virtues will be destroyed. It shall then moulder in the dust; but at last thy Salem will seek and awake thee; and if thou hast faithfully performed thy task on earth, will conduct thee, arrayed in celestial beauty, to the embraces of the Messiah, coming in the clouds to judge the world. Thus, enraptured, sang the juvenile spirits of heaven. (III.73–74)

While the disciples sleep, Satan appears in a dream to Judas, in the form of his father. He shows Judas the inheritance prepared for John and Peter and tells Judas that they are receiving what rightfully belongs to him. When Jesus and John awake, they walk up the mount together to where the others are asleep.

While Caiaphas and the Sanhedrin are plotting Jesus' death, Jesus sends Peter and John to prepare the Passover meal (IV.105). When Mary, the mother of Jesus, comes searching for Jesus, John receives her and explains that Jesus is on his way from Bethany (IV.108). At the supper, after Jesus institutes the Eucharist, John is allowed a heavenly vision:

> When John, seized with a sudden transport, sunk down at his feet, kissed them, and wetted them with his tears.
>
> Jesus then looking up towards heaven, with a gracious smile, cried, O Father! permit him to see my glory. John then arising beheld at the end of the chambers a bright assembly of angels, who knew that he saw them. Rapt in an ecstatic transport, he beheld the sublime Gabriel, with motionless astonishment. . . . Now, turning his ravished eyes, he discovered in the Messiah's placid countenance, traces of his celestial glory, and sunk speechless on his bosom. Gabriel then rose on his extended wings, and transported with love, said to Jesus, O thou great Messiah, embrace me, as those embracest thy disciple! (IV.121)

Next, the Beloved Disciple's silence about the identity of the betrayer is explained:

> Sorrow was again spread over each countenance. Peter then made a sign to John, who still lay reclined on the breast of the Redeemer, and, whispering, asked, Who is it? He it is, said the Saviour with low voice, to whom I, with tender affection, and brotherly love, give this sop. He then gave it to Judas. John trembled; but his humanity kept him silent. (IV.122)

In the Garden of Gethsemane, Peter reclines on John, who sleeps tranquilly while Salem hovers over him (V.144). Abbadonna, one of the fallen angels, mistakes John for Jesus, saying to himself as he looks at John sleeping: "thy countenance has the lineaments of celestial purity, and the traces of a tender and generous soul. Yes, thou art he!" (V.145). John's distress at the arrest of Jesus is recorded in an extended internal monologue (VI.162–64). Later, outside the courtyard, Peter confesses to John that he has denied Jesus (VI.175). When Jesus is taken to Herod, John catches a distant glimpse of him (VII.200). At the cross, Peter feels unworthy to be associated with John (IX.240). John stands with Jesus' mother. After Jesus' words to them, "John and Mary transported, looked at each other filled with surprise, and shedding tears of gratitude" (IX.250).

After Jesus' death, John brings the funeral linen for his burial (XII.334), and after the burial, he leads Mary to his own house (XII.338), where many of the disciples have gathered to comfort Mary. Later, John sleeps and dreams of Lebanon and Eden, continuing to weep even as he sleeps (XII.355). The discovery of the tomb empty follows the account in John 20, adding picturesque details. As they run to the tomb, John tells the others, "The lower way, by those bushes is the shortest" (XIV.385). John runs ahead of the others and sees the linen lying on the ground, "but, checked by timid reverence, [he] avoided going in" (XIV.386). When Mary Magdalene reports that she has seen the risen Lord, "John took hold of her, and she stood leaning on him" (XIV.390). When, after the appearance to the two on the road to Emmaus, the disciples debate why Jesus has appeared to certain of them but not to others— not to Thomas, and not to his own mother—John takes up for Thomas and confesses that he too is grieved that Jesus has not appeared to him either (XIV.416). When the Lord does appear to the disciples, "the affectionate John long held his right hand, long with joyful eyes looked up in his face, desirous of expressing hearty thanks, and petitions; but did not! He began, but stopped and was silent" (XIV.419). Shortly thereafter, when Jesus asks if they have any meat, it is John who sets before him a piece of honeycomb and some broiled fish, which the risen Lord eats in the presence of the disciples (XIV.420–421).

By means of pious imagination, therefore, Klopstock embroidered the Gospel narratives of the passion and resurrection, filling in details and making the account more vivid and wondrous. In the process, the role of John is enhanced and expanded, so that his character is praised even by the angels.

Friedrich Hölderlin

Friedrich Hölderlin (1770–1843) was a fellow student at Tübingen with Hegel and Schelling. He wrote a thesis on Greek art and took examinations in theology. Like others of the time, he was first filled with enthusiasm for the French Revolution and then bitterly disappointed. Loneliness, melancholy, and mental illness troubled him later in life.

In "Patmos" (1803) Hölderlin tells of his being snatched up and carried on a tour of the Greek islands, one of which is Patmos. There, he is reminded of John, whom he describes as a young man—an image of the evangelist similar to that in medieval art. Hölderlin then describes the Last Supper scene in John 13.

> . . . . So once
> Patmos fostered god's friend,
> The visionary, who in joyous young manhood strolled
>
> Arm in arm
> With the son of the Almighty, inseparable, for
> The thunder-bearing God loved his simplicity
> And the intent young man feasted he eyes and saw
> The face of the god directly
> When, in the mystery of the vine, they
> Sat together, at the hour of the feast,
> And the great foreboding soul looking inwards
> Spoke calmly of death and the extremity of his love,
> For no words ever
> Were enough for him then to tell of goodness
> Or to quiet, as he saw it, the world's quarreling.[38]

The rest of the poem relates common early Christian experience, using the voice of John as the paradigm.[39]

Henry Wadsworth Longfellow

The legend of John's wandering the earth until the return of Christ, which is depicted on the tomb of Edward the Confessor, is featured in Henry Wadsworth Longfellow's "Saint John," which is subtitled "Saint John Wandering Over the Face of the Earth":

> The Ages come and go,
> The Centuries pass as Years;
> My hair is white as the snow,
> My feet are weary and slow,
> The earth is wet with my tears!
> . . . .
> There is war instead of peace,
> Instead of Love there is hate;
> And still I must wander and wait,
> Still I must watch and pray,
> Not forgetting in whose sight,
> A thousand years in their flight

Are as a single day.

The life of man is a gleam
Of light, that comes and goes
Like the course of the Holy stream,
The cityless river, that flows
From fountains no one knows,
Through the Lake of Galilee,
Through forests and level lands,
Over rocks, and shallows, and sands
Of a wilderness wild and vast,
Till it findeth its rest at last
In the desolate Dead Sea!
But alas! alas for me
Not yet this rest shall be!

.   .   .   .

And Him evermore I behold
Walking in Galilee,
Through the cornfield's waving gold,
In hamlet, in wood, and in wold,
By the shores of the Beautiful Sea.
He toucheth the sightless eyes;
Before Him the demons flee;
To the dead He sayeth, "Arise!"
To the living, "Follow Me!"
And that voice still soundeth on
From the centuries that are gone
To the centuries that shall be![40]

In the poem "St. John's, Cambridge," Longfellow also recalls the legend based on John 21:20–23 that the apostle John did not die, but wanders the earth awaiting the Lord's return.

I stand beneath the tree, whose branches shade
Thy western window, Chapel of St. John!
And hear its leaves repeat their benison
On him, whose hand thy stones memorial laid;
Then I remember one of whom was said
In the world's darkest hour, "Behold thy son!"
And see him living still, and wandering

And waiting for the advent long delayed.[41]

Robert Browning

"A Death in the Desert" was published in 1864 as part of Robert Browning's *Dramatis Personae.*[42] The poem has been called both Browning's "most elaborate and closely reasoned *apologia* for Christianity" and the work of "a brilliant amateur."[43] William Temple said it was "the most penetrating interpretation of St. John that exists in the English language."[44] Citing Browning and Temple approvingly, John A. T. Robinson adds that John is concerned "to present the *truth* of the history. It is not the whole truth. But it is a primal vision. . . ."[45] Both Temple and Robinson were aware of the complexity of the relationship between history and theology in John, and we need not attempt to describe their interpretations of that relationship. In light of both the recent attention to the function of the Gospels as narratives and the continuing concern for their basis in history, however, it is worth recalling Robert Browning's poetic response to higher criticism and his nuanced view of the relationship between the Gospel of John and the historical events that lie behind it.

It is now generally accepted that Robert Browning (1812–1889) was familiar with higher criticism and that he was responding to the work of David Friedrich Strauss and Ernest Renan in particular.[46] Strauss's *The Life of Jesus Critically Examined* was first published in 1835.[47] Strauss (1808–1874) rejected both rationalist and supernaturalist views of Jesus in favor of a "mythical" interpretation of the texts.

Renan (1823–1892) began the first draft of his *Life of Jesus* when he traveled to Syria and Palestine in 1860. Published in 1863, the work became enormously popular—going through ten editions in a year—and was thus the means of Renan's bringing the question of Jesus out of the ghetto of theological discussion and laying it before the cultured world: "Men's attention was arrested, and they thought to see Jesus, because Renan had the skill to make them see blue skies, seas of waving corn, distant mountains, gleaming lilies, in a landscape with the Lake of Gennesareth for its centre, and to hear with him in the whispering of the reeds the eternal melody of the Sermon on the Mount."[48] Renan considered that although neither the discourses nor the miracles of the Fourth Gospel were authentic, John was the best biographer of Jesus. In this sense, Renan was a counterpoint to Strauss.

Renan's Jesus was "a romantic historian's portrayal of the human, historical Jesus."[49] While Renan was less skeptical of the Gospel accounts than Strauss, he was nevertheless free from the creedal Christ of French Catholicism. Renan's Jesus emerges as a wise, simple, gentle, charming rural prophet of the Galilean countryside. In his beloved Galilee, Jesus "found again his heavenly

Father in the midst of the green hills and the clear fountains—and among the crowds of women and children, who, with joyous soul and the song of angels in their hearts, waited the salvation of Israel."[50] In sum, therefore, Renan placed Jesus "at the highest summit of human greatness"—he was "the one who gave birth to true religion, the religion of the heart."[51]

Renan believed that the author of the Fourth Gospel was not John but someone who wished to pass for the apostle:

> The author always speaks as an eye-witness; he wishes to pass for the apostle John. If, then, this work is not really by the apostle, we must admit a fraud of which the author convicts himself. Now, although the ideas of the time respecting literary honesty differed essentially from ours, there is no example in the apostolic world of a falsehood of this kind. Besides, not only does the author wish to pass for the apostle John, but we see clearly that he writes in the interest of this apostle. On each page he betrays the desire to fortify his authority, to shew that he has been the favourite of Jesus; that in all the solemn circumstances (at the Lord's supper, at Calvary, at the tomb) he held first place. . . . We are tempted to believe that John, in his old age, having read the Gospel narratives, on the one hand, remarked their various inaccuracies, on the other, was hurt at seeing that there was not accorded him a sufficiently high place in the history of Christ.[52]

In particular, Renan used the other Gospels to show that the disciples had fled before the crucifixion.

Therefore, argued Renan, John's claim to have been present at the cross cannot be judged credible:

> This is, in my opinion, one of those features in which John betrays his personality and the desire he has of giving himself importance. John, after the death of Jesus, appears in fact to have received the mother of his master into his house, and to have adopted her (John 19.27). The great consideration which Mary enjoyed in the early church, doubtless led John to pretend that Jesus, whose favourite disciple he wished to be regarded, had, when dying, recommended to his care all that was dearest to him. The presence of this precious trust near John, insured him a kind of precedence over the other apostles, and gave his doctrine a high authority.[53]

Clearly, Browning took exception to Renan's treatment of the apostle. It is striking, therefore, that in Browning's "A Death in the Desert," the apostle appears to confess that indeed he was not present at the cross (ll. 301–11).[54]

Browning's poem was published in 1864, following the publication of Renan's *Life of Jesus* on June 23, 1863. A letter from Browning to Miss Blagden dated November 19, 1863, confirms that he had read Renan's book within months of its publication:

> I have just read Renan's book, and find it weaker and less honest than I was led to expect. I am glad it is written; if he thinks he can prove what he says, he has fewer doubts on the subject than I, but mine are none of his. As to the Strauss school, I don't understand their complacency about the book, he admits many points they have thought it essential to dispute, and substitutes his explanation, which I think impossible. . . . His admissions & criticisms on St. John are curious. I make no doubt he imagines *himself* stating a fact, with the inevitable license, so must John have done.[55]

Browning was incensed by Renan's suggestion that the resurrection of Lazarus was staged by Lazarus, possibly with the help of his sisters:[56] "miracles were cheats, and their author a cheat! What do you think of the figure *he* cuts who makes his hero participate in the wretched affair with Lazarus, and then calls him all the pretty names that follow?"[57] It appears, therefore, that Browning wrote or revised "A Death in the Desert" between the time he read Renan and the publication of the poem six months later.[58]

Browning was fascinated by Renan, although he differed sharply from both Strauss and Renan on the matter of miracles and on John's motives in writing the Gospel. Their suggestion that the Gospel was actually composed by the school of disciples that gathered around the apostle in Asia Minor was to exert a tremendous influence on later Johannine scholarship. Hidden in the conclusion to the section on the twelve disciples in Strauss's *Life of Jesus* one finds the following judgment on the authorship of the Fourth Gospel: "but the venerator of John, perhaps from a Johannine school [translation corrected], might very naturally be induced to designate the revered apostle, under whose name he wished to write, in this half honorable, half mysterious manner."[59] Similarly, Renan wrote:

> If we are to speak candidly, we will add that probably John himself had little share in this [the writing of the Gospel]; that the change was made around him rather than by him. One is sometimes tempted to believe that precious notes, coming from the apostle, have been employed by his disciples in a very different sense from the primitive Gospel spirit. . . . and without doubt many surprises would be in store for us, if we were permitted to penetrate the secrets of that mysterious school of Ephesus.[60]

To my knowledge, these are the earliest references to the Johannine school.[61] In Renan's view, the Gospel contains touches of verisimilitude added because the apostle relished relating circumstances that he alone as the last surviving eyewitness could know. Nevertheless, the Gospel suffers from disjointedness and gives every appearance of being "the remembrances of an old man, sometimes of remarkable freshness, sometimes have undergone strange modifications."[62]

The contention that Browning was responding to the work of Strauss and Renan when he wrote "A Death in the Desert" appears to be well-founded. One misinterprets Browning, however, if one reads him either as a man who piously rejects the skepticism of historical criticism or as a poet who dispenses with history as unimportant to the meaning of the Gospels. "A Death in the Desert" absorbs and recasts many of the features of the higher critics' view of the composition of the Gospels: oral tradition, manuscripts of uncertain origin, the recollections of an aged apostle, the need to reconstruct a process of composition and transmission, the recognition that the Gospel was ultimately the product of those who had gathered around the apostle, and the necessity of distinguishing fact from fiction.

"A Death in the Desert" begins with a twelve-line description of a scroll. The present owner of the scroll never reveals his identity, but he does tell us that he is married to the niece of Xanthus and that "*Mu* and *Epsilon* stand for my name" (l. 9). Kept hidden in a "chosen chest" (l. 5), the scroll is believed by its current owner to have been the work of Pamphylax the Antiochene. As a result of this ambiguity in the situation that Browning establishes at the poem's outset, the reader of "A Death in the Desert" is put in the position of a modern critic dealing with a document whose origin, author, and history are uncertain.

The second section of the poem reports, with first-person narration, the setting of the apostle John's last words. The present owner of the parchment says that the narrator is Pamphylax, but the first line of the poem forces the reader to maintain some question regarding this identification, since it says: "Supposed of Pamphylax the Antiochene." Only at the end of the poem—in a gloss, itself of uncertain origin—does the narrator identify himself as Pamphylax (l. 683), apparently confirming the owner's judgment as to the origin of the parchment and the identity of the narrator.

Slowly the scenario emerges. For sixty days, five of the aged apostle's friends have hidden him from persecution in a cave near Ephesus. The "I" narrator, Xanthus, Valens, and a boy had carried the apostle to a place where his face could be seen and attempted to revive him, while the Bactrian convert kept watch, pretending to graze a goat. Neither the attempts of the narrator nor those of Xanthus succeeded in rousing the apostle from his sleep. The boy, however, "stung by the splendour of a sudden thought," retrieved "the seventh plate of graven lead" from the secret chamber and read the words "I am the Resurrection and the Life" (ll. 58–64; John 11:25). As a result of the inspiration of the boy and the power of the written and spoken word, the apostle opened his eyes and sat up.

The third and central part of the poem contains the last words of the apostle (ll. 71–81, 105–642). Almost immediately after his words begin, they are interrupted by the interpolation of a gloss (ll. 82–104), which concludes with the statement "I give the glossa of Theotypas" (l. 104). Presumably the "I" who gives the gloss is also the narrator "I," whom we may identify as Pamphylax. But these identifications are far from certain. Why would Pamphylax interpolate a gloss in his own account of the apostle's words? Neither is Theotypas identified further.

The narration resumes at the end of the apostle's words, where the narrator (apparently Pamphylax) reports that the apostle was dead. The five companions buried him, and then each went his own way. Xanthus "escaped to Rome, / Was burned, and could not write the chronicle" (ll. 56–57). Valens was lost, and the narrator does not know his whereabouts (l. 648). The Bactrian convert was "a wild childish man, / And could not write nor speak" (ll. 649–50). Nothing is said about what happened to the boy. Pamphylax, assuming that he alone was left to tell the story (just as the apostle had once been the last who could say "I saw"; ll. 116–18, 129–33, 156), reports that he told the story to Phoebas on the day before he was to fight the beasts (ll. 651–53) and urges readers to believe Phoebas. This reference adds yet another layer to the tradition, for the author must now be Phoebas, who gives the words of Pamphylax, who reports the words of John. The conclusion of the poem adds a final layer: Cerinthus read the parchment and mused (l. 665), and an anonymous commentator contributed a final gloss (ll. 666–88), in which he condemns Cerinthus and associates himself with Pamphylax, the presumed narrator.

In sum, Browning created a document that purports to be the end result of a lengthy series of events, oral tradition, glosses, and stages of transmission. Pamphylax reported the words of John to Phoebas, who presumably wrote them down (but may have passed them on orally before they were put in writing); Theotypas wrote a gloss, which someone else inserted; Cerinthus read the account; someone else added a concluding gloss condemning Cerinthus; and the present owner of the parchment (was his wife's uncle the same Xanthus who was present at the apostle's death?) added the introductory notice at a time when believers still feared persecution. There is enough intrigue here to delight any higher critic!

Browning wrote a poem in the form of an early Christian document that purports to tell of the death of John. But he did so in such a way that the uncertain identity of the narrator in various sections of the poem and the obscure references to the scroll's own history of transmission would defeat any effort to unravel its origin or establish its historical legitimacy. The poem leads the reader simultaneously to imagine that there could be such a document yet undiscovered and to realize that even if we did have an account of the death of the apostle, its own veracity would be questionable.

The apostle's monologue in Browning's poem weaves a remarkable blend of perspectives. First, as his opening words indicate, there is confusion about his identity. Browning combines aspects of John the son of Zebedee, John the evangelist, John the Elder, and the seer.[63] Beyond the mix of these historical figures, who were already being distinguished by the historical critics, one can detect the biblical John (the subject), the poetic John (the character), and the authorial John (the mouthpiece for the author's response to higher criticism).[64] Temporal perspectives are mixed—past, present, and future.[65]

Even the apostle is not clear about his own identity or what he remembers. He could believe that Valens and the other man were James and Peter and that "this lad" (presumably the boy) was John, "so is myself withdrawn into my depths, / The soul retreated from the perished brain" (ll. 76–77). This is the setting for Browning's reflections on fact and truth. Memory and eyewitness testimony have their place, but it is secondary to inspiration:

> And I am only he, your brother John,
> Who saw and heard, and could remember all.
> Remember all! It is not much to say.
> What if the truth broke on me from above
> As once and oft-times? (ll. 116–20)

Browning has John concede the point the higher critics labored to make: the Gospel did not contain an account of what actually happened. The Gospel was more than a historical record. John did not call down fire on the Antichrists or do signs, as in the early days,

> But patient stated much of the Lord's life
> Forgotten or misdelivered, and let it work:
> Since much that at the first, in deed and word,
> Lay simply and sufficiently exposed,
> Had grown (or else my soul was grown to match,
> Fed through such years, familiar with such light,
> Guarded and guided still to see and speak)
> Of new significance and fresh result;
> What first were guessed as points, I now knew stars,
> And named them in the Gospel I have writ. (ll. 166–75)

In the end, therefore, the apostle foresees the rise of the higher critics who will question, even as he himself in his confusion had to search,

Feeling for a foot-hold through a blank profound,
Along with unborn people in strange lands,
Who say—I hear said or conceive they say—
"Was John at all, and did he say he saw?
Assure us, ere we ask what he might see!" (ll. 193–97)

Some would even doubt that John was the author of the Gospel, but how could he assure them? He saw nothing else but that life and death about which he wrote:

Is not God now i' the world His power first made?
Is not His love at issue still with sin
Visibly when a wrong is done on earth?
Love, wrong, and pain, what see I else around? (ll. 211–14)

Here the poet's John comes clearly into focus, sensing God's presence everywhere in the world. But it requires the inspiration of the Spirit for one to be able to see. It would require an optic glass the reverse of a telescope, a lens that could make objects lying too close seem far enough away to be distinct and clear (ll. 230–34).[66] So truth might be reduced to fact:

Just thus, ye needs must apprehend what truth
I see, reduced to plain historic fact. (ll. 235–236)

How will it be when there is no one left to say "I saw"? The poet answers that the "points" were "guessed" (l. 174). He has projected "plain historic fact" so that others might see truth distinctly and clearly. When one stands before the fact of the life and death of Christ, one has a chance to learn truth:

For life, with all it yields of joy and woe,
And hope and fear,— believe the aged friend,—
Is just our chance o' the prize of learning love,
How love might be, hath been indeed, and is. (ll. 244–47)

But we can hardly attain to truth, grasp it, and go on. Flesh will not allow that to happen, and inherent in the nature of truth is the fact that it cannot be grasped and acknowledged. The worth of Christ is not to be compared with gold or purple:

Could he give Christ up were His worth as plain?
Therefore, I say, to test man, the proofs shift,
Nor may he grasp that fact like other fact,

> And straightway in his life acknowledge it,
> As, say, the indubitable bliss of fire. (ll. 294–98)

Faithfulness was no easier then than now, however. John was tested and failed his test. At the arrest of Jesus, John too forsook his Lord and fled (ll. 302–11) as in Mark 14:50, but contrary to the Gospel of John, where the Beloved Disciple appears at the cross. Again, Browning appears to accept Renan's portrayal of John but turns it in another direction.

Indeed, truth is never safe because it needs "love's eye to pierce the o'erstretched doubt" (l. 321). The account of the death of Christ had been so corrupted by false teachers, Ebion, Cerinthus, or others, that John felt he had to write. But writing history only invites a questioning of history:

> Whereon I stated much of the Lord's life
> Forgotten or misdelivered, and let it work.
> Such work done, as it will be, what comes next?
> What do I hear say, or conceive men say,
> "Was John at all, and did he say he saw?
> Assure us, ere we ask what he might see!" (ll. 331–36)

There was so much more, "more glow outside than gleams he caught" (l. 348). Ephesus will be only "blank heaps of stone and sand" (l. 360). Truth cannot be told "the second day" (l. 371), nor can miracles prove doctrine (l. 372). Only love remains. But how can we know that love comes from God and not from man?

Miracles are not needed to prove the Gospel's truth (ll. 443–44). John says that he himself once gave a blind man sight (ll. 459–60), but faith grows to the point where miracles would hinder rather than help because they compel too much (ll. 472–73). Indeed, faith confers a level of knowledge which surpasses the process by which it is gained.

The essence of death is when man's loss comes from his gain (ll. 482–83). If progress leads to loss rather than gain, it is death. Surely the gain of historical criticism should not lead to the loss of faith. God answered our need by giving the written word (ll. 491–92), which points not only to God's might but to God's love. If one accepts his own love, which points to Christ's, but rejects Christ's love, that one dies (ll. 500–513).

But that one may respond that John's story of the historical particulars of Christ's life is just a trick. Why must one be drawn into distinguishing that which is historical from that which is not? The wise may cry that "the fact is in the fable" (l. 534). If one asks John, "Why breed in us perplexity, mistake, / Nor tell the whole truth in the proper words?" (ll. 538–39), he answers that the primal thesis is that "Man is not God but hath God's end to serve" (l. 542):

Grant this, then man must pass from old to new,
From vain to real, from mistake to fact,
From what once seemed good, to what now proves best.
How could many have progression otherwise? (ll. 545–48)

Neither might nor will is supreme. Man is lower than God but higher than the beasts; he can know, but there is a limit to what he can know (ll. 577–79). Progress is peculiar to man; neither God nor beasts are capable of it (ll. 586–87). Man, therefore, knows more now than he did at the first, but today's knowledge will be displaced by tomorrow's:

God's gift was that man should conceive of truth
And yearn to gain it, catching at mistake,
As midway help till he reach fact indeed. (ll. 605–7)

The last sentences from the apostle's mouth seem to point one last time to the poet's concern:

Such is the burthen of the latest time.
I have survived to hear it with my ears,
Answer it with my lips: does this suffice? (ll. 634–36)

The novelty of "A Death in the Desert" is the way in which Browning created a legend of the apostle's death to answer the onslaught of higher criticism. The period of naive legend-making had long since passed. Any new legend would be rigorously examined. But in Browning, we see the creation of legend in the form of a fictional document from early Christianity. The legend, moreover, challenges the skepticism of the historical critics of Browning's day while both sharing in that skepticism and refusing to grant to historical investigation any authority over matters of truth and faith. Browning sharply separates love, intuition, spirit, inspiration, and experience on the one side from reason, knowledge, and history on the other. In this way, Browning protects a place for faith and challenges the historical critics to go beyond examining the historicity of the Gospels to the Christ to whom they point. The apostle's question still stands both for modern interpreters and for Browning: "Does this suffice?"[67]

CONCLUSION

The story of the role of the apostle in art and poetry carries one from the piety of the Middle Ages to the historical consciousness of the modern period.

Greek and Latin religious art portrayed John as a youthful apostle, the aged evangelist, and the seer of Revelation. Episodes from the later legends—such as John's drinking the poisoned chalice, the story of the two who sold everything to follow John and then regretted their decision, the raising of Drusiana, and the legend of John and Edward the Confessor—were vividly brought to life in medieval art. So popular were these subjects that the windows devoted to John at Chartes and Bourges do not contain a single event drawn from the New Testament.

The evolution of John's role in poetry is particularly striking. Adam of Saint Victor praises John as the soaring eagle. In a charming and witty verse, Herder retells the story of John and the partridge. In his *The Messiah,* Klopstock imaginatively embroiders the role of John in the Gospels and so elevates his character that even the angels praise his virtue. Similarly, Hölderlin describes a vision of his being transported to Patmos, where he hears John, the fair, young disciple of John 13. Even Longfellow turned to the legend of John and Edward the Confessor for inspiration, describing John wandering the face of the earth. Browning's "A Death in the Desert" is without peer, however, as a penetrating poetic analysis of the nature of tradition, modern scholarship, and the enduring testimony of the aged apostle. As we have seen, Browning's work is in significant respects both informed by and sharply responsive to those who had subjected the traditions to critical analysis. In the next chapter therefore, the present study turns to the works of those who sought to reconstruct the life of John during the latter part of the nineteenth century and the early decades of the twentieth century.

NOTES

1. I did not have an opportunity to make use of the Index of Christian Art at Princeton University, which provides valuable resources for research on the place of John in Christian art.

2. For a dated but still valuable synopsis of artistic representations of the apostle, see Anna Jameson, *Sacred and Legendary Art* (Boston: Houghton Mifflin, 1900), 1:158–75. The preface to the first edition of Jameson's book is dated 1848. Gregor Martin Lechner has collected extensive documentation on representations of John in Christian art; see "Johannes der Evangelist (der Theologe)," in *Lexikon der christlichen Ikonographie,* ed. Wolfgang Braunfels (Rome: Herder, 1974), 7:108–30. Johannes H. Emminghaus, *St. John the Apostle,* text of story and legend by Leonhard Küppers, The Saints in Legend and Art, vol. 13, trans. Hans Hermann Rosenwald (Recklinghausen: Aurel Bongers, 1967), came to my attention after this chapter was written.

3. Jameson, *Sacred and Legendary Art* 1:160.

4. Jameson, *Sacred and Legendary Art* 1:161.

5. Jameson, *Sacred and Legendary Art* 1:163.

6. Jameson, *Sacred and Legendary Art* 1:163.

7. Jameson, *Sacred and Legendary Art* 1:164.

8. James M. McDonald, *The Life and Writings of St. John* (New York: Scribner, Armstrong, and Co., 1877), 26.

9. Jameson, *Sacred and Legendary Art* 1:166.

10. Jameson, *Sacred and Legendary Art* 1:166.

11. Manolis Chatzidakis, *Icons of Patmos: Question of Byzantine and Post-Byzantine Painting* (Athens: National Bank of Greece, 1985), 96 and plates 106–07.

12. Jameson, *Sacred and Legendary Art* 1:167–74.

13. Jameson, *Sacred and Legendary Art* 1:168 n.1.

14. Herbert Thurston and Donald Attwater, eds., *Butler's Lives of the Saints* (New York: P. J. Kenedy and Sons, 1956), 623.

15. See above, p. 000.

16. See above, p. 000.

17. See above, p. 000.

18. See above, p. 000.

19. Jameson, *Sacred and Legendary Art* 1:170–71.

20. See above, p. 000.

21. See above, p. 000.

22. Jameson, *Sacred and Legendary Art* 1:172.

23. Johannis Brompton, *Cronicon,* 955; cited in Jameson, *Sacred and Legendary Art* 1:173–74.

24. See above, p. 000.

25. F. S. Ellis, *The Golden Legend or Lives of the Saints as Englished by William Caxton* (London: J. M. Dent and Sons, 1900), 2:175–76; cf. 6:26–28.

26. Farmer, *The Oxford Dictionary of Saints,* 228–29. See also "Cuthbert and St. John," in Clinton Albertson, S.J., *Anglo-Saxon Saints and Heroes* (New York: Fordham University Press, 1967), 81–82.

27. Albertson, *Anglo-Saxon Saints and Heroes,* 42 n. 17.

28. *Life of Bishop Wilfrid,* chap. 10, trans. Bertram Colgrove, *The Life of Bishop Wilfrid by Eddius Stephanus* (Cambridge: Cambridge University Press, 1927), 21.

29. Isa Ragusa and Rosalie B. Green, trans., *Meditations on the Life of Christ: An Illustrated Manuscript of the Fourteenth Century Meditations on the Life of Christ* (Princeton: Princeton University Press, 1977), 150.

30. Emile Mâle, *The Gothic Image: Religious Art in France of the Thirteenth Century* (New York: Harper and Row, 1958), 221.

31. *The Gothic Image,* 299–302. Other legendary scenes from the life and death of John are discussed in M. R. James, *The Apocalypse in Art* (London: The British Academy, 1931), 48–49, 54–55.

32. Trans. Digby S. Wrangham, in *The Liturgical Poetry of Adam of St. Victor* (London, 1881), 2:156–69; cited in Philip Schaff, *History of the Christian Church* (Grand Rapids: Wm. B. Eerdmans, 1950), 1:588.

33. See above, p. 000.

34. See above, p. 000.

35. Johann Gottfried Herder, *Herder's Werke,* BDK (Berlin: Aufbau-Verlag, 1969), 1:54–55. My translation.

36. E. S. Shaffer, *'Kubla Khan' and the Fall of Jerusalem: The Mythological School in Biblical Criticism and Secular Literature, 1770–1880* (Cambridge: Cambridge University Press, 1975), 71–72; see also the discussion that follows, 72–85.

37. Friedrich Gottlieb Klopstock, *The Messiah* (Bungay: C. Brightly, 1808). The Roman numeral refers to the book number in *The Messiah,* and the Arabic numeral to the page number in this edition.

38. Friedrich Hölderlin, "Patmos," trans. E. S. Shaffer; cited in Shaffer, *'Kubla Khan' and the Fall of Jerusalem,* 298.

39. See Shaffer, "Hölderlin's 'Patmos' Ode and 'Kubla Khan': Mythological Doubling," in her *'Kubla Khan' and the Fall of Jerusalem,* 145–90, esp. 170–71, where she comments: "Hölderlin maintains in name only the identity of the apostle John with the visionary John; the experience given as John's is the communal experience of early Christianity. . . . The intimacy of John with Christ and the direct intensity of John's vision of the presence of Christ establish his traditional credentials; yet the poem conspicuously does not assert the identity of John the Apostle with John the Apocalyptic."

40. Longfellow,"St. John," ll. 1–5, 18–37, 53–64 in *The Complete Poetical Works of Henry Wadsworth Longfellow* (Boston: Houghton Mifflin, 1902), 685–86.

41. Longfellow, "St. John's, Cambridge," ll. 1–8 in *Complete Poetical Works,* 419.

42. See John Pettigrew, ed., *Robert Browning: The Poems* (New Haven: Yale University Press, 1981), 1:787–804.

43. Donna G. Fricke, "'A Death in the Desert': The Gospel According to Robert Browning," in *Aeolian Harps: Essays in Literature in Honor of Maurice Browning Cramer,* ed. Donna G. Fricke and Douglas C. Fricke (Bowling Green, Ohio: Bowling Green University Press, 1976), 167–68, citing respectively William O. Raymond and C. H. Herford. What Raymond actually wrote is: "With the single exception of the Pope's dialogue in *The Ring and the Book, A Death in the Desert* is the most elaborate and closely reasoned *apologia* for Christianity throughout Browning's poetry"; see William O. Raymond, "Browning and Higher Criticism," in his *The Infinite Moment and Other Essays in Robert Browning* (Toronto: University of Toronto Press, 1950), 32–33.

44. William Temple, *Readings in St. John's Gospel* (London: Macmillan, 1963), xx.

45. John A. T. Robinson, *The Priority of John,* ed. J. F. Coakley (London: SCM Press, 1985), 33.

46. See Kingsbury Badger, "'See the Christ Stand!': Browning's Religion," in *Robert Browning: A Collection of Critical Essays,* ed. Philip Drew (London: Methuen, 1966), 72–95; Fricke, "'A Death in the Desert': The Gospel According to Robert Browning," in *Aeolian Harps,* 167–78; Raymond, "Browning and Higher Criticism," 19–51; Shaffer, "Browning's St. John: The Casuistry of the Higher Criticism," in *'Kubla Khan' and the Fall of Jerusalem,* 191–224; Makio Yoshikado, "Browning and Higher Criticism in 'A Death in the Desert'" (Master's thesis, Baylor University, 1986).

47. For a handy edition of Strauss's work, see David Friedrich Strauss, *The Life of Jesus Critically Examined,* trans. George Eliot, ed. Peter C. Hodgson, LJS (Phila-

delphia: Fortress, 1972). For a brief summary of Strauss's place in the history of research, see below, p. 281.

48. Albert Schweitzer, *The Quest of the Historical Jesus: A Critical Study of Its Progress from Reimarus to Wrede* (New York: Macmillan, 1950), 181.

49. Dennis C. Duling, *Jesus Christ through History* (New York: Harcourt Brace Jovanovich, 1979), 191.

50. Ernest Renan, *The Life of Jesus* (Cleveland: World Publishing Co., 1941), 34.

51. Duling, *Jesus Christ through History,* 195, commenting on Renan, *The Life of Jesus,* 206.

52. Renan, *The Life of Jesus,* xxv–xxvi.

53. Renan, *The Life of Jesus,* 193 n. 1.

54. This interpretation has been disputed by Yoshikado in "Browning and Higher Criticism in 'A Death in the Desert,'" 89.

55. A. Joseph Armstrong, ed., *Letters of Robert Browning to Miss Isa Blagden* (Waco, Texas: Baylor University Press, 1923), 100–101.

56. See Renan, *The Life of Jesus,* 164–65.

57. Armstrong, ed., *Letters of Robert Browning to Miss Isa Blagden,* 100–101.

58. This is the conclusion reached by Raymond in "Browning and Higher Criticism," 32–35.

59. Strauss, *The Life of Jesus Critically Examined,* 330, cf. xxxix.

60. Renan, *The Life of Jesus,* xxviii.

61. See my *The Johannine School: An Evaluation of the Johannine-School Hypothesis Based on an Investigation of the Nature of Ancient Schools,* SBLDS 26 (Missoula, Mont.: Scholars Press, 1975), 1–4.

62. Renan, *The Life of Jesus,* xxvi.

63. This point has been noted by Virginia M. Hyde in "The Fallible Parchment: Structure in Robert Browning's *A Death in the Desert,*" *Vict Poet* 12, no.2 (1974): 128.

64. Cf. Fricke ("'A Death in the Desert,'" 174), who distinguishes the "historical" John, Calvin's John, and Browning's John.

65. See William Gruber, "Temporal Perspectives in Robert Browning's *A Death in the Desert,*" *Vict Poet* 17, no. 4 (Winter 1979): 329–42.

66. See Virginia Hyde, "Robert Browning's Inverted Optic Glass in *A Death in the Desert,*" *Vict Poet* 23, no. 1 (Spring 1985): 93–96.

67. For further reflection on this question, see my essay "Guessing Points and Knowing Stars: History and Higher Criticism in Robert Browning's 'A Death in the Desert,'" in *The Future of Christology: Essays in Honor of Leander E. Keck,* ed. Abraham Malherbe and Wayne Meeks (Minneapolis: Fortress Press, 1993). The section on Browning in the present study was adapted from that essay and is used here by permission.

CHAPTER 9

Historical Figure
The Apostle in Nineteenth- and Early Twentieth-Century Research

During the late nineteenth and early twentieth centuries, historians turned to the pages of the New Testament and to the early Christian writers with great confidence that these sources could yield a reliable characterization of the apostle John. The result was a succession of portraits of the apostle by New Testament scholars and others interested in the "historical John." These works generally survey the biblical references to John—some in a more scholarly fashion, some in a more popular manner. The style is invariably reverential, and vivid pictures emerge from these descriptions. In the following survey, only the distinctive interpretations and not the commonly repeated points will be summarized. Only a selection of these histories can be reviewed, but from them, the popular image of the apostle between 1870 and 1935 emerges with vibrant clarity. Other titles from this period are listed in the first section of the bibliography.

CHRISTOPH ERNST LUTHARDT

By the time Luthardt, professor of theology at Leipzig, published *St. John the Author of the Fourth Gospel* (1875), debate over the apostolic authorship of the Gospel of John was already nearly a century old.[1] An appendix in this volume contains an annotated bibliography of seventy-seven pages which surveys the literature on the authorship of the Gospel from 1792 to 1875. Edward Evanson (1792) attributed the Gospel to a second-century Platonist. The first serious critique of the traditional position, however, came from Karl Gottlieb Bretschneider in 1820. Bretschneider contended that the Gospel of John could not be the work of an eyewitness, a native of Palestine, or a Jew. The Jesus of the Fourth Gospel and his discourses differ markedly from the

280

portraits presented by the synoptics. The author's deficient understanding of Jewish affairs and the celebration of Passover shows that the Gospel could not have been written by one of Jesus' companions. Instead, Bretschneider suggested, it was written by a gentile Christian presbyter—probably in Egypt, in the second century—and reflects a clear polemical bias against hostile Jews. A wave of protest followed. The Gospel of John was the darling of the Schleiermacher school, and Bretschneider himself eventually withdrew his objections to Johannine authorship.[2]

David Friedrich Strauss's (1808–1874) *The Life of Jesus Critically Examined,* published in 1835, was a bombshell. Strauss rejected both rationalist and supernaturalist views of Jesus in favor of a "mythical" interpretation of the Gospels. The reaction to the book was explosive, altering the course of its author's life, German theology, and subsequent Jesus research.[3] Strauss was dismissed from Tübingen, where only three friends supported him and even F. C. Baur distanced himself from him. In 1838, shortly before the third edition of the book appeared, Strauss was appointed to a position in Zürich, but he was dismissed by the government because of widespread opposition to him, and he never held another church or university position again.

The third edition of Strauss's *Life of Jesus* is famous for the concessions it makes: espousing a less skeptical attitude toward the Gospel of John and making more room for Christology, Strauss had moved closer to Schleiermacher in his views. Strauss later regretted having published this edition, however, and retracted those concessions. In the fourth edition (1840), he returned to his original position and mounted an all-out attack on orthodox theologians. In so doing, Strauss focused sharply three areas of concern: (1) the issues of miracle and myth; (2) the connection between the Christ of faith and the Jesus of history; and (3) the relationship of the Gospel of John to the synoptics.[4]

Strauss proposed his mythical Jesus dialectically as an alternative to both the orthodox Jesus and the rationalist Jesus. Strauss's use of the term "myth" embodies neither the modern understanding of primitive myth, nor the romantics' concept of myth. Rather, for Strauss, myth was the way primitives depicted events and realities. Strauss defined "evangelical myth" as narrative related to Jesus that is not the expression of fact but the product of an idea or image of Jesus' earliest followers. Strauss astutely observed the discrepancies among the various Gospel stories. In contrast to Schleiermacher, he held that the Gospel of John was the most mythical—and hence the least historical of the Gospels.

C. H. Weisse (1801–1866) applauded Strauss's work and stands in direct succession to him. According to Albert Schweitzer, Weisse maintained "the impossibility that the historic Jesus can have preached the doctrine of the Johannine Christ. . . . It is not so much a picture of Christ that John sets forth, as a conception of Christ; his Christ does not speak *in* His own Person, but *of* His own Person."[5] John attempted to find a system in the Lord's teachings, and when he had worked out such a system in his own mind, he recalled the Lord's teachings in light of this system of thought. After the death of the apostle, some of his followers added the narrative portions of the Gospel, which are manifestly secondary. The effect was that as a source for the study of the historical Jesus, the Fourth Gospel was effectively ruled out. The result of Weisse's work, therefore, was that John, which had been the pillar of Jesus studies, was dismissed from future work, and Mark, which had been seen as a secondary abbreviator, was vaulted into prominence as the earliest Gospel.

Ferdinand Christian Baur (1792–1860) was the son of a Lutheran pastor. Baur was trained at a seminary in Blaubeuren and then at Tübingen, during the period when supernaturalism was taught there. Nevertheless, he read Plato, Kant, the German romantics, and Schleiermacher. He taught in the seminaries at Schöntal and Blaubeueren before his appointment to the faculty at Tübingen in 1826. In 1831 he published an influential article entitled "The Christ Party in the Corinthian Church" in which he developed the idea of a conflict between the parties of Peter and Paul. In Baur's work on Christian Gnosticism in 1835, the influence of Hegel is for the first time evident in his thought.

Baur is famous as the founder of the "Tübingen School," with its basis in Hegel's view of history, "tendency criticism," and the resulting dating of the New Testament documents. Relying heavily on the epistles of Paul, Baur interpreted early Christianity in terms of its conflicts. As a historian, he was interested in Jesus as the founder of Christianity, and thought that the essence of the movement could be traced to the personality of its founder. Of the various current theories regarding the synoptics, Baur accepted the Griesbach hypothesis but sought to establish the "tendency" of each Gospel. His studies led him to agree with Strauss over against Schleiermacher that the Gospel of John was of little value for the historical study of Jesus: "The fundamental difference between John's gospel and the synoptic gospels pressed itself so convincingly on me, that the view of the character and origin of the former . . . at once formed itself in my mind."[6] The Gospel of John, Baur contended, was written to put an end to the antagonism between the Pauline and Judaistic parties. At the earliest, he said, it was written about 160, and from the beginning, it was attributed to John "because it united itself to his genuine book, the rugged, Jewish, anti-Pauline Revelation, ennobling this by its high, free spirit; and therefore, from the outset, put itself under the aegis of that honoured apostle."[7]

Baur's position was buttressed by the work of his students. Eduard Zeller reviewed the patristic materials and concluded that the Gospel cannot be traced back beyond A.D. 170, and that it could not have been the source of Justin's concept of the Logos. Opposition to the Tübingen school also rallied.

Luthardt himself defended the unity and historical character of the Fourth Gospel in a work first published in 1852.[8] Gradually, the Gospel began to be dated earlier. In 1867, Theodor Keim contended that the Gospel originated at the beginning of the second century, under the emperor Trajan, between 110 and 117, but Keim denied John's residence in Asia Minor and explained the tradition about an Ephesian residence as a misunderstanding that arose from the confusion of the apostle with John the Elder.[9]

Such was the situation at the time Luthardt wrote *St. John the Author of the Fourth Gospel,* which reviews the testimony of the church, the testimony outside the church, the evidence for John's residence at Ephesus, the Passover controversy, the internal evidence regarding the Gospel's authorship, the difference between the Gospel of John and the character of second-century literature, the force of the differences between the Gospel of John and the synoptics, and the relationship between the Gospel and Revelation. The concluding chapter argues that it is psychologically possible that the Gospel of John's Christology originated with the apostle. Reversing the argument of the Tübingen school, Luthardt contended for Justin's dependence on the Fourth Gospel and surmised that Justin knew the Gospel of John as an apostolic writing, probably already bearing the name of John. Likewise, Polycarp "reaches far enough back into John's time to be secure from the danger of letting a book be palmed off on him as John's when the apostle had nothing to do with it."[10] Similarly, Luthardt argues, the school of Basilides used the Fourth Gospel and Marcion knew the Gospel and knew it as John's Gospel. Luthardt concludes, therefore, that as far back as A.D. 130 the Gospel of John "was known, and regarded as apostolic in Gnostic circles."[11]

Luthardt cites Erhard Friedrich Vogel (1801) as the first to deny the tradition of John's residence at Ephesus.[12] Heinrich Reuterdahl (1826) contested aspects of the tradition, and E. C. J. Lützelberger (1840) rejected it entirely, contending that John died before 55–57 and never lived in Ephesus or Asia Minor.[13] Lützelberger's reason was that if the apostle John had lived to an advanced age in Ephesus, a Gospel not from him yet bearing his name could not have appeared shortly thereafter. Therefore, the error must be in one of the premises, namely that John lived to an advanced age in Ephesus. Luthardt supplies a detailed summary of both Lützelberger's argument and the debate that followed between Grimm and Keim. Luthardt reviews the patristic evidence and the excerpts from Papias in particular, arguing that where the writings of John were known, the tradition of the Ephesian residence was also known, even from the middle of the second century. In sum, Luthardt advanced scholarship with a judicious review of both the patristic evidence and the arguments being advanced by the Tübingen school. Much can still be learned from his marshalling of the arguments and his command of the primary sources.

JAMES M. MACDONALD

James Madison MacDonald was a Presbyterian minister, a graduate of the Theological Seminary at Yale, and Vice President of Princeton Theological Seminary before his death in 1876. As its title suggests, *The Life and Writings of St. John* is a large book, over 400 pages, which treats first the life of John and then each of the writings attributed to the apostle.[14]

Published in 1877, the book is a loosely compiled collection of traditions about the apostle. Beginning with a description of the historical and geographical setting of the apostle's life, MacDonald volunteers that John was born to Zebedaeus and Salome in Bethsaida (which he locates on a beautiful bay just north of Capernaum). Salome is in turn suggested to be the daughter of Joseph by a former marriage, hence the step-daughter of Mary the mother of Jesus.[15] The family lived in comfortable circumstances and held a respectable position. Citing an unspecified tradition that the family was of noble origin, MacDonald writes: "Possibly Zebedaeus and his sons pursued fishing more for pleasure and recreation, than as a means of livelihood."[16] Because the mother of the sons of Zebedaeus is mentioned in the Gospels without Zebedaeus (Matt. 20:20, 27:56), MacDonald infers that he may have died shortly after James and John became disciples. Taking clues from the reference to the sons of Zebedee as *Boanerges,* MacDonald describes James and John as "earnest, bold, and fervid in their manner of address or their mode of action." John "possessed a temperament, indeed, which, if it had not been subjected to the influence of this grace, might have made him fiery and fierce, if not cruel and unforgiving."[17] That strength, however, was turned to love rather than violent hatred.

MacDonald conjectures that the young men from Bethsaida had joined John the Baptist and received baptism at his hands before he appeared publicly and attracted crowds to the Jordan. "It is very evident" that they became his disciples early in his ministry, so "there cannot be the least doubt" that they were present when John pointed out Jesus to his followers.[18] Likewise, "there cannot be the least doubt" that John was the unnamed disciple of John the Baptist who followed after Jesus along with Andrew (John 1:35–40).[19] That day spent with Jesus set the course for the rest of John's life.

MacDonald then follows the course of the ministry of Jesus according to John's Gospel, narrating the travelogue and supplying geographical information and local color, and occasionally working into the account events recorded in the synoptics. Following the demonstration in the temple in Jerusalem, John overheard the conversation between Jesus and Nicodemus:

> There is nothing improbable in the supposition that John, who had accompanied Jesus to Jerusalem, was present on this occasion.

How impressive the sight when this master in Israel, with grave and venerable aspect, approached the young Teacher, to listen to His wondrous words! John, too, could hear them, and hear the soughing of the wind among the mountains, to which the rabbi's attention was directed, as the Lord instructed him on the mysterious subject of the nature and necessity of regeneration.[20]

Evidently, MacDonald infers, John alone among the evangelists was present on this occasion.

The miraculous catch of fish recorded in Luke 5 represents a turning point for the disciple. James and John were in another vessel: "Whatever may have been the secret thoughts and purposes of John and his companions heretofore," says MacDonald, "as to the future course of their lives, their plans were now fully formed." They would forsake any worldly career and follow Christ in discipleship. Peter, James, and John formed "a kind of inner circle; the innermost nearest circle of the loving hearts that gathered around Him,"[21] but it was John who enjoyed the closest intimacy with the Lord. MacDonald wonders if, when the disciples were sent out by twos, John's companion was Peter or James—and decides it was probably the latter. As the "sons of thunder," they "no doubt prosecuted their mission with a zeal and fervour becoming of the title they had received." On this occasion, they exercised their newly acquired power of performing miracles.[22]

At the end of Jesus' ministry, it was Peter and John who prepared the Last Supper, as recorded in Luke 22:8. At the arrest, John fled with all the rest: "It was not long, however," MacDonald writes, "before John recovered his natural bravery of spirit, and we find him again by his Master's side. He shrank not again from any of the terrors of that gloomy night, nor of the succeeding day, the day of crucifixion." In the courtyard of the high priest's palace, John's "Galilean bravery of spirit" returned, and he stood by Jesus as "His only visible friend."[23] John, therefore, was the only disciple to witness the sad scene of Peter's defection.

Following the crucifixion, John took Jesus' mother to his home and cared for her until her death. The spear wound showed John that Jesus' death was a real death, and John "no doubt" was with the women of Galilee as they watched the burial of Jesus.[24] After the resurrection of Jesus, John saw and heard the risen Lord on numerous occasions, including the time the disciples went to Galilee to await the promised appearance of the Lord. Seven of them had decided to go fishing when the Lord appeared on the shore. Another miraculous catch of fish followed.

MacDonald vividly imagines the meeting between John and Paul reported in Galatians 2:1–10:

St. Paul fully appreciated the character of his brother, and recognized in him one of the strong and beautiful pillars of the house of God. He never could forget his cordial grasp as he departed again to his work among the heathen. The incident indeed is very expressive and significant. St. John had been silent in the assembly in which the other two "pillars," Peter and James, were so conspicuous. But at the close of it he thus expressed his hearty union with the great apostle to the Gentiles, in his opposition to the Jewish party, in the work of spreading the gospel.[25]

MacDonald follows the tradition that Peter worked among the Parthians, and conjectures that John joined him in this effort. As evidence, MacDonald cites Augustine's reference to 1 John as "the Epistle to the Parthians" (*Quaest. Evang.* 100.19).[26] During this period of work in the area where the Israelites had languished in exile, John reviewed the words of Daniel and Ezekiel, which had seemed so fresh in his mind when he wrote the Apocalypse.

At the end of his work among the Parthians, John returned to Jerusalem, where he had stayed for a short time during the turbulent period of the mid-60s. When the church fled to Pella, or shortly thereafter, John "embarked either at Tyre or at Caesarea for Asia Minor."[27] MacDonald conjectures that the ship may have put in at Miletus, and he cites with favor the tradition that John met with shipwreck as he was approaching the end of his journey.[28] Before he could do more than establish himself in Ephesus, however, he was banished to Patmos during the persecution of Christians which preceded Nero's death in A.D. 68. On Patmos, John wrote the Apocalypse in a thoroughly Semitic Greek idiom. From the language of the Apocalypse, MacDonald infers that John had only recently arrived in a Greek culture. Overreaching his argument, MacDonald claims we may infer that the Apocalypse was "one of the earliest books of the New Testament."[29]

Returning from his exile on Patmos shortly after the death of Nero in A.D. 68, John was told of the horrors of the persecution and of the destruction of Jerusalem. Not much over sixty-five years of age, John was now the sole surviving apostle, or one of the last of them. Here, MacDonald quotes from D. F. Bacon's *Lives of the Apostles:* "The ardent friends, the dear brother, the faithful father, the fondly ambitious mother, who made up his little world of life and joy and hope! Where were they? All were gone; even his own former self was gone too, and the joys, the thoughts, the views of those early days, were buried as deeply as the friends of his youth, and far more irrecoverably."[30] MacDonald himself vividly describes a tour of the seven churches that John probably made before his exile to Patmos.

Later, in Ephesus, the apostle wrote the Gospel (A.D. 85–86), and still later, the Epistles (ca. A.D. 90). By the time John wrote the Second and Third

Epistles, MacDonald says, "he had begun to feel some of the infirmities of age." At not less than a hundred years of age, the apostle died a natural death in Ephesus and was buried among the tombs on Mount Prion.[31] MacDonald also recalls several of the stories about the apostle that circulated in the *Acts of John* and among the early church fathers, many of which, he judges, are historically credible.

JAMES STALKER

Stalker wrote *The Two St. Johns of the New Testament* (1895) for popular consumption, with no notes or references to his sources.[32] The first 186 pages are devoted to the apostle, and the rest of the book to John the Baptist. The chief point of interest is Stalker's pious, psychologizing interpretation of the character of the apostle.

Stalker accepts the chain of inferences that identifies John as a cousin of Jesus, the son of Salome, who was the wife of Zebedee and the sister of Mary.[33] In character, "he was especially strong in the region of the affections—profoundly loving and sympathetic; the heart of Jesus could not have gone out so cordially to him unless it had met with a corresponding turn."[34] John was a thinker, though—a man of contemplative and mystical depth: "there slumbered in him the possibility and the intention of a priceless service; and he brought it to perfection when, in his gospel, he gave to mankind the final and incomparable portrait of the Son of God."[35] Stalker predicts that while Peter dominated Christendom for fourteen centuries, and Paul the Protestant Reformation, John's spirit will dominate the millennial age.[36] Similarly, John may be viewed as the patron saint of old age, when tolerance and love dominate over the zeal (Peter) of youth and the steady work (Paul) of middle age.

Like other writers, Stalker worried over the incongruities of the name *Boanerges*. It is not difficult to follow the interpretive moves that Stalker makes in the following passage to arrive at a suitable, devotional interpretation of the name given in Mark 3:17. After rejecting the interpretation that *Boanerges* referred to John's loud voice, Stalker cites the tradition that James and John wanted to call down fire on a Samaritan village (Luke 9:54), and adds:

> It is, indeed, difficult to reconcile with this image of St. John the charity and lovableness of his later years; but the fact seems undeniable. The Book of Revelation is the transfigured form of this disposition; and it is a book full of thunders, lightnings and voices from heaven. The character which is gentlest and most tolerant in maturity may have, hidden at its core, a temper once

hot but long subdued by grace. The idea, then, is that Jesus was alluding to this imperfection of the two brothers, marking it with a name, that they might watch against temptation and overcome its failing. They did overcome it, and this accounts for the fact that the name occurs nowhere else; the peculiarity at which it pointed having disappeared it ceased to be applicable, and was forgotten.[37]

Stalker's interpretation of the character of John, as the Beloved Disciple, yields a new twist, however. In a chapter entitled "St. John's Besetting Sin," Stalker writes: "St. John's was a refined and reserved nature, and pride was his besetting sin."[38] Because John was given the privilege of an especially elevated position, he had to guard against criticizing others "from the height of his own ideal" or being scornful and overbearing. James and John, Stalker suggests, put their mother up to asking for them to be given the left and right hand seats in the kingdom.[39]

Nevertheless, John was privileged to share the secret at the Last Supper that Judas would betray his Lord. John and Judas are therefore extreme opposites: "The same incident which drove forth Judas to his fate installed John more firmly than ever in the confidence and affection of his master."[40]

C. E. SCOTT-MONCRIEFF

Scott-Moncrieff states his purpose clearly in the preface to *St. John: Apostle, Evangelist and Prophet* (1909): "My aim had been to show that the objections alleged against St. John as the author of the works traditionally ascribed to him are far from conclusive."[41] In the chapters that follow, he surveys the history of the objections to apostolic authorship of the Johannine writings, reviews the internal and external evidence, and dismisses both the mediating views that the Gospel was written by a follower of the apostle and the attribution of any of the writings to the elder, whose existence Scott-Moncrieff calls into question.[42]

D. A. HAYES

The overriding concern of Hayes's *John and His Writings* is the defense of the apostolic authorship of each of the five books attributed to John.[43] Following an opening section on the apostle, the remainder of Hayes's book describes John's writings and develops the evidence for their authorship. In the opening chapter, entitled "John the Little Known," Hayes laments the sparsity of the New Testament record. There are more references to John the

Baptist than to John the apostle. From this, Hayes infers a reticence of character:

> On the other hand, if John's mother, Salome, lay sick with a fever and you knew nothing about it when you called at their home, John would receive you and talk with you about other matters and allow you to make your call and go away again without saying a word to you about his mother's illness; and when you heard of it through the neighbors afterward you would be likely to think that John was a queer fellow and unduly close-mouthed, and that he had been a little less than cordial in not telling you, an old friend of the family, something at least about it.
> That was the sort of man John was.[44]

As a result of John's reticence, the New Testament tells us five times as much about Peter as John, and Acts mentions Paul ten times more frequently than it does John: "Luke did not care particularly for the apostle John," asserts Hayes, "and he does not seem to have been a favorite with any of the other writers of the New Testament historical books."[45] Peter liked John—but then again, he liked everybody. The other evangelists did not like John and mentioned him only to find fault with him. One reason for this dislike may have been that Salome, James, and John considered themselves to belong to the aristocracy among the disciples. Their feeling could have grown out of their social status, Salome's relationship with Mary, or John's special relationship with Jesus.

In contrast to Paul, John may serve as a model of the Christian who could not point to a definite time of conversion because he had grown up in a devout home. Nevertheless, Jesus gave him the name *Boanerges:* "Jesus gave him this name because he had that in him which could flash fire at times. A man cannot flash fire unless he has some flint in him. It runs up and down his backbone and it shows in his face": "John's hair was neither brown nor blond nor bleached. On the contrary, in all probability it was as black as coal. His eyes too were black; and they could flash fire from their somber depths. John was a Boanerges. He was no weakling; he was a warrior."[46] With such a character, John should not surprise us when he calls spade a spade:

> To him Judas is a devil and the son of perdition. The Jews are the children of the devil. Every professing Christian who walks in the darkness is a liar, and he makes God a liar. The antichrist is a liar. Every sinner is a child of the devil. Whosoever hateth his brother is a murderer. . . . This is the spirit of a Boanerges.[47]

The same fiery spirit can be seen in the later stories of the apostle's fleeing the bathhouse where Cerinthus was bathing or denouncing the bishop to whom he had entrusted the care of the young man who became a robber captain.[48]

WILLIAM DALLMANN

Dallmann's *John: Disciple, Evangelist, Apostle* (1932) is a handsome, devotional commentary on the life of John, the Gospel, and the Epistles.[49] The short chapter on the apostle's life summarizes the relevant passages of scripture and illustrates the apostle's life with etchings, plates, and poetry.

With no equivocation, Dallmann informs his readers that John was the son of Zebedee and Salome and that he was born at Beth Saida.[50] After summarizing the passages in which John is mentioned in the synoptics and Acts and filling gaps with commentary on the history and geographical surroundings of Jesus' ministry, Dallmann turns to the reports regarding the apostle's later life. John left his homeland sometime during the war of A.D. 66–70 along with the evangelist Philip and Aristion, "and after shipwreck reached Ephesus."[51] Citing Eusebius, Dallmann says that John was banished to Patmos by Domitian in 95. As an old Latin hymn put it,

> To desert islands banished,
> With God the exile dwells
> And sees the future glory
> His mystic writing tells.[52]

After returning from Patmos, John restored the young man who had become a robber captain. John was also responsible for the practice of celebrating the Last Supper on the 14th of Nisan and, three days later, on Easter, regardless of which day of the week it fell on—"and here began the great split between the Greek and Latin Church."[53]

The last chapter in Dallmann's section on the apostle is entitled "John's Pupils." Quoting Irenaeus to the effect that John taught "presbyters in Asia," Dallmann identifies the following as John's pupils: Ignatius; Quadratus, "a Greek philosopher, [who] became a pupil of John and presented the first Apology, or Defense, of Christianity to Hadrian when that emperor came to Athens in 125"; Polycarp, who was martyred in A.D. 155; Papias; and Pothinus, bishop of Lyon, martyred in A.D. 177.[54]

A. T. ROBERTSON

As with the other volumes of this era we have surveyed, the first part of Robertson's *Epochs in the Life of the Apostle John* (1935) is devoted to the life of the apostle,[55] but without the kind of historical and geographical survey that fills out a book like Dallmann's. A survey of the Johannine writings follows in the second part of Robertson's work. In some respects, this book marks the end of the era in which scholars wrote lives of the apostle. After Robertson, scholarly attention turned elsewhere, as will be chronicled in the next chapter of this study. Indeed, the degree to which scholarship has changed in the last half-century can be seen by comparing Robertson's study to the present one, especially since both were written by occupants of the James Buchanan Harrison chair of New Testament Interpretatiom at the Southern Baptist Theological Seminary in Louisville, Kentucky.

Robertson begins by characterizing John as a mystic, recognizing that while the details of his life are scarce, the impression created by him is clear and distinct.[56] Showing more caution than many other writers of this period, Robertson says, "It is often supposed that she [John's mother] is Salome," and then adds, "This is entirely possible, but not quite certain."[57] On the basis of Mark 6:45, Robertson maintains that there were two towns called Bethsaida, one on the eastern side of the lake and one not far from Capernaum. This western Bethsaida was the home of others of the disciples and may have been the birthplace of John. John was "clearly" one of the two disciples directed to Jesus by John the Baptist.[58]

Before turning to trace John's career in more detail, Robertson feels compelled to "dispose of that shadowy figure whom Papias calls 'the elder John' according to Eusebius."[59] Robertson agrees with L. John Chapman that Eusebius was the first interpreter to find two Johns in Papias.[60] Irenaeus and Polycarp knew only one, the apostle. The term "elder," which is also used in the Epistles, does not mean that he was not an apostle also. Hence, Robertson agrees with Hayes: "We conclude that Papias is not distinguishing between two persons at all, but simply between two methods of gathering his material—one by report of what the apostle had said, and one by hearing the apostle himself."[61] The chief outcome of our accepting the existence of a second John, Robertson contends, is confusion.[62]

Having ruled out the possibility of a second John in Ephesus, Robertson affirms that John was the Beloved Disciple and the author of each of the five books attributed to him. He is also the "other disciple" mentioned in John 18:15. Arguing that the disciple must have been one of the Twelve and one of the "inner three," Robertson is led to the conclusion that the Beloved Disciple can only have been the apostle John. Robertson rejects Stalker's contention that pride was John's "besetting sin," saying that John had earned the title "Beloved Disciple" by being the one closest to the incarnate one.[63] The name *Boanerges* refers to the temperament of James and John, "the impetuosity of their natural character."[64] As evidence of the appropriateness of the name, Robertson cites the offer to call down fire on a Samaritan village, John's intolerance of the unauthorized exorcist, the ambitious request for the seats of honor in the kingdom, John's courage at the trial of Jesus, and his fiery denunciation of sin in the Epistles.

In the next chapter Robertson treats the close relationship between John and Peter, describing each of the scenes in the New Testament where the two are together: their work as fishermen; their being sent to prepare for the last Passover meal; their presence at the trial of Jesus, at the empty tomb, at the appearance by the Sea of Galilee, and at the Beautiful Gate; their appearance before the Sanhedrin; their work in Samaria; and, possibly, their being sent out together on mission in Galilee and their being sent to prepare for the triumphal entry.

Robertson characterizes John as "a man of spiritual insight." The apostle was the first to believe in the resurrection of Jesus, the first to recognize the Lord at the appearance by the lake. John was also the seer of Revelation, a mystic, and the theologian whose sign was the eagle. At the cross, Jesus gave John to his mother, and John immediately took her to his abode in Jerusalem: "Whether this was temporary or permanent we do not know."[65] John could have owned a house in Jerusalem, but the Gospel of John does not mandate this interpretation. By the time John returned to the cross, Jesus had already died, and John witnessed the water and blood flow from his side. Later, John is named as one of the pillars of the church whom Paul met in Jerusalem. It is the only recorded meeting between John and Paul, but John evidently accepted Paul's work among the Gentiles warmly and without reluctance.

Little is known about the apostle's life after the Jerusalem conference. The testimony of Papias, Polycarp, Irenaeus, and Polycrates that John settled in Ephesus, where he wrote the Gospel, should be taken as authoritative. Some of the legends about the apostle "reflect the impressions made by John's life and work in Ephesus."[66] Here, Robertson recalls the story of John's flight from the bathhouse, which Irenaeus attributes to Polycarp; the story of the robber captain; and Jerome's report that the aged apostle used to repeat the words "Little children, love one another." The picture of John as the elder in the epistles, the endorsement of the Gospel (John 21:24) by the elders of Ephesus, and the exile to Patmos fill in the details, such as they are, of the residence in Ephesus. We do not know whether John died a natural death or was martyred. Probably neither of the two tombs in Ephesus is genuine. With John's death, however, the greatest of the apostles, rivaled in genius and service only by the apostle Paul, passed from the scene.

CONCLUSION

The rise of modern historical consciousness and the beginnings of critical scholarship profoundly altered the course of the Johannine legends. The impetus for apocryphal stories and pious embellishments was severely reduced. As a result, the growth of the legends could not continue as it had for the previous sixteen hundred years. Instead, as we have seen, two new streams can be traced: imaginative recastings of the legend by poets, and investigative reconsiderations of the tradition by historians. Nevertheless, the legend flourished in these new genres, especially in the work of New Testament historians.

Debate over the authorship of the Gospel gave rise to feverish reassessments of the patristic materials. Strauss and the Tübingen School rejected the tradition of apostolic authorship and assigned a late date to the Gospel. Luthardt exposed flaws in this attack on the tradition, identified the crucial issues that have continued to shape the debate, and contended that the early tradition in support of the apostolic attribution of the Gospel is stronger than its critics had recognized.

MacDonald composed one of the first substantial biographies of John, portraying the apostle as a son of nobility. As in many of the lives surveyed in this chapter, the reports of the synoptic gospels and John are taken at face value and strung together to provide vivid glimpses of episodes in John's relationship with Jesus. In turn, the tradition of Irenaeus (John's residence in Ephesus and his authorship of the five writings attributed to him) forms the basis for MacDonald's account of the apostle's later life. Throughout MacDonald's account of the apostle's life, imaginative details and embellishments add interest to the book.

Psychological interpretation is particularly evident in the book on John written by Stalker. The Gospel and Revelation give complementary views of the inner character of the apostle, who was called both *Boanerges* and the Beloved Disciple. Fiery in nature, John labored to resist pride—his "besetting sin." Yet at the same time, he was capable of profound love.

Following the path charted by Luthardt and MacDonald, Scott-Moncrieff and Hayes wrote to refute the challenges to the traditional view of the authorship of the Johannine corpus. Hayes read the character of the apostle somewhat differently than his predecessors had, however—claiming that the record gives evidence that John was close-mouthed and reticent, yet fiery and direct when he spoke. Dallmann marshalled the geographical data to illumine the apostle's early life and strung together the patristic references to establish a direct relationship between John and the early apologists. Robertson continued the pattern of harmonizing the Gospel accounts with one another, while bringing his enormous scholarly acumen to the task. As a result, in Robertson's biography of John, one already begins to see a greater degree of restraint on the authorial urge to supply imaginative details. John the apostle is characterized there as a mystic, and John the Elder is dismissed from consideration.

Even before the publication of Robertson's life of John, others were exploring alternative constructions of the data, and in less than a decade, Bultmann's commentary on the Gospel would change the landscape of discussion about its origin and composition. In the next chapter, the life of the legend will be brought up to the present by taking notice of three divergent directions in current study.

NOTES

1. Christoph Ernst Luthardt, *St. John the Author of the Fourth Gospel*, rev. and trans. Caspar Rene Gregory (Edinburgh: T. & T. Clark, 1875).
2. Luthardt, *St. John*, 17
3. See Leander E. Keck, ed., *The Christ of Faith and the Jesus of History: A Critique of Schleiermacher's Life of Jesus by David Friedrich Strauss*, LJS (Philadelphia: Fortress Press, 1977).
4. Albert Schweitzer, *The Quest of the Historical Jesus: A Critical Study of Its Progress from Reimarus to Wrede* (New York: Macmillan, 1950), 97–98.
5. Schweitzer, *The Quest of the Historical Jesus*, 125.
6. F. C. Baur, *Theologische Jahrbücher* (Tübingen, 1851), 295; cited in Luthardt, *St. John*, 20–21.
7. Luthardt, *St. John*, 21.
8. Christoph Ernst Luthardt, *Das Johanneische Evangelium nach seiner Eigenthümlichkeit geschildert und erklärt* (Nuremberg, 1852–1853); cited by Luthardt, *St. John*, 22.
9. Theodor Keim, *Geschichte Jesu von Nazara in ihrer Verkettung mit dem Gesamtleben seines Volkes frei untersucht und ausführlich erzählt* (Zurich, 1867), esp. 1:103–72; cited in Luthardt, *St. John*, 24, 341.
10. Luthardt, *St. John*, 70.
11. Luthardt, *St. John*, 109–10.
12. Luthardt, *St. John*, 115.
13. See Luthardt, *St. John*, 115, 306.
14. James M. MacDonald, *The Life and Writings of St. John* (New York: Scribner, Armstrong, and Co., 1877).
15. MacDonald, *The Life and Writings of St. John*, 17 n. 3. Also see above, p. 8.
16. MacDonald, *The Life and Writings of St. John*, 19.
17. MacDonald, *The Life and Writings of St. John*, 28.
18. MacDonald, *The Life and Writings of St. John*, 39.
19. MacDonald, *The Life and Writings of St. John*, 41.
20. MacDonald, *The Life and Writings of St. John*, 58.
21. MacDonald, *The Life and Writings of St. John*, 68–69.
22. MacDonald, *The Life and Writings of St. John*, 75–76.
23. MacDonald, *The Life and Writings of St. John*, 94–95.
24. MacDonald, *The Life and Writings of St. John*, 110.
25. MacDonald, *The Life and Writings of St. John*, 135–36.
26. MacDonald, *The Life and Writings of St. John*, 138–39. Also see above, p. 169.

27. MacDonald, *The Life and Writings of St. John,* 144.
28. MacDonald, *The Life and Writings of St. John,* 145 n. 3. For the origins of the tradition that John was shipwrecked near the end of his journey, see above, the *Acts of John at Rome* (pp. 205–6) and the *Acts of John by Prochorus* (pp. 206–7).
29. MacDonald, *The Life and Writings of St. John,* 154. I am using a copy of MacDonald's book that was donated to the library of the Southern Baptist Theological Seminary, Louisville, Kentucky, by Mrs. A. T. Robertson. The copy has handwritten notes in the margins. Unfortunately, while the content of the notes is consistent with Robertson's views, the handwriting does not appear to be his. The notes on this page, for example, say: "He thinks / Ap. *produced* a dialect, \ w. / Apocal. represents / crude state. And / inference that this was one of the earliest books of the N.T. is very curious. He himself puts it A.D. 64–8. Then it was certainly preceded by nearly all / Ep. \ Paul, by James, prob. by [?] / Peter, not to insist on Luke's writings, + Mark's. What an argument!" And at the bottom of the page: "There is a very good argt. fr. / Hebraism genl. roughness of the style \ Rev. to show that it was written earlier than *John's* other writings, but not at all to show that it was earlier than most books of the N.T."
30. D. F. Bacon, *Lives of the Apostles;* cited in MacDonald, *The Life and Writings of St. John,* 258.
31. MacDonald, *The Life and Writings of St. John,* 380. Cf. the chronology given in the *Acts of John by Prochorus* (see above, p. 221).
32. James Stalker, *The Two St. Johns of the New Testament* (New York: American Tract Society, 1895), 9–10.
33. Stalker, *The Two St. Johns,* 9–10
34. Stalker, *The Two St. Johns,* 13.
35. Stalker, *The Two St. Johns,* 18.
36. Stalker, *The Two St. Johns,* 21.
37. Stalker, *The Two St. Johns,* 63.
38. Stalker, *The Two St. Johns,* 80.
39. Stalker, *The Two St. Johns,* 83.
40. Stalker, *The Two St. Johns,* 98.
41. C. E. Scott-Moncrieff, *St. John: Apostle, Evangelist and Prophet* (London: James Nisbet, 1909), vi.
42. Scott-Moncrieff, *St. John: Apostle, Evangelist and Prophet,* 194–98.
43. Doremus Almy Hayes, *John and His Writings* (New York: The Methodist Book Concern, 1917).
44. Hayes, *John and His Writings,* 17.
45. Hayes, *John and His Writings,* 21.
46. Hayes, *John and His Writings,* 47–48.
47. Hayes, *John and His Writings,* 53.
48. See above, pp. 125, 154, and pp. 142–43.
49. William Dallmann, *John: Disciple, Evangelist, Apostle* (St. Louis: Concordia, 1932).
50. Dallmann, *John: Disciple, Evangelist, Apostle,* 3.
51. Dallmann, *John: Disciple, Evangelist, Apostle,* 90. Also see above, pp. 205–7.

52. Dallmann, *John: Disciple, Evangelist, Apostle,* 102.
53. Dallmann, *John: Disciple, Evangelist, Apostle,* 104.
54. Dallmann, *John: Disciple, Evangelist, Apostle,* 108, 111.
55. A. T. Robertson, *Epochs in the Life of the Apostle John* (New York: Fleming H. Revell, 1935), 11.
56. Robertson, *Epochs in the Life of the Apostle John,* 11.
57. Robertson, *Epochs in the Life of the Apostle John,* 13–14.
58. Robertson, *Epochs in the Life of the Apostle John,* 16–17.
59. Robertson, *Epochs in the Life of the Apostle John,* 22. Also see above, pp. 109–12.
60. See L. John Chapman, *John the Presbyter and the Fourth Gospel* (Oxford: Clarendon Press, 1911), 33.
61. Robertson, *Epochs in the Life of the Apostle John,* 24; citing Hayes, *John and His Writings,* 139.
62. Robertson, *Epochs in the Life of the Apostle John,* 29.
63. Robertson, *Epochs in the Life of the Apostle John,* 39–40.
64. Robertson, *Epochs in the Life of the Apostle John,* 43; quoting Henry Barclay Swete, *The Gospel According to St. Mark* (London: Macmillan, 1898), 57.
65. Robertson, *Epochs in the Life of the Apostle John,* 94.
66. Robertson, *Epochs in the Life of the Apostle John,* 109. Also see above, pp. 125, 142–43, and 165.

CHAPTER 10

Eclipse and Acclaim
The Apostle in Recent Research

Since 1935, when A. T. Robertson's life of John was published, the apostle has slipped into a period of eclipse, overshadowed by other concerns in contemporary scholarship. Although its impact was felt only slowly among English-speaking scholars, Rudolf Bultmann's *The Gospel of John: A Commentary,* published in 1971, turned completely away from traditional questions about authorship and historicity and opened a whole series of new issues: the identification of sources, the displacements and rearrangement of the text, the work of the redactor, and the extent of Gnostic influence on the Gospel. Increasingly, attention turned to the social context in which the Gospel and the Epistles were written. As a result, the apostle John himself has largely been displaced by attention to the Johannine school or community.

This chapter will not attempt to review the past fifty years of debate over the authorship of the Johannine writings. Much of this debate has already been summarized in earlier chapters. Instead, we will continue to follow the development of what we may now speak of as the Johannine legend. While some proposals diffused the role of the apostle through reconstructions of the history of the Johannine school, Martin Hengel in particular has reasserted the figure of John the Elder as the theologian of Asia Minor. We will review works that have given particular attention to John the Elder, some of which set the course for later discussion, and others which merit restatement because of the creativity with which they marshall and remint the evidence. In contrast, Hengel's recent volume, *The Johannine Question* (1989), clearly moves the discussion onto a more substantial foundation.

The role of the apostle has not dropped completely from view, however. Evangelical New Testament scholars have continued to rely on B. F. Westcott's classic arguments for apostolic authorship. More recently, the defense of apostolic authorship has been taken up by Leon Morris, John A. T. Robinson,

Stephen S. Smalley, and D. A. Carson. These three lines of thought—the resurgence of John the Elder, the quest for the Johannine school, and the reaffirmation of the apostle—will occupy our attention in this chapter.

THE RESURGENCE OF JOHN THE ELDER

Most Johannine scholars would probably agree with the sentiment of Robert Eisler that nowhere in the whole realm of history is there a more elusive ghost than "John the Elder."[1] In fact, even the existence of John the Elder has been contested. D. A. Carson recently concluded: "it is far from certain that there was an 'elder John' independent of the apostle, and if there was, it is still less certain that he wrote anything."[2] The ambiguity of the evidence, which makes disparate interpretations virtually inevitable, lends the whole issue of John the Elder a phantom quality. Although B. W. Bacon strove valiantly to lay "the Elder John of Ephesus" to rest, he has survived Bacon's onslaught and reemerged in the work of such different scholars as Robert Eisler and Martin Hengel. As Bacon observed, "Until the ghost of an 'Elder John at Ephesus' is either materialized or laid the problem of the fourth Gospel must fall short of satisfactory solution."[3]

B. W. Bacon

As an exponent of critical theory in the earlier part of this century, Bacon maintained that scholarship had shown beyond reasonable doubt that the Gospel and the Epistles were not written by the apostle John. From his early work until the last article to come from his pen, however, the Yale New Testament scholar repeatedly attacked the popular notion that they were the work of John the Elder of Ephesus. In his view, "the Elder John of Ephesus is a higher-critical myth" spawned above all by Eusebius, Zahn, and Harnack.[4] After quoting Eusebius's interpretation of the reference to the Elder John in Papias, Bacon comments: "At last we have reached the authentic birthplace of the mythical 'other John.' The bright star of critical speculation has led us to the spot. Heaped on the altar still lie the gold of Zahn, the frankincense of Harnack and the myrrh of Gutjahr."[5] Perceptively, but apparently from anti-millenarian bias, Dionysius questioned the apostolic authorship of Revelation. Knowing of no other John in Ephesus, he suggested that the book came from John Mark. It was left to Eusebius to discover the reference to the Elder John in Papias and identify him as the Elder of Ephesus and the author of Revelation.

A brief summary can hardly reproduce the arguments in support of each of Bacon's conclusions—arguments developed over more than thirty years in a daunting series of chapters and articles.[6] Here we will attempt only to reproduce an overview of his solution to the Johannine riddle with passing reference to arguments central to his thesis.

Being persuaded by the testimony of the De Boor fragment of Papias, Bacon agreed with Eduard Schwartz and R. H. Charles that both of the sons of Zebedee were martyred in Jerusalem, "killed by the Jews."[7] James was martyred in A.D. 42, but John did not die until twenty years later, probably at the time of the martyrdom of the other James in A.D. 62. These latter two are probably the martyrs referred to in Revelation 11:1–8. Responding to the objections J. H. Bernard had raised against the case for the "red" martyrdom of John, Bacon argued that Papias held the early view (attested in Epiphanius) that John was exiled on Patmos "under Claudius."[8] Hence, Papias had no difficulty in maintaining that John, who had seen the vision on Patmos, was martyred by the Jews before A.D. 70.

The Revelation was probably written by the married daughter of Philip of Caesarea (Acts 21:9), a prophetess whose death and burial in Ephesus is reported by Polycrates. The editor of Revelation attributed the work to John to give its warnings apostolic weight.[9] The Gospel and the Epistles were written by an otherwise anonymous elder of the church in Ephesus, but not the Elder John mentioned by Papias.

The only likely candidate for the identity of the Elder John mentioned by Papias is the John who is the seventh elder listed by Eusebius and Epiphanius[10] in the Jerusalem succession. Epiphanius adds that John lived "until the nineteenth year of Trajan" (A.D. 117), which would make him Papias's contemporary. The linchpin in the argument is that Dionysius knew the writings of Papias and would have welcomed the opportunity to attribute Revelation to another Ephesian John. We may safely conclude, therefore, that Dionysius knew of no other John in Ephesus and found nothing in Papias to lead him to consider the existence of such a figure. Moreover, Papias does not give the impression that John the Elder was in Asia. Rather, he questioned those who came his way to ascertain what Aristion and John were saying.[11]

Polycrates of Ephesus accepted the current view that the Gospel and probably Revelation also were written by the apostle John, but he does not mention an "Elder John of Ephesus," whose authority he might be expected to cite in his argument with Rome over the date of Easter.[12] Eusebius saw that Irenaeus had been deceived by the similarity of the names and by his own desire to trace an apostolic line for the Fourth Gospel and for himself. As a result, Irenaeus maintained that Papias was a disciple of the apostle John, when in reality he was not even a disciple of John the Elder. The John that Polycarp had seen was not the apostle, as Irenaeus believed, but the Elder.[13] Irenaeus is therefore responsible for the confusion between the Elder John and the apostle John.[14] Neither Papias nor his sources reveal any interest in the Fourth Gospel. Believing that he had discovered the identity of the author of

Revelation, Eusebius nevertheless maintained that the Elder John mentioned by Papias was John the seer of Revelation. Hence was born "the Elder John of Ephesus."

What we know of Papias's elders, however, points not to Ephesus but to a Palestinian provenance. Irenaeus says that Papias attributed to the elders the description of the miraculous fertility of the land of the saints in the Messianic age. This description itself parallels 2 Baruch 39:5 and is based on the Hebrew text of Genesis 27:28. Moreover, Papias regards the elders as "the disciples of the apostles," who were therefore able to pass on their words. Bacon states his conclusion in the form of a challenge: "Our question is whether we should not go even beyond the correction of Eusebius distinguishing this 'Elder John' from the Apostle, and locate him in Jerusalem, whence Papias could obtain his 'traditions' only at second hand."[15]

Pressing his case further in two articles published in 1927, Bacon contended that Irenaeus mistakenly thought it was in Ephesus that Polycarp had contact with "John and the others who had seen the Lord," when it is much more likely that whatever association he had with John (in reality an elder, not the apostle) was in Jerusalem rather than Ephesus. Polycarp was born of Christian parents in A.D. 69, and Pionius says he was brought from "the east" to Smyrna in his youth.[16] As corroborating evidence, Bacon argues that "Ignatius, Polycarp and Justin have no idea of Asia as the seat of apostolic tradition."[17] Nor is there any indication that the elder of 2 John 1 and 3 John 1 was named John, as Bacon caustically observes: "Of course Ephesus, like any other church, has its 'elders.' Keen-eyed Origen, noting the superscription of the two smaller epistles it ascribed to its Apostle, shrewdly suspected the hand of one of these. But he does not make the naif suggestion that perhaps this 'elder' of II Jo 1_1; III Jo 1_1 bore the same name. That brilliant idea he left for moderns."[18] Elsewhere, Bacon is more direct: "The Ephesian Elder mentioned in the Second and Third John (and probably connected also with the First Epistle and Gospel) has nothing in common with the Elder John of Papias save the title of 'Elder'; and to what church leader of A.D. 100–120 could not the title 'elder' be applied in one or other of its diverse meanings?"[19]

In the end, therefore, Bacon not only denied that there was an "Elder John of Ephesus," he also maintained that the attribution of all five of the Johannine writings to John was the work of the later "canon-makers." Not only were there not two Johns in Ephesus, there wasn't even one.[20]

Robert Eisler

In 1938, Eisler published a volume in which he sets out to resolve what he terms in the book's title as *The Enigma of the Fourth Gospel*. His thesis is reviewed here not because it is of historical value but because it illustrates once again the creative, regenerative power of legend—particularly when mixed with a powerful imagination.

Eisler's starting point is the theory of Dom Donatien de Bruyne and Adolf von Harnack regarding the ancient Latin prologues to the Gospels.[21] Eisler distinguishes a shorter version of the prologues, which he attributes to Fortunatian the African (ca. A.D. 313), from the longer version found in the so-called Visigothic Bibles. Eisler points out that the anti-Marcionite prologue (quoted above, p. 129) does not identify the evangelist with the son of Zebedee. That identification depends on identifying the Beloved Disciple as John the son of Zebedee, and that equation, Eisler contends, originated with the Leucian *Acts of John.* It is not explicitly stated anywhere in Irenaeus, Theophilus of Antioch, Clement of Alexandria, or the *Muratorian Canon.*[22]

From a further statement in the *Acts of John,* Eisler concludes that the *Acts* deny that John the apostle was the author of the Gospel, for the apostle says: "I am neither able to declare unto you nor to write the things which I both saw and heard" (cf. 1 John 1:3).[23] Since the prologue to Luke identifies John as one of the Twelve,[24] Eisler reasons that this phrase must have been added to the prologue after Irenaeus and probably after Dionysius (third century).

Eisler turns next to the testimony of Polycrates of Ephesus, who says that John was a priest who had worn the golden frontlet. Polycrates introduces Philip as one of the apostles but not John. Neither does Polycrates affirm that John wrote the Gospel. From this reference Eisler concludes that the John of Asia known to Polycrates had been a Jewish high priest and was the John named in Acts 4:6—" . . . Annas the high priest, Caiaphas, John, and Alexander, and all who were of the high-priestly family." Eisler proposes that John was known to Josephus as Theophilus, son of Annas, who was high priest from A.D. 37 to A.D. 41. From a fragment attributed to Hilarius in a ninth-century manuscript of various works by Augustine, Eisler next identifies the boy that Jesus took in his arms as John the Evangelist.[25] The identification of John the Evangelist as the apostle entered orthodox tradition through Origen, who was probably influenced by the Leucian *Acts,* an inference made plausible by the report that Origen emasculated himself. This identification was then passed on from Origen to Dionysius, Eusebius, Epiphanius, and Jerome.

Eisler accepts the tradition of the martyrdom of John the son of Zebedee along with his brother.[26] From the *Toldoth Jeshu*—a Jewish anti-Christian document—and an emendation of Acts 12:2, Eisler concluded that John and James were martyred by Herod Agrippa I before A.D. 44. Revelation 11:3–7, moreover, should be understood as a reference to the role of James and John during the famine of A.D. 41. From the martyrologies and the references to three and a half days in Revelation, Eisler fixed the date of John's martyrdom in Jerusalem as December 28, A.D. 42, three and a half days before the

Roman New Year. The tombs in Ephesus were the tombs of John the high priest, who died there in exile and was later reburied.[27]

The confusion of the two Johns can be traced to the editor of the anti-Marcionite prologue to Luke, who was also the editor of the Apocalypse. The same editor deleted from Luke the oracle predicting the martyrdom of the sons of Zebedee and deleted from Acts 12:2 the reference to John. This editor identified the Ephesian John (the former high priest) with John the son of Zebedee.[28]

From the shorter version of the anti-Marcionite prologue, which Eisler attributes to Fortunatian, Eisler reasons that Papias could not have been John's scribe, or else Eusebius would surely have seized on this fact. By repunctuating the prologue, Eisler arrives at the following reading:

> The Gospel of John was revealed and given
> to the Churches by John whilst he was still alive in his body,
> as Papias, called the Hierapolitan,
> the beloved disciple of John,
> has reported in his five books of "Exegetics".
> But (he who) wrote down the Gospel, John dictating correctly
> the true (evangel), (was)
> Marcion the heretic. Having been disapproved by him for
> holding contrary views, he was expelled by John.
> He had, however, brought him writings, or letters,
> from the brethren who were in the Pontus.[29]

The scribe to whom John dictated the Gospel, Eisler contends, was none other than Marcion, and traces of Marcion's teachings can still be found lurking in the Fourth Gospel.[30] Marcion, therefore, gained the confidence of the old man who had once been high priest by presenting him with certain writings from Pontus. He then offered to take down John's dictation and abused his position by producing unfaithful copies of the Gospel interpolated with his own views. The Gospel and the First Epistle were written during the Jewish revolt of 115–117 under Trajan and sent to Parthia.[31]

The identity of the corrector of the Fortunatian prologue, who repunctuated it, Eisler discovered from one of the ancient texts of the prologue: Patricius of Ravenna (sixth century). Alternative traditions that identified John's amanuensis as either Timothy or Prochorus spread in the East:

> The tradition about Timothy, the first Bishop of Ephesus, acting
> as John's secretary, is preserved in a manuscript of Mount Athos,
> published by Usener in his edition of the "Acts of Timothy."[32]

This seems to have been the official Ephesian version of the anti-Marcionite preface of which, so far no Greek text has been found.

When Ephesus had been sacked in A.D. 1090, and the alleged original copy of John's Gospel had perished with the famous basilica of St. John, the founder of the new monastery of St. John on the island of Patmos, St. Christodulus (A.D. 1088), who until the Seljouk invasion was abbot of a convent in Heraclea at the foot of Mount Latmos, seems to have supplanted the Ephesian tradition by another "legend." According to this new invention, popularized through the efforts to attract pilgrims to the new sanctuary, John dictated his Gospel "standing" (*hestōs*) on the summit of a mountain—*katapausis,* near Karos on the Island of Patmos—to Prochorus, one of the first deacons, mentioned in Acts vi. 5, who wrote it on papyrus and made a first clean copy on parchment which remained in Patmos while the original papyrus was taken by John and Prochorus to Ephesus.

The story is one of the many pious legends fabricated in order to authenticate a particular relic, in this case probably the famous Gospel manuscript (N) written with silver and gold on purple parchment, brought to Patmos by Christodulus, of which a part is still in Patmos, while others have been dispersed by the greed of relic-hunters and relic-mongers. We find it incorporated in a Catholicized version of the old Ps.-Leucian "Wanderings of John" which contains almost unaltered a number of chapters from the old heretical "Acts of John."[33]

Eisler's interpretation is mistaken, however. The legend that John dictated the Gospel to Prochorus was not invented by Christodulus in 1088. The account of the dictation to Prochorus during the exile at Patmos appears in the *Acts of John by Prochorus,* which dates from the fifth century.[34] Therefore, it cannot be a legend invented to authenticate Codex N of Patmos.

Eisler puts the finishing touches on the picture he has painted by identifying the Beloved Disciple who rested his head on Jesus' breast as Lazarus, who was also the boy Jesus had taken in his arms. On the authority of Ambrose of Milan (ca. A.D. 390), Epiphanius of Salamis (ca. A.D. 400), and Peter Chrysologus of Ravenna (ca. A.D. 450), Eisler identifies John the high priest as the young man who fled naked from the garden (Mark 14:50–52). John knew that the Beloved Disciple's testimony was true because he too had been in the garden at the arrest and then had fled to his quarters at the high priest's house. Since Mark 15:31 and Matthew 27:41 say that "the high priests" were at the crucifixion, Eisler suggests that as a boy, John had been taken to witness the execution and that he had seen Lazarus, who was known to the high priest there. Years later, when Marcion brought him writings from the Beloved Disciple which contained these recollections, he testified to the truth of the witness of that disciple, Lazarus of Bethany.

In conclusion, Eisler claims to have resolved the enigma by breathing life into Papias's elusive John the Elder. John was born the son of Annas, the high priest (A.D. 6–15), probably during the last year of that period. As a boy, he followed Jesus in Jerusalem and believed that Jesus was the God-sent liberator. He had been taken in the arms of Jesus. He followed Jesus to the garden and witnessed the arrest, and probably also the trial and crucifixion. Later he sat with the court in judgment on Peter and John the son of Zebedee and cast his vote with Gamaliel. From 37 to 41, he was high priest, but was deposed by Herod Agrippa I, who executed John the son of Zebedee on December 28, A.D. 42. During the revolt of A.D. 66–70, the former high priest commanded one of the armies, experienced the crushing defeat, and was exiled to Ephesus. There, he was attracted to the Pauline believers and waited for the Second Coming of the Redeemer. His fame spread, and Papias would question travelers regarding what John had said. Luke devoted his two volumes to John (*Johanan*), who was also known as Theophilus! Finally, Marcion, a shipowner from the Black Sea, brought him "scriptures," among them the reminiscences of Lazarus of Bethany, who was well-known to John and his family. John gave in to Marcion's offer and agreed to dictate his recollections in the form of a new Gospel.

When Marcion's corruptions of John's thought to advance his own ultra-Paulinism came to John's attention, he had to correct as best he could the Gospel which had already been sent to Parthia, to the "elect lady" in Jerusalem, and which had been rejected by many a Diotrephes in the towns around Ephesus. Worse yet, Cerinthus had circulated the Apocalypse under his name and under that of the apostle, the son of Zebedee. There was nothing left for him to do therefore but drink the poison cup. Some held that the poison was not effective, or that he was asleep in his rock tomb. Deprived of the Gospel of John, which was now reissued in a revised form and with an anti-Marcionite preface, Marcion sailed to Ostia to renew his efforts with an edited version of Luke, which had been dedicated to "Theophilus." At the conclusion of the book, Eisler promises another volume, to explain the "scriptures" that Marcion brought to John, but apparently such a work was never published.

Martin Hengel

The work of Martin Hengel is, of course, of quite a different nature. As wild and uncontrolled as Eisler's thesis is, Hengel's is restrained and worthy of serious consideration. The only similarity between the two is their focus on the figure of John the Elder.

Hengel has launched a counteroffensive against all source theories in his reassessment of the early evidence regarding the authorship of the Fourth Gospel. *The Johannine Question* grew out of the Stone Lectures which Hengel delivered at Princeton Theological Seminary in 1987 and is part of a larger manuscript which has not yet been published.[35] Its brevity is deceiving. With the thoroughness and precision that his readers have come to expect, Hengel proposes a reassessment of second-century references to John that overturns established views and rehabilitates both Papias and John the Elder. Hengel's thesis in short is that the Gospel and the Epistles of John (and probably an early version of the Apocalypse) were composed by one "towering theologian, the founder and head of the Johannine school."[36] This influential teacher of Asia Minor, however, was not the apostle but John the Elder.

Beginning with Irenaeus and working back into the earlier decades of the second century, Hengel observes that John is referred to not as the apostle but as "John the Lord's disciple" or as a teacher. The inscription *Euangelion kata Iōannēn* is preserved in p[66] and, Hengel contends, should probably be traced back to the circulation of the text at the beginning of the second century. Hengel traces the attribution of the Gospel to the apostle John to Ptolemy (ca. A.D. 150) and cites the *Acts of John* as supporting evidence of the apostle's growing reputation. Hengel finds the references and allusions to John in the middle of the second century to be more substantial than most other recent interpreters have allowed. Hengel's judgment of the tricky references in Justin is that Justin knew the Gospel "quite well" but did not use it,[37] perhaps because it was not generally accepted by Roman Christians. Irenaeus's report that Polycarp knew John of Ephesus is credible. On the other hand, so are the reports of the early martyrdom of John the son of Zebedee, which can be traced to the second volume of Papias's work. The martyrdom of John must then have been deliberately suppressed by Eusebius in order to support the apostolic authorship of the Johannine corpus.

John the Elder, mentioned by Papias and known by Polycarp, was the elder who wrote the Johannine Epistles (2 John 1; 3 John 1). The similarity of style and thought is such that all three Epistles must have been composed by the elder. Similarly, the close relationship in style and thought between the Epistles and the Gospel points to common authorship at the hand of the Elder. The arguments for the stylistic, literary unity of the Gospel have never been answered.[38] One cannot distinguish either a signs Gospel or extensive later redaction from a different hand, though the idealized references to the Beloved Disciple have the character of insertions. On balance, it is likely that the Elder wrote the Apocalypse at an early stage and that it was revised by one of his followers after his death. The Epistles do not presume a widely accepted Gospel, so the final redaction of the Gospel probably did not occur until after the death of the Elder.

The result, therefore, is a vivid picture of a Judean disciple who established a Christian school in Asia Minor (Ephesus) late in the first century. As his name and Semitic Greek idiom indicate, John came from a Palestinian home. John knew the topography of Judea and explained the meaning of Aramaic terms. He knew the Jewish law, and numerous parallels to the Qumran documents point to Palestine. John was also at home in the Hellenism that had pervaded the eastern Mediterranean since Alexander the Great. It is probable that the author came from the aristocracy in Jerusalem, since most of the characters around Jesus belonged to the upper class (the royal steward, Nicodemus, Mary and Martha and Lazarus, Joseph of Arimathea). The John of the Apocalypse was banished to Patmos. Insignificant persons were not sent into exile: "For John to be banished to Patmos," writes Hengel, "indicates that he had high social status."[39] Affinities with the Hellenists of Acts indicate the general context rather than direct contacts with this group. Similarly, the references to the disciples' being put out of the synagogue reflect the troubled history of tension with the Jewish authorities since the earliest days rather than a bloody persecution at the time the Gospel was written.

Hengel speculates that the turmoil of the early 60s in Palestine forced John to emigrate to Asia Minor, "where at about the age of fifty he founded his school, which flourished for about thirty-five years."[40] Hengel suggests that the Apocalypse was written by John the Elder about 68–70 and reworked by his disciples after his death. The Gospel was written primarily for a gentile community; separation from the synagogue lies well in the past. The school had contacts with other Christian communities, however, so that Paul and the other Gospels were known to it. For the Elder, John the son of Zebedee was the ideal disciple (in contrast to Peter), but his followers superimposed the two by means of the references to "the Beloved Disciple":

> Given the unique way in which the figures of John son of Zebedee and the teacher of the school and author of the Gospel are deliberately superimposed in a veiled way, it would be conceivable that with the "beloved disciple" "John the elder" wanted to point more to the son of Zebedee, who for him was an ideal, even *the* ideal disciple, in contrast to Peter, whereas in the end the pupils impressed on this enigmatic figure the face of *their* teacher by identifying him with the author in order to bring the Gospel as near to Jesus as possible. Therefore I cannot believe that this ideal figure is pure fiction. In the teaching of the Evangelist and in the discussions of the school the beloved disciple had not only an ideal but also some kind of "historical" significance which was— ultimately—related to two figures: the "apostle" John from the Twelve and the author himself.[41]

Thirty or forty years after the death of John the Elder, church tradition identified him as the evangelist and seer, and John the son of Zebedee.

Hengel's *The Johannine Question* is a treasury of scholarship on the early references to John and the Johannine writings. It calls us back to the substantial scholarship of the Harnack, Lightfoot, Schlatter, Zahn, and others who had a high respect of the historical value of the second-century patristic writers. Hengel has forged a challenging thesis as a reasonable explanation of the riddles posed by the five Johannine writings, their relationships with the synoptic Gospels, their setting in the Johannine school, and the references in the second century to John the Elder, the apostle John, and the Johannine corpus. The scope and coherence of the thesis add to its strength.

On the other hand, the thesis, while a plausible and reasonable construction of the evidence, is unconvincing at key points. The linchpin of the argument— the identification of the Elder John (from the single reference in Papias) with the elder of 2 John 1 and 3 John 1—will not bear the weight of the argument that is built on it. For many, the evidence for the early martyrdom of John the son of Zebedee remains problematic. Yet so does the credibility of Irenaeus's report that he had heard Polycarp tell of hearing John, the great teacher of Asia Minor. If the report is accepted, why should one believe that Irenaeus has recalled the memory of Polycarp correctly but confused the Elder with the apostle? Why is it more credible that Eusebius suppressed the evidence of the early martyrdom of John the son of Zebedee than that Irenaeus shortened the chain of tradition leading back to John?

THE QUEST FOR THE JOHANNINE SCHOOL

During the 1960s and 1970s, an old theory about the origins of the Johannine writings was revived and expanded. The origins of the hypothesis that the Johannine writings come not from one author (the apostle) but from a school of writers can be traced to the writings of Strauss, Renan, and J. B. Lightfoot.[42] The early development of the hypothesis need not detain us here. Suffice it to say that the notion of the Johannine school originally functioned either as confirmation of the traditional view that the apostle wrote the Gospel or as a mediating view, establishing an indirect link between the apostle and the Gospel or the corpus of the Johannine writings. The school was conceived of as a group of disciples who had gathered around John the apostle and either wrote or edited the Gospel, the Epistles, and the Apocalypse. Differences among these writings could then be explained in terms of the different authors, while the similarities among the writings and their later attribution to John could be explained on the basis of origin from a closely knit community around the apostle.

C. K. Barrett

As illustrative of such a view of the role of the Johannine school, the position taken by C. K. Barrett in his influential commentary on the Gospel (originally published in 1955) may be cited. The crux of the problem, he contends, is "the moral certainty that the gospel was not written by John the son of Zebedee."[43] In the second edition of his commentary (1978), Barrett adds the following defense of this judgment:

> It must be allowed to be not impossible that John the apostle wrote the gospel; this is why I use the term "moral certainty." The apostle may have lived to a very great age; he may have seen fit to draw on other sources in addition to his own memory; he may have learnt to write Greek correctly; he may have learnt not only the language but the thought-forms of his new environment (in Ephesus, Antioch, or Alexandria); he may have pondered the words of Jesus so long that they took shape in a new idiom; he may have become such an obscure figure that for some time orthodox Christians took little or no notice of his work. These are all possible, but the balance of probability is against that having all actually happened.[44]

Nevertheless, "the Johannine literature exists, and is marked by differences, which forbid the view that all the works concerned come from the same hand, and similarities, which demand some kind of interrelation."[45] The following solution, Barrett proposes, would satisfy the requirements of the data before us:

> John the Apostle migrated from Palestine and lived in Ephesus, where, true to character as a Son of Thunder, he composed apocalyptic works. These, together with his advancing years, the death of other apostles, and predictions such as Mark 9:1, not unnaturally gave rise to the common belief that he would survive to the *parousia*. A man of commanding influence, he gathered about him a number of pupils. In course of time he died; his death fanned the apocalyptic hopes of some, scandalized others, and induced a few to ponder over the meaning of Christian eschatology. One pupil of the apostle incorporated his written works in the canonical Apocalypse; this was at a date about the close of the life of Domitian—*c.* A.D. 96. Another pupil was responsible for the epistle (probably 1 John came from one writer, and 2 and 3 John

from another). Yet another, a bold thinker, and one more widely read both in Judaism and Hellenism, produced John 1–20. . . . [Later] The gospel was now edited together with ch. 21. . . . The evangelist, perhaps, after Paul, the greatest theologian in all the history of the church, was now forgotten. His name was unknown. But he had put in his gospel references to the beloved disciple— the highly honoured apostle who years before had died in Ephesus. These were now partly understood, and partly misunderstood. It was perceived that they referred to John the son of Zebedee, but wrongly thought that they meant that this apostle was the author of the gospel.[46]

In the 1960s and early 1970s, several Johannine scholars focused attention on the nature of the Johannine community, while allowing the issues of authorship and the role of the apostle to fade into the background. The construction of a profile of the Johannine community was important apart from these issues because of its potential for shedding light on the social context in which the Johannine writings were produced. The role of the apostle went into eclipse.

J. Louis Martyn

The eclipse can be seen in several pacesetting works on the Johannine community from this period, first and foremost the works of J. Louis Martyn, *History and Theology in the Fourth Gospel* (1968), and *The Gospel of John in Christian History* (1978). Beginning from the observations that the Gospel reflects a sharp conflict with the synagogue leaders and that this situation reflects the period of the writing of the Gospel rather than the conditions of Jesus' ministry, Martyn proposes that the Gospel is written as a two-level drama, which simultaneously reflects both the period of Jesus' ministry and that of the conflict between the Johannine community and the synagogue. The expression "excluded from the synagogue" (John 9:22; 12:42; 16:2), Martyn contends, refers to the "Benediction against Heretics" that was formulated by the Jewish leaders meeting at Jamnia late in the first century. The Johannine Christians suffered both social dislocation and persecution from the local Jewish authorities, and these conditions are reflected in the Gospel. On the other hand, neither the apostle nor the Beloved Disciple play a significant role in Martyn's view of the history of the Johannine community.[47]

Wayne A. Meeks

Analyzing the metaphorical language of the Gospel and the Epistles, Wayne A. Meeks demonstrates that these writings were produced within and for a community which had separated itself from the world. The Johannine metaphorical system was well understood by the insiders for whom true faith in Jesus meant joining the Johannine community. The Gospel is not a missionary tract, however. One of its primary functions was "to provide a reinforcement for the community's social identity which appears to have been largely negative."[48] The Gospel reflects the Christological motifs which this community developed and which in turn drove it into further isolation. The Johannine letters show us a later stage of the isolation, estrangement, and disruption of the community.[49]

R. Alan Culpepper

In my doctoral dissertation, *The Johannine School* (1975), I attempt to test the hypothesis that the Johannine community should be identified as a school by isolating features common to ancient schools and then asking whether these features are reflected in the Gospel and the Epistles attributed to John. The dissertation, therefore, is more concerned with historical and sociological issues than with the question of authorship or the role of the apostle. The hypothesis that the community should be viewed as an ancient school does push to the forefront the role of the school's founder. The dissertation proposes that the self-understanding of the community is vitally linked to its regard for the Beloved Disciple as the founder of the community. He served as its authority and source for the traditions about Jesus, and was venerated as an eyewitness and the ideal disciple, though he was probably not one of the Twelve, and hence not the apostle John.[50] The dissertation accepts the notion that "the linguistic and theological similarities and dissimilarities among the Johannine writings can be explained best by assuming that they were written by several writers working in one community—hence probably a school."[51] On the other hand, the dissertation does not venture to identify the process by which the Gospel was composed. The Beloved Disciple, the evangelist, the redactor, the elder, and the seer are viewed as different persons, and their relationship to one another may be best understood on the basis of the pattern of an ancient school in which disciples carry on the work and teachings of an esteemed founder. The hypothesis of a Johannine school serves, therefore, to illuminate one aspect of the origin and setting of the Johannine writings, and it offers a contemporary sociological model which seems to have been influential in the way the community conceived of itself and was perceived by others—as a school. With this work, however, the role of the apostle John is effectively separated from the hypothesis of a Johannine school, and the latter no longer serves a means of relating the Johannine writings directly or indirectly to the apostle.

Oscar Cullmann

After years of reflection on the origin of the Gospel of John, Oscar Cullmann published *The Johannine Circle* in 1976 (German ed. 1975). The distinctive contribution of this monograph can be sketched in the following points, but such a brief summary cannot convey its nuances. Cullmann locates the Johannine circle within Judaism during the early decades of the development of the Christian community in Jerusalem. The Johannine circle maintained a close relationship with heterodox Judaism, especially but not exclusively Samaritanism, the disciples of John the Baptist, and the Hellenists mentioned in Acts 6–8. In fact, Cullmann posits a two-stage relationship between heterodox Judaism and the Johannine community, first in the origin of the community itself and then in the Transjordan, or in Syria, after the community's flight from Jerusalem before 70. Cullmann rejects both the identification of the Beloved Disciple as the apostle John and the suggestion of F.-M. Braun, Raymond E. Brown, and Rudolf Schnackenburg that the Beloved Disciple was merely the authority and not actually the author of the Gospel. On the other hand, Cullmann feels that differences between John and the synoptics may be explained by assuming that Jesus gave a special teaching (the Johannine) to the inner group of his followers. Once again, in this view the apostle John plays no role in the production of the Gospel attributed to him.

Raymond E. Brown

In the first volume of his monumental commentary *The Gospel According to John* (1966), Brown proposed a five-stage process to explain the composition of the Gospel of John. The first stage was the existence of a body of tradition concerning the words and works of Jesus. The origin of this tradition was independent of the synoptic Gospels and can be traced to the Beloved Disciple, who Brown concludes is best identified as the apostle John.[52] In the second stage, this material was developed in Johannine patterns, and written forms of material that had been preached and taught began to take shape. Brown posits a close-knit school of thought in which the evangelist (who was a disciple of the apostle) was the principal preacher, the elder was a later leader of the community, and the seer may have been less closely related to the same community. During stage three, the first edition of the Gospel was written. Later (stage four), a second edition was produced by the evangelist. Finally (stage five), the Gospel was revised and completed by a redactor, who was also a member of the Johannine community. Though Brown recognizes that in the nature of the case, such a theory cannot be proved, it serves admirably to account for the development of the Johannine tradition, the aporias in the Gospel, the Gospel's testimony to the Beloved Disciple, and the attribution of the Gospel to the apostle John in the second century.

Thirteen years after the publication of the first volume of the Anchor Bible commentary on the Gospel, Brown published *The Community of the Beloved Disciple* (1979), which offers a more comprehensive presentation of his understanding of the history of the Johannine community. We need not attempt to summarize even the principal points of Brown's fascinating portrayal of the life of the Johannine community in this volume. Two points call for attention, however. First, Brown indicates that he changed his mind regarding the identification of the Beloved Disciple as the apostle John and now rejects the view that the Beloved Disciple was the apostle.[53] Brown agrees with Cullmann's proposal that the Beloved Disciple had been a disciple of John the Baptist, but continues to reject Cullmann's contention that the Beloved Disciple was the author of the Gospel. Secondly, Brown persuasively argues that the school of Johannine writers should be distinguished as a special group within the Johannine community.[54] In *The Community of the Beloved Disciple,* we have the most detailed hypothesis to date of the history of the Johannine community, but once again, the apostle John plays no role in this history.

George R. Beasley-Murray

John, the Word Biblical Commentary written by George R. Beasley-Murray, offers yet another significant statement of the view that the Johannine writings derive from a Johannine school which cannot be connected to the apostle John. Beasley-Murray summarizes his view in eight points, which are reproduced here without the comments that accompany each point:

> (*a*) The Beloved Disciple is presented as a historical figure among the early disciples of Jesus and in the continuing Church.
> (*b*) The Beloved Disciple is not a member of the Twelve, nor a well-known person in the early Church. It is difficult to supply a cogent reason for the Evangelist consistently and completely hiding his identity if he were a prominent leader like John the apostle or Paul, or a well-known individual like John Mark or Lazarus.
> (*c*) The Beloved Disciple is not the author of the Gospel—neither of chaps. 1–20 nor of chap. 21.
> (*d*) The Beloved Disciple is presented as an eyewitness of certain crucial events in the Gospel, notably in connection with the end of the ministry of Jesus and the resurrection appearances.

(e) The authority of the Beloved Disciple extends beyond the events which he may have witnessed.

(f) The relationship of the Beloved Disciple to Peter requires examination in the exegesis of the passages.

(g) As the authority figure to which the Johannine communities looked, the Beloved Disciple appears to have had a group of teachers about him.

(h) The identity of the leader of this group remains the secret of the Evangelist.[55]

Beasley-Murray's endorsement of the thesis that the Gospel was written by "a master interpreter of the school of the Beloved Disciple"[56] is important both for its clarity and for its having been published in the Word Biblical Commentary series, which shows that this thesis has grown in popularity, even among Evangelical scholars.

REAFFIRMATION OF THE APOSTLE

The diversity of views surveyed in this chapter should discourage anyone from claiming that the question of the origin of the Johannine writings has been settled, or even that scholarship has rendered a negative judgment on that issue. Indeed, in recent years there has also been a resurgence of the traditional view that the apostle John was the author of the Gospel, and of the other writings attributed to him. This resurgence in English scholarship is best illustrated in the works of Leon Morris, John A. T. Robinson, Stephen S. Smalley, and D. A. Carson.

Leon Morris

Two chapters in Morris's *Studies in the Fourth Gospel* address the issue of the authorship of the Gospel. In the first, entitled "Was the Author of the Fourth Gospel an 'Eyewitness'?" Morris argues at length that the vivid reporting of names, times, places, and incidental details—which are not only appropriate to the context but, to every appearance, historically accurate—is forceful evidence that the Fourth Gospel was indeed written by an eyewitness to the events. For Morris, as for William Temple, whom he cites, the account "has the 'feel' of exact memory."[57] Morris's case for apostolic authorship rests therefore primarily on the internal evidence from the Gospel itself and involves the further contention that the Gospel preserves and records "exact memory." At one point he recognizes but repudiates the obvious objection to this mode of argument:

Against this kind of approach some critics have countered that the vividness belongs to the mind of the writer (any good writer of fiction is vivid!), not to the circumstances of the narrative. I imagine that this cannot be ruled out as impossible. But the argument is not convincing, if only for the reason that writers of fiction in antiquity did not normally insert the kind of detail that carries conviction here.[58]

In response, it must be said that the alternatives Morris sets up—exact memory or fiction—do not allow for the kind of conditioning process of tradition or the creative handling of a tradition that is rooted in history that many interpreters of John find in the Gospel. His view of the ancient writers of fiction, moreover, is indefensible.[59]

His second essay, "The Authorship of the Fourth Gospel," is more substantial. In it, Morris revisits Westcott's famous fivefold argument that the Gospel was written by (1) a Jew, (2) a Jew of Palestine, (3) an eyewitness, (4) an apostle, and therefore (5) the apostle John.[60] The first two points are now widely accepted and need not detain us. The third point Morris argues in the same fashion as he argues the case in the preceding chapter: vivid details are evidence of eyewitness reporting. In a page and a half, Morris simply restates Westcott's contention that the author of the Gospel was an apostle because he has "'intimate acquaintance' with the feeling of the disciples" and remembers their words and the erroneous impressions that were later corrected.[61] Morris himself recognizes that these passages are not convincing to those who do not think the Gospel was written by the apostle, but admits that even though the passages do not prove the point, "at least they are not incongruous with that supposition."[62]

The fifth point, of course, is the crux. Indeed, the fourth and, to a lesser extent, the third points in Westcott's argument really depend on the strength of the case for the fifth point: that the author was the apostle John. As support for identifying the author as the apostle, Morris follows Westcott in saying that John 21 leads us to identify the Beloved Disciple as one of the sons of Zebedee, who along with Peter were especially close to Jesus. Since James was martyred, the Beloved Disciple must have been John. The observation that John the Baptist is simply called "John" in the Fourth Gospel is curiously turned into an argument for concluding that the author of the Gospel was also named John. Morris also acknowledges two objections that Westcott refuted—that the author would not call himself the Beloved Disciple and that he would not elevate himself above Peter. In the process, Morris also responds to Barrett on these matters, arguing that the Fourth Gospel acknowledges the primacy of Peter just as clearly as the other Gospels do. He is more persuaded by the objection that "Beloved Disciple" is not likely to have been a self-designation but concludes that this subjective judgment cannot stand against the rest of the evidence which indicates that the author of the Gospel was indeed the apostle John.

John A. T. Robinson

The Priority of John, published two years after Robinson's untimely death in 1983, represents the culmination of his repeated arguments that the Gospel of John is grounded in early, Palestinian tradition and was written at an early date by one who had direct links with Jesus and the earliest Christian community. There is, therefore, no basis for identifying written sources or finding theological developments or historical events from the latter part of the first century reflected in the Gospel. The Gospel of John should be viewed, rather, as *a* first Gospel, not necessarily the first Gospel chronologically. It was early, independent of the synoptics, and has close links in space, time, and person to Jesus himself. This was no recently adopted view for Robinson, since it consistently reflects the positions he had sketched in his influential paper "The New Look on the Fourth Gospel," which he delivered at the conference on the Gospels held at Oxford in 1957, the last point of which is an affirmation that the Gospel of John was indeed written by the apostle John.[63]

Robinson accepts the patristic tradition that locates the origin of the Gospel in Ephesus, but argues that equally important are the evidences within the Gospel of its origin in Judea and its intimate knowledge of the topography of Judea and Jerusalem. Dismissing the widely accepted view that the Gospel was not finished until the last decade of the first century, Robinson argues that the references to the disciples' being put out of the synagogue (John 9:22; 14:42; 16:2) are not allusions to the *birkat ha-minim.* Consequently, there are no reasons to date the Gospel any later than A.D. 65.[64] In his review of the external evidence regarding the authorship of the Gospel, Robinson calls the evidence for the early martyrdom of John "palpably inferior."[65]

On the other hand, Irenaeus's citation of the testimony of Polycarp credibly purports that Polycarp had known John in Asia and that John was the author of the Gospel. Similarly, Papias gives no evidence of a generation gap between the apostles and the elders.[66] As author of the Gospel, John the Elder is "a mere construct of modern scholarship."[67] Nevertheless, on the basis of the internal evidence, Robinson rejects Irenaeus's view on the authorship and date of the Apocalypse, maintaining instead that it was written by a second John in Asia shortly after the death of Nero. The concluding verses of the Gospel stand midway between external and internal evidence, since they are either integral to the Gospel or constitute the earliest external testimony, added to the Gospel by a member of the Johannine community. Responding to the position that the Beloved Disciple was an otherwise unknown Judean disciple, Robinson asks why such a disciple "should be found fishing in Galilee in ch. 21 in the same boat as Peter."[68] To Robinson, the traditional view that the Beloved Disciple was John the son of Zebedee is still preferable.

What, then, of the identity of the evangelist? From the Gospel itself, one can see that he is a Jew who writes in passable Greek with an Aramaic accent. The homogeneity of style in the Gospel continues to pose problems for any who would assign parts of it to different hands, and though Robinson concedes that the matter of the common authorship of the Gospel and the Epistles is more open to question, he finds fewer objections to common authorship than to the alternatives.

The links between the Gospel narrative and Galilee focus primarily on Capernaum, where Robinson suggests the Zebedees had their business. If that is so, what of Barrett's cumulative listing of the assumptions one must make if one identifies the evangelist as John the son of Zebedee?[69] Robinson maintains that his arguments do not depend on any of the assumptions Barrett cited. Greek was the *lingua franca;* Acts 4:13 means only that John did not have a rabbinic education, and fishing was such a good business that John could have been known to the servant of a high priestly household in Jerusalem from his business there. In sum, Robinson concludes: "This does not in the least mean that apostolic authorship is a hypothesis without difficulties, nor is it one, as I said at the beginning of this section, on which everything turns. Yet I have gradually been driven back to regard it as the one least open to objection and therefore the most scientific."[70]

If apostolic authorship can be maintained, however, then we are very close to "source" indeed, for the Beloved Disciple was Jesus' "bosom friend," one of the inner group of disciples, and (on the basis of the references we have reviewed at the outset of chapter 1) possibly Jesus' first cousin—a relationship which may explain Jesus' act of leaving his mother to the care of the Beloved Disciple (John 19:26–27). Such a relationship would also make John a first cousin to John the Baptist—a tie which would explain why James and John joined the movement of John the Baptist in the first place.[71] The priestly contacts which the family had—at least through Elizabeth's marriage to Zechariah—could also explain why John was known to the high priestly family in Jerusalem and why Polycrates later claimed that John was a priest and wore the sacerdotal plate. Robinson's last word on the matter is typically equivocal: "Of course all these connections are highly tentative and *nothing* hangs on them. But at least a good deal begins to come together and make sense if the hypothesis is accepted, on its own merits, that the man behind John's Gospel, the beloved disciple, is indeed the son of Zebedee, as tradition has unanimously asserted."[72]

Stephen S. Smalley

Smalley builds on the work of both Robinson and Barrett. Indeed, he alludes to the "new look" in Johannine studies at the outset of *John: Evangelist and Interpreter* and returns to this allusion from time to time throughout the book.[73] He also follows a line of argument similar to Robinson's. Polycarp is accepted as the single intermediary between the apostle John and Irenaeus, who authoritatively reports that John "gave out" his Gospel at Ephesus after the other Gospels had been written.[74] After reviewing the external evidence, Smalley concedes:

> External attestation to the apostolic authorship of the Gospel is neither strong nor uniform before Irenaeus. Those early witnesses who might reasonably be expected to mention a link between the apostle and the Gospel are at times completely silent on the point; and it is difficult to find a clear consensus of opinion at any time about the eventual fate of John, and whether or not he could have produced a Gospel late in his life at Ephesus, as Irenaeus maintains he did.[75]

Smalley proceeds to analyze the testimony of Papias regarding John the Elder, and concludes that the references are to one and the same John—the apostle.[76] Even if it could be proved that there was a John the Elder, Smalley contends, there is nothing to establish that he lived at Ephesus or had anything to do with the composition of the Gospel. When he examines the internal evidence, Smalley concludes that none of the objections to identifying the Beloved Disciple as the apostle is insurmountable. He also favors the interpretation which takes the participle in John 21:24 in a causal sense, paraphrasing the verse, "The beloved disciple is responsible for the tradition recorded in this Gospel; he caused the tradition to be written down, and the authors can vouchsafe for its reliability."[77] His solution, therefore, is that the Beloved Disciple and the evangelist were different persons. John the apostle, the Beloved Disciple, was responsible for preserving the tradition underlying the Gospel, but the Gospel was actually written by others, hence the ambiguity of the early evidence regarding the authorship of the Gospel.

In his commentary on the Epistles, *1, 2, 3 John,* Smalley maintains that "the community around John can be traced from the gospel to the three letters," that 1, 2, and 3 John were written in that order, that 2 and 3 John were written by the presbyter, and 1 John by the same author or "someone very close to him."[78] Smalley continues:

But it is not unreasonable to suppose that the inspiration behind
the tradition and distinctive theology of the Fourth Gospel came
from John the apostle, the beloved disciple, himself; that some
followers of John published the final version of his Gospel at
Ephesus after his death (around A.D. 85); and that these
Christians were not directly involved in the production of 1, 2, and
3 John.[79]

The intent of the last clause of this sentence is to affirm that "those who were
responsible for the final version of John's Gospel were not necessarily involved in the composition of the Johannine letters."[80]

In the Manson Memorial Lecture in 1986, published the following year as
"John's Revelation and John's Community," Smalley returned to the issue of
the authorship of the Johannine writings, adding considerations for the probability that all five writings are to be traced to the apostle. The Gospel, he
maintains, gives evidence of a living community, and the relationship between
the Gospel and the Epistles is clearly closer than that between the Gospel and
the Revelation. The lecture points to "subtle but striking resemblances"
between the Gospel and Revelation in five areas: ethos, theology (esp. cosmology, Christology, and eschatology), testimony tradition, language, and
structure (as dramatic pieces).[81] On the basis of his review of the evidence in
these areas, Smalley concludes that Revelation is an integral part of the
Johannine corpus. In turn, Revelation gives further information regarding the
extent of Johannine Christianity. The seven churches of Revelation are Johannine congregations related to one another and to the "mother church" at
Ephesus. Putting together the various pieces of the puzzle, Smalley concludes
that the Revelation was the first document, not the last, of the Johannine
corpus to be written. John moved to Ephesus with his followers in the 50s,
doubtless as a result of persecution. At Ephesus, one or more of those
followers began to formulate the tradition they had received from John for
worship and instruction. Some time during the 60s, John was exiled on
Patmos. After his release, in the 70s, John returned to Ephesus, where he
began to write the Apocalypse. Its dualism and theme of "salvation *through*
judgment" were later taken up in the Gospel and Epistles.[82] In the 80s, after
the apostle's death, the Gospel was edited and published by the Johannine
church. Although the individual arguments themselves cannot be repeated
here, Smalley's summation bears quoting in full:

My suggestion is, therefore, that Revelation belongs to an early
period in the life of the community for which it was composed,
and that the history of John's circle may be traced from it through
to 3 John. In that initial place, furthermore, the Apocalypse seems

to fit naturally. Although structurally John's Revelation and Gospel are very similar, other features of the Apocalypse, in relation to the Fourth Gospel, are more primitive. Its ethos is less Hellenistic; its theology is less developed; its exegesis of Old Testament tradition is less advanced; and its use of the Greek language is less expert.[83]

For those who are convinced of the community context of the Johannine writings and see the need to explain the similarities between Revelation and the Gospel, there is much here with which one can agree. The debated point, of course, is whether Smalley is correct in identifying John the seer as the apostle and the Beloved Disciple.

D. A. Carson

The Gospel According to John, a full-scale commentary on the Gospel published in 1991 by D. A. Carson, vigorously renews the case for the apostolic authorship of the Gospel and consistently interprets the Gospel from this perspective. Crucial to Carson's reassessment of the external evidence is his reading of Papias: (1) whereas Eusebius distinguishes between apostles and elders, "Papias himself makes no such distinction"; (2) John is called "elder" because he is grouped with the elders just mentioned; (3) the distinction Papias is making in the two lists is not between two generations (apostles and elders) but between the witnesses who have died and those of the first generation who are still alive; and (4) Eusebius's interpretation of Papias reflects his own dislike for Revelation. "In short," Carson concludes, "it is far from certain that there was an 'elder John' independent of the apostle, and if there was, it is still less certain that he wrote anything."[84]

Turning to the internal evidence, Carson judges, no doubt rightly, that most now accept the first two of Westcott's cumulative arguments (discussed above) for the identity of the author of the Fourth Gospel as John the son of Zebedee: (1) he was a Jew, (2) a Palestinian, (3) an eyewitness, (4) an apostle, and (5) the apostle John. After reviewing the references to the Beloved Disciple in the Gospel, Carson refutes five arguments that have been used against the position of those who identify the Beloved Disciple as the apostle: (1) although John was a Galilean, he could have later become familiar with other locales; (2) that John was unlearned (Acts 4:13) does not mean he did not possess a creative intellect; (3) although John was a "son of thunder," the transforming power of the Spirit (as in the life of Paul) and "the mellowing effect of years of Christian leadership" could have made him the apostle of love reflected in the Gospel; (4) the "other disciple," known to the high priest's household, may have had a house in Jerusalem and functioned there as his father's agent; and (5) recent studies of the use of Greek in Galilee remove any objection that John could not have written the Greek of the Fourth Gospel. Having dealt with these objections, Carson judges that "the internal evidence is very strong, though not beyond dispute, that the beloved disciple is John the apostle, the son of Zebedee."[85]

One final issue remains to be considered: the relationship between the Beloved Disciple and the evangelist. Rejecting the view of those (including Beasley-Murray and Smalley) who distinguish between the Beloved Disciple and the evangelist, Carson favors the view of Morris and Robinson, that the two are one and the same person. The difficulty of believing that the evangelist would refer to himself as "the Beloved Disciple" has often been advanced as a reason for thinking that the term is used by the evangelist in reference to his esteemed mentor or the apostle. Carson dismisses this argument, however, saying that it "betrays a profound ignorance of the psychological dynamics of Christian experience."[86] As support, he quotes a hymn by George W. Robinson (1838–1877) that speaks in the first-person singular and condemns the view which distinguishes between the Beloved Disciple and the evangelist as actually self-defeating: "It implies that the Evangelist (someone other than the beloved disciple, on this view) thought Jesus loved certain disciples and not others."[87] Carson also advances the judgment that the lack of references to John in the Gospel is a consideration favoring the conclusion that the evangelist was himself the apostle. The case is further extended by the argument that "these things" in John 21:24 cannot refer only to chapter 21, that John 21:22–23 is a caveat coming from the aging apostle rather than a correction after the death of the Beloved Disciple, and that the view that the Beloved Disciple wrote the Gospel is simpler than the view that he caused it to be written. Carson, like Robinson, quotes Barrett's list of reasons for rejecting the view that the apostle wrote the Gospel, and finds the evidence unconvincing. In conclusion, he also rejects the thesis of a Johannine school or community, claiming that "the view that this Gospel was written by John the son of Zebedee (whether with an amanuensis or not) tends to prompt a fairly sceptical evaluation of the evidence advanced to offer a detailed delineation of the Johannine community."[88]

Inevitably, the arguments on both sides of the issue of apostolic authorship are not all of equal weight. It is unlikely, however, that even those who are disposed to affirm that the Beloved Disciple was the apostle John will find all of Carson's arguments convincing. Both Robinson and Smalley, for example, maintain the apostolic authorship of the Gospel while affirming the value of interpreting the Gospel in relation to the ongoing history of the Johannine community.[89]

CONCLUSION

At present, there seems to be no weakening of any of the three trends reviewed in this chapter. Just when one might think that the Elder John had been consigned to the curiosities of New Testament scholarship, the Elder's ghost reappears in a more substantial form. The recognition that the Johannine writings reflect both a community setting and the work of a group of several closely related writers has commended the thesis of a Johannine school both to those who connect the school to the apostle (or the Elder) and to those who do not. At the same time, the declaration of the "moral certainty" that the apostle John did not write the Gospel attributed to him continues to incite others to defend apostolic authorship along the lines laid down by Westcott and Robinson. If no consensus is in sight, debates among and within these three camps promise that the legends about the apostle John will continue to be revisited with no lessening of energy or interest for the foreseeable future.

NOTES

1. Robert Eisler, *The Enigma of the Fourth Gospel* (London: Methuen, 1938), 204.
2. D. A. Carson, *The Gospel According to John* (Grand Rapids: Wm. B. Eerdmans, 1991), 70. Stephen S. Smalley adopts a similar interpretation of Papias; see *John: Evangelist and Interpreter* (Greenwood, S.C.: Attic Press, 1978), 73. For Papias's reference to John the Elder, see above, pp. 109–12.
3. B. W. Bacon, "The Elder of Ephesus and the Elder John," *HibJ* 26 (1927): 127.
4. B. W. Bacon, "The Mythical 'Elder John' of Ephesus," *HibJ* 29 (1931): 313.
5. Bacon, "The Mythical 'Elder John' of Ephesus," 321.
6. See the entries under Bacon in the bibliography. In his *An Introduction to the New Testament* (London: Macmillan, 1900), 249, Bacon contended that attaching the name "John" to the Ephesian Elder is fallacious (249). That thesis was refined and repeated by Bacon in *The Fourth Gospel in Research and Debate* (London: T. Fisher Unwin, 1910), and in a series of articles, including "John and the Pseudo-Johns," *ZNW* 31 (1932): 132–50, which was published after Bacon's death on February 1, 1932.
7. Bacon, "John and the Pseudo-Johns," 137–39. See Eduard Schwartz, "Über den Tod der Söhne Zebedaei," in *Johannes und sein Evangelium*, ed. K. H. Rengstorf (Darmstadt: Wissenschaftliche Buchgesellschaft, 1973), 202–72; and R. H. Charles, *The Revelation of St. John*, ICC (Edinburgh: T. and T. Clark, 1920), 1:xlv–l. For the De Boor fragment, see above, p. 171.
8. See the quotation from Epiphanius, *Panarion* 51.12.2, cited above, p. 158.
9. Bacon, "John and the Pseudo-Johns," 142–43. See also B. W. Bacon, "The Authoress of Revelation—A Conjecture," *HTR* 23 (July 1930): 235–50; and "The Elder of Ephesus and the Elder John," 120–21.

10. See Eusebius, *E.H.* 4.5.3 (LCL 1:311); Epiphanius, *Panarion* 66.20 (trans. Amidon, 229).

11. See B. W. Bacon, "The Elder John, Papias, Irenaeus, Eusebius and the Syriac Translator," *JBL* 27 (1908): 1–23.

12. Bacon, "The Mythical 'Elder John' of Ephesus," 317.

13. B. W. Bacon, "Date and Habitat of the Elders of Papias," *ZNW* 12 (1911): 178 n. 2.

14. Bacon, "The Elder of Ephesus and the Elder John," 125.

15. Bacon, "Date and Habitat of the Elders of Papias," 182.

16. B. W. Bacon, "The Elder John in Jerusalem," *ZNW* 26 (1927): 192–93. See also "The Elder of Ephesus and the Elder John" (1927).

17. Bacon, "The Elder John in Jerusalem," 199. Bacon takes up this aspect of his argument in more detail in "The Mythical 'Elder John' of Ephesus," where he maintains that "no church writer, between the death of Paul and the advancement by Dionysius, ca. A.D. 250, of his ingenious theory of *two* Johns at Ephesus, betrays the slightest knowledge of any other John in Asia than just the seer of Patmos, whom Justin (converted in Ephesus *ca.* A.D. 125) explicitly declares to have been the Apostle" (314).

18. Bacon, "The Elder John in Jerusalem," 199. Cf. Martin Hengel, who asserts in *The Johannine Question,* trans. John Bowden (Philadelphia: Trinity Press International, 1989): "But if Ephesus, the great metropolis in Asia Minor, is most probable as a place for the letters, then it is hard to see why this unique elder of the second and third letters of John should not be identical with the unique John the elder mentioned by Papias the Bishop of Asia Minor, who was writing about a generation after these letters had been sent" (30). In response to Bacon, Hengel writes: "The identification by A. Schlatter and B. W. Bacon of the 'elder John' in Papias with the otherwise unknown John in the list of fifteen 'bishops of Jerusalem' given by Hegesippus is quite out of place. Why should Papias, as a bishop in Phrygia, have had any interest in such a remote and insignificant figure?" (28).

19. Bacon, "The Elder of Ephesus and the Elder John," 116.

20. See Bacon, "John and the Pseudo-Johns."

21. See above, pp. 129–30.

22. Eisler, *The Enigma of the Fourth Gospel,* 26.

23. *Acts of John* 88.3–5, in Eric Junod and Jean-Daniel Kaestli, *Acta Iohannis,* CChr (Turnhout: Brepols, 1983), 1:191.

24. See above, p. 130.

25. Eisler, *The Enigma of the Fourth Gospel,* 46–47. Also see above, p. 170.

26. See above, pp. 170–74.

27. See above, pp. 147–50.

28. Eisler, *The Enigma of the Fourth Gospel,* 131–32.

29. Eisler, *The Enigma of the Fourth Gospel,* 156. Cf. the text of the anti-Marcionite prologue quoted above, p. 129.

30. See Eisler, *The Enigma of the Fourth Gospel,* 178–84.

31. For this datum, Eisler cites Augustine, *Quaest. evang.* 2.39 (*The Enigma of the Fourth Gospel,* 169).

32. See Hermann Karl Usener, ed., "Acta S. Timothei," *Bonner Universitätsprogramm* (Bonn: Caroli Georgi, 1877).

33. Eisler, *The Enigma of the Fourth Gospel,* 163–64.

34. See above, pp. 220–21.

35. Martin Hengel, *Die johanneische Frage,* WUNT, 67 (Tübingen: J. C. B. Mohr, 1993), was published while this volume was in press.

36. Martin Hengel, *The Johannine Question,* trans. John Bowden (Philadelphia: Trinity Press International, 1989), ix.

37. Hengel, *The Johannine Question,* 13.

38. On this point, see also Eugen Ruckstuhl, "Zur Antithese Idiolekt—Soziolekt im johanneischen Schrifttum," in his *Jesus im Horizont der Evangelien,* Stuttgarter biblische Aufsatzbände 3 (Stuttgart: Verlag Katholisches Bibelwerk, 1988), 219–64.

39. Hengel, *The Johannine Question,* 126.

40. Hengel, *The Johannine Question,* 134.

41. Hengel, *The Johannine Question,* 131–32.

42. See above, p. 270, and my *The Johannine School: An Evaluation of the Johannine-School Hypothesis Based on an Investigation of the Nature of Ancient Schools,* SBLDS 26 (Missoula, Mont.: Scholars Press, 1975), 1–38.

43. C. K. Barrett, *The Gospel According to St. John,* 2d ed. (Philadelphia: Westminster Press, 1978), 132.

44. Barrett, *The Gospel According to St. John,* 132 n. 2.

45. Barrett, *The Gospel According to St. John,* 133.

46. Barrett, *The Gospel According to St. John,* 133–34.

47. For an insightful review of the influence of Martyn's work, see D. Moody Smith, "The Contribution of J. Louis Martyn to the Understanding of the Gospel of John," in *The Conversation Continues: Studies in Paul & John in Honor of J. Louis Martyn,* ed. Robert T. Fortna and Beverly R. Gaventa (Nashville: Abingdon Press, 1990), 275–94.

48. Wayne A. Meeks, "The Man from Heaven in Johannine Sectarianism," *JBL* 91 (1972), 70.

49. Meeks, "The Man from Heaven," 71.

50. Culpepper, *The Johannine School,* 264–67.

51. Culpepper, *The Johannine School,* 261.

52. Raymond E. Brown, *The Gospel According to John,* AB 29 (Garden City: Doubleday, 1966), xxxiv, xcviii, c.

53. Raymond E. Brown, *The Community of the Beloved Disciple* (New York: Paulist Press, 1979), 33. Schnackenburg also changed his mind, rejecting his earlier identification of the Beloved Disciple as the apostle; see above, p. 73.

54. Brown, *The Community of the Beloved Disciple,* 102. This suggestion is helpful in that it recognizes that the community encompassed many who were not involved in the writing of the Johannine documents. On the other hand, it obscures the similarities between the community and other ancient schools which looked back to their founders and transmitted their traditions. As a point of clarification, it

should be noted that nowhere in *The Johannine School* do I "make the community the author of the Gospel" as Brown charges (101 n. 196).

55. George R. Beasley-Murray, *John,* WBC 36 (Waco, Texas: Word Books, 1987), lxxiii–lxxv.

56. Beasley-Murray, *John,* lxxv.

57. Leon Morris, *Studies in the Fourth Gospel* (Grand Rapids: Wm. B. Eerdmans, 1969), 142.

58. Morris, *Studies in the Fourth Gospel,* 147.

59. In response to Morris's allegation that ancient writers of fiction did not insert vivid details to give their narratives credibility, see Robert Scholes and Robert Kellogg, *The Nature of Narrative* (New York: Oxford University Press, 1966), 246–47; quoted in my *Anatomy of the Fourth Gospel* (Philadelphia: Fortress Press, 1983), 48 n. 63.

60. See B. F. Westcott, *The Gospel According to St. John* (Grand Rapids: Wm. B. Eerdmans, 1971), v–xxv.

61. Morris, *Studies in the Fourth Gospel,* 244–46.

62. Morris, *Studies in the Fourth Gospel,* 245.

63. For John A. T. Robinson's earlier work on John, see the essays on John in his *Twelve New Testament Studies,* SBT, no. 34 (London: SCM Press, 1962), esp. "The New Look on the Fourth Gospel," 94–106; and his *Redating the New Testament* (Philadelphia: Westminster Press, 1976).

64. John A. T. Robinson, *The Priority of John,* ed. J. F. Coakley (London: SCM Press, 1985), 64–65.

65. Robinson, *The Priority of John,* 99.

66. Robinson, *The Priority of John,* 102–3.

67. Robinson, *The Priority of John,* 103.

68. Robinson, *The Priority of John,* 108.

69. See above, n. 43.

70. Robinson, *The Priority of John,* 118.

71. Robinson, *The Priority of John,* 121.

72. Robinson, *The Priority of John,* 122.

73. Smalley, *John: Evangelist and Interpreter,* 8, 11ff. See also Robinson, "The New Look on the Fourth Gospel," in *Twelve New Testament Studies,* 94–106.

74. Smalley, *John: Evangelist and Interpreter,* 69 (see also 119–21).

75. Smalley, *John: Evangelist and Interpreter,* 72.

76. Smalley, *John: Evangelist and Interpreter,* 73–74.

77. Smalley, *John: Evangelist and Interpreter,* 81.

78. Stephen S. Smalley, *1, 2, 3 John,* WBC, vol. 51 (Waco, Texas: Word Books, 1984), xxii.

79. *1, 2, 3 John,* xxii.

80. I am grateful to the Very Reverend Dr. Smalley for clarifying this matter in a personal letter, March 10, 1992.

81. Stephen S. Smalley, "John's Revelation and John's Community," *BJRL* 69 (1987): 551ff.

82. Smalley, "John's Revelation and John's Community," 569.

83. Smalley, "John's Revelation and John's Community," 570.

84. D. A. Carson, *The Gospel According to John* (Grand Rapids: Wm. B. Eerdmans, 1991), 69–70. See the discussion of Papias above, pp. 109–12.

85. Carson, *The Gospel According to John*, 75.

86. Carson, *The Gospel According to John*, 76.

87. Carson, *The Gospel According to John*, 77.

88. Carson, *The Gospel According to John*, 81.

89. Robinson refers to "the perfectly reasonable view advocated by Barrett and Brown in their commentaries or subsequently by Culpepper that a group of teachers or disciples were instrumental in producing the Gospel" (*The Priority of John*, 20). Similarly, Smalley begins his "John's Revelation and John's Community" by saying: "if the Fourth Gospel came to birth in the context of a living *community*, and was addressed to the individual and corporate needs of such a circle (a conclusion which to my mind seems inescapable) . . . " (549).

Reflections

The journey has been fascinating. Repeatedly we have seen the power of the legend of the apostle John to feed on itself and on other legends and thereby to regenerate itself in new and creative forms. The gaps and uncertainties in the legend feed its later development. Among these gaps, the following have exerted a particularly powerful influence.

First, the New Testament does not tell us what happened to the apostle after his work in Samaria, reported in Acts 8. The clues or possible references are unclear. Was the apostle banished to Patmos, where he wrote the Revelation, or was that a different John? Was John the Beloved Disciple, or was the latter not one of the Twelve at all? Did John the apostle write anything, and if so, why is it that references to his work as the seer of Revelation do not appear before Justin Martyr, and references to his role as the evangelist appear even later, when the Gospel was in the process of being accepted in orthodox circles?

Second, we have no solid evidence regarding the later life or the death of the apostle. The Gospel records suggest two possibilities: (1) that he died a martyr's death prior to the writing of the Gospel of Mark (Mark 10:39), and (2) that he did not die a martyr's death, in contrast to Peter, but lived a long life (John 21:22–23). Whether the traditions were generated by these references or not, it is significant that both Gospel references are reflected in the later legends. According to the traditional view, John moved to Ephesus, where he lived a long life. According to the other view, John died a martyr's death at the hands of the Jews. Various other stories of the death of John are added later: that he was boiled in oil (but survived); that he was forced to drink poison or was bitten by a snake (but survived—the longer ending of Mark promises that poison and snakes will not hurt the disciples); that he was starved to death, or that he took leave of his disciples, was buried, and then no trace of his body could be found; or that he continued to wander the face of the earth for centuries, appearing to King Edward the Confessor.

326

Another of the pivotal points in the development of the legend is the testimony of Papias. Did Papias know of the death of John as a martyr? Did he know of a second John, John the Elder, whom he distinguished from the apostle John? Differing interpretations of Papias, from Irenaeus on, have fueled the development of the legend. Some read Papias as confirming the death of John as a martyr, while others use Papias to argue that there was no John the Elder in Ephesus. Can we trust Irenaeus's report that Polycarp had heard the apostle John? Had Irenaeus confused John the Elder with John the apostle, or was he using an uncertain tradition to establish both the authority of the Gospel and his own place in the line of succession from the apostle?

Undergirding our review of the development of the traditions about the apostle John—and being confirmed by it—has been the insight that legend has shaped the tradition from its very beginnings. In the synoptic Gospels, we see the legends of John as fisherman, Boanerges, and member of the "inner three" (Peter, James, and John). Since it is hardly likely that the metaphor "fishers of men" in the story of the call gave rise to the Gospel accounts that the first disciples were fishermen from Galilee, this much seems to be grounded in historical bedrock.

The legend of John as the Beloved Disciple arose out of interpretations of references to this idealized and representative figure in the Gospel of John. In themselves, these references are the product of a separate tradition that lionized the founder of the Johannine community. The Fourth Evangelist and the Elder (the author of the Johannine Epistles) provided leadership for this community after the death of the Beloved Disciple. None of the Johannine writings appears to have been written by the apostle John, however. John the seer was a contemporary leader of the churches in Asia Minor, but seems to have been related to the Johannine community only tangentially or indirectly.

The first half of the second century forms a kind of tunnel period during which we have only echoes, parallels, or uncertain allusions to the Gospel of John and references to the Epistles in Polycarp. Justin Martyr, in the middle of the second century, is the first to identify John the seer as John the apostle. The first attribution of apostolic authorship for the Gospel came about the same time, from the Valentinian Gnostics (esp. Ptolemy). Between 150 and 180, there is evidence—centered in Rome and secondarily in Antioch—for the growing acceptance and use of the Gospel of John. Justin seems to have been reluctant to use it, and it was expressly rejected by Gaius. On the other hand, the *Epistula Apostolorum,* the Quartodecimans, Melito of Sardis, Tatian, and Theophilus provide evidence of the Gospel's increasing acceptance and authority. Claims of apostolic origin followed. These claims were apologetic and polemical, defending the authority of a Gospel that was rapidly gaining acceptance. The place of the Johannine writings was decisively secured by

Irenaeus, who defended the orthodoxy of the Gospel against the Gnostics, the Montanists, and Gaius. Other defenses followed, and as early as A.D. 200, we have manuscripts of the Gospel bearing the superscription "According to John."

The Beloved Disciple had been identified as one of the Twelve. The elder of the Epistles was identified as the evangelist, and hence also the Beloved Disciple and the apostle John. And, John the seer, the author of Revelation, had been identified as an apostle. The nexus was complete: apostolic authorship was certified for all five Johannine writings.

From the third century (or even late second century), we also witness the origins of the legends about John that were to be perpetuated for centuries in the rich and developing forms of the apocryphal *Acts of John* (through Leucius, Prochorus, and the Irish *Life of John the Evangelist*). Although the apocryphal *Acts* were opposed by the Church, they continued to flourish, and even orthodox writers continued to transmit stories of the later life of the apostle in Ephesus. Eventually, two tombs in Ephesus were identified as the apostle's resting place, and a basilica was built there in his honor.

Following the Enlightenment and the rise of modern concern for historical accuracy and the critical examination of sources, the free development of the legend of the apocryphal John ceased, and legend-making turned in new directions. Poetry still provided freedom for imagination and creativity, and historical analysis of perplexing sources provided fertile territory for the ingenuity of historians who wrote various lives of the apostle. Even John the Elder, who is referred to so briefly by Papias, has enjoyed a renewal of plausibility. In their various forms, each of these Johns is the product of legend created by the human drive to recover history, perpetuate tradition, interpret earlier stages of the tradition, and embellish that tradition with pious or plausible detail. Efforts to defend or attack traditional ecclesiastical positions and arguments intending to confirm or demolish scholarly positions have also contributed to the ongoing reassessment and reinterpretation of the traditions themselves.

The vitality of the legends about John is directly related to the uncertainties of the New Testament record and the second-century witnesses. Mystery, fascination, and controversy feed legends. The result has stirred pious imagination, enriched both culture and church, and evoked enormous ingenuity and creativity from those who have attempted to resolve the uncertainties. If a resolution to the historical difficulties surrounding the apostle is not forthcoming, one can only hope that the future will be as fruitful as the past, that the legend will continue to inspire both piety and imagination, art, and scholarship. Who can measure the power of the legend or its influence on persons, cultures, and communities of faith? So let the legend live: "Little children, love one another . . . it was the precept of the Lord, and . . . it is enough."[1]

NOTE

1. Jerome, *Commentary on Galatians* 6.10 (Migne, *PL* 26:462).

Bibliography

BOOKS ON THE APOSTLE JOHN AND THE BELOVED DISCIPLE

Benham, William. *St. John and His Work.* The Temple Series of Bible Handbooks. Philadelphia: J. B. Lippincott, 1902.

Broomfield, Gerald Webb. *John, Peter, and the Fourth Gospel.* New York: Macmillan, 1934.

Culross, James. *John, Whom Jesus Loved.* New York: Robert Carter and Brothers, 1878.

Dallmann, William. *John: Disciple, Evangelist, Apostle.* St. Louis: Concordia, 1932.

Eller, Vernard. *The Beloved Disciple: His Name, His Story, His Thought.* Grand Rapids: Wm. B. Eerdmans, 1987.

Fouard, Constant Henri. *Saint John and the Close of the Apostolic Age.* New York: Longman, Green, and Co., 1906.

Gloag, Paton James. *The Life of St. John.* Bible Class Primers. Edinburgh: T. and T. Clark, 1891.

Griffith-Thomas, W. H. *The Apostle John: Studies in His Life and Writings.* 1923. Reprint. Grand Rapids: Wm. B. Eerdmans, 1946.

Hayes, Doremus Almy. *John and His Writings.* New York: The Methodist Book Concern, 1917.

Hemleben, Johannes. *Johannes der Evangelist.* Reinbek bei Hamburg: Rowohlt Taschenbuch Verlag, 1972.

Krenkel, Max. *Apostel Johannes.* Berlin: F. Henschel, 1871.

Larfield, Wilhelm. *Die beiden Johannes von Ephesus, der Apostel und der Presbyter, der Lehrer und der Schüler: Ein Beitrag zur Erklärung des Papias Fragments bei Eusebius.* Munich: C. H. Beck, 1914.

Lenski, R. C. H. *Saint John.* Columbus, Ohio: The Book Concern, 1928.

Llwyd, John Plummer Derwent. *Son of Thunder: A Study of the Life and Work of John of Bethsaida, Fisher of Men.* New York: Ray Long and Richard R. Smith, 1932.

Luthardt, Christoph Ernst. *St. John the Author of the Fourth Gospel.* Revised and translated by C. R. Gregory. Edinburgh: T. and T. Clark, 1875.

330

McDonald, James M. *The Life and Writings of St. John.* New York: Scribner, Armstrong, and Co., 1877.

Robertson, A. T. *Epochs in the Life of the Apostle John.* New York: Fleming H. Revell, 1935.

Scott-Moncrieff, C. E. *St. John: Apostle, Evangelist and Prophet.* London: James Nisbet, 1909.

Stalker, James. *The Two St. Johns of the New Testament.* New York: American Tract Society, 1895.

Trench, Francis. *The Life and Character of St. John the Evangelist.* London: Longman, Brown, Green, and Longmans, 1850.

RELATED WORKS

Abogunrin, S. O. "Three Variant Accounts of Peter's Call: A Critical and Theological Examination of the Texts." *New Testament Studies* 31 (1985): 587–602.

Achtemeier, Paul J. *Mark.* Proclamation Commentaries. 2d ed. Philadelphia: Fortress Press, 1986.

———. "Toward the Isolation of Pre-Markan Miracle Catenae." *Journal of Biblical Literature* 89 (1970): 265–91.

Adler, Ada, ed. *Suidae Lexicon.* Vol. 1 of *Lexicographi Graeci.* Sammlung wissenschaftlicher Commentare. Stuttgart: Verlag B. G. Teubner, 1967.

Aland, Kurt, and Barbara Aland. *The Text of the New Testament.* Translated by E. F. Rhodes. Grand Rapids: Wm. B. Eerdmans, 1987.

Albertson, Clinton, S. J. *Anglo-Saxon Saints and Heroes.* New York: Fordham University Press, 1967.

Allberry, C. R. C., ed. *Manichaean Psalm-Book.* 2 vols. Manichaean Manuscripts in the Chester Beatty Collection. Stuttgart: W. Kohlhammer, 1938.

Andersen, J. Vikjaer. "L'apôtre Saint-Jean grand-prêtre." *Studia Theologica* 19 (1965): 22–29.

Arav, Rami, and John J. Rosseau. "Elusive Bethsaida Recovered." *The Fourth R* 4 (January 1991): 1–4.

Armstrong, A. Joseph, ed. *Letters of Robert Browning to Miss Isa Blagden.* Waco, Tex: Baylor University Press, 1923.

Attridge, Harold W., and George W. MacRae, S.J. "The Gospel of Truth." In *Nag Hammadi Codex I (The Jung Codex),* edited by Harold W. Attridge, 55–122. Nag Hammadi Studies 22. Leiden: E. J. Brill, 1985.

———. "The Gospel of Truth (I,3 and XII,2)." In *The Nag Hammadi Library,* 2d ed., edited by James M. Robinson, 38–51. San Francisco: Harper and Row, 1988.

Augustine, Saint. *St. Augustine: Tractates on the Gospel of John 1–10.* Translated by John W. Retting. Fathers of the Church 78. Washington, D.C.: Catholic University of America Press, 1988.

Aune, David E. "The Prophetic Circle of John of Patmos and the Exegesis of Revelation 22:16." *Journal for the Study of the New Testament* 37 (1989): 103–16.

———. "The Social Matrix of the Apocalypse of John." *Biblical Research* 26 (1981): 16–32.

Aus, R. D. "Three Pillars and Three Patriarchs: A Proposal Concerning Gal 2:9." *Zeitschrift für die neutestamentliche Wissenschaft* 70 (1979): 252–61.

Bacon, Benjamin Wisner. "The Authoress of Revelation—A Conjecture." *Harvard Theological Review* 23 (July 1930): 235–50.

———. "Date and Habitat of the Elders of Papias." *Zeitschrift für die neutestamentliche Wissenschaft* 12 (1911): 176–87.

———. "The Elder John, Papias, Irenaeus, Eusebius and the Syriac Translator." *Journal of Biblical Literature* 27 (1908): 1–23.

———. "The Elder John in Jerusalem." *Zeitschrift für die neutestamentliche Wissenschaft* 26 (1927): 187–202.

———. "The Elder of Ephesus and the Elder John." *The Hibbert Journal* 26 (1927): 112–34.

———. *The Fourth Gospel in Research and Debate.* London: T. Fisher Unwin, 1910.

———. *An Introduction to the New Testament.* London: Macmillan, 1900.

———. "John and the Pseudo-Johns." *Zeitschrift für die neutestamentliche Wissenschaft* 31 (1932): 132–50.

———. "Marcion, Papias, and 'the Elders.'" *Journal of Theological Studies* 23 (1921–1922): 134–60.

———. "The Mythical 'Elder John' of Ephesus." *The Hibbert Journal* 29 (1931): 312–26.

Badger, Kingsbury. "'See the Christ Stand!': Browning's Religion." In *Robert Browning: A Collection of Critical Essays.* Ed. Philip Drew, 72–95. London: Methuen, 1966.

Bailey, John Amedee. *The Traditions Common to the Gospels of Luke and John.* Supplements to Novum Testamentum 7. Leiden: E. J. Brill, 1963.

Baran, Musa. *Ephesus and Its Surroundings.* Trans. Hulya Terzioglu. Izmir: Molay Matbaacilik, n.d.

Barnard, L. W. *Justin Martyr: His Life and Thought.* Cambridge: Cambridge University Press, 1967.

Baron, Salo Wittmayer. *A Social and Religious History of the Jews.* New York: Columbia University Press, 1952.

Barrett, C. K. *The Gospel According to St. John.* 2d ed. Philadelphia: Westminster Press, 1978.

———. "Paul and the 'Pillar' Apostles." In *Studia Paulina in honorem Johannis de Zwaan,* 1–19. Haarlem: Erven F. Bohn N.V., 1953.

———. "The Theological Vocabulary of the Fourth Gospel and the Gospel of Truth." In *Current Issues in New Testament Interpretation: Essays in Honor of Otto A. Piper,* edited by W. Klassen and G. F. Snyder, 210–24. New York: Harper and Row, 1962.

Bartlet, J. Vernon. "Papias's 'Exposition': Its Date and Contents." In *Amicitiae Corolla: A Volume of Essays Presented to James Rendel Harris,* edited by H. G. Wood, 15–44. London: University of London Press, 1933.

Bauer, Walter. *A Greek-English Lexicon of the New Testament and Other Early Christian Literature.* 2d ed. Revised by Frederick W. Danker. Translated and edited by William F. Arndt and F. Wilbur Gingrich. Chicago: University of Chicago Press, 1979.

Bean, George E. *Aegean Turkey: An Archaeological Guide.* New York: F. A. Praeger, 1966.

Beasley-Murray, George R. *The Book of Revelation.* New Century Bible. Greenwood, S.C.: Attic Press, 1974.

————. *John.* Word Biblical Commentary, vol. 36. Waco, Texas: Word Books, 1987.

Beattie, D. R. G. "Boanerges: A Semiticist's Solution." *Irish Biblical Studies* 5 (1983): 11–13.

Beck, Brian E. "'Imitatio Christi' and the Lucan Passion Narrative." In *Suffering and Martyrdom in the New Testament,* edited by W. Horbury and B. McNeil, 28–47. Cambridge: Cambridge University Press, 1981.

Beckwith, I. T. "The Two Johns of the Asian Church." In *The Apocalypse of John,* 362–93. London: Macmillan, 1919.

Bellinzoni, A. J. *The Sayings of Jesus in the Writings of Justin Martyr.* Supplements to Novum Testamentum 17. Leiden: E. J. Brill, 1967.

Bernard, J. H. "The Traditions as to the Death of John, the Son of Zebedee." In *Studia Sacra,* 260–84. London: Hodder and Stoughton, 1917.

Best, Ernest. *Following Jesus: Discipleship in the Gospel of Mark.* Journal for the Study of the New Testament, Supplement Series 4. Sheffield: JSOT Press, 1981.

————. "Mark's Use of the Twelve." *Zeitschrift für die neutestamentliche Wissenschaft* 69 (1978): 11–35.

————. "The Role of the Disciples in Mark." *New Testament Studies* 23 (1976–1977): 377–401.

Best, Thomas F. "The Transfiguration: A Select Bibliography." *Journal of the Evangelical Theology Society* 24 (1981): 157–61.

Betz, Hans Dieter. *Galatians.* Hermeneia. Philadelphia: Fortress Press, 1979.

Betz, Otto. "Donnersöhne, Menschenfischer und der davidische Messias." *Revue de Qumran* 3 (1961): 41–70.

Bishop, E. F. F. "Jesus and the Lake." *Catholic Biblical Quarterly* 13 (1951): 398–414.

Bodenheimer, F. S. "Fish." In *Interpreter's Dictionary of the Bible* 2:272–73. Nashville: Abingdon Press, 1962.

Böcher, Otto. "Johanneisches in der Apokalypse des Johannes." *New Testament Studies* 27 (1981): 310–21.

————. "Das Verhältnis der Apokalypse des Johannes zum Evangelium des Johannes." In *L'Apocalypse johannique et l'Apocalyptique dans le Nouveau Testament,* 289–301. Bibliotheca Ephemeridum Theologicarum Lovaniensium 53. Louvain: Louvain University Press, 1980.

Bonnet, Maximilianus. *Acta Apostolorum Apocrypha.* 1898. Reprint. Hildesheim: Georg Olms Verlagsbuchhandlung, 1959.

Bonsack, Bernhard. "Der Presbyteros des dritten Briefs und der geliebte Jünger des Evangeliums nach Johannes." *Zeitschrift für die neutestamentliche Wissenschaft* 79 (1988): 45–62.

Boobyer, G. H. "St. Mark and the Transfiguration." *Journal of Theological Studies* 41 (1940): 119–40.

————. *St. Mark and the Transfiguration Story.* Edinburgh: T. and T. Clark, 1942.

Bovon, François, et al. *Les actes apocryphes des apôtres: Christianisme et monde païen.* Geneva: Labor et Fides, 1981.

Braun, François-Marie. *Jean le théologien et son évangile dans l'église ancienne.* 3 vols. Paris: J. Gabalda, 1959.

Brodie, Thomas L. *The Gospel According to John: A Literary and Theological Commentary.* New York: Oxford University Press, 1993.

Brooke, A. E. *The Johannine Epistles.* International Critical Commentary. Edinburgh: T. and T. Clark, 1912.

Broomfield, George Welele. *John, Peter and the Fourth Gospel.* New York: Macmillan, 1934.

Brown, Raymond E. *The Community of the Beloved Disciple.* New York: Paulist Press, 1979.

———. *The Epistles of John.* Anchor Bible 30. Garden City: Doubleday, 1982.

———. *The Gospel According to John.* 2 vols. Anchor Bible 29 and 29a. Garden City: Doubleday, 1966–1970.

Brownrigg, Ronald. *The Twelve Apostles.* New York: Macmillan, 1974.

Bruce, F. F. *The Acts of the Apostles.* Grand Rapids: Wm. B. Eerdmans, 1951.

———. *Peter, Stephen, James, and John: Studies in Early Non-Pauline Christianity.* Grand Rapids: Wm. B. Eerdmans, 1979.

———. "St. John at Ephesus." *Bulletin of the John Rylands University Library* 60 (1978): 339–61.

Bruns, J. Edgar. "John Mark: A Riddle within the Johannine Enigma." *Scripture* 15 (1963): 88–92.

———. "The Confusion between John and John Mark in Antiquity." *Scripture* 17 (1965): 23–26.

Bryne, Brendan. "The Faith of the Beloved Disciple and the Community in John 20." *Journal for the Study of the New Testament* 23 (1985): 83–97.

Buchanan, George Wesley. "Jesus and the Upper Class." *Novum Testamentum* 7 (1964): 195–209.

Budge, Ernest A. Wallis. *The Contendings of the Apostles.* 2 vols. 1901. Reprint. Amsterdam: Apa-Philo Press, 1976.

———. *Coptic Apocrypha in the Dialect of Upper Egypt.* London: British Museum, 1913.

Bultmann, Rudolf. *The Gospel of John: A Commentary.* Translated and edited by G. R. Beasley-Murray et al. Philadelphia: Westminster Press, 1971.

———. *The History of the Synoptic Tradition.* Revised, edited, and translated by John Marsh. New York: Harper and Row, 1963.

Buth, Randall. "Mark 3:17 *BONEREGEM* and Popular Etymology." *Journal for the Study of the New Testament* 10 (1981): 29–33.

Caird, G. B. *The Revelation of St. John the Divine.* Black's New Testament Commentaries. London: Adam and Charles Black, 1966.

Cameron, Ron. *Sayings Traditions in the Apocryphon of James.* Philadelphia: Fortress Press, 1984.

Carlston, C. E. "Transfiguration and Resurrection." *Journal of Biblical Literature* 80 (1961): 233–40.

Carson, D. A. *The Gospel According to John.* Grand Rapids: Wm. B. Eerdmans, 1991.

Chabot, J.-B. *Chronique de Michel le Syrien Patriarche Jacobite d'Antioche (1166–1199).* 1899. Reprint. Brussels: Culture et Civilisation, 1963.

Chapman, L. John. *John the Presbyter and the Fourth Gospel.* Oxford: Clarendon Press, 1911.

Charles, R. H. *The Revelation of St. John.* 2 vols. International Critical Commentary. Edinburgh: T. and T. Clark, 1920.

Chatzidakis, Manolis. *Icons of Patmos: Question of Byzantine and Post-Byzantine Painting.* Athens: National Bank of Greece, 1985.

Chilton, Bruce D. "The Transfiguration: Dominical Assurance and Apostolic Vision." *New Testament Studies* 27 (1980): 115–24.

Chrysologus, Peter. *Saint Peter Chrysologus, Selected Sermons, and Saint Valerians, Homilies.* Translated by George E. Ganss, S.J. Fathers of the Church 17. New York: Fathers of the Church, 1953.

Clement of Alexandria, *Clement d'Alexandrie, Extraits de Théodote.* Translated by François Sagnard. Paris: Éditions du Cerf, 1948.

Colgrove, Bertram, trans. *The Life of Bishop Wilfrid by Eddius Stephanus.* Cambridge: Cambridge University Press, 1927.

Collins, Adela Yarbro. *Crisis and Catharsis: The Power of the Apocalypse.* Philadelphia: Westminster Press, 1984.

Colson, Jean. *L'Énigme du disciple que Jésus aimait.* Théologie historique 10. Paris: Beauchesne, 1969.

Connolly, R. H. "The Diatessaron in the Syriac Acts of John." *Journal of Theological Studies* 8 (1906–1907): 571–81.

———. "The Original Language of the Syriac Acts of John." *Journal of Theological Studies* 8 (1906–1907): 249–61.

Conybeare, Fred C. "Ein Zeugnis Ephräms über das Fehlen von c. 1 und 2 im Texte des Lucas." *Zeitschrift für die neutestamentliche Wissenschaft* 3 (1902): 192–97.

Corbo, Virgilio. *The House of St. Peter at Capharnaum.* Translated by S. Saller. Publications of the Studium Biblicum Franciscanum, 5. Jerusalem: Franciscan Printing Press, 1972.

Corbo, Virgil, and Stanislaus Loffredda. *New Memoirs of Saint Peter by the Sea of Galilee.* Translated by G. Bushell. Jerusalem: Franciscan Printing Press, n.d.

Cribbs, F. Lamar. "The Agreements that Exist between John and Acts." In *Perspectives on Luke-Acts,* edited by Charles H. Talbert, 40–61. Special Studies Series 5. Danville, Va.: Association of Baptist Professors of Religion, 1978.

———. "St. Luke and the Johannine Tradition." *Journal of Biblical Literature* 90 (1971), 422–50.

Cullmann, Oscar. *The Johannine Circle.* Translated by John Bowden. Philadelphia: Westminster Press, 1976.

Culpepper, R. Alan. *1, 2, 3 John.* Knox Preaching Guides. Atlanta: John Knox Press, 1985.

———. "Guessing Points and Knowing Stars: History and Higher Criticism in Robert Browning's 'A Death in the Desert.'" In *The Future of Christology: Essays in Honor of Leander E. Keck,* edited by Abraham J. Malherbe and Wayne A. Meeks, 53–65. Minneapolis: Fortress Press, 1993.

———. *The Johannine School: An Evaluation of the Johannine-School Hypothesis Based on an Investigation of the Nature of Ancient Schools.* SBL Dissertation Series 26. Missoula, Mont.: Scholars Press, 1975.

Cyril, Saint. *The Works of Saint Cyril of Jerusalem.* 2 vols. Translated by Leo P.McCauley and Anthony A. Stephenson. Fathers of the Church 61. Washington, D.C.: Catholic University of America Press, 1969.

Dalman, Gustaf. *Sacred Sites and Ways: Studies in the Topography of the Gospels.* Translated by Paul P. Levertoff. London: S.P.C.K., 1935.

Danby, Herbert, trans. *The Mishnah.* London: Oxford University Press, 1933.

Dauer, Anton. "Das Wort des Gekreuzigten an seine Mutter und den "Jünger, den er liebte: Eine traditionsgeschichtliche und theologische Untersuchung zu Joh 19, 25–27." *Biblische Zeitschrift* 12 (1968): 80–93.

Davey, D. M. "Justin Martyr and the Fourth Gospel." *Scripture* 17 (1965): 117–22.

De Boor, C. "Neue Fragmente des Papias, Hegesippus und Pierius in bisher unbekannten Excerpten aus der Kirchengeschichte des Philippus Sidetes." *Texte und Untersuchungen* 5 (1888): 165–84.

De Bruyne, Donatien. "Les plus anciens prologues latins des évangiles." *Revue Benedictine* 40 (1928): 193–214.

Delehaye, H. *The Legends of the Saints: An Introduction to Hagiography.* Translated by V. M. Crawford. New York: Longman, Green, and Co., 1907.

———. *Synaxarium Ecclesiae Constantinopolitanae.* Brussels: Socios Bollandianos, 1902.

Devreesse, Robert. *Essai sur Théodore de Mopsueste.* Studi e Testi 141. Città del Vaticano: Biblioteca Apostolica Vaticana, 1948.

Dibelius, Martin. *From Tradition to Gospel.* Translated by Bertram Lee Woolf. London: Ivor Nicholson and Watson, 1934.

———. "Papias." In *Religion in Geschichte und Gegenwart* 4:892–93. 2d ed. 5 vols. Edited by Hermann Gunkel and Leopold Zscharnack. Tübingen: J. C. B. Mohr, 1927—31.

Diekamp, Franz., ed. *Hippolytus von Theben.* 4th ed. Texte und Untersuchungen. Münster: D. Aschendorff, 1898.

Dietrich, Wolfgang. *Das Petrusbild der lukanischen Schriften.* Beiträge zur Wissenschaft vom Alten und Neuen Testament 94. Stuttgart: W. Kohlhammer, 1972.

Dittenberger, Wilhelmus, ed. *Orientis Graeci Inscriptiones Selectae.* Lipsiae: S. Hirzel, 1905.

Dix, G. H. "The Use and Abuse of Papias on the Fourth Gospel." *Theology* 24 (1932): 8–20.

Dodd, C. H. "The Appearances of the Risen Christ: An Essay in Form-Criticism of the Gospels." In *Studies in the Gospels: Essays in Memory of R. H. Lightfoot,* edited by D. E. Nineham, 9–35. Oxford: Basil Blackwell, 1955.

———. "The First Epistle of John and the Fourth Gospel." *Bulletin of the John Rylands University Library* 21 (1937): 129–56.

———. *Historical Tradition in the Fourth Gospel.* Cambridge: Cambridge University Press, 1963.

———. *The Johannine Epistles.* Moffatt New Testament Commentary. London: Hodder and Stoughton, 1946.

Donahue, John R. "Tax Collectors and Sinners: An Attempt at an Identification." *Catholic Biblical Quarterly* 33 (1971): 39–61.

Draper, H. Mudie. "The Disciple Whom Jesus Loved." *Expository Times* 32 (1920–1921): 428–29.

Drum, W. "The Disciple Known to the High Priest." *Expository Times* 25 (1913–14): 381–82.

Drummond, James. *An Inquiry into the Character and Authorship of the Fourth Gospel.* London: Williams and Norgate, 1903.

Duchesne, L. *Christian Worship, Its Origin and Evolution: A Study of the Latin Liturgy up to the Time of Charlemagne.* 5th ed. Translated by M. L. McClure. London: Society for Promoting Christian Knowledge, 1949.

Duling, Dennis C. *Jesus Christ through History.* New York: Harcourt Brace Jovanovich, 1979.

Duncan, J. Garrow. "The Sea of Tiberias and Its Environs." *The Palestine Exploration Fund Quarterly* (1926): 15–22.

Dunkel, P. Franz. "Die Fischerei am See Gennesareth und das Neue Testament." *Biblica* 5 (1924): 375–90.

Dupont-Sommer, A. *The Essene Writings from Qumran.* Translated by Geza Vermes. Cleveland: World Publishing Co., 1961.

Eckhardt, Karl August. *Der Tod des Johannes als Schlüssel zum Verständnis des johanneischen Schriften.* Studien zur Rechts- und Religionsgeschichte 3. Berlin: De Gruyter, 1961.

Edwards, Hubert Edwin. *The Disciple Who Wrote These Things: A New Inquiry into the Origins and Historical Value of the Gospel According to St. John.* London: J. Clarke, 1953.

Eisler, Robert. *The Enigma of the Fourth Gospel.* London: Methuen, 1938.

Eller, Vernard. *The Beloved Disciple: His Name, His Story, His Thought. Two Studies from the Gospel of John.* Grand Rapids: Wm. B. Eerdmans, 1987.

Ellis, F. S., ed. *The Golden Legend or Lives of the Saints as Englished by William Caxton.* 7 vols. London: J. M. Dent and Sons, 1900.

Emminghaus, Johannes H. *St. John the Apostle.* Text of story and legend by Leonhard Küppers. The Saints in Legend and Art, vol. 13. Trans. Hans Hermann Rosenwald. Recklinghausen: Aurel Bongers, 1967.

Enslin, M. S. "John, Acts of." In *Interpreter's Dictionary of the Bible* 2:930–32. Nashville: Abingdon Press, 1962.

Epiphanius, Saint. *The Panarion of Epiphanius of Salamis.* Translated by Frank Williams. Nag Hammadi Studies 35. Leiden: E. J. Brill, 1987.

———. *The Panarion of St. Epiphanius, Bishop of Salamis: Selected Passages.* Translated and editied by Philip R. Amidon, S.J. New York: Oxford University Press, 1990.

Epstein, Isidore, ed. *The Babylonian Talmud.* 35 vols. London: Soncino Press, 1935– 60.

Erbes, C. "Der Apostel Johannes und der Jünger, welcher an der Brust des Herrn lag." *Zeitschrift für Kirchengeschichte* 33 (1912): 159–239.

Etheridge, Wayne. "John, His Life and Times." *Biblical Illustrator* 4 (Winter 1978): 53–58.

Eusebius of Caesarea. *Eusebius Werke, 5: Die Chronik.* Edited by Josef Karst. Griechischen christlichen Schriftsteller. Leipzig: J. C. Hinrichs'sche Buchhandlung, 1911.

———. *Eusebius Werke, 7: Die Chronik des Hieronymous,* ed. Rudolf Helm. Grischischen christlichen Schriftsteller, 47. Berlin: Akademie-Verlag, 1956.

————. *Eusebius: Ecclesiastical History.* Translated by Kirsopp Lake. Loeb Classical Library. 2 vols. Cambridge, Mass.: Harvard University Press, 1926.

Farmer, David Hugh. *The Oxford Dictionary of Saints.* 2d ed. New York: Oxford University Press, 1987.

Faure, Alexander. "Das 4. Evangelium im muratorischen Fragment." *Zeitschrift für systematische Theologie* 19 (1942): 143–149.

Feltoe, C. L. "St John and St James in Western 'Non-Roman' Calendars." *Journal of Theological Studies* 10 (1909): 589–92.

Ferguson, John. "Philippians, John and the Traditions of Ephesus." *Expository Times* 83 (1971): 85–87.

Feuillet, A. "La coupe et le baptême de la passion (Mc, x, 35–40; cf. Mt, xx, 20–23; Lc, xii, 50)." *Revue biblique* 74 (1967): 356–91.

Filson, Floyd V. "Who Was the Beloved Disciple?" *Journal of Biblical Literature* 68 (1949): 83–88.

Finegan, Jack. *The Archaeology of the New Testament: The Life of Jesus and the Beginning of the Early Church.* Princeton: Princeton University Press, 1969.

Fitzmyer, Joseph A. *The Gospel According to Luke.* 2 vols. Anchor Bible 28 and 28a. Garden City: Doubleday, 1981–1985.

Foerster, Werner. *Gnosis: A Selection of Gnostic Texts.* Translated and edited by R. McL. Wilson. Oxford: Clarendon Press, 1972.

Foss, Clive. *Ephesos after Antiquity.* Cambridge: Cambridge University Press, 1979.

Freyne, Seán. *Galilee from Alexander the Great to Hadrian, 323 B.C.E. to 135 C.E.: A Study of Second Temple Judaism.* Wilmington, Del.: Michael Glazier, 1980.

————. *The Twelve: Disciples and Apostles, A Study in the Theology of the First Three Gospels.* London: Sheed and Ward, 1968.

Fricke, Donna G. "'A Death in the Desert': The Gospel According to Robert Browning." In *Aeolian Harps: Essays in Literature in Honor of Maurice Browning Cramer,* edited by Donna G. Fricke and Douglas C. Fricke, 167–78. Bowling Green, Ohio: Bowling Green University Press, 1976.

Fuller, Reginald H. *The Formation of the Resurrection Narratives.* 2d ed. Philadelphia: Fortress Press, 1980.

Galbiati, J. ed. *Iohannis Evangelium apocryphorum arabice.* 2 vols. Milan: In aedious Mondadorianis, 1957.

Gardner, Percy. *The Ephesian Gospel.* London: Williams and Norgate, 1915.

Garvie, Alfred E. *The Beloved Disciple.* London: Hodder and Stoughton, 1922.

Geerard, Maurice. *Clavis Apocryphorum.* Turnhout: Brepols, 1992.

Ginzberg, Louis. *The Legends of the Jews.* Philadelphia: Jewish Publication Society of America, 1968.

Godet, Frederic Louis. *Commentary on John's Gospel.* 1886. Reprint. Grand Rapids: Kregel Publications, 1978.

Goodenough, E. R. *The Theology of Justin Martyr.* Jena: Verlag Frommannsche Buchhandlung, 1923.

Goodspeed, Edgar J. *Die ältesten Apologeten.* Göttingen: Vandenhoeck and Ruprecht, 1914.

Grant, Robert M. *Gnosticism.* New York: Harper and Brothers, 1961.

————. "The Oldest Gospel Prologues." *Anglican Theological Review* 23 (1941): 231–45.

————. *Second-Century Christianity: A Collection of Fragments.* London: S.P.C.K., 1946.

Grayston, Kenneth. *The Johannine Epistles.* New Century Bible. Grand Rapids: Wm. B. Eerdmans, 1984.

Griffith, B. Grey. "The Disciple Whom Jesus Loved." *Expository Times* 32 (1920–1921): 379–381.

Gruber, William. "Temporal Perspectives in Robert Browning's *A Death in the Desert.*" *Victorian Poetry* 17, no. 4 (Winter 1979): 329–42. \

Gunther, John J. "Early Identifications of Authorship of the Johannine Writings." *Journal of Ecclesiastical History* 31 (1980): 407–27.

————. "The Elder John, Author of Revelation." *Journal for the Study of the New Testament* 11 (1981): 3–20.

Haenchen, Ernst. *The Acts of the Apostles: A Commentary.* Philadelphia: Westminster Press, 1971.

————. *John.* 2 vols. Translated and edited by Robert W. Funk. Hermeneia. Philadelphia: Fortress Press, 1984.

Hall, Stuart G. *Melito of Sardis: On Pascha and Fragments.* Oxford: Clarendon Press, 1979.

Harnack, Adolf von. "Die ältesten Evangelien-prologe und die Bildung des Neuen Testaments." In *Sitzungsberichte der preussischen Akademie der Wissenschaften,* 322–41. Philosophisch-historische Klasse, 24. Berlin: G. Reimer, 1928.

Harrison, Roland K. "Fish." In *International Standard Bible Encyclopedia,* 2:308–09. Grand Rapids: Wm. B. Eerdmans, 1982.

Hawkin, David J. "The Function of the Beloved Disciple Motif in the Johannine Redaction." *Laval Theologique et Philosophique* 33 (1977): 133–50.

Hay, David M. "Paul's Indifference to Authority." *Journal of Biblical Literature* 88 (1969): 36–44.

Heard, R. G. "The Oldest Gospel Prologues." *Journal of Theological Studies* n.s., 6 (1955): 1–16.

Heitmueller, Wilhelm. "Zur Johannes-Tradition." *Zeitschrift für die neutestamentliche Wissenschaft* 15 (1914): 189–209.

Hengel, Martin. *Die johanneische Frage.* Wissenschaftliche Untersuchungen zum Neuen Testament, 67. Tübingen: J. C. B. Mohr, 1993.

————. *The Johannine Question.* Translated by John Bowden. Philadelphia: Trinity Press International, 1989.

————. *The Charismatic Leader and His Followers.* Translated by James Greig. New York: Crossroad, 1981.

Hennecke, Edgar. *New Testament Apocrypha.* 2 vols. Edited by Wilhelm Schneemelcher. Translated by R. McL. Wilson. Philadelphia: Westminster Press, 1963–1965.

Heracleon. *The Fragments of Heracleon.* Edited by A. E. Brooke. Texts and Studies 1, no. 4. Cambridge: Cambridge University Press, 1891.

Herder, Johann Gottfried. *Herder's Werke.* 5 vols. Bibliothek Deutscher Klassiker. Berlin: Aufbau-Verlag, 1969.

Hester, James D. "The Use and Influence of Rhetoric in Galatians 2:1–14." *Theologische Zeitschrift* 42 (1986): 386–408.

Hicks, E. L. *Priene, Iasos, and Ephesos.* Vol. 3 of *The Collection of Ancient Greek Inscriptions in the British Museum.* Edited by C. T. Newton. Oxford: Clarendon Press, 1890.

Hillmer, M. R. "The Gospel of John in the Second Century." Th.D. diss., Harvard Divinity School, 1966.

Hills, Julian. *Tradition and Composition in the Epistula Apostolorum.* Harvard Dissertations in Religion 24. Minneapolis: Fortress Press, 1990.

Holl, Karl. *Epiphanius (Ancoratus und Panarion).* Die griechischen christlichen Schriftsteller der ersten drei Jahrhunderte. Leipzig: J. C. Hinrischs'sche Buchhandlung, 1933.

Holtzmann, H. J. "Das Problem des ersten johanneischen Briefes in seinem Verhältnis zum Evangelium." *Jahrbücher für protestantische Theologie* 7 (1881): 690–712; 8 (1882): 128–52, 316–42, 460–85.

Holweck, Frederick George. *A Biographical Dictionary of the Saints.* St. Louis: B. Herder Book Co., 1924.

Horstmann, Maria. *Studien zur markinischen Christologie.* Münster: Aschendorff, 1969.

Howard, Wilbert Francis. "The Anti-Marcionite Prologues to the Gospels." *Expository Times* 47 (1936): 534–38.

———. "The Common Authorship of the Johannine Gospel and Epistles." *Journal of Theological Studies* 48 (1947): 12–25.

Hunt, Arthur S., and J. Gilbart Smyly, eds. *The Tebtunis Papyri.* 3 vols. London: Oxford University Press, 1933.

Hyde, Virginia. "Robert Browning's Inverted Optic Glass in *A Death in the Desert.*" *Victorian Poetry* 23, no. 1 (Spring 1985): 93–96.

———. "The Fallible Parchment: Structure in Robert Browning's *A Death in the Desert.*" *Victorian Poetry* 12, no.2 (1974): 125–35.

Jackson, H. Latimer. *The Problem of the Fourth Gospel.* Cambridge: Cambridge University Press, 1918.

James, Montague Rhodes. *The Apocalypse in Art: The Schweich Lectures of the British Academy 1927.* London: The British Academy, 1931.

———. *The Apocryphal New Testament.* Oxford: Clarendon Press, 1953.

Jameson, Anna. *Sacred and Legendary Art.* 2 vols. Boston: Houghton Mifflin, 1900.

Jaschke, H. J. "Das Johannesevangelium und die Gnosis im Zeugnis des Irenaeus von Lyon." *Münchener theologische Zeitschrift* 29 (1978): 337–76.

Jerome, Saint. *The Homilies of Saint Jerome.* Translated by Marie Liguori Ewald. Fathers of the Church 57. Washington, D.C.: Catholic University Press of America, 1966.

———. *S. Hieronymi Presbyteri Opera.* Corpus Christianorum, Series Latina 77. Turnhout: Brepols, 1969.

———. *Saint Jerome: Dogmatic and Polemical Works.* Translated by John N. Hritzu. Fathers of the Church 53. Washington, D.C.: Catholic University of America Press, 1965.

Johnson, Lewis. "Who Was the Beloved Disciple?" *Expository Times* 77 (1966): 157–58.

———. "The Beloved Disciple—A Reply." *Expository Times* 77 (1966): 380.

Johnson, N. E. "The Beloved Disciple and the Fourth Gospel." *Church Quarterly Review* 167 (1966): 278–91.

Jones, A. H. M. *The Greek City from Alexander to Justinian.* Oxford: Clarendon Press, 1940.

Jonge, Marinus de. "The Beloved Disciple and the Date of the Gospel of John." In *Text and Interpretation. Studies in the New Testament presented to Matthew Black,* edited by E. Best and R. McL. Wilson, 99–114. New York: Cambridge University Press, 1979.

Josephus. *Josephus.* Translated by H. St. J. Thackeray, et al. Loeb Classical Library. 10 vols. Cambridge, Mass: Harvard University Press, 1926–1981.

Junod, Eric. "La virginité de l'apôtre Jean: recereche sur les origines scripturaires et patristiques de cette tradition." In *Lectures anciennes de la Bible,* 113–36. Cahiers de Biblia Patristica 1. Strasbourg: Centre d'analyse et de documentation patristiques, 1987.

Junod, Eric, and Jean-Daniel Kaestli. *L'histoire des actes apocryphes des apôtres du IIIe au IXe siècle: le cas des Actes de Jean.* Cahiers de las Revue de théologie et de philosophie, 7. Geneva: Revue de théologie et de philosophie, 1982.

———, eds. *Acta Iohannis.* 2 vols. Corpus Christianorum. Turnhout: Brepols, 1983.

Kaestli, Jean-Daniel. "L'exégèse valentienne du quatrième évangile." In *La communauté johannique et son histoire,* edited by Jean-Daniel Kaestli, Jean-Michel Poffet, and Jean Zumstein, 323–50. Le monde de la Bible. Geneva: Labor et Fides, 1990.

———. "Le mystère de la croix de lumière et le johannisme. Actes de Jean ch. 94–102." *Foi et Vie* 86 (1987): 35–46.

———. "Le rapport entre les deux Vies latines de l'apôtre Jean." In *Apocrypha 3* (1992).

———. "Le rôle des textes bibliques dans la genèse et le développement des légendes apocryphes: Le cas du sort final de l'apôtre Jean." *Augustinianum* 23, nos. 1–2 (1983): 319–36.

Keck, Leander E., ed. *The Christ of Faith and the Jesus of History: A Critique of Schleiermacher's Life of Jesus by David Friedrich Strauss.* Lives of Jesus Series. Philadelphia: Fortress Press, 1977.

Keil, J. "XIII Vorlaüfiger Bericht über die Ausgrabungen in Ephesus." *Jahreshefte des österreichischen archäologischen Instituts in Wien* 24 (1929), Beiblatt, cols. 8–67.

———. "XIV Vorläufiger Bericht über die Ausgrabungen in Ephesus." *Jahreshefte des österreichischen archäologischen Instituts in Wien* 25 (1929), Beiblatt, cols. 5–52.

———. "Die Wiederauffindung des Johannesgrabes in Ephesus." *Biblica* 13 (1932), 121ff.

Kelber, Werner. "Mark 14:32–42: Gethsemane. Passion Christology and Discipleship Failure." *Zeitschrift für die neutestamentliche Wissenschaft* 63 (1972): 166–87.

Kenny, Anthony. "The Transfiguration and the Agony in the Garden." *Catholic Biblical Quarterly* 19 (1957): 444–52.

Kilpatrick, George Dunbar. "What John Tells About John." In *Studies in John Presented to Professor J. N. Sevenster on the Occasion of his Seventieth Birthday,* 75–87. Leiden: E. J. Brill, 1970.

Kittel. Gerhard and Gerhard Friedrich, ed. *Theological Dictionary of the New Testament.* 10 vols. Translated by G. Bromiley. Grand Rapids: Wm. B. Eerdmans, 1964–1976.

Klein, Günter. "Galater 2, 6–9 und die Geschichte der Jerusalemer Urgemeinde." *Zeitschrift für Theologie und Kirche* 57 (1960): 275–95.

Kline, Leslie L. *The Sayings of Jesus in the Pseudo-Clementine Homilies.* SBL Dissertation Series 14. Missoula, Mont.: Scholars Press, 1975.

Klopstock, Freidrich Gottlieb. *The Messiah.* Bungay: C. Brightly, 1808.

Koester, Helmut. *Ancient Christian Gospels: Their History and Development.* London: SCM Press; Philadelphia: Trinity Press International, 1990.

———. "History and Cult in the Gospel of John and in Ignatius." *Journal for Theology and the Church* 1 (1965): 111–23.

Kopp, Clemens. "Christian Sites Around the Sea of Galilee: II. Bethsaida and El-Minyeh," *Dominican Studies* 3 (1950): 10–40.

———. *The Holy Places of the Gospels.* Translated by Ronald Walls. Freiburg: Herder and Herder, 1963.

Kragerud, Alv. *Der Lieblingsjünger im Johannesevangelium.* Oslo: Universitätsverlag, 1959.

Krautheimer, Richard. *Early Christian and Byzantine Architecture.* 3d ed. Harmondsworth: Penguin Books, 1979.

Kügler, Joachim. *Der Jünger, den Jesus liebte: Literarische, theologische und historische Untersuchungen zu einer Schlüsselgestalt johanneischer Theologie und Geschichte. Mit einem Exkurs über die Brotrede in Joh 6.* Stuttgarter biblische Beiträge 16. Stuttgart: Verlag katholisches Bibelwerk, 1988.

Kümmel, W. G. *Introduction to the New Testament.* 17th ed. Translated by Howard Clark Kee. Nashville: Abingdon Press, 1975.

———. *The New Testament: The History of the Investigation of Its Problems.* Translated by S. McLean Gilmour and Howard C. Kee. Nashville: Abingdon Press, 1972.

Kürzinger, Josef. *Papias von Hierapolis und die Evangelien des Neuen Testaments.* Eichstätter Materialien 4. Regensburg: Verlag Friedrich Pustet, 1983.

———. "Papias von Hierapolis: Zu Titel und Art seines Werkes." *Biblische Zeitschrift* 23 (1979): 172–186.

Kuhn, Heinz-Wolfgang, and Rami Arav. "The Bethsaida Excavations: Historical and Archaeological Approaches." In *The Future of Early Christianity: Essays in Honor of Helmut Koester,* edited by Birger A. Pearson, 77–107. Minneapolis: Fortress Press, 1991.

Lagrange, M.-J. *Évangile selon Saint Jean.* 3d edition. Études bibliques. Paris: Librairie Victor Lecoffre, 1927.

Lake, Kirsopp, trans. *Apostolic Fathers.* Loeb Classical Library. 2 vols. Cambridge, Mass.: Harvard University Press, 1912–1913.

Lane, William L. *The Gospel According to Mark.* Grand Rapids: Wm. B. Eerdmans, 1974.

Larfield, Wilhelm. "Das Zeugnis des Papias über die beiden Johannes von Ephesus." In *Johannes und sein Evangelium*, edited by K. H. Rengstorf, 381–401. Darmstadt: Wissenschaftliche Buchgesellschaft, 1973.

Layton, Bentley. *The Gnostic Scriptures.* Garden City: Doubleday, 1987.

Lechner, Gregor Martin. "Johannes der Evangelist (der Theologe)." In *Lexikon der christlichen Ikonographie*, edited by Wolfgang Braunfels, 7:108–30. Rome: Herder, 1974.

Lee, G. M. "Eusebius, *H. E.* 3, 39, 4." *Biblica* 53 (1972): 412.

———. "The Presbyter John: A Reconsideration." In *Studia Evangelica, VI*, 311–20. Texte und Untersuchungen 112. Berlin: Akademie-Verlag, 1973.

Légasse, S. "Approche de l'épisode préévangélique des Fils de Zébédée (Marc x.35–40 par.)." *New Testament Studies* 20 (1974): 161–77.

Leloir, Louis. *Écrits apocryphes sur les apôtres: Traduction de l'édition arménienne de venise.* Corpus Christianorum. Turnhout: Brepols, 1986.

Lewis, Agnes Smith. *The Mythological Acts of the Apostles.* Horae Semiticae 4. London: C. J. Clay and Sons, 1904.

Lewis, Frank Warburton. "The Disciple Whom Jesus Loved." *Expository Times* 33 (1921–1922): 42.

Lieu, Judith. *The Second and Third Epistles of John: History and Background.* Edited by John Riches. Edinburgh: T. and T. Clark, 1986.

Lightfoot, Joseph Barber. *The Apostolic Fathers.* 2d ed. 5 vols. London: Macmillan, 1889.

———. "External Evidence for the Authenticity and Genuineness of St. John's Gospel." In *Biblical Essays,* edited by Joseph Barber Lightfoot, 47–122. London: Macmillan, 1904.

Lindars, Barnabas. *The Gospel of John.* New Century Bible. London: Oliphants, 1972.

Lippelt, Ernestus. *Quae Fuerint Justini Martyris Apomnemoneumata Quaque Ratione cum Forma Evangeliorum Syro-Latina Cehaeserint.* Halis Saxonum: E. Karras, 1901.

Lofthouse, William Frederick. *The Disciple Whom Jesus Loved.* London: Epworth, 1934.

Lohmeyer, Ernst. "Die Verklärung Jesu nach dem Markus-Evangelium." *Zeitschrift für die neutestamentliche Wissenschaft* 21 (1922): 185–215.

Longfellow, Henry Wadsworth. *The Poetical Works of Henry Wadsworth Longfellow.* Boston: Houghton Mifflin, 1902.

Lorenzen, Thorwald. *Die Lieblingsjünger im Johannesevangelium. Eine redaktionsgeschichtliche Studie.* Stuttgarter Bibelstudien 55. Stuttgart: Katholiches Bibelwerk, 1971.

Lowenich, Walther von. *Das Johannesverständnis im zweiten Jahrhundert.* Giessen: A. Töpelmann, 1932.

Lüdemann, Gerd. *Early Christianity According to the Traditions in Acts.* Minneapolis: Fortress Press, 1989.

———. "Zur Geschichte des ältesten Christentums in Rom: I. Valentin und Marcion, II. Ptolemäus und Justin." *Zeitschrift für die neutestamentliche Wissenschaft* 70 (1979): 86–114.

Lührmann, Dieter. "Gal 2:9 und die katholischen Briefe: Bemerkungen zum Kanon und zur regula fidei." *Zeitschrift für die neutestamentliche Wissenschaft* 72 (1981): 65–87.

————. "Das neue Fragment des PEgerton 2 (PKöln 255)," in *The Four Gospels 1992: Festschrift for Frans Neirynck.* Ed. F. Van Segbroek et al. Bibliotheca ephemeridum theologicarum lovaniensium 100, 2239–55. Leuven: University Press, 1992.

Luthardt, Christoph Ernst. *Das johanneische Evangelium nach seiner Eigenthümlichkeit geschildert und erklärt.* Nuremberg, 1852–1853.

McBirnie, William Steuart. *The Search for the Twelve Apostles.* Wheaton, Ill.: Tyndale House, 1973.

McGuckin, John Anthony. *The Transfiguration of Christ in Scripture and Tradition.* Studies in the Bible and Early Christianity 9. Lewiston, N.Y.: Edwin Mellen Press, 1986.

McNamara, Martin, M.S.C. *The Apocrypha in the Irish Church.* Dublin: Dublin Institute for Advanced Studies, 1975.

———— and Máire Herbert, eds. *Irish Biblical Apocrypha: Selected Texts in Translation.* Edinburgh: T. & T. Clark, 1989.

Mack, Burton. *A Myth of Innocence: Mark and Christian Origins.* Philadelphia: Fortress Press, 1988.

Mahoney, Robert. *Two Disciples at the Tomb: The Background and Message of John 20.1–10.* Theologie und Wirklichkeit 6. Bern: Herbert Lang, 1974.

Mâle, Emile. *The Gothic Image: Religious Art in France of the Thirteenth Century.* New York: Harper and Row, 1958.

Manek, Jindrich. "Fishers of Men." *Novum Testamentum* 2 (1957): 138–41.

Manson, T. W. "The Fourth Gospel." In *Studies in the Gospels and Epistles,* edited by M. Black, 105–22. Manchester: The University Press, 1962.

————. *On Paul and John.* London: SCM Press, 1963.

Marshall, I. Howard. *The Gospel of Luke.* New International Greek Testament Commentary. Grand Rapids: Wm. B. Eerdmans, 1978.

Martyn, J. Louis. *The Gospel of John in Christian History.* New York: Paulist Press, 1978.

————. *History and Theology in the Fourth Gospel.* 2d ed. Nashville: Abingdon, 1979.

Masterman, Ernest W. Gurney. *Studies in Galilee.* Chicago: University of Chicago Press, 1909.

Maurer, Christian. *Ignatius von Antiochien und das Johannesevangelium.* Abhandlungen zur Theologie des Alten und Neuen Testaments 18. Zurich: Zwingli Verlag, 1949.

Meeks, Wayne A. "The Man from Heaven in Johannine Sectarianism." *Journal of Biblical Literature* 91 (1972): 44–72.

Meinardus, Otto. "The Christian Remains of the Seven Cities of the Apocalypse." *Biblical Archaeologist* 37, no. 3 (1974): 69–82.

————. *St. John on Patmos and the Seven Churches of the Apocalypse.* New Rochelle, N.Y.: Caratzas Bros., 1979.

Migne, Jacques Paul, ed. *Patrologiae cursus completus . . . Series graeca.* 161 vols. Paris: Sea Petit-Montrouge, 1857–1866.

————. *Patrologiae cursus completus . . Series latina.* 221 vols. Paris: J. P. Migne, 1844–65.

Miles, Margaret R. *Image as Insight: Visual Understanding in Western Christianity and Secular Culture.* Boston: Beacon Press, 1985.

Minear, Paul S. "The Beloved Disciple in the Gospel of John: Some Clues and Conjectures." *Novum Testamentum* 19 (1977): 105–23.

————. "The Original Functions of John 21." *Journal of Biblical Literature* 102 (1983): 85–98.

Mingana, Alphonse. "The Authorship of the Fourth Gospel." *Bulletin of the John Rylands University Library* 14 (1930): 333–39.

Miyoshi, Michi. *Der Anfang des Reiseberichts Lk 9,51–10,24: Eine redaktionsgeschichtliche Untersuchung.* Analecta Biblica 60. Rome: Biblical Institute, 1974.

Mohn, Werner. "Gethsemane (Mk 14:32–42)." *Zeitschrift für die neutestamentliche Wissenschaft* 64 (1973): 194–208.

Montgomery, James A. "Brief Communications." *Journal of Biblical Literature* 100 (1981): 94–95.

Morris, Leon. *Studies in the Fourth Gospel.* Grand Rapids: Wm. B. Eerdmans, 1969.

Neirynck, F. "The 'Other Disciple' in Jn 18, 15–16." *Ephemerides theologicae lovaniensis* 51 (1975): 113–41.

Neusner, Jacob. *The Tosefta: Neziqin.* New York: KTAV, 1981.

Nickelsburg, George W. E. "Enoch, Levi and Peter: Recipients of Revelation in Upper Galilee." *Journal of Biblical Literature* 100 (1981): 575–600.

Nützel, Johannes M. *Die Verklärungserzählung im Markusevangelium: Eine redaktionsgeschichtliche Untersuchung.* Forschung und Bibel 6. Würzburg: Echter Verlag, 1973.

Nun, Mendel. *The Sea of Galilee and Its Fishermen in the New Testament.* Kibbutz Ein Gev: Kinnereth Sailing Co., 1989.

Nunn, H. P. V. *The Authorship of the Fourth Gospel.* Oxford: Blackwell, 1952.

————. "The Fourth Gospel in the Early Church." *Evangelical Quarterly* 16 (1944): 173–91, 294–99.

O'Grady, John F. "The Role of the Beloved Disciple." *Biblical Theology Bulletin* 9 (1979): 58–65.

ó hUiginn, Ruairí. "Beatha Eoin Bruinne." In *Neutestamentliche Apokryphen,* 5th ed., edited by Wilhelm Schneelmelcher, 2:191–93. Tübingen: J. C. B. Mohr, 1989.

Osborn, Eric F. *Justin Martyr.* Beiträge zur historischen Theologie 47. Tübingen: J. C. B. Mohr, 1973.

Otero, Aurelio de Santos. *Die handschriftliche Überlieferung der altslavischen Apokryphen.* 2 vols. Patristische Texte und Studien 20–21. New York: Walter de Gruyter, 1978.

————. "Jüngere Apostelakten." In *Neutestamentliche Apokryphen,* 5th ed., edited by W. Schneemelcher, 2:385–91. Tübingen: J. C. B. Mohr, 1989.

Pagels, Elaine H. *The Johannine Gospel in Gnostic Exegesis: Heracleon's Commentary on John.* SBL Monograph Series 17. Missoula, Mont.: Scholars Press, 1973.

Parker, Pierson. "John and John Mark." *Journal of Biblical Literature* 79 (1960): 97–110.

————. "John the Son of Zebedee and the Fourth Gospel." *Journal of Biblical Literature* 81 (1962): 35–43.

Perkins, Pheme. "Johannine Traditions in *Ap. Jas.* (NHC 1, 2)." *Journal of Biblical Literature* 101 (1982): 403–14.

————. *Resurrection: New Testament Witness and Contemporary Reflection.* Garden City: Doubleday, 1984.

Perler, Othmar. *Méliton de Sardes: Sur la Pâque et fragments.* Paris: Éditions du Cerf, 1966.

Pervo, Richard I. "Johannine Trajectories in the *Acts of John*." *Apocrypha* 3 (1992): 47–68.

Pesch, Rudolf. *Das Markusevangelium.* 2 vols. Herders theologischer Kommentar zum Neuen Testament. Freiburg: Herder, 1976.

————. *Der reiche Fischfang.* Düsseldorf: Patmos-Verlag, 1969.

Poland, Lynn M. "The New Criticism, Neoorthodoxy, and the New Testament." *Journal of Religion* 65 (1985): 459–77.

Porter, J. R., and Donald G. Rogers. "Who Was the Beloved Disciple?" *Expository Times* 77 (1966): 213–14.

Porter, Stanley E. "The Language of the Apocalypse in Recent Discussion." *New Testament Studies* 35 (1989): 582–603.

Procopius of Caesarea. *Procopius.* Translated by H. B. Dewing and Glanville Downey. Loeb Classical Library. 7 vols. Cambridge, Mass.: Harvard University Press, 1954–1959.

Quast, Kevin. *Peter and the Beloved Disciple: Figures for a Community in Crisis.* Journal for the Study of the New Testament, Supplement Series 32. Sheffield: JSOT Press, 1989.

Quasten, Johannes. *Patrology.* 3 vols. Westminster, Maryland: Newman Press, 1960.

Quispel, Gilles. "The Jung Codex and Its Significance." In *The Jung Codex: A Newly Recovered Gnostic Papyrus,* edited and translated by F. L. Cross, 35–78. London: A. R. Mowbray, 1955.

Radcliffe, William. *Fishing from the Earliest Times.* Chicago: Ares Publishers, 1974.

Ragusa, Ias, and Rosalie B. Green, trans. *Meditations on the Life of Christ: An Illustrated Manuscript of the Fourteenth Century.* Paris: Bibliothèque Nationale, MS Ital. 115; Princeton: Princeton University Press, 1977.

Raymond, William O. *The Infinite Moment and Other Essays in Robert Browning.* Toronto: University of Toronto Press, 1950.

Reames, Sherry L. *The Legenda aurea: A Reexamination of Its Paradoxical History.* Madison: University of Wisconsin Press, 1985.

Regul, Jürgen. *Die antimarcionitischen Evangelienprologe.* Vetus Latina, Die Reste der altlateinischen Bibel: Aus der Geschichte der lateinischen Bibel 6. Freiburg: Herder, 1969.

Renan, Ernest. *The Life of Jesus.* Cleveland: World Publishing Co., 1941.

Rice, George E. "Luke's Thematic Use of the Call to Discipleship." *Andrews University Seminary Studies* 19 (1981): 127–32.

Rigg, H. "Was Lazarus 'the Beloved Disciple'?" *Expository Times* 33 (1921–1922): 232–34.

Riggenbach, D. "Neue Materialien zur Beleuchtung des Papias-zeugnisses über den Märtyrertod des Johannes." *Neue kirchliche Zeitschrift* 32 (1921): 692–96.

Robbins, Vernon K. "Mark 1.14–20: An Interpretation at the Intersection of Jewish and Graeco-Roman Traditions." *New Testament Studies* 28 (1982): 220–36.

Roberts, Alexander, and James Donaldson, eds. *The Ante-Nicene Fathers.* 10 vols. 1867–1897. Reprint. Grand Rapids: Wm. B. Eerdmans, 1986.

Robinson, John A. T. *The Priority of John.* Edited by J. F. Coakley. London: SCM Press, 1985.

———. *Redating the New Testament.* Philadelphia: Westminster Press, 1976.

———. *Twelve New Testament Studies.* Studies in Biblical Theology, no. 34. London: SCM Press, 1962.

Roeder, Helen. *Saints and Their Attributes.* Chicago: Henry Regnery Co., 1956.

Rogers, Donald G. "Who was the Beloved Disciple?" *Expository Times* 77 (1966): 213–14.

Roloff, Jürgen. *Apostolat—Verkündigung—Kirche.* Gütersloh: Gerd Mohn, 1965.

———. "Der johanneische 'Lieblingsjünger' und der Lehrer der Gerechtigkeit." *New Testament Studies* 15 (1968–1969): 129–51.

Rook, John T. " 'Boanerges, Sons of Thunder' (Mark 3:17)." *Journal of Biblical Literature* 100 (1981): 94–95.

Ross, J. M. "The Rejected Words in Luke 9:54–56." *Expository Times* 84 (1972–1973): 85–88.

Rostovtzeff, Michael I. *The Social and Economic History of the Hellenistic World.* 3 vols. Oxford: Clarendon Press, 1941.

Ruckstuhl, Eugen. *Jesus im Horizont der Evangelien.* Stuttgarter biblische Aufsatzbände 3. Stuttgart: Verlag Katholisches Bibelwerk, 1988.

Russell, E. A. "A Plea for Tolerance (Mk. 9.38–40)." *Irish Biblical Studies* 8 (1986): 154–60.

Russell, Ralph. "The Beloved Disciple and the Resurrection." *Scripture* 8 (1956): 57–62.

Salom, A. P. "Some Aspects of the Grammatical Style of I John." *Journal of Biblical Literature* 74 (1955): 96–102.

Sanders, E. P. *The Tendencies of the Synoptic Tradition.* SNTS Monograph Series 9. Cambridge: Cambridge University Press, 1969.

Sanders, Joseph N. *The Fourth Gospel in the Early Church.* Cambridge: Cambridge University Press, 1943.

———. "St. John on Patmos." *New Testament Studies* 9 (1962–1963): 75–85.

———. "Those Whom Jesus Loved (John XI, 5)." *New Testament Studies* 1 (1954–1955): 29–41.

———. "Who Was the Disciple Whom Jesus Loved?" In *Studies in the Fourth Gospel,* edited by F. L. Cross, 72–83. London: A. R. Mowbray, 1957.

Schäferdiek, Knut. "Johannesakten." In *Neutestamentliche Apokryphen,* 5th ed., edited by Wilhelm Schneelmelcher, 2:138–90. Tübingen: J. C. B. Mohr, 1989.

———. "Die 'Passio Johannis' des Melito von Laodikeia und die 'Virtutes Johannis.' " *Analecta Bollandiana* 103 (1985): 367–82.

Schaff, Philip. *Apostolic Christianity, A.D. 1–100.* Vol. 1 of *History of the Christian Church.* Grand Rapids: Wm. B. Eerdmans, 1950.

————, and Henry Wace, eds. *A Select Library of the Nicene and Post-Nicene Fathers of the Christian Church*. First series, 14 vols.; second series, 14 vols. New York: Christian Literature Co.,1886–1890, 1890–1900.

Schenke, Ludger. *Studien zur Passionsgeschichte des Markus: Tradition und Redaktion in Markus 14, 1–42*. Forschung zur Bibel 4. Würzburg: Echter Verlag, 1971.

Schermann, Theodor. *Propheten- und Apostellegenden nebst Jüngerkatalogen des Dorotheus und verwandter Texte*. Texte und Untersuchungen 31,3. Leipzig: J. C. Hinrichs'sche Buchhandlung, 1907.

Schlosser, J. "L'exorciste étranger (*Mc*, 9, 38–39)." *Revue des sciences religieuses* 56 (1982): 229–39.

Schmahl, Günther. *Die Zwölf im Markusevangelium: Eine redaktionsgeschichtliche Untersuchung*. Trierer Theologische Studien 30. Trier: Paulinus Verlag, 1974.

Schmidt, Andreas. "Zwei Anmerkungen zu P. Ryl. III 457." *Archiv für Papyrusforschung* 35 (1989): 11f.

Schmidt, Karl L. *Der Rahmen der Geschichte Jesu*. Berlin: Trowitzsch, 1919.

Schmiedel, Paul W. "John, Son of Zebedee." In *Encyclopaedia Biblica,* edited by Thomas Kelly Cheyne and J. Sutherland Black, 2:2503–2562. London: A. and C. Black, 1901.

Schnackenburg, Rudolf. *The Gospel According to St. John,* vol. 1. Translated by Kevin Smyth. Herder's Theological Commentary on the New Testament. New York: Herder and Herder, 1968.

————. *The Gospel According to St. John,* vol. 3. Translated by David Smith and G. A. Kon. New York: Crossroad, 1982.

————. "Der Jünger, den Jesus liebte." In *Evangelisch-katholischer Kommentar zum Neuen Testament,* 97–117. Vorarbeiten 2. Neukirchen-Vluyn: Neukirchener-Verlag, 1970.

Schneider, Paul G. *The Mystery of the Acts of John: An Interpretation of the Hymn and the Dance in Light of the Acts' Theology*. San Francisco: Mellen Research University Press, 1991.

Schneiders, Sandra M. "The Face Veil: A Johannine Sign (John 20.1–10)." *Biblical Theology Bulletin* 13 (July 1983): 94–97.

Scholes, Robert, and Robert Kellogg, *The Nature of Narrative*. New York: Oxford University Press, 1966.

Schürer, Emil. *The History of the Jewish People in the Age of Jesus Christ*. 3 vols. Revised and edited by Geza Vermes, Fergus Millar, and Matthew Black. Edinburgh: T. and T. Clark, 1973–1986.

Schüssler Fiorenza, Elisabeth. *The Book of Revelation: Justice and Judgment*. Philadelphia: Fortress Press, 1985.

Schütz, John. *Paul and the Anatomy of Apostolic Authority*. SNTS Monograph Series 26. Cambridge: Cambridge University Press, 1975.

Schwartz, Eduard. "Über den Tod der Söhne Zebedaei." In *Johannes und sein Evangelium,* edited by K. H. Rengstorf, 202–72. 1904. Reprint. Darmstadt: Wissenschaftliche Buchgesellschaft, 1973.

————. "Noch Einmal der Tod der Söhne Zebedaei." *Zeitschrift für die neutestamentliche Wissenschaft* 11 (1910): 89–104.

————. "Johannes und Cerinthos." In *Gesammelte Schriften,* edited by E. Schwartz, 5:170–82. Berlin: Walter de Gruyter, 1963.

Schweitzer, Albert. *The Quest of the Historical Jesus: A Critical Study of Its Progress from Reimarus to Wrede.* New York: Macmillan, 1950.

Schweizer, Eduard. *The Good News According to Mark.* Translated by Donald H. Madvig. Atlanta: John Knox Press, 1970.

————. *The Good News According to Luke.* Translated by David E. Green. Atlanta: John Knox Press, 1984.

Segovia, Fernando F. *Discipleship in the New Testament.* Philadelphia: Fortress Press, 1985.

————. *Love Relationships in the Johannine Tradition: Agape/Agapan in I John and the Fourth Gospel.* SBL Dissertation Series 58. Chico, Cal.: Scholars Press, 1982.

Shaffer, E. S. *'Kubla Khan' and the Fall of Jerusalem: The Mythological School in Biblical Criticism and Secular Literature, 1770–1880.* Cambridge: Cambridge University Press, 1975.

Sirker-Wicklaus, Gerlinde. *Untersuchungen zu den Johannes-Akten.* Beiträge zur Religionsgeschichte 2. Witterschlick: Verlag M. Wehle, 1988.

Smalley, Stephen S. *1, 2, 3 John.* Word Biblical Commentary, vol. 51. Waco, Texas: Word Books, 1984.

————. *John: Evangelist and Interpreter.* Greenwood, S.C.: Attic Press, 1978.

————. "John's Revelation and John's Community." *Bulletin of the John Rylands University Library* 69 (1987): 549–71.

Smith, Charles W. F. "Fishers of Men." *Harvard Theological Review* 52 (1959): 187–203.

Smith, D. Moody. "The Contribution of J. Louis Martyn to the Understanding of the Gospel of John." In *The Conversation Continues: Studies in Paul & John in Honor of J. Louis Martyn,* edited by Robert T. Fortna and Beverly R. Gaventa, 275–94. Nashville: Abingdon Press, 1990.

Smith, Joseph Daniel, Jr. "Gaius and the Controversy over the Johannine Literature." Ph.D. diss., Yale University, 1979.

Smith, Morton. "The Origin and History of the Transfiguration Story." *Union Seminary Quarterly Review* 36 (1980): 39–44.

Soards, Marion L. "*ton ependytēn diezōsato, ēn gar gymnos.*" *Journal of Biblical Literature* 102 (1983): 283–84.

Söder, Rosa. *Die apokryphen Apostelgeschichten und die romanhafte Literatur der Antike.* 1932. Reprint. Stuttgart: W. Kohlhammer Verlag, 1969.

Solages, Bruno de. "Jean, fils de Zébédée et l'énigme du 'disciple que Jésus aimait.'" *Bulletin de Litterature Ecclesiastique* 73 (1972): 41–50.

Sotiriou, G. A., J. Keil and H. Hörmann, "Die Johanneskirche," pt. 3 of *Forschungen in Ephesos,* 4. Vienna: Verlag des oesterreichischen archaeologischen Institutes, 1951.

Sperber, Daniel. *Nautica Talmudica.* Leiden: E. J. Brill, 1986.

————. "Some Observations of Fish and Fisheries in Roman Palestine." *Zeitschrift der deutschen morgenländischen Gesellschaft* 118 (1968): 265–69.

Spitta, Friedrich. "Die neutestamentliche Grundlage der Ansicht von E. Schwartz über den Tod der Söhne Zebedaei." In *Johannes und sein Evangelium,* edited by K. H. Rengstorf, 291–313. Darmstadt: Wissenschaftliche Buchgesellschaft, 1973.

Stein, R. H. "Is the Transfiguration (Mark 9:2–8) a Misplaced Resurrection Account?" *Journal of Biblical Literature* 95 (1976): 79–86.

Strabo. *The Geography of Strabo.* Translated by Horace Leonard Jones. Loeb Classical Library. 8 vols. Cambridge, Mass.: Harvard University Press, 1954.

Strauss, David Friedrich. *The Life of Jesus Critically Examined.* Translated by George Eliot, edited by Peter C. Hodgson. Lives of Jesus Series. Philadelphia: Fortress Press, 1972.

Strecker, Georg. "Die Anfänge der johanneischen Schule." *New Testament Studies* 32 (1986): 31–47.

Sundberg, A. C., Jr. "Canon Muratori: A Fourth-Century List." *Harvard Theological Review* 66 (1973): 1–41.

———. "Muratorian Fragment." In *Interpreter's Dictionary of the Bible,* Supplementary Volume, 609–10. Nashville: Abingdon, 1976.

Swete, Henry Barclay. *The Apocalypse of St. John.* 1906. Reprint. Grand Rapids: Wm. B. Eerdmans, 1954.

———. "The Disciple Whom Jesus Loved." *Journal of Theological Studies* 17 (1916): 371–74.

———. *The Gospel According to St. Mark.* London: Macmillan, 1898.

———. "John of Ephesus." *Journal of Theological Studies* 17 (1916): 375–78.

Tacitus. *Tacitus: The Annals.* Translated by John Jackson. Loeb Classical Library. 4 vols. Cambridge, Mass.: Harvard University Press, 1953.

Talbert, Charles H. *Reading John: A Literary and Theological Commentary on the Fourth Gospel and the Johannine Epistles.* New York: Crossroad, 1992.

Tannehill, Robert C. "The Disciples in Mark: The Function of a Narrative Role." *Journal of Religion* 57 (1977): 386–405.

Taylor, Vincent. "Detached Note on the Alleged Papias Tradition regarding the Death of James and John." In *The Gospel According to St. Mark,* 442. London: Macmillan, 1952.

Temple, William. *Readings in St. John's Gospel.* 1939–1940. Reprint. London: Macmillan, 1963.

Thompson, Steven. *The Apocalypse and Semitic Syntax.* SNTS Monograph Series 52. Cambridge: Cambridge University Press, 1986.

Thucydides. *Thucydides.* Translated by Charles Foster Smith. Loeb Classical Library. 4 vols. Cambridge, Mass.: Harvard University Press, 1953.

Thurston, Herbert, and Donald Attwater, eds. *Butler's Lives of the Saints.* 4 vols. New York: P. J. Kenedy and Sons, 1956.

Thyen, Hartwig. "Entwicklungen innerhalb der johanneischen Theologie und Kirche im Spiegel von Joh. 21 und der Lieblingsjüngertexts des Evangeliums." In *L'Évangile de Jean: Sources, rédaction, théologie,* 259–99. Bibliotheca Ephemeridum Theologicarum Lovaniensium 44. Gembloux: J. Duculot, 1977.

Tissot, Gabriel. *Traité sur l'évangile de s. Luc.* Sources Chrétiennes. Paris: Éditions du Cerf, 1958.

Titus, Eric L. "The Identity of the Beloved Disciple." *Journal of Biblical Literature* 69 (1950): 323–28.

Torrey, Charles Cutler. *The Four Gospels.* 2d ed. New York: Harper and Brothers, 1947.

Trites, Allison A. "The Transfiguration of Jesus: The Gospel in Microcosm." *The Evangelical Quarterly* 51 (1979): 67–79.

Turner, C. H. "Latin Lists of the Canonical Books. I. The Roman Council under Damasus, AD 382." *Journal of Theological Studies* 1 (1900): 544–60.

Turner, Nigel. *Style.* Vol. 4 of *Grammar of New Testament Greek,* by J. H. Moulton. Edinburgh: T. and T. Clark, 1976.

Usener, Hermann Karl, ed. "Acta S. Timothei." In *Bonner Universitätsprogramm.* Bonn: Caroli Georgi, 1877.

Vaganay, Léon. *An Introduction to New Testament Textual Criticism.* 2d ed. Revised and edited by C.-B. Amphoux. Translated by J. Heimerdinger. Cambridge: Cambridge University Press, 1991.

Van Unnik, W. C. "The 'Gospel of Truth' and the New Testament." In *The Jung Codex: A Newly Discovered Gnostic Papyrus.* Translated and edited by F. L. Cross. London: A. R. Mowbray, 1955.

Völker, Walther. *Quellen zur Geschichte der christlichen Gnosis.* Sammlung ausgewählter kirchen- und dogmengeschichtlicher Quellenschriften, n.F. 5. Tübingen: J. C. B. Mohr, 1932.

Wachsmann, Shelley. "The Galilee Boat—2,000-Year-Old Hull Recovered Intact." *Biblical Archaeology Review* 14, no. 5 (1988): 18–33.

Walker, Williston, et al. *A History of the Christian Church.* 4th ed. New York: Charles Scribner's Sons, 1985.

Weiss, Johannes. "Zum Märtyrertod des Zebedaeiden." *Zeitschrift für die neutestamentliche Wissenschaft* 11 (1910): 167.

Westcott, B. F. *The Gospel According to St. John.* Grand Rapids: Wm. B. Eerdmans, 1971.

Wiles, M. F. *The Spiritual Gospel: The Interpretation of the Fourth Gospel in the Early Church.* Cambridge: Cambridge University Press, 1960.

Wilhelms, Eino. "Der fremde Exorzist." *Studia Theologica* 3 (1950–1951): 162–71.

Wilson, W. G. "An Examination of the Linguistic Evidence Adduced against the Unity of Authorship of the First Epistle of John and the Fourth Gospel." *Journal of Theological Studies* 49 (1948): 147–56.

Wrangham, Digby S. *The Liturgical Poetry of Adam of St. Victor.* London: Kegan Paul, Trench & Co., 1881.

Wright, G. E. "There Go the Ships." *The Biblical Archaeologist* 1, no. 3 (1938): 19–20.

Wright, William. *Apocryphal Acts of the Apostles.* 2 vols. in 1. 1871. Reprint. Amsterdam: Philo Press, 1968.

Wuellner, Wilhelm H. *The Meaning of "Fishers of Men."* The New Testament Library. Philadelphia: Westminster Press, 1967.

Wynne, G. R. "Mending Their Nets." *Expositor,* 7th ser., 8 (1909): 282–85.

Yamauchi, Edwin. *The Archaeology of New Testament Cities in Western Asia Minor.* Grand Rapids: Baker Book House, 1980.

———. *New Testament Cities in Western Asia Minor.* Grand Rapids: Baker Book House, 1980.

Yonge, C. M. *The Pupils of St. John the Divine.* N.p.: Macmillan, 1868.

Yoshikador, Makio. "Browning and Higher Criticism in 'A Death in the Desert.'" Master's thesis, Baylor University, 1986.

Zahn, Theodor, ed. *Acta Joannis*. Erlangen: Verlag von Andreas Deichert, 1880.

———. "Die Wanderungen des Apostels Johannes." *Neue kirchliche Zeitschrift* 10 (1899): 191–218.

Ziesler, J. A. "The Transfiguration Story and the Markan Soteriology." *Expository Times* 81 (1970): 263–68.

Index

SCRIPTURE

ANCIENT SOURCES

MODERN AUTHORS